Making a Difference

Making a Difference

Behavioral Intervention for Autism

Edited by
Catherine Maurice
Gina Green
Richard M. Foxx

pro·ed
An International Publisher

8700 Shoal Creek Boulevard
Austin, Texas 78757-6897
800/897-3202 Fax 800/397-7633
www.proedinc.com

© 2001 by PRO-ED, Inc.
8700 Shoal Creek Boulevard
Austin, Texas 78757-6897
800/897-3202 Fax 800/397-7633
www.proedinc.com

Library of Congress Cataloging-in-Publication Data

Making a difference: behavioral intervention for autism / [edited by] Catherine Maurice,
  Gina Green, Richard M. Foxx.
    p.   cm.
  Builds upon and expands: Behavioral intervention for young children with autism. c1996.
  Includes bibliographical references and index.
  ISBN 0-89079-871-0 (alk. paper)
  1. Autistic children—Rehabilitation 2. Behavior modification 3. Behavior therapy for
children I. Title: Behavorial intervention for autism II. Maurice, Catherine. III. Green,
Gina IV. Foxx, Richard M. V. Behavorial intervention for young children with autism.
  [DNLM: 1. Autistic Disorder—rehabilitation. 2. Behavior Therapy—Child. WM 203.5
M235 2001]
RJ506.A9 M35 2001
618.92'898206—dc21

00-046023
CIP

This book is designed in Goudy.

Printed in the United States of America

3 4 5 6 7 8 9   11 10 09 08 07 06

Contents

◆　◆　◆　◆　◆　◆　◆　◆　◆　◆　◆　◆　◆　◆　◆　◆　◆

Preface

◆ ◆

This work is an attempt to build upon and expand the work of *Behavioral Intervention for Young Children with Autism: A Manual for Parents and Professionals* (Maurice, Green, & Luce, 1996). The guiding principle behind both books is the same: Claims about the effectiveness of treatments for autism, and suggestions as to intervention, must be backed by credible research and robust data. Where such data do not yet exist, authors in both manuals have been guided to inform the reader of this fact. Thus, parental or clinical experience, where included, is clearly described as such, and no sweeping claim or recommendation is made for any intervention strategy or teaching procedure that cannot be backed by objective data from methodologically sound, peer-reviewed, published studies.

The editors of this present book work with and interact with large numbers of parents and professionals who are concerned about individuals with autism of all ages, from toddler to adult. We have seen and heard firsthand how desperate such people are for concrete information about effective intervention. We know that there is an urgent need to get information about high-quality applied behavioral research and practice—so far restricted to only a few programs and providers in this country—"out there" to people thirsty for knowledge. There is an urgent need to translate treatment research into understandable terms, and to render it accessible to the lay public as well as to professionals and academicians. We recognize that no book can ever substitute for direct training in the requisite skills, or take the place of a behavior analyst to orchestrate and supervise each child's program directly and continuously. Until enough competent professional support exists, however, we hope that this book will satisfy some of that thirst for knowledge, and bring at least some help to people with autism, to their families, and to those who teach and work with them.

In Chapter 1, Catherine Maurice discusses the tumultuous ideological conflicts that tend to complicate the search for credible information about autism and its proposed treatments. She reviews some of the common themes of this political sparring, and suggests that the best hope for effective treatment lies not in personalities, promises, angry accusations of abuse, or fervent protestations of "caring," but rather in the principles of science employed in search of truth, in the exercise of human reason inspired by compassion.

In Chapter 2, Pamela F. Dawson provides a real-life illustration of the difficulties to which Maurice alludes, as she

shares the heart-wrenching story of her attempts to find effective treatment for her young daughter. Eloquently, Dawson describes the pressures and confusion that parents of newly diagnosed children have to endure, as they seek the best possible help for their child.

In Chapter 3, Deborah Fein, Diana Robins, Miriam Liss, and Lynn Waterhouse present a clearly written overview of autism, including the definitions and characteristics of autism and related disorders, findings from research on cognitive and biological features of these disorders, and implications for treatments. This chapter should prove helpful to parents and professionals alike, as it offers a lucid and well-grounded discussion of several debated topics.

Gregory S. MacDuff, Patricia J. Krantz, and Lynn E. McClannahan discuss in Chapter 4 the critically important techniques of prompting and effective "fading," or diminishing, of prompts. The chapter, solidly anchored in research, also reflects the authors' 25 years of experience in serving scores of children and young adults with autism.

In Chapter 5, William A. Ahearn provides help for a problem that troubles many parents and practitioners: the situation of a child who persists in eating only one or two food items, to the point where his or her health may be undermined. Ahearn discusses feeding problems—why they occur, whether we should intervene, and when and how we should intervene. His guidelines and recommendations should prove invaluable to many.

Edward C. Fenske, and his colleagues, Patricia J. Krantz and Lynn E. McClannahan, make the critically important point, in Chapter 6, that "incidental teaching has been part of the behavior analysis armamentarium for more than three decades." This chapter corrects the common misperception that applied behavior analysis consists exclusively of sitting a child in a chair and practicing drills for 40 hours a week, and offers clear illustrations and examples of incidental teaching.

Bridget A. Taylor and Suzanne Jasper have contributed two chapters on the topic of social skills, a vital area that behavior analysis is mistakenly criticized for ignoring. In Chapter 7, Taylor provides an overview of research on teaching peer interaction skills to children with autism, and discusses procedures for teaching such skills. The next chapter, written by Taylor and Jasper, provides a concrete set of programs for helping children develop age-appropriate social behavior.

In Chapter 9, Margery F. Rappaport, a speech–language pathologist, describes some of the strategies she has used over the years to help children begin to use language in a flexible manner and in a wide array of social contexts. She focuses on that nebulous area where a child tests well on measures of cognition and language knowledge, but where his or her *use* of language remains stilted and limited. Her chapter is thus geared toward children who have made appreciable progress in developing communication skills, but who need help to overcome some additional hurdles.

The editors and authors of this manual are ever mindful of the children and adults who do not progress so far, so fast. Richard M. Foxx turns in Chapter 10 to the topic of what to do when things do not go well. How do we troubleshoot? How do we analyze what is or is not working in our programs? How do we make certain, at all times, that we are not "blaming the learner" when our strategies seem to stall? He discusses lessons learned from 30 years' experience in using applied behavior analysis methods to treat problem behaviors.

We end the book with the voice of another parent, Lora Perry, who is striving to give her own and other children the gifts of language, learning, and communication. To every endeavor, from helping found The Association for Science in Autism Treatment,[1] to editing its newsletter, to dealing with an autism diagnosis in both of her twin sons, Perry brings a singular purity of heart. "Never, ever give up," she writes—and she does not. She decided early on that her children, whether they recovered or not, would receive treatment based on the best available scientific evidence, even if she had to move mountains to get them that help—which she did. It is the editors' hope that her chapter, and all the chapters in this work, will make the journey somewhat easier for all the parents and professionals who are trying to help someone with autism receive the best possible treatment that science and compassion can provide.

Reference

Maurice, C., Green, G., & Luce, S. C. (1996). *Behavioral intervention for young children with autism: A manual for parents and professionals.* Austin, TX: PRO-ED.

---

[1]The Association for Science in Autism Treatment (ASAT), 175 Great Neck Road, Suite 406, Great Neck, NY 11021; phone: 516/466-4400, Fax: 516/466-4484. ASAT is a national, not-for-profit group of parents and professionals, dedicated to the dissemination of science-based information about autism and treatments for autism, and to improving access to such treatments for all people with autism, regardless of age, severity of condition, income, or place of residence.

Acknowledgments

This work is a collaborative effort with some people who keep me humble by always keeping me aware of what I know and what I don't know, and who constantly challenge my thinking.

Without Richard M. Foxx, my co-editor, this book would not have seen the light of day. At several critical points, when I was about to throw the project out the window, he stepped forward and guided me with his wisdom, his professionalism, and his calm counsel. I learn from his experience, I appreciate his compassionate insights regarding people with autism, and I am grateful to be able to work with him. Foxx's responsibilities as editor included the chapters written by Deborah Fein, Diana Robins, Miriam Liss, and Lynn Waterhouse; William H. Ahearn; Margery F. Rappaport; and Lora Perry. He also contributed his own chapter, an invaluable set of reflections and guidelines offered by someone who has spent several decades caring for children, including children with severe, challenging behaviors.

Gina Green, also a co-editor on this manual, always inspires my deepest admiration for the high standards she sets when it comes to treatment for people with autism, and for her courage in speaking the truth about science and pseudoscience. In all endeavors, in all respects, she will not compromise with the truth. If a treatment has the evidence to support its use with vulnerable human beings, she will say so. If it does not, she will say so. She brought these standards to her work on this manual, and I know that the authors she worked with appreciate, as much as I do, her critical insights and keen intellect. Her editorial responsibilities for this manual included the chapters written by Pamela F. Dawson; Gregory S. MacDuff, Patricia J. Krantz, and Lynn E. McClannahan; Edward C. Fenske, Krantz, and McClannahan; and Bridget A. Taylor and Suzanne Jasper.

I would like to thank our authors, who tolerated so patiently the long delays and multiple setbacks of the project. Without these authors, of course, there would be nothing to offer you but my own limited experience, my own thoughts. What they can offer is the concrete help, the research knowledge, the experience of working with other children—in some cases many children, over many years.

Finally, I would like to add a personal note of thanks to my husband and my children, who uplift and comfort me always. And to my mother, whose life has ended, but whose love lives on.

Catherine Maurice

My work on this book was supported in part by National Institutes of Health Grant PO1 DC03610 to the E.K. Shriver Center for Mental Retardation, and by The New England Center for Children. I am grateful for that and the other forms of support provided by my employers and colleagues at both agencies. Heartfelt thanks go to Catherine Maurice, Richard Foxx, PRO-ED, and all the contributors to this text not only for their extraordinary skill and dedication, but also for their extraordinary patience with my delays. Finally, I gratefully acknowledge all the people with autism and their families who have taught me so much over the years, and whose accomplishments are a constant source of inspiration.

Gina Green

Several people deserve thanks for helping me with the editing process. First and foremost, my Pennsylvania State University colleague Kimberly Schreck provided me with valuable feedback on much of the material I reviewed and edited. I greatly appreciated her help in determining what should and should not be published. Keith Williams, who runs the behavioral feeding program at the Penn State University Medical School in Hershey, provided me with detailed and important feedback on Bill Ahearn's feeding chapter. I also would like to thank Daria Sessamen, staff assistant in the psychology program at Penn State, for doing such an outstanding job at every step in the editing process. Last, I would like to thank Catherine Maurice for inviting me to join the project. I have very much enjoyed working with her and having the opportunity to be exposed to such a caring, clearheaded, intelligent, and incisive thinker and writer.

Richard M. Foxx

1

Autism Advocacy or Trench Warfare?

Catherine Maurice

For the past decade or so, I have been trying to do some advocacy work in the field of autism, and I have to report a mixture of hope and discouragement. In 1993 I published a book, *Let Me Hear Your Voice: A Family's Triumph Over Autism* (Maurice, 1993), chronicling my own family's struggles with autism in two of our children. In that work, I described our own experiences with, on the one hand, an array of conflicting claims and popular treatments and, on the other hand, the treatment that was ultimately to prove the most evidence-based and scientifically grounded, at least to date, of all those proposed options for autism. That treatment was the teaching technology called applied behavior analysis (ABA).

Then in 1995, following an upsurge of interest in ABA and recognizing that I did not have the expertise to answer all the questions that parents were asking, I asked a prominent scientist, Gina Green, and a respected director of a treatment program for children with autism, Stephen Luce, to help me compile a manual for those who wanted to learn more about ABA (Maurice, Green, & Luce, 1996). In chapters ranging from theory to practice, from research to real-world applications, the parents and professionals who contributed to the manual further explored and illustrated the principles and practices of behavior analysis for young children with autism. In that book, we also tried to guide the readers through the maze of treatments for autism. We did this not by telling anyone what to do, but by offering a concise overview of the existing scientific evidence on current autism treatments, and by clearly laying out the distinguishing features of scientific versus pseudoscientific approaches. In other words, one of our goals was to teach people how to weigh the evidence, that is, how to seek outcome measures, good science, and credible data.

I began this chapter by saying that after a decade of such work, I needed to report some hope and some discouragement. My hope springs from the letters, calls, and corroborating documents that flooded in from all over this country—indeed from all over the world—after the publication of these works, all reporting the same phenomenon: Children with autism who were receiving quality intervention based on ABA were making unprecedented strides forward. They were surpassing the low expectations and bleak predictions laid out for them. They were overcoming the historical absolutism of the diagnosis. Some of the children, although by no means all, were actually beginning to lose the diagnosis, attaining normal cognitive, intellectual, and emotional functioning—something that had been pronounced impossible since autism was first named 50 years ago. Ample reason for hope, for thanks, for joy.

No change, however, especially not the fundamental sea change entailed in the historical prognosis for autism and the traditional ways of treating autism, is met without some resistance and cynicism. Many people have vested much in their own theories, beliefs, and pronouncements about autism. Entire careers and reputations have been structured around those theories. The notion that other theories and methods were better substantiated than their own did not sit well with many in the autism establishment. Moreover, the whole idea of what has been commonly called behavior modification simply does not go over well with many. The backlash—against ABA, against the very idea of recovery—was not long in coming, and it was virulent.

"What can we make of *Let Me Hear Your Voice?*" began a book review, written by Pat Amos (1994), president of a group called the Autism National Committee (ANC), and disseminated widely over the Internet. "Well, with responsible paper recycling, probably quite a bit" (p. 1). The review descends steadily from there, piling on ever more sarcastic mockery not only of *Let Me Hear Your Voice* and its author, but apparently of anyone so stupid and cruel as to opt for behavioral intervention. As for applied behavior analysis itself, Amos paints it as child abuse, an approach that tramples over the rights of people with autism and forces them, often through the use of electric shocks, ammonia squirts, and the like, into rigid obedience. The degree of vitriol in this review, the abundant caricatures, and the misrepresentations and distortions about behavioral intervention would be frightening and discouraging enough. Unfortunately, however, Amos also spends a good deal of time extolling the benefits of several of the more preposterous and destructive autism treatment fads, including the thoroughly discredited Facilitated Communication.[1] This theme—that behavioral intervention is a dangerous, unethical, and outmoded form of child abuse—appears frequently in publications of the ANC, and no extreme of rhetoric is spared in making this point. In the Fall 1995 edition of *The Communicator*, the newsletter of the ANC, Kathy Lissner-Grant drew a parallel between behaviorally based treatment and Nazi torture of people with disabilities. The "distinguished disservice awards" of *The Communicator* listed people whose ideas the ANC opposed, their names surrounded by a drawing of barbed wire, evocative perhaps of concentration camps (The Autism National Committee, 1995).

In any case, while particularly lurid in their attacks, the Autism National Committee was by no means alone. In personal correspondence or in conversation with me, scores of parents began to share further evidence that behavioral intervention was still being dismissed out of hand, routinely disparaged by the psychologists, psychiatrists, or special educators such parents turned to for help. In conferences or seminars they attended and in their consultations with autism professionals, many parents reported hearing behavioral intervention still described as "dog training," as "feeding children candy so that they behave," or as a shallow attempt to force children into rigid compliance before they were "developmentally ready."

After the publication of *Behavioral Intervention for Young Children with Autism* (Maurice et al., 1996), where we laid out the evidence (such as it was) behind many popular treatments, I began to receive letters from people who always seemed to be threatening me that many other letters would follow shortly. "Hundreds of members of our organization will be writing to you soon, Catherine Maurice," warned the angry letter writers, whose authority was often amplified by long strings of letters after their names (Jane Doe, OTR/L FAAP, MECED, FAOTA, COM, CA . . .). (Such titles may have impressed and scared me more if I had ever seen them before.)

Some of the attacks were more personal. One California authority, author of one of the ubiquitous "let's describe the symptoms of autism one more time" books, publicly derided my children, whom she has never met, and mocked the notion of their recovery. A special educator, Shirley Cohen, published a book (1998) in which she repeatedly suggests that I promise recovery to everyone who follows the meth-

ods that my colleagues and I promote. Cohen sprinkles this pastiche with some gossipy comments about my physical appearance, and indulges in some creative cutting and pasting in order to twist the intended meanings of my words.

More disturbing than her commentary on my work or me, however, is her sustained and subtle attack against intensive behavioral intervention for autism. Recognizing its importance, she cannot dismiss it out of hand. Thus, she resorts to damning it with faint praise, conceding that behavioral intervention may help some children make some progress, but at what cost? Very adroitly, while never actually using the kind of intemperate rhetoric employed by other antibehaviorists, she succeeds in painting ABA as predominantly intrusive, coercive, and cruel:

> In programs based on or derived from the Lovaas Young Autism Project model, intrusion begins immediately. . . . Directions are often given in a loud voice. Physical guidance is used to ensure that the child follows the adult's directions, with food or other rewards being used to reinforce the child's compliance. Some young children cry and seek to escape . . . for days or even weeks as they are initiated into treatment programs. . . . This starting point not only paves the way for later program objectives such as imitation of speech sounds but also establishes a pattern for child/therapist interactions: the adult directs, models, and reinforces; the child responds with imitation and compliance. Lack of attention and stereotyped activities . . . are often responded to with sharpness. (Cohen, p. 89)

Where have we read such a frightening and one-sided caricature before? Why does this portrayal of behavioral treatment as an intrusive attempt to force children into "compliant imitation" sound so familiar? Because it has been around for a very long time. As Bruno Bettelheim wrote in 1967,

> Here I wish to comment on current efforts to deal with infantile autism through operant conditioning—that is, by creating conditioned responses through punishment and reward. Temporarily this breaks down the child's defenses . . . and arouses him to some action. But the actions are not of his devising. They are those the experimenter wants. . . . Autistic children are reduced to the level of Pavlovian dogs. . . . Conditioned response regimes may turn autistic children into more pliable robots. (pp. 410, 412)

The model of parents and therapists forcing children into meaningless imitation in order to turn them into com-

---

[1]Facilitated Communication entails a "facilitator's" touching the hand or arm of a person with autism, while spelling out words and phrases on a keyboard. Over 40 well-designed studies have clearly debunked it as a treatment for autism, but not before hundreds of thousands of dollars were wasted, families were torn apart by false accusations of sexual abuse (accusations produced through Facilitated Communication), and children were exploited. As those studies demonstrated, it is the facilitator and not the person with autism who authors the messages spelled out with this technique.

pliant robots has an all too familiar ring. In Cohen's (1998) book and many others on the market today, those of us who have opted for behavioral intervention are cast as rather cruel, while the professional writing the book or article portrays himself or herself as exquisitely understanding and respectful of the needs of autistic children.

Those of us who have chosen a behavioral approach are also portrayed in Cohen's (1998) book as pretty dumb, as cult followers blindly following something called the Young Autism Project in a futile attempt to recover our children. This too is a distortion. Most parents I know fully understand the basic principle that behaviorally based programs *must* be tailored to each individual child. Cohen simply glosses over the clear and repeated articulation of this point, by me and many others, that there is no one "model" for behavioral intervention. Indeed, there never can be.

In light of the fact that Cohen is a special educator and, as she informs us, has been one for 30 years, perhaps her work may be read as an obvious attempt to deflect attention from the historical failure of the special education establishment, that is, its inability to adequately address our children's learning needs. This book was received with ecstatic praise from certain quarters upon its publication. Why? One reason may be that it is a strong defense of the status quo, and that defense includes multiple "treatment" options that have failed to meet even rudimentary standards of empirical validation. True to its genre, its conclusions rely, to a troubling degree, on the author's personal observations and opinions rather than on an objective review of outcome data. "What we know and don't know" is the rather grandiose subtitle. But who is "we"? Perhaps the subtitle would be better phrased, "What I know; What I don't know; What I think and believe."

The Autism Society of America (ASA), historically founded as an advocacy and support group, was one of the first major organizations to weigh in. I had had only limited contact with the ASA. When my child was diagnosed, I called the ASA, in desperation. In response, the organization sent me a long reading list of outdated books, including one titled *Autism, Nightmare Without End* (Beavers, 1982). They also sent me a list of symptoms for autism and a newsletter replete with advertisements for every alternative and fad treatment ever invented for autism. There was not one word, in all of this material, about applied behavior analysis, about the necessity or the means to evaluate treatment options, or about how to distinguish between scientific and pseudoscientific evidence. The publication of my book, however, had apparently brought them an increase in parental questions about ABA, and they decided to publish in *The Advocate* the following review (Johnson, 1994):

> *Let Me Hear Your Voice* falls into the genre I have come to think of as "Other People's Miracles," which, like Other People's Money (something the Maurices clearly

have plenty of, too) possesses only limited entertainment value. In these pages young Anne-Marie and her brother Michel metamorphose from very autistic small children into privileged and precocious little beings who . . . sit around the table musing about—I'm not kidding—the nature of infinity. We are invited to listen in wonderment as Maurice voices her awe and gratitude over being expressly chosen by God to experience the benefits of divine intervention—a benefit that, one cannot help reflecting, has thus far eluded her hapless reader. By the end of the book I felt like one of the losers in the Miss America contest; my job as a reader seemed to be to squeal with delight that Ms. Maurice is the one who won. (p. 32)

Well. A child abuser, a fraud, an embezzler of Other People's Money, a mother of privileged and precocious brats, a religious fanatic—*and* a Miss America Queen?

Of course, it serves no purpose to respond in kind. Most *ad hominem* attacks are best left unanswered. However, again, it may clarify things to set Johnson's review into a wider historical and political context. It is important to discuss some of its specific arguments, because, in a very short space and most concisely, it encapsulates so much of what parents are up against today: continued attacks against ABA, remarkably positive assertions about failed treatment models, outright dismissal of the very notion of recovery.

First, there is in Johnson's (1994) review something that I have observed in virtually all of these backlash works—that is, a device employed by folks who do not know much about ABA, who do not have the research knowledge or the clinical experience to accurately discuss it, yet who recognize that it would probably be unwise to trash it completely. So their tactic is to claim a learned understanding of the approach, while reducing it to some simplistic formula, such as "training for compliance," or "managing bad behaviors," or "teaching rote skills." Johnson's review follows suit, as she assures us of her extensive experience in behavioral intervention, but then goes on to describe it rather simplistically as a kind of "behavior management" for problem behaviors. This behavior management assumption is shared by many educators, psychologists, and others who have been charged with the care of our children. The fact that ABA has been used successfully to teach communicative language and other high-level skills to people with autism is news to many of these authorities. Nevertheless, they wax pedantic on a discipline that has so far published over 500 peer-reviewed studies.

Johnson's (1994) review then moves on to another dominant theme in autism politics today, which is to attack, in every way possible, the very idea of recovery. First, recovery is simply dismissed ("false hope," etc.). This is common. Many parents report to me that they cannot even say the word "recovery" to their local autism professional without being regarded as sadly delusional. The word, if it appears at all in the works of antagonistic authorities, is always surrounded by quotation marks: "Recovery" (wink). Very few can find someone who at the very least will even concede the possibility. "No. No way. It has never happened, it never will happen, it never can happen" seems to be an all too familiar response.

Well, at least that would be a consistent response. Johnson (1994), however, tries to debunk recovery with yet another argument, one that begins to trip over its own logic. These recovered kids, we are told, were all "high functioning" to begin with. Moreover, Johnson goes on to cite an obscure study that asserts, at least in her interpretation, that "if you choose children who are high-functioning to start, you'll get a 47% 'recovery' rate, behavior management or no" (p. 31).

What data are offered to support this astonishing claim? Johnson (1994) gives no indication of whether this study included any independent assessments of children's functioning, any definition of how "recovery" was determined to have occurred or not, or any independent verification of outcome measures. What is offered, however, as corroborating support of this study is the authoritative opinion of a "renowned autism specialist."

It is worth underscoring, moving out again from this particular review to autism politics in general, that, again, the appeal to authority often forms the bedrock support of this kind of ideological critique. For decades, autism treatment has been guided and shaped not by science, but by an overreliance on the opinions and theories and "clinical intuition" of the people who happen to be in power. This is the what "we know and don't know"/"who cares about data" mentality. Thus Bruno Bettelheim reigned unchallenged for decades, and his disciples—inventors of therapeutic nurseries, play therapy, and other surrogate parenting approaches—still dominate treatment programs today.

The autism specialist cited by Johnson (1994) is Dr. B. J. Freeman, who has publicly denigrated ABA and stated, apparently without embarrassment, that special education has proven itself "the one treatment that has stood the test of time, and is effective for all children" (cited in Johnson, 1993, p. 8). Now, I know many special educators (including two of my sisters) who are very fine people, trying their best to help kids, and even they would find that statement a stretch, to put it mildly. Most of the special educators I know are frustrated by the lack of specialized training opportunities provided for them by their discipline. Many have confessed their consternation and genuine concern when they are thrust, willy-nilly, into a classroom with five autistic kids, three kids with Down syndrome, and two with mental retardation, and informed that they have to give each child the very special attention he or she deserves.

Moving along, Johnson's (1994) review continues to hammer away at the notion of recovery, but, as it tries to undercut the idea from all possible angles, contradictions

and logical impossibilities begin to abound. The next assertion in this review is that children can be both "high functioning" to begin with and "severely autistic at outcome." "They remain autistic . . . they continue to have difficulties . . . severe difficulties" (p. 31). In other words, these "very high functioning" children "who would have recovered anyway" have been taught to behave more compliantly, but of course, deep down, they are still "*severely* autistic." Clear?

And *besides* (a new theme in this particular article, but as we're beginning to see, a repeated assertion of the establishment), "intensive behavior management can actually teach these children to be more autistic, because it reinforces their rote-learning style" (p. 31).

Really? I have heard some variation of this statement over and over again in my 10 years of work in this field, and I have seen not one—*not one*—published, peer-reviewed study, anywhere, to support this assertion. Yet it is repeated constantly, forcefully, with absolute conviction in the pages of *The Advocate*, in popular books, in Ivy League halls of learning, at major teaching hospitals, everywhere. Applied behavior analysis, according to Dr. B. J. Freeman and to many of those in power, is

> *for treating behavior, not for teaching academic or social skills.* . . . You can teach a parrot to talk, but you can't teach it to *communicate* . . . behavior management teaches rote skills . . . You hear that children with autism have trouble generalizing, but one reason for that is the way they're taught: If you use behavior management to teach a child to put a block in the box, and you use the same block and the same box every time . . . all he's learned is to put that particular block into that particular box. He hasn't learned the *concept* [italics added through quote]. (p. 8)

These comments are of course so denigrating, so misleading, and so inaccurate that one cannot help but wonder why these distortions persist. "Not for teaching academic or social skills"? "Putting the same block in the same box every time"? What is being described here? How could any "autism specialist" not know that prompt fading, generalization, and the careful teaching of academic and social skills have been part of the behavior analytic scene for years? All of these components of good behavioral teaching are embedded not only in the copious research literature on applied behavior analysis, but feature prominently in quality behavior analytic programs. As my own family discovered (once we *fortunately* decided to ignore these negative stereotypes), behavior analysis methods can be used to teach anything that a child can learn, including complex social, academic, and communication skills. What kind of behavioral intervention is being described in the pages of *The Advocate?* It seems to me that these dismissive comments stem from a very incomplete understanding of this discipline. If so, perhaps it is time to rethink such arrogant presumptions and assumptions—children's futures are, after all, at stake.

It is impossible, however, to exaggerate how often this mantra is affirmed—never by reason of a growing body of objective evidence, but because it could be, might be, hypothetically, true: "One needs to consider the hypothesis that the types of overly rigid and structured interventions that have been organized on behalf of these infants and toddlers in part support rather than remediate their more mechanical behavior" (Greenspan, 1992, p. 5). And here we go again: Behavioral intervention will turn a child into a more compliant robot. Greenspan's language is scary indeed. The very words "infant" and "toddler" coupled with these hard descriptors—"rigid," "structured," and "mechanical"—make for a chillingly persuasive argument. After hearing so much about how rote learning can irrevocably damage their child, how ABA is neither "child friendly" nor "developmentally appropriate," parents I know have *agonized* over these fears. So did I when my daughter was diagnosed and I heard or read these denigrating comments. So did I when I was sternly warned how severely her "bonding" and relationship with me would suffer if I subjected her to this cruelty.

But let's think about all of this. *Of course* one has to start with a fair degree of rote learning. Does anyone know any child with autism who learns naturally and spontaneously from the environment, the way typically developing peers do? If they could learn that way, they would not actually have the diagnosis of autism, would they? They would all flourish in regular education. Most children with autism, however, need highly individualized, precise teaching, at least for a while. They need multiple opportunities to practice what they have learned, because they do not simply hear a new word, repeat it, and begin using it spontaneously when they are "developmentally ready." If only they could, if only they would, parents and professionals would not have to subject them to any structure or repetition. Children with autism could simply be put into a nice therapeutic nursery, with some nice kids, some warm and gentle parent substitutes, some "developmentally appropriate" toys, and they would talk and interact "when they were ready." If only . . .

Is ABA all rote learning, practice, and drills? No quality ABA program that I have observed ignores generalization, incidental teaching, academic skills, play, and socialization. No parent or professional I know has claimed that sitting a child in a chair and practicing rote drills all day long is a sufficient or effective approach, and it seems to me to be a deliberate distortion of the truth to keep telling parents that that is what this intervention is about. The buzzword *developmental* is used to imply love and kindness, as opposed to the aversive and robotic drills of behavioral intervention. But this is a false opposition, as most parents involved in behavioral teaching know. I used incidental teaching 10 years ago, because it just made sense. I knew about and was guided by "typical developmental milestones" 10 years

ago, because my therapists and I discussed the developmental appropriateness of every phase of our treatment program. The parents and professionals whom I know have always attempted, most lovingly, to incorporate incidental teaching, academics, life skills, generalization, and socialization into every child's program. Exactly which rigid programs, unfeeling parents, and abusive therapists are these renowned authorities and angry advocates describing?

Has Johnson's (1994) review exhausted all possible lines of attack? Not at all. Steadily building up to a veritable froth of self-righteousness, Johnson finally rolls out the big gun: a bid for the moral high ground. How? By castigating those of us who have not learned to accept our children for *whom they are*, of course, and who have not learned to "make friends with autism" as she implies that she herself has learned to do.

This rather sanctimonious attempt to claim a higher degree of love for autistic children, however, while utilized quite frequently in the autism wars, has met with only limited success. It is quite a stretch, even for people who are more ideological than logical, to propose that parents who don't love autism don't love their children. It is quite arrogant to propose that parents who choose ABA are somehow less caring than those who decide to subject their children to hormone injections, powerful medications, megadoses of vitamins, and on and on. Why are they doing that, if they have learned to "make friends with autism"? How odd that the same folks who promote an array of failed treatments and fads, in the clear hope of "changing" a child's autistic symptoms, would challenge the morality of others who are trying to help their children through educational initiatives.

It is hard, and discouraging, to keep responding to these lethal attacks against a treatment that truly helps so many kids, and I have not even *begun* to discuss the controversies that swirl around all the latest "breakthroughs" for treating autism. It is of course disturbing to read that one is a liar, a cult follower, a cult figure, or a proponent of child abuse. It is disconcerting to read an anonymous statement, sent to millions of Internet readers, that "Catherine Maurice believes that autism is merely a problem of behavior," when I have stated publicly and without ambivalence that science's best guess about autism, to date, is that it is a neurobiological disorder of possibly genetic etiology. It is frustrating to read yet another authority from yet another Ivy League institution pronounce that "Operant Conditioning is good for treating symptoms, but not the root cause of autism." I always feel like responding, "Until you can tell me what the 'root cause' is, I'll continue to promote the treatment that I know can help children learn." It is an astonishing irony that these "experts" constantly accuse me and those I work with of promoting a treatment that only the rich can afford, when it is their animosity and their public denigration of ABA that renders it so difficult for families to access this treatment. Throughout this country, families are routinely denied behavioral treatment for their children because schools and funding agencies can refuse them such services, backed by the opinions and beliefs and "clinical intuition" of these powerful and influential anti-ABA authorities.

It is especially appalling to read public mockery of one's children, especially after making the hard decision to share such private moments of love and pain.

So why persist? Because there are wider issues at stake. There are children who need help, who need the most effective treatment that scientific research and human compassion can provide, right now. I listen to my friends, the passionate mothers, fathers, and professionals who are fighting these battles with me, and I agree with them: If we let opinion triumph over fact, then real children and real families will suffer. All the turf warfare, the huffing and puffing about who "truly cares" or does not, cannot obscure what is true, and that is something that professionals and parents keep discovering for themselves: Applied behavior analysis is a powerful approach that not only helps children behave compliantly, but helps them learn. It can help them learn to get dressed, eat with the family at the dinner table, take care of their hygiene. It can help them to overcome self-injury. It can help people of any age to overcome isolation, sitting in a corner, rocking, finger flicking, and moaning. It can help people with autism to engage meaningfully with those who cherish them. It can help many of them to communicate more effectively. It can help many to talk, to listen, and to express themselves. In some cases, it can help them learn to tell a joke, listen to a friend, understand innuendo, and share another's pain. It can free children and adults with autism to become all that they are capable of becoming, under our present system of knowledge.

Applied behavior analysis may not help all kids recover, but nobody I know ever claimed that it could. It is an outright and perhaps even deliberate distortion of the truth to keep claiming that those of us who support behavioral intervention are promising recovery to all children, as Cohen's (1998) book and others repeatedly insinuate. In *Let Me Hear Your Voice* (Maurice, 1993), I sought out and published the stories of several parents whose children had not progressed very far, very fast, under ABA. In every speech I make, in every book I write, I emphasize this point. Do those who attack, discredit, or undermine access to ABA care equally about the truth? Do they seek out the stories of kids who recover? Do they publish any objective validation or outcome measures on their own approaches? Are they listening to the parents who want to tell them about the reality of their children's progress, both fast and slow? Or do they persist in clinging to their view of reality, to what they "know" rather than to what the evidence demonstrates?

ABA is not a panacea, is not the "end of all our exploring" (Eliot, 1943), and has helped only a minority of kids recover from autism. It is important to keep researching causes and potential cures for all forms of autism. I support those who are conducting quality biological and brain research. If some magic pill were found tomorrow that would cure autism, I would promote it in any way I could. It is equally important, however, to continue to provide care for the children who are alive today, as we seek that biological cure. It is important to defend and promote ABA not because it is a religion, but because it has proven itself to be a means of helping almost all children make substantial progress in overcoming some of the communication and behavioral problems associated with autism.

Finally, to address what has perhaps sparked the most virulent attacks: As a matter of fact, ABA actually does seem to help some children overcome autism—truly overcome autism, as in "they are no longer autistic." How does ABA do that, exactly? I don't know, but as my friend Lora Perry once pointed out, neither do I know how the body recovers from a common cold, and yet it can. There is growing scientific evidence that, given the right kind and degree of active engagement with the environment, the brain can sometimes heal itself, make new neural connections, overcome damage or underdevelopment.

In other words, if "cure" means "eradicating the cause of autism," then no, that has not yet been done because no one has yet identified, with certainty, the cause or causes of autism. But if *cure* can also mean, as *The New Merriam-Webster Dictionary* (1989) allows, "a recovery," and if "to cure" can mean "to restore to health" or "to regain a normal condition, as of health," then actually, in that sense, there is not a whole lot of difference between the word *cure* and the word *recovery*, is there? If some children can be brought to the point where they no longer display the characteristic signs of autism, if they have been restored to health, to normal functioning, to the capacity to interact linguistically, socially, and intellectually with others, in flexible, animated, and creative discourse, why exactly may we not call them "recovered" or "cured" or both?

But whichever word one uses, the old guard does not like applying such words to autism and furiously rejects the possibility of either outcome ever. In a special issue of the *Journal of Autism and Developmental Disorders*, the predictable laceration of "those who promise total cures" appears with numbing frequency. In the introductory article, written by Mesibov (1997), the assertion that there is no cure, ever, ever, ever is repeated no fewer than four times on a single page:

> Four articles are included in this section. B. J. Freeman begins with a superb discussion of major issues in the preschool area for children with autism. . . . Freeman reminds us . . . that there is no known cure. . . . [The child] has a lifelong, chronic disability. . . . This last point is especially important because many parents are vulnerable to suggestions of possible cures and the field has suffered greatly from those suggesting this is a possible outcome of certain early intervention efforts. . . . She warns parents to be wary of those promising cures as there is no evidence that this is a possible outcome. (p. 638)

To paraphrase Shakespeare, methinks these folk do protest too much. Why? Perhaps one way of understanding this angry resistance to even the possibility of recovery may be found in one of Mesibov's (1997) statements, a statement that I find very disturbing: ". . . the field has suffered greatly from those suggesting this is a possible outcome." Who or what is "the field"? Children with autism? Parents of children with autism? How have those populations suffered from the fact that there is now documented evidence that some children can *and do* recover from autism? Who, precisely, is "the field"? Professionals or academicians who have built their careers around their own confident assumptions, presumptions, and pronouncements about autism? How has this field suffered? Through wounded pride, loss of status, loss of authority? As a parent who knows what it is like to have two children diagnosed with autism, I admit to a certain prejudice, perhaps. However, to my thinking, protecting "the field" from suffering is not quite as important as raising the bar for children with autism, giving them every opportunity to reach their fullest potential, by providing them with *evidence-based* intervention.

Is the recovery real? Or are the kids just "acting normal"? Another cliché, replete in many popular books on autism, is that children who recover are merely "pretending to be normal." I hope that this assertion will one day fizzle out as the children grow older and begin to speak out for themselves, but given the animosity surrounding this topic, perhaps that hope is naïve. Certainly, I know that no follow-up case reports or school reports that I produce about my own children can convince the skeptics—we tried that (Perry, Cohen, & DeCarlo, 1995), and putting our children on television is not something my family chooses to do. Why would we, when we know that nothing our children could ever say or do would ever be enough for those whose minds are set, when we know that there are people who would be actively seeking any "residua." Would our children ever be allowed to stumble? To fall? To fail a course one day? To break up with a girlfriend or boyfriend? To feel shy or awkward in their teen years? It seems not. In her book, Cohen (1998) describes attending a speech by a woman who has claimed to have recovered from autism. Cohen acknowledges that the young woman, who is married and has graduated from college *magna cum laude,* conducts herself with charm and grace. However, Cohen sits in the audience, observing her closely, expressly "searching for residual signs of autism" (p. 169). This scene actually sickens me. I wonder how many of us, including Cohen, would survive such microscopic analysis of our "normalcy."

"High-functioning robots," a phrase employed often by the old guard, is an offensive term, belying the creative, imaginative, and richly affective lives that some children who were formerly diagnosed with autism are now living. I live with three children, two of whom have recovered from autism, and, however galling it may prove to some, they still *do* wonder about, question, and delight in their world. They *do* reflect about anything and everything under the sun, including God, including infinity. Children, after all, with or without autism, are far closer to God than we are: Such questions are a part of their nature, and if given the gift of language, they will persist in exploring, in their innocence, the profound truths of life, spirit, being, and time. At my dinner table, we still indeed talk about philosophy and ethics and art, mixed in with plenty of more mundane concerns, such as homework, dessert options, politics, trying out for the school play, and the sadness of the autism wars, of which they are well aware.

Sometimes, we talk about recovery, about what it means to be "normal." I talk aloud to myself, sometimes in public elevators. Am I normal? My husband can be hyperfocused on any task he sets his mind to. Is he normal? We talk about recovery with our children, because we have to. Knowing what nonsense awaits them in the world, we have had to arm them. We have taught them, carefully, about their early history of autism, and about the brain's ability to keep growing and changing to meet new challenges. We have taught them to be confident and sure, and to rejoice in their accomplishments. We have taught them to be aware of, and to laugh at, the absurdities, the distortions. "Hey! I see three unmade beds here! I thought I trained you all to be compliant robots!"

And let's be very careful about this charge of child abuse. Some people may genuinely decide that autism is just another personality variation, and that nothing at all should be done to change it or treat it. This appears to be the position (occasionally) of the Autism National Committee, when they are not promoting Facilitated Communication. That does not give those individuals the right to impose that ideology upon their neighbor, who might be trying to guide, teach, and maximize the potential of his or her own child. That does not give any group or individual the right to paint other caring parents as Nazi storm troopers, oppressors of the weak. People may disagree on what autism is, but one fact is certain. If not treated effectively, autism radically impairs a child's ability to communicate through language (spoken or written or signed), which is the cornerstone of human learning. What parent would not do all in his or her power to seek any effective and safe means of improving, even a little, a child's capacity to communicate his wants, needs, desires? That is not oppressing them. That is not "rejecting" them because they are autistic. That is freeing them, whether they recover or not, to exercise more autonomy, to make more decisions, to express independent choices.

My daughter and son were not traumatized by any early experience they had with their therapists. In fact, they have an understanding that is pretty straightforward and truthful. They were diagnosed autistic. Autism gets in the way of smart kids learning how to talk. Bridget and Kelly and Robin and Mary Beth came in and helped them get over that hurdle—helped them learn how to talk! Where is the problem?

My daughter, whom we called Anne Marie in *Let Me Hear Your Voice,* is 14 now, and thankfully growing out of the phase where her chief embarrassment in life is her mother. She will walk down the main street in our town with me now, provided that I promise her I will behave myself, and not sing or talk aloud in public. She just asked to have her ears pierced, and she loves Dave Barry books, *The Sixth Sense,* poetry, video games, and humor. Recently, in a self-esteem workshop that the school had the kids attend as part of health class, her classmates had to write comments about each other, then compile a list of compliments for each child. The two most frequent compliments for Anne Marie were "kind" and "funny."

"Do you remember those teaching sessions?" I have asked her.

"Oh yes."

"What do you remember?" I have asked this question several times, and each time, she comes up with a surprisingly detailed memory of interactions and events that I did not tell her about, but I know she is remembering them accurately. For instance, she recalled, in precise detail, a series of teaching cards called "Tell-a-Story," where the object was to place five or six picture cards in a logical narrative order, and construct a story around them. She recalls the pictures and the stories she made up. She recounts things that I have forgotten, as I recall some things she has forgotten.

"And was it hard?"

"It was fun! I liked those little wind-up toys Bridget would bring. Remember the little duck that walked across the table?"

"I do. What is one of the favorite things you remember?"

"I liked it when Bridget would bring Daniel into the room, and we would play cops and robbers."

"Yes. You used to ask for him. But let me ask you something. Do you remember how hard you cried when Bridget first tried to put you in a chair?"

"Not really."

"It's a repressed memory. One day you will go to a shrink and your shrink will help you get in touch with your Inner Child and your Inner Child will discover lots of repressed memories and posttraumatic stress disorder and it will all be Mama's fault."

"I know. But if you let me have another turn at Final Fantasy Seven I will be a happy, well-adjusted girl."

"Nice try."

I don't know what else to say. Both children are doing fine in school, without the need of tutors or therapists of any kind. More important, both have friends, care about their friends, suffer for others, and are capable of expressing sympathy, pain, understanding, and affection. Anne Marie is very shy in new groups, but when she relaxes, she is, as her classmates say, "kind and funny."

Other than that, I hesitate to reveal any more details about my children. Given the tone and level of public discussion on autism today, it seems unwise. I have no wish to expose them to any more mockery, adult bitterness, or cynicism. Besides, the publication of any more information about them will have to be their choice, not mine.[2]

I will continue, however, to the best of my ability while protecting my family's privacy, to defend the truth of recovery, because it is true. I defend the validity of the research on applied behavior analysis because it is real. I resist the distortions because they are distortions, misleading, damaging, and ultimately hurtful to children with autism.

Yes, hurtful to children with autism. The backlash is very strong, and as any glance at the current autism scene will reveal, the people who deride ABA are chairs of departments, professors of special education, "renowned experts." Why do we parents allow these authorities and institutions to speak for us? These are the gatekeepers of our children's future, powerful guardians of what is funded, what is sanctioned, what is approved. Can these statements not damage our children? Talk to the mothers and fathers who are desperately trying to access quality ABA for their son or daughter, and who have to contend with this kind of prejudice. Talk to the psychologists and behavior analysts and special educators and therapists who *are* trying to provide such treatment for children. Listen to the rhetoric to which they have been subjected, the threats and the accusations that they are abusing children for personal gain.

Why such hostility? Who has time to spend the next hundred pages writing or reading an academic treatise on the historical, ideological, and political reasons why? Perhaps hostility is born because power gets in the way of humility, and people begin to feel that they have nothing left to learn. Perhaps animosity is rising because people have spent the last two decades touting their "structured, developmental approach," and are irritated that they are being challenged to produce anything resembling outcome data. Maybe some people are angry because ABA is effective, but not effective enough to bring all children far enough, fast enough. Maybe there are some arrogant or unskilled practitioners of behavior techniques out there (there are), just as there are some arrogant or unskilled practitioners of medicine. So let's not throw away the practice of medicine, just because some physicians are incompetent. Let's work to ensure adequate training opportunities, uniform certification requirements, and professional standards of conduct for anyone who works with our children.

In all honesty, I would have to say that some of my own hesitation about behavioral treatment rose from my wariness

---

[2]Anne Marie read the dialogue above, and says it's ok for me to write that.

around those who strike me as true believers, those who seem to embrace behaviorism as a religion, one that explains and accounts for all human actions, interactions, human purpose, and human nature. This religiosity about behaviorism, if indeed it exists, is not a sentiment I share. I have my own religion, my own philosophical and theological leanings, and my own God. Skinner puts me to sleep, and behavioral jargon, in its sometimes absurdly mechanistic formulations, sets my teeth on edge. But is this the essential? I don't have to "believe in" behaviorism as a philosophy or a theology in order to appreciate its contributions to learning theory.

But, again, who has time for any of this philosophical analysis? Parents need help for their children. Most are so busy just trying to access that help that they cannot be expected to join committees and gently tinker with an entrenched and powerful system.

I don't know how to change the system, either. What I can do is speak out, praying for the wisdom to know the truth and the courage to speak it. The other thing I can do is to try to get parents and professionals as much practical information as possible, through the written word. That is what I have attempted to do in this manual, in collaboration with the gifted co-editors and contributors with whom I am privileged to work. It is my hope that anyone who reads this book will find concrete help and renewed courage, as you work with the child or adult you cherish.

References

Amos, P. (1994, Spring). Review of *Let Me Hear Your Voice*. Autcom: Book Review, pp. 1, 4. Retrieved from the World Wide Web: www.autcom.org

Autism National Committee. (1995, Fall). The Autism National Committee is pleased to announce the 2nd Annual Distinguished Disservice Awards. *The Communicator: A Publication of the Autism National Committee, 6*(2), 15.

Beavers, D. J. (1982). *Autism: Nightmare without end*. Port Washington, NY: Ashley Books.

Bettelheim, B. (1967). *The empty fortress: Infantile autism and the birth of the self*. New York: The Free Press.

Cohen, S. (1998). *Targeting autism: What we know, don't know, and can do to help young children with autism and related disorders*. Berkeley: University of California Press.

Eliot, T. S. (1943). Little Gidding. In *Four Quartets*. New York: Harcourt Brace.

Greenspan, S. (1992). Reconsidering the diagnosis and treatment of very young children with autistic spectrum or pervasive developmental disorder. *Zero to Three, 13*(2), 1–9.

Johnson, C. (1993, Fall). The Advocate interview with Dr. B. J. Freeman. *The Advocate*, pp. 8–10.

Johnson, C. (1994, March–April). Book reviews. *The Advocate*, pp. 31–33.

Lissner-Grant, K. (1995, Fall). One Christian's perspective on the right to die issue. *The Communicator: A Publication of the Autism National Committee, 6*(2), 12.

Maurice, C. (1993). *Let me hear your voice: A family's triumph over autism*. New York: Knopf.

Maurice, C., Green, G., & Luce, S. (1996). *Behavioral intervention for young children with autism: A manual for parents and professionals*. Austin, TX: PRO-ED.

Mesibov, G. (1997). Preschool issues in autism: Introduction. *Journal of Autism and Developmental Disorders, 27*(6), 637–640.

The New Merriam-Webster dictionary. (1989). Springfield, MA: Merriam-Webster.

Perry, R., Cohen, I., & DeCarlo, R. (1995). Case study: Deterioration, autism, and recovery in two siblings. *Journal of the American Academy of Child and Adolescent Psychiatry, 34*, 232–237.

2

♦ ♦ ♦ ♦ ♦ ♦ ♦ ♦ ♦ ♦ ♦ ♦ ♦ ♦ ♦ ♦ ♦ ♦ ♦

The Search for Effective Autism Treatment: Options or Insanity?

Pamela F. Dawson

On my desk is a photograph of my daughter Kelsey at the age of 19 months, sitting on the beach on Captiva Island, Florida, with the sun setting in the background. The photo shows a beautiful child with brown curly hair, large blue eyes, and the face of a cherub. At first glance, one does not notice the hauntingly empty look of her unfocused eyes or the total lack of expression on her face. For me, these are very evident reminders of the first indications of Kelsey's autism and the long distance we have traveled since then.

When Kelsey was born, I felt that my life could not have been more perfect. Kelsey's older brother Sean was thriving and proved to be a loving, bright, and articulate little boy. I was elated when Kelsey entered the world at 8 pounds 7 ounces, with a full head of dark brown hair and a perfectly healthy little body. As I held my daughter for the first time in the delivery room, I was struck by the volume of her piercing cries as she loudly protested her first interactions with the rest of the human race. The doctors proclaimed her to be healthy, and I allowed myself to begin to dream of the successes that would come so naturally to this beautiful and obviously assertive little girl.

There were no warning signs during the first year of Kelsey's life that the reality of our family life might be drastically different from my expectations. In fact, Kelsey's development was typical until the approximate age of 15 months when I noticed a very gradual loss of her first words. Several months later, I realized that it was becoming increasingly difficult to get her attention and eye contact, especially when I attempted to take photographs. Previously, Kelsey had been such a ham, smiling readily for the camera and quickly responding to her name. At approximately 20 months of age, Kelsey also began to exhibit certain oddities in her play. Strangely, I didn't link Kelsey's perseveration on the same activities and the unconventional way in which she often used her toys with her loss of language and eye contact. If all

of the warning signs had appeared more suddenly, perhaps my alarm would have been greater. As luck would have it, her regression coincided with a bout of continuous ear infections which lasted for the next 18 months.

My denial of the seriousness of these issues was facilitated by the lack of concern on the part of Kelsey's pediatrician. Whenever I expressed my anxiety to him, he seemed to prefer a "let's wait and see" approach that gave me a false sense of security. Finally, when Kelsey was 24 months of age, I could no longer deny that something was amiss, and I decided to have Kelsey's hearing tested without a referral from her doctor. The results were inconclusive because Kelsey was very uncooperative during the testing. In retrospect, I am sure that the audiologist had suspicions about the nature of Kelsey's problems. She recommended further developmental assessment but never hinted at what she felt such testing might uncover. I decided to wait until I discussed this further with Kelsey's doctor.

At Kelsey's 2½-year checkup, her pediatrician finally seemed more concerned and we arranged to have Kelsey's hearing tested again. After two hearing tests and an auditory brainstem response test, we were finally able to rule out a hearing loss as the reason for her total lack of language. When we tried to schedule an appointment to have her evaluated at the Child Development Unit of Children's Hospital of Pittsburgh, we were distressed to learn that we would have to wait more than 4 months for an appointment. Those 4 months proved to be the longest and most agonizing of my entire life.

While we waited, I began to search for professionals who could provide us with the services Kelsey needed to stimulate her language and social development. Oddly, her pediatrician never told us that she would qualify for federal- and state-funded early intervention services based on her significant developmental delays. It was another parent who told me that I should call our county's mental health and mental retardation program to have Kelsey tested for eligibility for early intervention services. Kelsey easily qualified, and in the summer of 1994 began to receive services from a speech therapist and a developmental specialist funded through Pennsylvania's Department of Public Welfare. The people who worked with Kelsey were obviously dedicated to their work, but it was apparent to me that the 2 hours a week of services she received were a mere fraction of what she needed. Furthermore, they used a play therapy type of approach, and it was almost impossible to engage Kelsey for any amount of time. After her fourth session, Kelsey's speech therapist commented that she had been unable to get even the most fleeting eye contact from Kelsey since their first session.

I began to ask a lot of questions of the people who worked with Kelsey, about her lack of speech and eye contact, her odd play repertoires, and her almost complete inattentiveness to others' efforts to engage her in even the most rudimentary play. Although these professionals and Kelsey's doctor did not mention the word *autism*, I knew from their questions about her behaviors that they had suspicions in this direction. I called the Autism Society of America and ordered their standard information packet, with the hope that the information would allay my fears. Surely, my daughter did not have autism; she didn't spin objects or rock, and I knew that autism is much less likely to occur in girls than boys. When the packet arrived, I opened it with shaking hands and quickly skimmed through the information until I found a list of 14 symptoms of autism. As I read the list, I counted and recounted the number of symptoms that fit Kelsey. According to the information, it was extremely likely that Kelsey had autism. As the reality of Kelsey's diagnosis hit me, I was quite literally unable to breathe.

For several weeks afterward I was so overcome with grief that I could barely care for Kelsey and her brother Sean. The only moments of the day that were free of the despair that was choking me were the few seconds each morning before I was fully awake. The reprieve was very brief, as very quickly the pain and fear crept into my consciousness. *Autism* invaded my thoughts from those first waking moments and overshadowed every second of my day. I could not look at my daughter without crying; I seemed to see only the autism instead of the child whom I had always loved.

It was unimaginable to me that I would ever again be capable of feeling true joy. I was terrified at the prospect of a future in which every holiday, every birthday, every happy event in my children's lives would be overshadowed by Kelsey's autism.

As I watched how Kelsey isolated herself from the neighborhood children at play in our backyard, I wondered if she would ever have friends. As I observed children much younger than Kelsey happily chattering with their parents in the grocery store or at the playground, I wondered if Kelsey would ever call me "Mommy," if she would ever be able to tell me what she wanted, or if she would ever share her hopes and dreams with me. But by far the greatest source of distress for me was wondering what would become of Kelsey after my husband and I were dead. Would she be able to care for herself? Would she have people in her life who would love her unconditionally as we did? I prayed desperately for the strength and guidance I knew that I would need to help my child.

Fortunately, 3 weeks after the packet arrived, I realized I could not afford to lose any more time to the depression that had taken control of my life. I knew that I would have to work very hard to ensure that Kelsey got the very best treatment available.

The Search for Effective Treatment

As I read and reread the information that the Autism Society of America had sent, I was shocked to discover that there were no established standards for treatment of individuals with autism. If Kelsey had been diagnosed with acute myeloid leukemia or cystic fibrosis, there would be treatment guidelines that had been validated by scientific research. Instead, the information packet that the Autism Society of America mailed to me stated,

> A wide variety of approaches have been found useful with persons with autism. These include: speech therapy, vocational training, sensory-motor therapy, social skills training, and positive behavior management. Parents may wish to explore and evaluate a variety of techniques to determine what will work best for their own child. . . . At this time, it appears that structured habilitative planning and programming is a lifelong requirement for virtually all persons with autism.

The packet contained an extensive list of resources for additional information on a wide assortment of approaches, including TEACCH, Options therapy, auditory training, Facilitated Communication, sensory integration, occupational therapy, vision therapy, and music therapy. I sent for information from the Autism Research Institute, which is operated by Bernard Rimland, and was even further overwhelmed by information on vitamin therapy, dietary interventions, allergies, and yeast overgrowth. How in the world was I to determine what would work for Kelsey? Was I to turn my child into a human guinea pig, performing my own uncontrolled experiments on her? My level of confusion and panic rose in direct proportion to the amount of material I read about autism treatment.

Soon afterward, while searching for reading material on autism in the psychology section of a local bookstore, I found a copy of *Son-Rise: The Miracle Continues* (Kaufman, 1994). In the book, the author contends that his severely autistic son recovered from autism after treatment in a very intensive home-based program developed by the child's mother,

Samahria. The mother said that she spent much of her son's day locked away with him in a small bathroom, at first imitating his self-stimulatory behaviors and gradually encouraging his attempts to interact and communicate. This approach, which is called Options therapy, stresses the importance of acceptance of the child and a "nonjudgmental attitude" in which therapists take the child's lead and imitate the child's play and actions. I called the Options Institute and learned there was a 6-month wait for a 5-day training session, which had a price tag of $6,000. My questions about the effectiveness of the program were met with the names of families who would talk to me about their experiences. Although I was unable to obtain research data on the Options approach, I decided to at least talk to the parents whose names and phone numbers I had been provided by the Options Institute. The families I spoke with told me of the gains that their children had made since beginning the Options program, but none had seen the type of success described in *Son-Rise*. None knew of any data available on the overall effectiveness of this approach.

Although the former banker in me wanted statistics and data quantifying the effectiveness of this approach, I decided that I would lock myself in the bathroom with my daughter as the mother in the book had done with her son, and see what happened. If Kelsey showed any signs of improvement from my attempts, we would look further into attending the Options training. It was within the confines of that small bathroom that I realized how very distant my daughter was, despite her physical proximity. I imitated her self-stimulatory behaviors and her obsessive lining up of objects, and I was as far away from Kelsey after 10 days of this as I had ever been.

While still awaiting the developmental assessment at Children's Hospital, I heard anecdotal reports of the positive effects of the use of dimethylglycine (DMG) and high doses of vitamin B6 and magnesium in children with autism. (These can be purchased without a prescription in most health food stores.) After purchasing the supplements and battling with Kelsey to get the foul-tasting B6 into her, I waited for the miracle of speech. Nothing happened. I continued to hope because I had been told by other parents that it could take up to 30 days for the B6 to have the maximum impact. The 30 days passed with little change in Kelsey's level of functioning. We discontinued use of both DMG and B6 because Kelsey experienced a large increase in sleeplessness while taking the supplements.

Despite the disappointment over the DMG and B6 approach, I continued in desperation to search for answers. After reading about the "yeast connection" theory, which purports that the overuse of antibiotics can result in a yeast overgrowth that causes autism (Crook, 1987), I became convinced that the large doses of antibiotics Kelsey took for her recurrent ear infections were somehow responsible for her autism. On some level, I am sure that I wanted to be able to blame some outside factor as the cause of Kelsey's autism. It

pained me to think that my husband and I might be responsible for passing on to Kelsey the genes that caused her autism.

As I searched for a doctor who would test her and treat her for such a disorder, I became convinced that Kelsey would be cured. The restrictive diet, which is part of the treatment for yeast overgrowth, would be tolerable if it would rid Kelsey of the autism that I felt I could never accept. After all the tests, I was shocked to learn that Kelsey had no "yeast overgrowth" on which we could blame her autism.

The Options therapy, vitamin therapy, and yeast overgrowth therapy were my first experiences of the emotional roller-coaster ride that had embittered so many of the parents of older children with autism with whom I talked. After the irrepressible buildup of hope, thinking "maybe *this* will be the answer," the inevitable crash is very difficult to handle.

In August 1994 while we were still waiting for our appointment at Children's Hospital to confirm Kelsey's diagnosis, I borrowed several textbooks on special education from neighbors and friends and pored over any information I could find on autism. Several of the books mentioned the promising results achieved using intensive behavioral intervention with young children with autism (Fenske, Zalenski, Krantz, & McClannahan, 1985; Harris, Handleman, Gordon, Kristoff, & Fuentes, 1991; Lovaas, 1987; McEachin, Smith, & Lovaas, 1993). What impressed me most about the work of these individuals was that it had been peer-reviewed and published in reputable professional journals. This was the first true glimmer of hope.

The next week, I bought the book *Let Me Hear Your Voice: A Family's Triumph Over Autism* by Catherine Maurice (1993), which I read from cover to cover in less than a day. The message of hope that I derived from the book convinced me that I must try an intensive behavioral program for Kelsey. It struck me that I did not recall reading anything about intensive behavioral programs in the information packet that I received from the Autism Society of America. I went back and read through the entire packet, and found not a single word about this type of treatment despite the fact that research validating the efficacy of behavioral programming in the treatment of autism had been available for decades.

The Formal Diagnosis

In September 1994, we took Kelsey to Children's Hospital for our long-awaited appointment. I was hopeful that they could help us find the resources for the services that Kelsey needed. I thought they would be able to assist us in putting together an intensive behavioral program for Kelsey by referring us to the appropriate professionals. I thought they would give us some hope for Kelsey's future.

Our actual experience was so far removed from what I had hoped that both my husband and I were devastated. We were shuffled from room to room to see the various members of the multidisciplinary team that assessed Kelsey. After months of waiting, I was disturbed that most of these individuals spent less than 5 minutes with her, and that we spent more time waiting for the next member of the team to arrive than in actual contact with that person. Finally, the psychologist in charge of the team confirmed that Kelsey had autism, and went on to say that it was in the moderate range. Of course we had read all the terms about "high functioning" versus "low functioning," and my husband dared to ask the question to which I dreaded the answer:

"Would you consider Kelsey to be high functioning?"

"Definitely not."

"Why not?"

"If she were high functioning, she would have developed meaningful language by now."

She proceeded to tell us that the majority of children with autism *never* develop meaningful language and that we had best put our efforts into finding a means of communication within Kelsey's capabilities. The implication that Kelsey would never communicate verbally was painfully apparent to both my husband and me.

I asked her about the research of Ivar Lovaas using intensive behavioral intervention for children with autism. Her response is one I will never forget: "Personally, most of us here *shudder* at the mention of Lovaas's name." I asked why she was so against this approach, and she stated that she hated to see families putting so much time and money into such a program "at the expense of their marriages and other children." When we asked what type of program she did recommend, she mentioned an inclusive preschool program located outside of our county, which was not an option for Kelsey due to the significant travel time involved.

If the diagnosing psychologist's intention was to destroy every bit of hope that we harbored for Kelsey, she certainly did a fine job. I sobbed the entire way home. It was not so much the diagnosis that caused me so much pain but the fact that my belief that these professionals would reassure us that Kelsey could be helped, and would provide some guidance in attaining that help, was completely crushed. We were given no answers, no guidance, no hope. In fact, we were given no advice other than to place Kelsey in one of the standard special education programs available within our county.

While awaiting the formal written report from Children's Hospital, I visited the programs in my county for which Kelsey would be eligible on her third birthday. One was a mixed disabilities preschool that contained 14 children with one teacher and an aide. I could not imagine Kelsey learning through imitation of the other children, because she had yet to pay attention to her own brother who made exhaustive attempts to interact with her. Also, considering the teacher–student ratio, I knew that she would receive far

more individual attention at home than in the special preschool. The teaching techniques that the teacher used were based on the assumption that the children already possessed basic attending and imitation skills, which were almost completely absent in Kelsey.

Our other placement option was an inclusive preschool setting, which on paper sounded great, but when I took Kelsey with me to visit the school, I knew it was completely inappropriate for her. The preschool operated under the "open classroom" concept and housed approximately 40 children in a large building with concrete block walls. The noise and confusion did not seem conducive to learning, especially for a child such as Kelsey, who was obviously overwhelmed by all the stimulation. I asked the special education administrators for outcome data for children with autism who had been placed in both of these programs, and was told that none were available.

My husband, angry and disgusted by the attitudes of the special education administrators and the psychologist from Children's Hospital, prevented me from falling over the edge into a state of total despair and convinced me that we should proceed on our own to put together an intensive behavioral program for Kelsey. What did we have to lose at that point in time? How could we possibly live with ourselves if we did not at least try this approach?

It took the multidisciplinary team from Children's Hospital 2 months from the date of her appointment to issue their report on Kelsey's evaluation. Fortunately, I had not expected the report to be any more helpful than our interactions with the staff at the appointment itself. The report, although seven pages in length, was obviously based on a standard template because there were numerous instances throughout the report in which my daughter was described using the pronouns "he" and "his." The report stated,

Kelsey was inconsistently responsive to visual and auditory stimuli. She was generally socially inattentive unless actively engaged by an adult in an energetic activity. She required repeated prompting before responding to the examiner and her responses were inconsistent and minimal. Her eye contact was fleeting, inconsistent and generally not used communicatively. Her use of gestures, facial expression and body postures to communicate was minimal as well. Interest in imitation was very limited.

She was attentive to exaggerated play with a small Barney toy, but even with repeated prompts and modeling of requesting behaviors, she was unable to indicate that he [sic] wanted the activity to continue or resume. She did display her unhappiness when the toy was removed, crying and trying to physically secure the toy. No other communicative gestures accompanied this.

Kelsey is impaired in her capacity for reciprocal social interaction although she is responsive at times. She generally does not initiate contact with others and is generally not responsive to interaction unless it is fairly intrusive. She cannot sustain interaction. She is demonstrating significant impairments in her capacity for verbal and non-verbal communication. She has not developed the capacity for symbolic or abstract thought and has restricted interests in her environment.

The Journey Begins

Fortunately, we had not waited for the report from Children's Hospital to begin our efforts to put together an intensive behavioral program for Kelsey. God was truly watching over me on the day that I learned, from the friend of a friend, of a local woman, Joan Cross, who had put together such a program for her son. Joan helped me in all of the areas in which the professionals had failed so miserably. She helped me find a behavioral consultant, gave me tips on how to hire therapists, and shared all of the knowledge regarding the science of applied behavior analysis (ABA) which she had learned through necessity. Joan spent hours on the phone with me, answering my questions and encouraging me during the times when I felt I couldn't possibly handle the emotional stress of dealing with Kelsey's problems. Joan encouraged my efforts to restore hope to our lives.

Within 2 months of Kelsey's appointment at Children's Hospital of Pittsburgh, we had interviewed over 20 applicants for the position of therapist, and had hired 5 to work with Kelsey. Because there was no local expertise in intensive behavioral programming, we decided to use a consultant from the Center for Autism and Related Disorders (CARD), located in California, to provide training for our team of therapists and to set up the curriculum for Kelsey's program. CARD's program is based on the model developed by O. Ivar Lovaas at the University of California at Los Angeles (UCLA). On the eve of our first workshop, I was in such a state of emotional turmoil that I did not sleep at all. If this didn't work, I didn't know where we would turn for help for Kelsey because I had seen how little impact the traditional interventions had on her despite the hard work and enthusiasm of the professionals who worked with her.

Kelsey was 38 months old when we began her program, and during the time since we first realized Kelsey had autism, she had made almost no progress. Kelsey still had no meaningful language. Her receptive language was also very poor. In fact the multidisciplinary team at Children's Hospital had determined her language skills to be clustered below the 12-month level.

Her toy play was restricted to repetitive activities, such as dropping toys through openings in other toys and lining up toys and other objects for hours on end. She was very difficult to engage and seemed to prefer to be off on her own in her solitary activities. She tolerated and even showed affection toward my husband and me, but treated other people (including her own brother) as nothing more than objects that were in her way.

My husband and I had been so happy when our children were born that they would have the opportunity to know both sets of grandparents, who lived nearby. We were puzzled and saddened when we saw that Kelsey wanted absolutely nothing to do with either set of grandparents who tried so desperately to get close to their beloved little granddaughter. It was typical of her to escape to her room when they visited, or to seek an empty room in which to hide in seclusion whenever we visited their homes.

Sean's determined efforts to play with his sister or to elicit her laughter, which once came so easily, were also met with similar rejection. It broke my heart when my son, who was almost 5 at the time, asked me with tears in his eyes why his sister didn't love him. How do you explain autism to a little boy who only knows that every time he tries to play with his sister or to make her laugh, she screams and pushes him away? Equally disturbing, Kelsey was beginning to engage in some self-injurious behavior, frequently smacking herself in the face and on the head when frustrated. One thing that never failed to set her off was being stopped in traffic. While we were cautiously hopeful that an intensive behavioral program would help Kelsey, we were fearful for her future if she did not respond favorably.

The first weeks of Kelsey's program were so difficult that I gladly would have walked away from the whole thing if I felt there was any other choice. Kelsey fought the therapists' efforts to get her to perform the simplest of tasks, even when we used the most enticing reinforcement. Her crying and tantrums left me so shaken that I often sat outside or went for a walk, sobbing the entire time. I was desperate for this program to help my daughter, and vowed to stick out those first horrible weeks despite my instincts that screamed for me to rush into the room and grab my daughter, hug and kiss her, and then banish the therapists from our home. Slowly over the first 3 weeks the crying and tantrums subsided, but Kelsey still seemed resolved to wear all of us down with her refusal to cooperate. Attempts to physically prompt her through nonverbal imitation were met with passive resistance, as Kelsey made every muscle in her body completely slack. Verbal imitation was equally frustrating as she refused to make any attempt to imitate the sounds and simple words that we knew she was capable of repeating. Nothing seemed a powerful enough motivator to get Kelsey to comply with our wishes.

Six weeks into her program, it was as though someone flicked a switch and Kelsey made the powerful connection that language was a tool to be used to get what she wanted. Kelsey's receptive and expressive language exploded. Up to that point, we had had no success with either her receptive label or expressive label programs; she had not mastered a single target in either program. We had not been able to get her to repeat sounds or words on a consistent basis in her verbal imitation program. And then, within a 1-week period, she acquired more than 40 receptive and expressive labels. I still remember the day that one of her therapists called me into the room saying, "Kelsey has something to show you." I was expecting Kelsey to correctly supply maybe one or two labels, and was amazed to hear Kelsey expressively label 14 of her favorite foods, 12 different animals, and almost 20 different toys. The next week she also began to verbally request her favorite foods spontaneously. She began to breeze through her block imitation program, duplicating even the most difficult structures with ease. She learned the names of family members and therapists from photographs. Three weeks later, a little more than 2 months since we began Kelsey's program, as I stood cooking at the stove, I heard a voice call to me from behind, "Mom!" Before I turned completely around, I responded, "What, Sean?" assuming it was my son. But instead, I found my daughter, from whom I had yearned to hear that one word for so long. My husband and I shared our exuberance with her entire team of therapists. We had been blessed with therapists who shared our vision for Kelsey and who had the perseverance to stick with us through those tough times.

At the 3-month mark of our program, our CARD consultant returned and she too expressed delight over Kelsey's progress. She gave us many new programs that were intended to boost Kelsey closer to her typically developing peers, but Kelsey's progress stalled because many of the new programs were too much of a jump forward. We were expecting her to perform a sequencing drill that required responses in full sentences, when she was incapable of articulating more than two-word phrases. We were also expecting her to use *he* or *she* correctly in sentences when she had not yet learned to distinguish between boys and girls. I grew frustrated because I felt that the consultant was not properly adapting Kelsey's programming to her level of functioning. In my opinion, we had failed to address a number of critical components of the more complex skills we were expecting Kelsey to learn.

Kelsey's own frustration over her repeated failures in these new programs alarmed me. She began to cry more and she grew more nonresponsive in therapy. I was frightened that she would find her therapy sessions so aversive that she would slowly revert back to the silent and socially nonresponsive child that she had once been.

Fortunately, before our fears were realized, we were able to retain the services of a new consultant from the Young Autism Project of Pittsburgh (YAPP), a UCLA replication site, who would be attempting to replicate the favorable outcomes that Lovaas had achieved with children with autism. Under our new consultant's supervision, we backtracked, broke tasks down into smaller steps, and were able to get Kelsey's program back on track.

The next 6 months were encouraging, as Kelsey mastered many new programs with little difficulty. Then she began to struggle with her articulation, with discrimination errors and behavioral issues. After quickly acquiring single labels, Kelsey was having difficulty articulating more than two or three words. She learned simple sentences with a tremendous amount of effort. She was able to generalize these sentences and use them appropriately outside of therapy, but it seemed that she would never be able to create unique sentences of her own. My fears mounted as her progress stalled once more.

At that time, several parents told me of an Auditory Integration Training (AIT) practitioner who would be coming to our area. AIT is based on the premise that sensory processing dysfunction is responsible for many of the characteristics of autism, and its proponents claim that by subjecting it to specially filtered music through headphones, the auditory system can be "retrained." The training consisted of two half-hour sessions per day conducted over a 10-day period, at a cost of about $1,200. I was provided with scores of anecdotal stories about AIT that claimed everything from moderate levels of positive behavioral change to complete recovery from autism. Although I was growing increasingly skeptical of any therapies marketed for autism, I decided to give it a try. Despite my efforts to remain realistic, I became caught up in the hope that maybe this really would help Kelsey "over the hump."

During the AIT, I was made aware of several practices of the people providing the therapy that deeply disturbed me. First, almost from the initial session, I was told that the effects of AIT were cumulative, and that most individuals with autism would benefit from repeating the training every 6 to 12 months. I recall feeling guilty because I immediately thought, "Well, gee, if these kids keep coming back for more AIT, eventually you would expect to see *some* amount of progress that would have occurred even without AIT."

Second, families who were interested in a second round of AIT could do so for free if they could sign up 10 other paying clients. This pyramid approach to marketing AIT reminded me of the methods used by the promoters of some overpriced vitamin supplements, in which consumers of the supplements are encouraged to "share the good news" with friends and relatives of how the supplements had supposedly improved their lives. By selling the supplements to friends and relatives, they are then able to earn free products. It was my opinion that if AIT were truly as effective as claimed, this type of marketing ploy should not be necessary.

Last, to qualify for this free repeat AIT program, you also had to complete a survey about your child's progress at 3 months and then at 6 months after completion of AIT. These surveys were being used to compile "data" for "research" into the efficacy of AIT.

I had serious concerns for the vulnerable parents who would be reading the results of this particular "research" in the future. Who would be more likely to complete and return the survey: parents who felt that AIT had been ineffective for their child, or parents who felt it had helped their child and were interested in the free follow-up round of therapy? Also, how can we as parents put aside our emotions, our desperation to objectively evaluate every treatment out there, to determine the validity of the research and claims of every proponent of the multitude of therapies and treatments for autism?

Despite my misgivings, we did the 20 sessions, and waited. There was no miracle; there was no improvement in Kelsey's rate of progress. In fact, the 6 months after her AIT were the most difficult since we began Kelsey's intensive behavioral program. I recall thinking that even if Kelsey had gone through an upswing in her rate of progress after AIT, how would I have determined what was responsible? We had seen Kelsey go through periods of rapid acquisition of new skills, and also periods where she seemed to plateau. I realized that it was virtually impossible to objectively evaluate the impact of any additional therapies we tried.

In October 1996, we enrolled Kelsey in a typical preschool with a shadow aide. Although Kelsey was not disruptive in her behavior, she was easily distracted and was much less responsive with her teacher and peers than in a therapy setting.

Immediately, our consultant from the Young Autism Project of Pittsburgh and Kelsey's developmental pediatrician began a campaign to convince us to try Ritalin and various other stimulants to treat Kelsey's distractibility. By this time, I had become increasingly skeptical of the many treatments being touted for autism. I did my own research on the use of Ritalin in children with a diagnosis of autism, and was shocked that professionals would recommend Ritalin after what I learned. First, I was dismayed to learn that there had been no testing of the effects of Ritalin on any children under the age of 6 (*Physicians' Desk Reference*, 1993). My daughter was only 5 at the time. Second, research has shown that the use of Ritalin in persons with autism was more likely to produce negative effects, such as increased stereotypic behaviors, than positive effects (Campbell, 1989). More recently, I have learned that *no* drugs have been approved by the FDA *specifically* for the treatment of autism (National Institute of Mental Health, 1997).

My husband and I had no difficulty in reaching the decision *not* to try Ritalin or any other drug. Kelsey's behaviors were not putting her or us at risk of bodily harm, and given her young age, we preferred to try a behavioral approach to address this issue. I cannot say that I would never consider medication for my child. However, I was frankly appalled at the proclivity of the professionals to initiate a game of pharmacological roulette in a child as young as my daughter, especially given the lack of aggressive or other dangerous behaviors.

At the 2½-year mark of her intensive ABA program, Kelsey's rate of progress picked up once again, as we saw a significant increase in her spontaneous language and wonderful imaginary play. However, several months later, we were dealt a blow that could have proved disastrous to her program.

During a workshop in June 1997, my consultant pulled me aside and informed me that Kelsey was being terminated as a client of the YAPP. The implications were significant, because Kelsey's entire staff of therapists was employed by YAPP. I was given just over 60 days to find and train an entire new team of therapists. What made this task especially difficult was the fact that behavioral programs for children with autism were fully funded in Pennsylvania, creating long waiting lists for services. The irony of the situation was that I was one of a key group of people who had led the effort to secure funding for ABA programs within our state, to inform others of the benefits of ABA, and to bring a UCLA replication site to Pittsburgh.

As Kelsey ran into the room and leaped into my lap for a hug, I sat, numb, listening to the consultant's rationale. I was told that YAPP had made a commitment to take on a given number of research children within certain time frames. Because of a freeze on hiring at Allegheny General Hospital, which housed the program at that time, the additional staff necessary to fulfill that research commitment could not be hired. Kelsey was never a research subject due to the fact that we had begun treatment prior to becoming clients of YAPP, and she therefore did not meet the criteria for research subjects. Apparently my precious child and her future were to be sacrificed so that staff could be freed to work with a new and obviously more valuable research child.

While Kelsey squirmed in my lap, the consultant launched into a long monologue about how difficult it was to hold the program together, what long hours she and her staff worked, and what horrible pressure they were under. I suppose this was intended to elicit sympathy from me, but instead I became angry over her egocentric view of the situation. I bit back the angry words that sprang to my lips, but finally, when I could not stand to hear another word, I hugged Kelsey to me and said, "Don't worry, honey. Mommy will make sure that you are taken care of."

Despite my anger, I realized that I could not afford to indulge in my desire to lash back. I tried to buy more time to find replacement staff, and was told that the termination date I was given was absolute. I asked if the YAPP could at least continue to provide workshop consultations every 2 to 3 months. The consultant reluctantly agreed, but I was told that it would be in Kelsey's best interest for me to find a new consultant as soon as possible. The consultant told me that since Kelsey was 5 at that time, I should find someone who had more experience in working with children of school age.

Within 2 weeks of the date I was first informed of Kelsey's termination from YAPP, I hired two new therapists directly, and used Kelsey's existing YAPP staff to begin an intensive training program for the new therapists. I also found a new provider of behavioral health services which, unlike most within our state, did not have a long waiting list for services. The new provider agreed to take over Kelsey's program the day after YAPP's termination, and also agreed to hire the two new therapists that I had trained, to ease the transition for Kelsey. When the YAPP consultant and I had a meeting 1 week prior to the termination date to finalize the details of Kelsey's transition to the new provider, I was told there would be *no* more workshops, as originally promised. I felt angry, abandoned, and frustrated at the prospect of having to pull together an entire program once again. We were fortunate to find a new consultant who had recently moved to western Pennsylvania from Florida, where she had been certified as a behavior analyst.

During the past year with our new provider and new consultant, Kelsey has made significant gains, most notably in her interactive play and expressive language. I feel that Kelsey's recent progress has been largely due to the fact that our new team has done an excellent job of task analysis of skills that are difficult for Kelsey, and has been much more creative in eliciting and rewarding spontaneous language.

Kelsey Today

When we began Kelsey's program, I had hoped that she would reach the point where she was indistinguishable from her peers. After almost 4 years of intensive behavioral therapy, this is not the case. However, today Kelsey is a very different child from the one described in the report from Children's Hospital of Pittsburgh. The child whose language skills were assessed to be clustered below the 12-month level now speaks in sentences and is wonderfully spontaneous in her observations and comments on the world around her. The child whose toy play once consisted of lining up objects for hours on end recently asked her dad to help her turn an empty cardboard box into a puppet theater, and has been entertaining us with her theatrical productions which incorporate various members of her extensive Disney character beanbag collection. The child who once sought isolation at all costs now asks, "Mommy, can I go outside and play with my friends?"

Four years ago Kelsey took no notice of the emotions of others, and displayed no empathy, even for those closest to her. Today, she is at times a little too sensitive to the feelings of the people she loves. She is very quick to offer an apology, a hug, or a smile because she does not want anyone to be angry, hurt, or sad. When her brother was recently hospitalized overnight following a tonsillectomy, Kelsey insisted on calling me several times at the hospital asking, "Mommy, how's Sean feeling? Mommy, please bring Sean home." And when Sean came home from the hospital the following day, she ran to greet him. But when she sensed his pain, her smile quickly faded into a look of genuine concern. She sat beside him looking intently for some sign of improvement, and then suddenly jumped to her feet and declared, "Sean, I have a surprise for you! I'll be right back." She ran from the room, and quickly returned with the smile back on her face and the biggest helium balloon I have ever seen, crying, "Look Sean, I got a balloon for you."

Four years ago, Kelsey spent most of her free time engaged in stereotypic behaviors that are characteristic of autism. Now when Kelsey is not in therapy or at school, I no longer have to exercise the constant vigilance that I once did to make sure she is engaged in appropriate behaviors. Last night, as I approached Kelsey's room to tell her it was time to prepare for bed, I heard my husband's laughter intermixed with Kelsey's giggles. I walked into the room and asked, "What's so funny, guys?" Kelsey responded, "Look, Mom! I made a Cri-Kee book." (Cri-Kee is a character from Disney's movie *Mulan*.) Kelsey then proceeded to narrate a comical story of her own creation of the adventures of Cri-Kee based on her elaborate drawings of the character. Cri-Kee visited Rudolph and gave him a carrot; went into a cave, saw a bear, and was scared; went to a Halloween party and was afraid of the ghost; and eventually got married and lived happily ever after (Kelsey had Cri-Kee, whom she claims is a boy, wearing a veil). Her syntax was far from perfect, but we were thrilled by the pleasure she took in telling us her story.

Despite her tremendous progress, Kelsey is still delayed in her expressive and receptive language and in her social skills. She still has difficulty answering some wh– questions and frequently uses pronouns incorrectly. She cannot sustain a conversation beyond two or three turns despite her desire to interact with others, and she has a tendency to perseverate on certain topics. She is still easily distracted in new environments, and is not very responsive socially in new settings.

This fall, Kelsey climbed aboard the school bus with her brother for the first time. She now attends the local elementary school where she is enrolled in a regular kindergarten classroom with an aide who is trained in behavioral intervention. The aide is focusing on developing Kelsey's social skills by using peer-training techniques to elicit socially appropriate language and behaviors. We are also working with Kelsey to develop the skills she will need to successfully transition from learning in one-on-one instruction to group instruction. Although Kelsey still has deficits, as she continues to make steady, systematic gains, our fear for her future subsides.

What about the dire warnings of the diagnosing psychologist about the impact of intensive behavioral programs on families? Today, our family is intact, and because of the gift of Kelsey's progress, our home is filled with more joy than I had ever dreamed possible after we first learned of Kelsey's diagnosis. I have found additional reasons to love the man I married as I witness his devotion and commitment to Kelsey. My son Sean has a sister who absolutely adores him and who has become a playmate. Oh, what a joy it is to hear Kelsey's sweet little voice calling, "Sean, you want to play with me?"

I have always worried about the impact on Sean of the attention that has been focused on Kelsey. After all, the psychologist at Children's Hospital warned about the tremendous negative impact on siblings when parents pursue intensive ABA programs for their children with autism. But Sean has amazed us with his desire and capacity to become one of

Kelsey's best teachers, and his success with her has become something in which he takes enormous pride. When his first-grade teacher asked each student to complete the sentence, "I feel proud of myself when . . . ," Sean's response was, "when I teach something to my sister Kelsey who has autism, and she does it right."

There are still days when the reality of Kelsey's disability overwhelms me, when the clouds seem to overshadow all. But in contrast to the very dark days when I first realized that Kelsey had autism, there is so much sunshine once again in our lives. Four years ago, my husband and I watched our daughter's odd behaviors and isolation with fear and despair. Now, almost daily, our eyes meet and we share a private smile of joy and of triumph as we observe our daughter saying or doing something many would never have thought possible. Kelsey is a true heroine and I know that the final chapter in her success story lies in the distant future.

What Made Our Fight for Kelsey So Difficult

The past 4 years since Kelsey's diagnosis have been very difficult, primarily because of the tremendous efforts required to effectively advocate for the services our daughter needs in order to reach her potential. Instead of getting support for our quest to ensure that Kelsey becomes as self-sufficient as possible, we have had to fight a system that has a very poor track record in terms of positive outcomes for persons with autism. My husband and I refused to meekly allow Kelsey to become another one of the two thirds of adults with autism who require lifelong supervision because they have failed to develop the skills requisite to independent functioning (Gillberg, 1991).

Although parents are no longer blamed for causing their children's autism, the autism community has not progressed very far toward ensuring free access to the best treatment available. Precious time is still being wasted as we search for answers. Fortunately, a growing number of people within the autism community are committed to ensuring access to scientifically validated treatment. From several of the early forerunners of this movement, I first read and heard concise descriptions of the impediments to access of such treatment. In my own experiences, I have found their assessments of the current autism culture to be painfully accurate.

Low-Outcome Expectations Become a Self-Fulfilling Prophecy

The majority of medical and educational professionals still view autism as a chronic condition from which very little improvement can be expected over the course of the individual's lifetime. Many do not believe that significant progress, let alone recovery, is possible except in very rare cases. At a

recent conference, Catherine Maurice (1998) spoke of this phenomenon, which she aptly called the "accommodation model." The premise of the model is that we must accommodate individuals with autism because we cannot change them.

Sadly, these low expectations have become a self-fulfilling prophecy for many children with autism. Medical professionals warn parents when their children are diagnosed not to expect too much. The psychologist who diagnosed Kelsey apparently felt compelled to force us to face the facts as she saw them. This same professional who told us that Kelsey was definitely *not* high functioning told another parent, "I hope you realize that any hopes you had for a normal family life just went right out the window."

These low expectations are typical among education professionals as well. I remember the incredulous looks I received when I first told people within the educational system of the type of program I felt my daughter needed. They could not understand why I was not satisfied with their programs. Many of the standard educational programs for children with autism that I have seen offer a very structured and predictable setting, for the purpose of accommodating the individual with autism. I could not help but believe that such a setting would make it virtually impossible for the individual with autism to live and function in the rest of the world, which unfortunately is neither structured nor predictable. In most of the standard educational placements for children with autism, long-term outcomes are generally not favorable.

Sadly, considering that a free and appropriate public education (FAPE) is supposedly guaranteed to children with autism under the Individuals with Disabilities Education Act (IDEA), the standards for what is deemed *appropriate* are based on low-outcome expectations. Parents who ask for anything more than the standard programs often are faced with an expensive and exhausting legal battle.

Pressure To "Accept" Rather than Rehabilitate

Within the autism community itself, there is a segment of people who seem to feel that we parents who want intensive behavioral programs for our children with autism are being cruel and unfair to our children. They feel we need to "accept" our children as they are and "let them be children." Apparently it is politically incorrect to aspire to more than the typically bleak prognosis that our children would face without proper treatment. Maurice (1998) commented on the plethora of "coping books" on autism, which offer advice to parents on how to accept and cope with their child's autism, but little or no advice as to how to bring about positive change in their children.

Unfortunately, not only the families of children with autism have difficulty "accepting" their children's autism; society as a whole does not accept our children's differences. I still have vivid recollections of the reactions of strangers to my daughter's behaviors before and in the early phases of her behavioral program. I remember the venomous remark, "Next time, take them camping," from the woman seated behind me on a 2-hour airplane flight during which Kelsey screamed continuously. I remember the dirty looks in restaurants when Kelsey shouted and refused to stay in her seat. I remember one woman's angry insistence that I "do something to stop her," when Kelsey engaged in self-injurious behavior in public.

With much trepidation for Kelsey's future, I have observed people within our local community angrily protesting the opening of a group home in their neighborhood for adults with mental retardation. During Kelsey's most difficult moments I never stopped loving her; I never failed to accept Kelsey herself. What I could not accept was the notion that her difficult behaviors could not be reduced or eliminated, that she could not be taught the skills she would need to function independently. I know that I will not be around for Kelsey's entire life to buffer her from the prejudices against the disabled that will more than likely not be eradicated within her lifetime.

My fear for Kelsey's future has driven me to provide her with early intensive behavioral intervention. But in the process, I have received criticism that I am robbing her of her childhood. Anyone who would observe my daughter for a short period of time would see that she is a very happy little girl who now is actively partaking of the joys and wonder of childhood. I have witnessed scores of other children who have similarly benefited from behavioral intervention. These children have not been abused; rather, they have been systematically taught the skills that have enabled them to become more active participants in their families and communities.

No one would dream of refusing rehabilitation services to persons who have suffered a stroke or a serious head injury. No one would dream of telling the families that it would be "cruel" to put their loved ones through arduous rehabilitation therapy, that they need to "accept" their loved ones as is. Why should it be any different for children with autism?

Lack of Treatment Guidelines

In the fall of 1997, I had the pleasure of hearing Gina Green speak on the topic of "Science, Pseudoscience, and Antiscience in Autism Treatment." Green's incisive speech illustrated clearly for me how the lack of treatment guidelines based on science has impeded access to the most effective treatment for children with autism. Without such guidelines, parents often waste precious time and resources on ineffective and sometimes dangerous treatments.

Many grassroots organizations for other diseases and disabilities have led the effort to establish treatment guidelines and standards of care for those particular diseases or disabilities. Such standards and guidelines include treatments that have been scientifically validated to be most effective. These organizations have then spearheaded the effort to push insur-

ance companies to provide coverage for these treatments. There are no such guidelines, no such standards of care for people with autism, and as a result, insurance coverage for the treatment of autism is the exception rather than the rule.

In Pennsylvania, children with autism are eligible for Medical Assistance, the state's Medicaid program, regardless of parental income under the Katie Beckett waiver. Parents of children with autism have been successful in getting funding for programs through Medical Assistance under the category of mental health wraparound services. This funding source was seriously jeopardized last year when the Pennsylvania Department of Public Welfare proposed changes to the state's definition of medical necessity for these types of services. Under the proposed definition, interventions that are not consistent with an "existing national standard of care" for the condition for which they are prescribed would not be funded. More than 400 families nearly lost funding for their children's behavioral programs because the autism community has focused its efforts on making parents feel good about their "choices" rather than on adherence to best practices based on science.

By emphasizing the parents' right to choices for treatment for their children, the Autism Society of America and other autism organizations not only have made it difficult to obtain funding, but also have opened the door to a virtual flood of options. There is no deterrent for those who would prey upon the desperation of parents in search of the ever-elusive "magic bullet." The array of supposed choices grows almost daily.

Recently, on an autism mailing list on the Internet, a parent advised another parent of a newly diagnosed child to "try everything and anything you can afford." I was saddened when I read of this recipe for emotional and financial bankruptcy.

I have met other parents who share my vision of access to fully funded and high-quality behavioral programming for all children with autism. Over the past 3 years, we have undertaken an intensive and exhausting campaign to educate those in control of the purse strings about the benefits of behavioral intervention for our children. As a result of these efforts, our parents' group has often been the subject of very caustic and unfounded attacks. Many feel that by advocating for science, we are in some fashion jeopardizing their own children's future by taking away their choices. It seems that many within the autism community equate free and indiscriminate choice with progress. We have repeatedly stated that we do not advocate against choice, but rather for *informed* choice based on scientific research and validation of treatment efficacy.

I do not feel that I have the right to dictate the choices parents make after they are given accurate information about treatment efficacy. However, it is a sad reality that today many are not given that information. Further, there is limited public funding for programs for our children, and I feel very strongly that when it comes to the allocation of public monies for autism treatment, scientific outcome data must be a prime consideration.

Parents as the Experts

A parallel to the outcry for choice and for options is the commonly held view that parents are the experts on their children with autism and can best determine the most effective course of treatment. Although I may be the expert regarding certain aspects of my child's behaviors and preferences, I hardly feel that I am qualified to sift through medical, psychological, and special education journals to determine the best course of treatment for my child. This is not meant to be a criticism of the many parents, myself included, who have been forced to make difficult treatment decisions in the absence of sound professional advice. I know firsthand of the desperation that drives parents to abandon logic and reason and try *anything* to try to help their child. The difficult decisions that we as parents of children with autism face on a daily basis are a constant source of anxiety. We will typically try treatment after treatment, not because we are convinced that any one of them is truly effective, but rather because we are terrified that we may bypass the one treatment that might help our child. Without data-based guidelines to help us through the maze of therapies and treatments, we turn to other parents for advice.

I have read with alarm contributions to Internet mailing lists on autism in which parents promote various types of treatment for autism. These treatments include dolphin therapy, the use of assorted vitamins and dietary supplements, secretin therapy, brushing and other sensory integration techniques, Lycra suits, intravenous immunoglobulin (IVIG) therapy, music therapy, play therapy, art therapy, Facilitated Communication, home-brewed mushroom tea, weighted vests, "paleo" diets, treatment for yeast overgrowth, Irlen lenses, gluten- and casein-free diets, drum therapy, therapeutic horseback riding, Universal Studios therapy, cranial massage, auditory training, human growth hormones, Epsom salt baths, and a wide array of over-the-counter and prescription drugs.

Through the Internet, parents have warned other parents not to give antibiotics to their children unless their illness was "life threatening" because, according to these parents, it was known that antibiotics caused autism and would also cause further regression in children with autism. Parents have regularly advised other parents to have their children checked for yeast overgrowth and have stated that 95% of children with autism suffer from this affliction. One parent was told that if she put her child on the special antiyeast diet, 90% of her son's autistic behaviors would disappear. What many parents do not realize is that there are no data to support these claims.

Many parents insist that they trust the opinions of other parents more than those of the mainstream medical and psychological communities because members of those same professions once blamed parents for causing their children's autism. I wondered if this was the source of the "parents are the experts" mentality. Yes, it is tragic that parents, and specifically mothers, were once blamed for causing their children's autism (Bettelheim, 1967). What parent of a child with autism has not heard of Bruno Bettelheim? How did he manage to woo the professional community and the popular press to accept his views? A recent biography (Pollak, 1997) reveals that Bettelheim was a ruthless man who fabricated not only his professional credentials but also the data upon which he based many of his published works on the topic of autism. His actions were deplorable, but should parents now shun *all* professionals in the field? Or should we set standards for the behavior of these professionals and demand that claims about autism treatments be subjected to the type of rigorous scrutiny described so well by Green (1996) in *Behavioral Intervention for Young Children with Autism: A Manual for Parents and Professionals*?

The Proliferation of "Pseudoexperts"

In addition to the "parent experts," there are a large number of pseudoexperts in the field of autism. They are the scores of people touting themselves as experts in the treatment of autism who have little true expertise to offer. A person can become "certified" as a practitioner of "therapy X" or "therapy Y" by attending a short training course. The framed certificate hanging on the wall may look impressive, but what does it tell us about the individual's ability to deliver effective services to our children?

There are scores of unqualified people marketing themselves as ABA consultants and collecting hefty fees from parents who are in a frantic race against the clock to put together a behavioral program for their children. Many of these so-called consultants may have their books of "drills," but have no or only rudimentary training in the science of behavior analysis. Many have no grasp of basic behavior analytic methods, such as how to gather and interpret data or how to analyze the causes of problem behaviors or learning difficulties. They have only the "cookie-cutter" approach in which they were trained, and do not know how to make the necessary adaptations to programming when children fail to progress. The blame is often placed on the child or the parents rather than the programmer.

At a past workshop, my daughter screamed when a new therapist "reinforced" her by vigorously tickling her. My daughter normally loves to be tickled by her family and by people she knows and likes, including her regular therapists. She does, however, show socially appropriate restraint with new people and with people she does not like. I was taken aback when the consultant told the therapist to continue tickling Kelsey until she stopped screaming because she would just have to get over her tactile defensiveness. Did it occur to the consultant that perhaps she had lost track of the definition of reinforcement here? Or that perhaps it was incorrect to interpret my daughter's screaming as tactile defensiveness without performing a functional analysis? Even if it was tactile defensiveness, was this really the appropriate way to address it?

My own experiences have been mild compared with some of the horror stories I have heard about incompetent and unethical "experts." But with the emphasis on treatment choices rather than treatment quality, it is not surprising that such abuses occur.

Hope for the Future

I have suffered through many sleepless nights in which my thoughts invariably turn to my daughter Kelsey. It is then, during the darkest hours of the night, that my fears for her future work their way into my consciousness. It is then that my pain and my frustration are the strongest. It is then that I dare to wonder how much better Kelsey would have fared if things within the autism community had been different when she was diagnosed.

I know that I am not alone in my painful contemplation of the past events in my child's life. I know that many other parents are currently dealing with the same emotions. I know that still today there are parents whose children are being diagnosed later than necessary, and for whom the information about services that could significantly alter their children's lives is not being provided by professionals. I know that many parents cannot afford to give their children the help that they deserve. No parent should have to lie awake at nights with the painful questions that plague all of us who know that there is much more that can and should be done for these precious children. No parent should have to undertake the all too common trial-and-error approach to finding effective treatment.

Over the past several years, there has been a growing movement within the autism community to ensure the dissemination of accurate information about treatment efficacy, and to increase access to high-quality intensive behavioral programs. It is my sincere hope that, through the efforts of these parents and professionals, the children and the families of the children who will be diagnosed with autism in the future will be spared the frustration and the anguish associated with the current "try everything and anything" mentality.

References

Bettelheim, B. (1967). *The empty fortress*. New York: The Free Press.

Campbell, M. (1989). Pharmacotherapy in autism: An overview. In C. Gillberg (Ed.), *Diagnosis and treatment of autism* (pp. 203–217). New York: Plenum Press.

Crook, W. G. (1987). Nutrition, food allergies, and environmental toxins [letter]. *Journal of Learning Disabilities, 20*, 260–261.

Fenske, E. C., Zalenski, S., Krantz, P. J., & McClannahan, L. E. (1985). Age at intervention and treatment outcome for autistic children in a comprehensive intervention program. *Analysis and Intervention in Developmental Disabilities, 5*, 49–58.

Gillberg, C. (1991). Outcome in autism and autistic-like conditions. *Journal of the American Academy of Child and Adolescent Psychiatry, 30*, 375–382.

Green, G. (1996). Evaluating claims about treatments for autism. In C. Maurice, G. Green, & S. C. Luce (Eds.), *Behavioral intervention for young children with autism: A manual for parents and professionals* (pp. 15–28). Austin, TX: PRO-ED.

Green, G. (1997, September). *Science, pseudoscience and antiscience in autism treatment*. Paper presented at the 7th Annual New York State Association for Behavior Analysis Conference, Tarrytown, NY.

Harris, S. L., Handleman, J. S., Gordon, R., Kristoff, B., & Fuentes, F. (1991). Changes in cognitive and language functioning of preschool children with autism. *Journal of Autism and Developmental Disorders, 21*, 281–290.

Kaufman, B. N. (1994). *Son-rise: The miracle continues*. Tiburon, CA: H J Kramer.

Lovaas, O. I. (1987). Behavioral treatment and normal educational and intellectual functioning in young autistic children. *Journal of Consulting and Clinical Psychology, 55*, 3–9.

Maurice, C. (1993). *Let me hear your voice: A family's triumph over autism*. New York: Knopf.

Maurice, C. (1998, March). *Autism and advocacy: Avoiding role confusion*. Paper presented at the Science in Autism Treatment Conference, Pittsburgh, PA.

McEachin, J. J., Smith, T., & Lovaas, O. I. (1993). Long-term outcome for children with autism who received early intensive behavioral treatment. *American Journal on Mental Retardation, 4*, 359–372.

National Institute of Mental Health. (1997). *Autism* (DHHS Publication No. NIH 97-4023). Washington, DC: U.S. Government Printing Office.

Physicians' desk reference (47th ed.). (1993). Montvale, NJ: Medical Economics Data Production.

Pollak, R. (1997). *The creation of Dr. B: A biography of Bruno Bettelheim*. New York: Simon & Schuster.

3

The Nature of Autism

Deborah Fein, Diana Robins, Miriam Liss, and Lynn Waterhouse

T his chapter, which provides a general introduction to the nature of autism and related disorders, is divided into three sections. The first deals with attempts to define the boundaries of autism and related disorders. The second section describes the cognitive difficulties most often found in children with autistic disorders and outlines some of the cognitive models of autism. The third section presents some of the major biological findings in autism research. Although each section presents an overview of a very extensive literature, coverage of each topic is necessarily incomplete. References at the end of the chapter will provide a starting point for the reader who wishes to acquire more in-depth information on each topic. An expanded overview of research and theory on autism can be found in Fein, Joy, Green, and Waterhouse (1996).

Definitions and Characteristics of Autism and Related Disorders

Defining Characteristics

Current definitions of psychological disorders are provided by the *Diagnostic and Statistical Manual–Fourth Edition* (DSM–IV) of the American Psychiatric Association (APA) (1994). In this manual, the term *pervasive developmental disorder* (PDD) is used to describe a group of childhood disorders with similar behavioral features. Others call this group "autistic spectrum disorders." The disorders that make up the pervasive developmental disorders are (1) autistic disorder, (2) Asperger's disorder, (3) childhood disintegrative disorder, (4) Rett's disorder, and (5) PDD–not otherwise specified.

Autistic disorder is defined by the presence of symptoms in three domains: impairments in social interaction, impairments in communication and play, and the presence of repetitive and restricted patterns of behavior. *Social interaction*

impairments can include poor eye contact, poor nonverbal communication, lack of mutual attention behaviors (showing or bringing things to a caregiver, pointing and looking where someone else is pointing), poor awareness of others' emotions, and poor peer relationships. *Communication and play impairments* can include poorly developed language, lack of conversational skill (for one's age), language that is stereotyped (i.e., language that is unusually repetitive, in which the child uses the same phrase or sentence over and over, often from a commercial or video), and play that is similarly stereotyped or lacks the quality of make-believe. *Repetitive and restricted behaviors* include very narrow interests, inflexible adherence to routines or rituals, repetitive motor movements, or preoccupations with parts of objects.

A tremendously wide range of behaviors can fulfill criteria for the symptoms in each of these domains, and therefore the group of children that meet criteria for having autistic disorder is a very diverse group. Much of the variability in symptom expression depends on level of intellectual functioning (Fein et al., 2000). For example, children who are very young or have significant retardation may express their social impairment by ignoring people or interacting only to have their needs met, whereas older or higher functioning children may desire social relationships but be insensitive to others' reactions and frequently violate unwritten social rules, such as rules governing interpersonal distance, staying on topic in a conversation, and not commenting on others' physical characteristics or weaknesses. In the communication domain, children with lower mental ages may completely lack spoken language, whereas children with higher mental ages may carry on one-sided conversations on topics of interest to them. In the domain of restricted behavior, lower functioning children may engage in repetitive self-stimulatory and motor stereotypies (e.g., finger flicking or rocking), whereas higher functioning children may perseverate on preferred activities, topics, or collections.

For the most part, this variability in symptoms has not been organized into different types or patterns of behavior. In the social domain, however, one useful typology was proposed by Wing and Gould (1979; see also Wing & Atwood, 1987). Examining a large group of children with broadly defined PDD, Wing and Gould identified three types of social impairment. First is the *aloof* type, in which the children are uninterested in interacting with others. This disinterest shows itself across all situations that the child encounters; some of these children will occasionally seek out interaction with others, especially their mother, but this is primarily to get fundamental needs met rather than for the pleasure of interaction. Second is the *passive* type, in which the children tolerate interaction with others but do not seek it out. Third is the *active-but-odd* type, in which the children initiate interactions with others but these attempts are one-sided and awkward. Although some researchers have found indications of possible biological differences among these three groups (Dawson, Klinger, Panatiotides, Lewy, & Castelloe, 1995; Modahl et al., 1998; Volkmar, Cohen, Bregman, Hooks, & Stevenson, 1989), it has not been shown that children stay in one group over the course of development.

Asperger's disorder is marked by impairments in social interaction and repetitive and restricted patterns of behavior, in conjunction with normal language and intellectual functioning. Individuals diagnosed with Asperger's disorder often show relatively good verbal functions, such as vocabulary, but have impaired visual–perceptual and visual–motor functions. These children may appear to be clumsy or have poor balance and coordination, while having vocabulary and grammatical skills that are at or near those of their same-age peers. Many researchers and clinicians believe that Asperger's disorder is distinct from autism, but research has not yet demonstrated conclusively that individuals with Asperger's disorder are suffering from a qualitatively different disorder than high-functioning individuals with autism.

Childhood disintegrative disorder is a rarely diagnosed disorder that differs from autistic disorder in that the child has at least 2 years of normal development, followed by a developmental regression marked by loss of social and cognitive skills. The level of functioning attained by such children is usually in the severely mentally retarded range. In practice, however, it may be difficult to reliably distinguish childhood disintegrative disorder from autistic disorder unless the regression is quite late or especially severe, because many children with a diagnosis of autism also show marked regression of skills, usually in the second year.

In contrast to Asperger's disorder and childhood disintegrative disorder, *Rett's disorder* seems to be well established as a true syndrome with a distinctive course. This disorder affects only females, in contrast to autistic disorder, which affects about four times as many males as females. Rett's disorder is marked by normal development for at least 5 months, followed by deceleration of head growth, loss of previously acquired hand skills (e.g., self-feeding, grasping and manipulating toys), and development of stereotyped hand movements, loss of social interest, language and cognitive retardation, and progressive incoordination of motor skills. Unlike other disorders on the PDD spectrum, Rett's disorder has been identified as having a specific genetic basis (Ellaway & Christodoulou, 1999).

Pervasive developmental disorder–not otherwise specified (PDD–NOS) is diagnosed when a child demonstrates impairments in any of the three areas of functioning previously described for autism, but when criteria for any of the specific syndromes are not fulfilled. In practice, however, PDD–NOS is often used to diagnose children who have mild autism, high-functioning (nonretarded) autism, or questionable autism, or when the clinician wishes to avoid use of the term *autism*.

Historical Development

Autism was first described in 1943 by Leo Kanner. For a brief period, it was regarded as an "inborn disturbance of affective contact," as Kanner suggested in his original paper, a conception that was probably very close to an accurate or at least a useful view. During the 1950s and 1960s and well into the 1970s, however, the psychodynamic view came to predominate; this view held that the symptoms of autism were a response to a deep emotional disturbance or poor mother–child relationship, subtly or not so subtly blaming parents for the child's dysfunction. Unfortunately for the affected children and their parents, research into causes and treatment focused during this period on parental attitudes and emotional reactions to their children. This led to great increases in parental suffering, and to the development of completely ineffectual treatment modes. Starting with publication of Rimland's (1964) landmark book, *Infantile Autism: The Syndrome and Its Implications for a Neural Theory of Behavior*, and accelerating in the 1970s, research efforts turned to describing the cognitive and behavioral details of the syndrome, as well as developing effective behavioral interventions; then in the 1980s and accelerating in the 1990s, biological research became a prime focus of much autism research. The view that autism and related syndromes are disorders of brain development is now virtually unanimous among American researchers. Some of the highlights of the cognitive and biological findings are outlined in the following sections.

Developmental Course

Autism is a developmental disorder and the clinical picture changes with time. The classic autistic "aloofness" from other people is more likely to characterize the preschooler than the older child with autism. Behavior in the older child or adult with autism may resemble the behavior of an individual with retardation or hyperactivity more than the behavior of classic autism. Social interest may increase around puberty, but behavioral disorganization, temporary cognitive regression, or onset of seizures sometimes interferes with continued development in early to middle adolescence. A number of long-term follow-up studies are reviewed in Fein, Joy, et al. (1996). It must be remembered, however, that these studies have followed individuals into adolescence or adulthood whose educational programs were those of 10 to 30 years ago. Preliminary longitudinal data from recent studies suggests that the improvements seen following aggressive and effective interventions (particularly those described in the remainder of this book) are stable over many years (McEachin, Smith, & Lovaas, 1993; Smith, Eikeseth, Klevstrand, & Lovaas, 1997). These studies, because they are so recent, have investigated relatively few children, and continuing this area of research will be crucial in the next few years.

It has long been held that communicative language by the age of 5 and high IQ are important prognostic features in young children with autism (Fein, Joy, et al., 1996; Rutter, Greenfield, & Lockyer, 1967). Recent data by Fein, Stevens, et al. (2000) confirm these earlier findings, and suggest that cognitive ability is a more potent predictor of outcome than is the severity of autistic symptoms. Assessment of intellect in children with autism can be just as reliable as in normally developing children, but the examiner must be acutely aware of the degree to which he or she has the child's cooperation. In clinical practice, it is not unusual for children to be virtually untestable because of noncompliant behavior (although an estimate of developmental level can be made from parent report), but later become reliably testable after their behavior is brought under control and compliance and cooperation are increased.

Comorbid Conditions

Individuals with autism are at risk for a number of other disorders and conditions, because comorbidity (the co-occurrence of two or more discrete disorders in the same individual) is high between autism and some specific other conditions. *Tourette's syndrome* (chronic motor and vocal tics) seems to occur more often than would be expected by chance in individuals with autism, and tics may be associated with a high-IQ subgroup (Burd, Fisher, Kerbeshian, & Arnold, 1987). Although an increased incidence of *schizophrenia* in individuals with autism has been reported by some investigators (Petty, Ornitz, Michelman, & Zimmerman, 1984), these increases are very small and are not found by all researchers. It seems unlikely, therefore, that individuals with autism are at significantly increased risk for schizophrenia.

The relationship between autism and *developmental language disorder* is unclear, and a differential diagnosis can be difficult in very young children. The main difficulty, as discussed later in more detail, is the role of language impairment in autism. Although one may reject (as we do) the notion that autism is in essence a disorder of language, nevertheless a significant number of children with autism have

inordinate difficulty in mastering language skills even in the best designed and implemented intervention programs. Our clinical observations suggest that some of these children do relatively well on nonverbal tests of reasoning, at least at preschool age. One may conclude, therefore, that these children may have a dense and specific language disorder that is comorbid with autism.

Another set of conditions that has a high comorbidity with autism is *seizure disorders*. Estimates of the prevalence of seizures in autism range from one quarter to one third of individuals with autism, far in excess of the prevalence of seizures in the general population (Tuchman, Rapin, & Shinnar, 1991). The most frequent types of seizure are generalized tonic-clonic (i.e., grand mal) and atypical absence (staring spells). Seizures in autism are associated with motor problems and with mental retardation, but not with difficult birth or family history of epilepsy (Tuchman et al., 1991). There seem to be two peaks in onset, one in early childhood, as is common with many other disorders, and a second, more unusual peak in early adolescence (Tuchman et al., 1991).

Mental retardation is also often comorbid with disorders on the PDD spectrum. At least half of all children with autism and related disorders have been found to function in the mentally retarded range (defined as an IQ of 70 or below), although, as noted above, long-term outcomes for children receiving optimum services, while exciting, are still largely unexplored. Typically, verbal IQ is lower than nonverbal IQ, although the opposite is usually true for individuals with Asperger's disorder. The real relationship between retardation and autism is unknown. It is possible that the low-functioning children have autism plus retardation. It is also possible that a different pattern of brain dysfunction affects the two groups, such that the high-functioning children have milder dysfunction that primarily affects brain areas related to social or motivational functioning, whereas the lower functioning children have more extensive involvement that affects brain areas underlying learning, memory, attention, language, and nonverbal reasoning, as well as social skills.

A number of *specific biomedical conditions* have also been found to be associated with the presence of autistic disorder or autistic symptomatology. These conditions are more likely to be the underlying cause of the autism, at least in some cases, than merely comorbid conditions. Gillberg (1992) described many such conditions, which include fragile X syndrome, tuberous sclerosis, hypomelanosis of Ito, phenylketonuria (PKU), rubella, and cytomegalovirus. Genetic contributions to autism are further discussed later in this chapter.

Of what practical importance for the parent, educator, or physician is a specific diagnosis (such as PDD–NOS vs. autistic disorder) or the identification of a comorbid disorder? With regard to the latter, significant information may be gained. If, for example, the child is found to have a seizure disorder, various treatment options may be considered. If the child is found to have a defined genetic disorder, genetic counseling for parents and siblings may be improved. With regard to distinguishing among disorders on the PDD spectrum, however, the answer is "very little." Somewhat different prognoses may be associated with such disorders as autistic disorder versus Asperger's disorder, and it may be easier to get intensive services for a child with a diagnosis of autistic disorder, but the optimum type, intensity, or setting of treatment is not dictated by these diagnoses. Rather, treatment choices are dictated by the child's clinical picture, including behavioral strengths and weaknesses and cognitive functioning in the areas of language, nonverbal reasoning, attention, memory, and so forth.

Cognitive Findings

Autism involves a variety of symptoms, some of which are included in the diagnostic criteria (e.g., social deficits, language deficits, perseverative behavior) and some of which are associated with the disorder (e.g., intellectual deficits, difficulties with attention, sensory abnormalities, sleeping and feeding problems). Different researchers have focused on these different aspects of autistic disorder in attempting to determine the primary deficit (if indeed there is one). Deficits in language, memory, attention, executive functioning, theory of mind, emotion, and motivation have all been proposed as the primary deficit in autistic disorder. These theories tend to focus on either the cognitive and intellectual deficits, or the emotional and social deficits.

Language

One of the oldest classes of cognitive theories views autism as fundamentally a disorder of language (Prior, 1979; Rutter, 1968). In addition to studies that argue that language deficits are primary in autism, a very large body of literature exists on language characteristics in autism. Studies consistently find that verbal skills are lower than nonverbal skills (Carpentieri & Morgan, 1994; Sandberg, Nydern, Gillberg, & Hjelmquist, 1993), and many individuals with autism are mute (Fein, Dunn, et al., 1996). Research has focused on phonology (speech sounds), syntax (grammar), semantics (word meanings), written language, expressive language versus receptive language, pragmatics (social use of language), and prosody (the intonation or "melody" of speech) (Lord & Paul, 1997). In general, research has shown that phonological and syntactic development are often delayed in autistic children, but they do not appear deviant from normally developing children, although there are individual exceptions (reviewed in Fein, Humes, Kaplan, Lucci, & Waterhouse, 1984). Research on semantics has demonstrated that high-functioning children with autism categorize and use semantic groupings (e.g., food, animals, clothing) in ways that are very similar to normally developing children (Tager-Flusberg, 1985). However, children with autism may give less typical answers when asked to give examples from a category (they may say "cheetah" or "orangutan" rather than "dog" or "cat" when asked to give examples of animals) (M. Dunn, Gomes, & Sebastian, 1996). Furthermore, there is evidence that children with autism do not use word meanings in a normal way (Tager-Flusberg, 1991) and that high-functioning children with autism may use peculiar (e.g., being overly literal or using idioms in an unconventional way) or pedantic (sounding like a teacher) language (reviewed in Lord & Paul, 1997).

Research on written, expressive, and receptive language has indicated that high-functioning individuals with autism may develop the ability to decode words for reading and writing at a relatively early age, whereas their spoken language usually lags behind (Lord & Paul, 1997). In those children who develop language, comprehension is often relatively impaired compared with expression (Fein, Lucci, Braverman, & Waterhouse, 1992), which is the reverse of the pattern seen in typical development or in children with developmental language disorder. Even children who demonstrate adequate comprehension for simple or concrete language usually have deficits in comprehending complex language and in formulating complex output.

Research on prosody and pragmatics has indicated that individuals with autism are particularly impaired in interactive language, including the ability to engage in a conversation, understand nonverbal communication, and use appropriate speech prosody (Waterhouse & Fein, 1982). Children with autism are often noted to have peculiar intonation, most frequently monotony (Lord & Paul, 1997). Although high-functioning children with autism can effectively use language to communicate their needs, they have difficulty using language as a tool for social communication. They are less likely than typical children to provide a relevant response to a comment, expand on other comments, or add new information (Tager-Flusberg & Anderson, 1991). High-functioning children with autism may also have a particularly difficult time understanding slang, puns, jokes, and words with double meanings.

Early researchers (Prior, 1979; Rutter, 1968) believed that language deficits in autism were indicative of dysfunction in the left hemisphere, the side of the brain on which language abilities are thought to primarily depend. However, a review of the arguments for left-hemisphere dysfunction concluded that evidence for left-hemisphere dysfunction is weak and that language difficulties likely reflected developmental lag rather than left-hemisphere pathology (Fein, Humes, et al., 1984). Furthermore, because many language functions are delayed rather than deviant and because many individuals with autism have adequate language abilities indicate that language pathology is unlikely to be the cause of autistic disorder.

Memory

Difficulties with memory functioning have also been proposed as the primary deficit in autism by some researchers (Boucher & Warrington, 1976; Delong, 1992). Compared with the study of language in autism, the study of memory must be regarded as in its infancy. These researchers propose that autism may be understood as a developmental amnesic syndrome. Similarities have been noted between some of the symptoms of autism and behavior shown by animals who have received lesions to the hippocampus, a brain area involved in the acquisition of memories. These symptoms include reduced responsiveness to novelty, increased general activity, motor stereotypies, and perseveration. Research on memory function indicates that individuals with autism do have some specific memory deficits, especially in the area of verbal memory for meaningful material such as stories (Fein, Dunn, et al., 1996). However, visual and rote auditory memory tends to be spared (Barth, Fein, & Waterhouse, 1995; Fein, Humes, et al., 1984), and many high-functioning individuals with autism display remarkable memory for certain facts such as bus routes, music, or events (Rimland & Fein, 1988). In a recent study of memory functioning (Bennetto, Pennington, & Rogers, 1996), individuals with autism were found to have intact long-term and short-term recognition memory and cued recall. They also were found, however, to have significant difficulty in temporal order memory, source memory, and two working memory tasks: sentence span and counting span. Another study compared individuals with autism and normal controls on a memory and learning test involving short-term memory, long-term memory, and recognition (Minshew & Goldstein, 1993). Although children with autism had significantly worse short-term recall and significantly more intrusions, there were no significant differences on long-term storage or recognition. Such a variation in memory function poses problems for theories viewing autism as a type of amnesia.

Attention

Abnormalities in attention and response to sensory stimulation have been viewed by some researchers as the primary deficit in autism, and research on sensory responsiveness goes back to the 1960s. Ornitz (1985, 1988) described autism as a disorder of directed attention and attributed the social deficits in autism to deficits in sensory modulation. According to Ornitz, the disturbed sensory system of individuals with autism results in a diminished capacity to direct attention to people and appropriate objects for play. He specifically attributed the disordered sensory system to dysfunction in brainstem and reticular formation. Research has partially confirmed Ornitz's theory and has demonstrated specific attention deficits. For example, individuals with autism tend to be overselective in their attention (paying attention to one thing to the exclusion of others) (Fein, Tinder, & Waterhouse, 1979; Lovaas, Schreibman, Koegel, & Rehm, 1971) and have difficulty shifting their attention both between modalities (e.g., from visual to verbal stimuli) (Courchesne et al., 1994) and between objects in space (Townsend, Courchesne, & Eggs, 1992). Other aspects of attention may not be specifically impaired, such as sustained attention under conditions of adequate reinforcement (Garretson, Fein, & Waterhouse, 1990).

Different theories of attention have proposed alternately that individuals with autism are underaroused and seeking stimulation (Rimland, 1964), or that they are overaroused and attempting to screen out stimuli that threaten to arouse them even further (Hutt, Hutt, Lee, & Ounsted, 1965). Both of these theories attempted to explain certain perseverative behaviors in autism. For example, motor stereotypies were seen by the former theory as increasing arousal and by the latter as reducing arousal.

Other researchers have argued that arousal in individuals with autism swings to both maladaptive extremes, producing fluctuating states of over- and underresponsiveness (Kinsbourne, 1987). Gaze avoidance and isolation are seen as attempts to fend off the arousing sensory stimulation, and perseverative behaviors are seen as ways to focus on one specific aspect of the environment in order to reduce overarousal. Novelty is seen as particularly arousing, which accounts for the insistence on sameness that is characteristic of individuals with autism (Dawson & Lewy, 1989). Advocates of the arousal hypothesis (Dawson & Lewy, 1989) view the social deficits characteristic of autism as arising from the fact that social behavior is particularly unpredictable, and thus particularly overstimulating.

Sensory disturbances, such as over- and undersensitivity to stimuli, are widely reported in first-hand accounts and often portrayed as central to the disorder (Grandin, 1995). However, a recent review concluded that systematic investigation of the nature of sensory deficits in autism is sorely needed before a causal theory can be properly developed (O'Neill & Jones, 1997). A Sensory Survey is currently being developed at the University of Connecticut (Saulnier & Liss, 2000) based on items from the Sensory Profile by Winnie Dunn (W. Dunn & Brown, 1997). This survey measures sensory oversensitivity, undersensitivity, and sensory-seeking behavior within each sensory domain. This tool may allow researchers to gain a better understanding of the nature of sensory disturbances in autism and how these disturbances relate to other functional difficulties. The presence of these sensory disturbances has led some parents to seek sensory integration therapy for their children; no controlled studies have validated this type of therapy for children with autism (Smith, 1996).

Executive Functioning

Still other researchers hold that other cognitive deficits, such as executive functioning deficits, are the primary cause of autistic behavior (Ozonoff, Pennington, & Rogers, 1991). Executive function is a term that describes problem-solving behaviors that are thought to be controlled in large part by the frontal lobes of the brain (Duncan, 1986). Executive functioning involves forming abstract concepts, having a flexible plan of action, being able to self-monitor and self-correct, and being able to inhibit impulsive responses. Some researchers (Ozonoff et al., 1991) hold that the perseverative, inflexible behaviors of individuals with autism, as well as their impulsivity and lack of social skills, indicate that they have deficits in executive functioning that are similar to deficits found in patients with prefrontal lesions.

Research has demonstrated that individuals with autism do poorly on certain executive functioning tasks, especially those that require mental flexibility and the ability to shift their approach to a cognitive task (Ozonoff & McEvoy, 1994; Ozonoff et al., 1991; Ozonoff, Strayer, McMahon, & Filloux, 1994; Prior & Hoffmann, 1990). The most robust finding is that individuals with autism exhibit more perseverative behavior than age-matched controls on the *Wisconsin Card Sorting Test* (WCST). This task involves sorting cards on a variety of dimensions (color, shape, and number). The subject does not know which is the appropriate way to sort the cards and must figure it out based on feedback from the examiner (each trial is rated correct or incorrect). To make things more complicated, the rules of the game change after 10 correct sorts (from color to shape to number). However, the subject is not informed that the rule has changed and must infer it from the examiner's feedback. Individuals with autism are more likely than mental age-matched controls to perseverate on a previously reinforced category. However, the implications of this result remain somewhat ambiguous. To successfully complete the WCST, one must have a knowledge of the concepts of number, shape, and form. Children who perform poorly on the WCST may do so because they lack the relevant concepts or for other reasons such as poor language comprehension, poor sustained attention, poor short-term memory, or lack of compliance.

One problem with using tests that measure perseverative behavior to determine whether individuals with autism have executive functioning deficits is that perseverative behavior itself is a diagnostic criterion for autism. Thus, it is not surprising that someone with a diagnosis of autism would perseverate on a task such as the WCST. Consequently, this finding may reflect a tendency that is part of the disorder but not necessarily the central feature.

Liss, Fein, Bullard, Robins, and Waterhouse (in press) investigated cognitive estimating (e.g., "How many seeds are in a watermelon?") in autism, as an example of executive functioning not involving perseveration. They found individuals with autism to be deficient in estimating in three of four domains (length, weight, and time, but not quantity) relative to typical individuals matched for overall fund of knowledge.

Some researchers have questioned whether executive functioning deficits can fully account for the social deficits of autism. A study of executive functioning and pretend play in autism (Jarrold, Boucher, & Smith, 1994) concluded that executive functioning deficits were unlikely to account for deficits in pretend play, one of the core diagnostic features of autism. In conclusion, executive functioning deficits seem to be an important associated feature of autism, but are unlikely to be the primary cause of the other symptoms.

Theory of Mind

One current view of autism holds that the primary deficit is an absence of "theory of mind." Theory of mind involves the ability to understand that other people have internal mental states such as knowledge, emotion, and expectation (Baron-Cohen, Leslie, & Frith, 1985). In a classic theory of mind task the subject is told a story with two characters, Sally and Anne. While Sally is out of the room, Anne moves one of Sally's marbles from a basket into a box. The subject is then asked where Sally will look for the marble. Although the correct answer is that Sally would look in the basket, many children with autism answer that Sally would look in the box, since that is where the marble really is. This is taken to mean that children with autism are not able to understand what others are thinking or to take the perspective of the other, since they do not understand that if Sally left the room she would have a mental state that is different from their own (still thinking that the marble is in the basket). It is consistent with their frequently observed tendency to take events at face value and to think literally. The ability to understand other people's mental states is critical in order to engage in pretend play, pragmatic communication, and empathy, all of which are impaired in autism (Baron-Cohen et al., 1985).

The theory of mind hypothesis has stimulated a great deal of research. Children with autism have been found to be impaired on a variety of theory of mind tasks (Ozonoff et al., 1991; Prior, Dahlstrom, & Squires, 1990). However, other research has shown that theory of mind deficits are not found in high-functioning children with autism or in individuals with Asperger's syndrome (Ozonoff, Rogers, & Pennington, 1993). Furthermore, others have shown that performance in theory of mind tasks is highly correlated with verbal ability, age, and IQ (Happe, 1994); when these variables are controlled and shorter less complex theory of mind tasks are used, group differences disappear (Tager-Flusberg & Sullivan, 1994).

Although findings show that children with autism are often impaired on theory of mind tasks, this task seems to be strongly influenced by IQ and is not found consistently in all individuals with autism. Consequently, in our view, theory of mind deficits are an important deficit associated with autism but are unlikely to be the central deficit.

Emotion and Motivation

Researchers who view the emotional aspects of autism as primary point out that the emotional difficulties of individuals with autism are not necessarily tied to their cognitive difficulties (Fein, Pennington, Markowitz, Braverman, & Waterhouse, 1986). Degree of social impairment has not been found to be correlated with IQ or other cognitive measures; high-functioning individuals with autism may display their social deficits in subtle but nevertheless apparent ways. Fein et al. (1986) argued that no cognitive deficit is universal in autism and that cognitive deficits do not adequately explain the autistic features (e.g., aloofness, lack of interest in people) that may be found in the first 12 to 18 months of life. On the other hand, failure to develop social and emotional reciprocity would lead to deficits in language and play, and consequently to deficits in higher levels of cognitive functioning.

Research has indicated that individuals with autism are selectively impaired on emotional tasks. Subjects with autism have difficulty matching pictures of people according to their displayed emotion or according to their identity, compared with their ability to match pictures of objects (Fein et al., 1992; Hobson, 1986). In a recent study (Hauck, Fein, Waterhouse, Feinstein, & Maltby, 1998), subjects with autism were found to be unimpaired relative to mental-age matched controls on an object memory recognition task, but significantly impaired on a face memory task.

Those who see emotional factors as primary view the deficits that individuals with autism demonstrate in cognitive tasks as partially attributable to deficits in motivation. That is, they hold that children with autism are most impaired on cognitive tasks that depend on attention to others or on communication, or that have social content (e.g., matching pictures of emotions). Children with autism, for example, have been found to show deficits on simple sustained attention tasks when praise was used as a reinforcer, but not when food was used (Garretson et al., 1990). On the WCST, individuals with autism have been found to perform significantly better with computerized administration than with administration by an examiner (Ozonoff, 1995).

Summary of Cognitive Findings

It is difficult to reconcile the variety of theories of autism. One solution may be to view each of these theories as contributing a portion to the total picture (Fein, Joy, et al., 1996). There is a great deal of heterogeneity among individuals with autism; this is reflected in the heterogeneity of the theories proposed to account for the deficits. It is possible that many cognitive and affective systems are involved in the development of autism and that disruption of any of these elements can lead to some form of the disorder. This supposition proposes that there may not be one single core deficit of autism,

but a variety of deficits that can come together to varying degrees in different individuals. Furthermore, there is a great deal of interaction between cognitive and affective systems. Thus, any deficit in one of these systems would probably lead to deficits in others. Untangling the complex interactions between the multiple systems affected in this disorder is an arduous but fundamentally important task.

Biological Findings

Just as no single theoretical model explains the causes of autism, no one brain area or neurochemical system has been implicated in the disorder. Research on the biological causes of autism has used information from a variety of disciplines and has included genetic research, postmortem exams of brain tissue, measures of cerebral activity, metabolic activity, and neurochemical research.

Genetics

Genetic research has indicated that the proportion of families having two children with autism is greater than would be expected by chance. In a review of family studies, Smalley, Asarnow, and Spence (1988) determined that the rate of siblings with autism is 2.7% (24 out of 886 siblings), which is considerably larger than the prevalence rate of autism in the population, which is between .04% and .2%. Other studies have found that the probability that any sibling born after a child with autism will also be autistic is 8.6% (Ritvo et al., 1989).

Twin studies have demonstrated that identical twins are considerably more likely to be concordant for autism than fraternal twins (Cook, 1998; Smalley et al., 1988). In a study of 23 monozygotic twin pairs and one triplet set, in each of which at least one member had autism, Steffenburg et al. (1989) found that 13 of the twin pairs and all of the triplets were found to be concordant (e.g., they also carried a diagnosis of autism), yielding a rate of 73%. A recent review concluded that there is agreement that autism is a strongly genetic disorder and that the genes for autism also make an individual susceptible to other forms of PDD such as Asperger's syndrome (Szatmari & Jones, 1998). Although autism is clearly a genetic disorder, there is no consensus on which genes are involved. The exception is the gene for Rett's syndrome, which has been found to be located on the distal arm of the X chromosome (Xq28) (Ellaway & Christodoulou, 1999).

To understand the genetics of autism, it is likely that more than one gene needs to be considered (Szatmari & Jones, 1998). Several large-scale investigations are currently under way. Initial results from these investigations have identified certain genes that may be involved. Specifically, abnormalities have been found on chromosomes 15 and

7 (Cook, 1998). Hopefully, these studies will continue to better identify the genes involved in this disorder.

Neuroanatomy

Studies of structural abnormalities in the brains of individuals with autism have used postmortem examinations as well as imaging techniques such as computerized tomography (CT) and magnetic resonance imaging (MRI). These studies have provided inconsistent results and have indicated a great deal of variation within individuals with autism.

Research using postmortem brain tissue (Bauman & Kemper, 1985) has provided evidence for the involvement of the hippocampus, amygdala, and cerebellum. Cells in the hippocampus and amygdala have shown decreased neuron size and increased cell packing density. In other words, the cells have been found to be too small and too close together. Case studies also have been reported in which individuals developed tumors or lesions in the amygdala and hippocampus and subsequently displayed autistic behaviors such as social isolation and perseverative behaviors (Hoon & Reiss, 1992).

The amygdala and hippocampus are parts of the limbic system, the brain area associated with emotion. The hippocampus is involved in memory and in the learning of new material. The amygdala is thought to be involved in the assignment of emotional significance to social and novel stimuli. Thus, brain abnormalities involving the limbic system might support a theory of autism that involves the central role of emotional factors (Waterhouse, Fein, & Modahl, 1996).

The cerebellum lies at the base of the brain and is thought to be involved in motor coordination and balance. More recently, the cerebellum has been implicated in higher cognitive functions such as learning, memory, and attention (Yamaguchi, Tsuchiya, & Kobayashi, 1998). The cerebellum has been suggested as playing a role in autism in both postmortem brain tissue studies (Bauman & Kemper, 1985) and research with magnetic resonance imaging (Gaffney, Tsai, Kuperman, & Minchin, 1987; Murakami, Courchesne, Press, Yeung-Courchesne, & Hesselink, 1989). Researchers have found Purkinje and granule cell loss within the cerebellar tissue (Bauman & Kemper, 1985) and smaller cerebellums in subjects with autism than in normal controls (Gaffney et al., 1987; Murakami et al., 1989).

The cerebellum modulates auditory startle responses and heart rate responses (Leaton & Supple, 1986), both of which have been found to be abnormal in subjects with autism (Courchesne, 1987). Disruption to the cerebellum has also been thought to lead to a disruption in the ability to coordinate rapid shifts of attention between stimuli (Courchesne et al., 1994). This has been hypothesized to induce a tendency to focus only on certain stimuli, leading to the restriction of activities that many individuals with autism exhibit.

Research has not demonstrated consistent abnormalities in the cerebral cortex of subjects with autism (see review by Fein, Joy, et al., 1996). If autism were due primarily to frontal pathology, one would expect differences in the neuroanatomy of the frontal lobes between subjects with autism and normal controls. Although current research does not support any structural differences, some research has demonstrated functional differences between subjects with autism and normal controls. For example, an investigation of phosphate and phospholipid metabolism in the prefrontal cortex found that subjects with autism had decreased metabolism, which was correlated with poor performance on language and other neuropsychological tests (Minshew, Goldstein, Dombrowski, Panchalingam, & Pettegrew, 1993).

Neurophysiology

Research on neurophysiology has focused on assessing sensory and perceptual functioning through the use of electrical recordings of brain activity, or electroencephalograms (EEGs). These provide a noninvasive recording of brain activity and are measured through recording devices on the scalp. Event-related potentials (ERPs) are obtained from averaging multiple EEG traces in different areas of the scalp in response to specific sensory, motor, or cognitive events (Burack, Ennis, Stauder, Mottron, & Randolph, 1997). Research measuring ERPs has found that individuals with autism have abnormalities in the way they handle sensory information. Research has shown that individuals with autism may not be able to "damp down" or inhibit intense sensory input. This finding was hypothesized to be due to a dysfunction in the vestibular system, which governs balance and orientation (Ornitz, Atwell, Kaplan, & Westlake, 1985). Studies focusing on the vestibular system have found abnormalities in some children with autism, including suppression of postrotatory nystagmus, which is eye movement that follows spinning behavior (Ornitz et al., 1985). More recent studies suggest that the early processing of auditory stimuli by the cerebral cortex may also be different (M. Dunn & Vaughan, 1999).

Research involving auditory ERPs has also implicated brainstem dysfunction (Fein, Skoff, & Mirsky, 1981; Skoff, Mirsky, & Turner, 1980; Wong & Wong, 1991), although other research has suggested no difference in brainstem evoked potentials between individuals with autism and normal controls (Courchesne, Courchesne, Hicks, & Lincoln, 1985).

After a stimulus is presented, a series of waves can be detected by an EEG. These consist of a series of amplitude highs and lows that are abbreviated by whether they are positive (P) or negative (N) and how many milliseconds they occur after onset events (Burack et al., 1997). The P3 wave, a positive wave that occurs 300 milliseconds after a stimulus has been presented, has been found to be consistently smaller in individuals with autism than in normal controls (Lincoln, Dickstein, Courchesne, Elmasian, & Tallal, 1992). This wave is thought to reflect the ability to detect and classify stimuli, especially unexpected and novel stimuli. This finding is consistent with a model of autism as a disorder of attention or information processing.

In summary, neurophysiological studies have indicated that some of the neurological processes of selecting, attending to, understanding, and responding to sensory stimuli may be abnormal in individuals with autism.

Neurochemistry

Research on the neurochemistry of autistic disorder has involved looking at levels of various neurotransmitters in the bloodstream and in the cerebrospinal fluid. Although results have shown some consistent differences between neurotransmitter levels in individuals with autism and normal controls, the interpretation of these results remains unclear. Disturbances in blood levels of a neurotransmitter may reflect disturbances in the synthesis, metabolism, or receptor function of the transmitter. Furthermore, any differences in chemistry may indicate associated deficits of autism, rather than causes of the disorder. Research on neurochemical correlates such as serotonin has led to a variety of drug treatments for autism, some of which have been found to be effective for certain symptoms in certain individuals.

Serotonin

Research on serotonin levels has consistently demonstrated higher levels of blood plasma serotonin in children with autism than in normal controls (Anderson et al., 1987). Serotonin is thought to be involved in the regulation of learning, memory, sensory, and motor processes, many of which are impaired in children with autism (Ciaranello, VandenBerg, & Anders, 1982). Higher levels of serotonin have been found in approximately 30% of children with autism (Anderson et al., 1987), and levels of serotonin in children with autism have been found to be correlated with serotonin levels in their family members (Kuperman, Beeghly, Burns, & Tsai, 1985). Although there seems to be a distinct subgroup of children with autism who have elevated levels of serotonin, a specific behavioral or cognitive profile for these children has not been found. It remains unclear whether the increased blood levels of serotonin reflect increased synthesis or decreased metabolism. Furthermore, although significant differences between children with autism and normal controls have been found for blood levels of serotonin, no consistent evidence for differences in levels of serotonin in the brain has been found.

Despite the uncertain meaning of the serotonin findings, fenfluramine (a drug that blocks the uptake of serotonin) is effective in treating specific symptoms for some children with autism, leading to decreased levels of hyperactivity, stereotypies, and inattentiveness (see McDougle, 1998). However, the effects of this drug on social and cognitive functioning have been generally shown to be insignificant and its overall effect is similar to that of other stimulants (reviewed in McDougle, 1998).

Dopamine

The dopamine system is thought to be related to a variety of behaviors that are particularly relevant to autism. It has been implicated in motivational behavior, selective attention, motor activity, and cognition (Young, Kavanagh, Anderson, Shaywitz, & Cohen, 1982). Researchers have hypothesized that dopamine systems may be involved in the motor stereotypies of autism (Damasio & Maurer, 1978; McDougle, 1998), as well as the social–cognitive deficits (Coleman & Gillberg, 1985).

Research on dopamine levels in individuals with autism has examined neurotransmitter and metabolite (by-product) levels in the blood, plasma, urine, and cerebrospinal fluid, and has led to inconsistent results. Although some research has found that higher levels of a metabolite of dopamine was related to autistic symptoms (Gillberg & Svennerholm, 1987), this result has not been replicated (Ross, Klykylo, & Anderson, 1985).

Nevertheless, clinical trials of medications that involve the dopamine system have provided more consistent results for the involvement of dopamine in autism. Drugs that act by increasing the activity of dopamine (dopamine agonists) have been found to exacerbate symptoms, whereas drugs that inhibit dopamine function (dopamine antagonists) have been found to reduce some symptoms (reviewed in McDougle, 1998). Specifically, abnormal speech patterns, social relatedness, stereotypies, and inattention and hyperactivity have been found to be improved by the administration of neuroleptics, which act as dopamine antagonists. A large-scale double-blind placebo-controlled study of risperidone (a dopamine antagonist) was recently completed, and risperidone was found to be better than placebo in reducing repetitive behavior, aggression, anxiety, depression, and irritability, although no change was found in social behavior or language (McDougle et al., 1998). Any decision to use risperidone to treat autism, however, must be made with extreme care since risperidone can cause side effects such as sedation, increased salivation, weight gain, and occasional worsening of symptoms. Parents should discuss with their physician the likelihood, severity, and reversibility of adverse reactions and side effects to any medications being considered.

Peptides

Some similarities between the symptoms of autism and those of individuals addicted to opiates (Kalat, 1978) have led researchers to hypothesize a role for endorphins in autism. Specifically, higher levels of endorphins have been hypothesized to lead to self-injurious behavior, as well as deficits in attachment and social interaction (Panksepp, 1979). Children with autism have been found to have higher endorphin levels than normal controls, and elevated endorphin levels have been shown to be related to decreased pain sensitivity (Gillberg, Terenius, & Lonnerhold, 1985), a characteristic also seen in some children with autism.

Clinical trials of drugs that block opiate function (opiate antagonists) such as naloxone and naltrexone have shown them to be inconsistent in ameliorating autistic symptoms. Decreases in self-injurious and stereotypic behavior and hyperactivity, and increases in social communicative behaviors have been found with these drugs (Leboyer et al., 1992); however, these results have not been consistently obtained (Willemsen-Swinkels, Buitelaar, Nijhof, & van Engeland, 1995). A recent review suggested that naltrexone reduces motor hyperactivity in some children, but does not significantly affect the core symptoms of autism and self-injurious behavior (McDougle, 1998).

Recent research has investigated the role of oxytocin, which is known to regulate affiliative behavior in animals (Modahl, Fein, Waterhouse, & Newton, 1992). Analyses indicated lower levels of oxytocin in individuals with autism than in normal controls (Modahl et al., 1998), although significant within-group variability was also found.

Summary of Biological Findings

Although certain consistent biological differences have been found between subjects with autism and normal controls, there are many inconsistent results and the most striking feature of the literature is the great variety of suggested abnormalities. There is scarcely a brain area or neurochemical system that has not been suggested to underlie autistic symptomatology. Furthermore, with few exceptions, research into the biological aspects of autism has failed to establish a relationship between the hypothesized core deficits of autism and the biological substrates.

The complexity of the symptoms and the variety of biological findings suggest that autism is a heterogeneous disorder. Some biological findings may be relevant for a portion of the population with autism, whereas other findings may be relevant for another subpopulation. The nervous system is extremely complex and provides a vast number of opportunities for deviation. It is unlikely that there is a single biological cause, just as we noted that there is probably no one core deficit of autism. In any given individual with autism, various biological systems are probably malfunctioning to different degrees. This individual variation may lead to the heterogeneity seen in the clinical presentation of autism. Research to date has probably identified only a small portion of the process. Much remains to be done in understanding this complex disorder.

Implications for Medical Treatment

When making a decision whether to embark on a medical treatment for a child with autism, several factors must be considered. First, medical treatment should never be used as a substitute for behavioral and quality educational interventions. Currently, behavioral intervention is usually preferable to medical intervention because of the possible long-term gains and the absence of negative side effects. However, in some cases medical treatment can be used to ameliorate some of the symptoms in order to make a child more able to focus attention and gain more from the behavioral intervention.

Second, it is extremely important to obtain good medical consultation and supervision over any proposed medical treatment. Some drugs used for autism have potentially harmful side effects and some interactions between drugs can be dangerous.

Finally, no drug can act as a cure for autism. At best, the drugs described above can alleviate some of the symptoms for some of the children. When considering the use of medical treatment, one should target specific symptoms. Symptoms that may interfere with functioning and that may be targeted by medications include especially poor attention, obsessionality, aggression, and poor sleep. Furthermore, different children will have different reactions to different treatments, and some physicians consider children with autism to be particularly unpredictable in their reactions to medication. What is effective in alleviating symptoms in one child may be ineffective or produce adverse reactions in another. There will be individual differences in the severity of side effects as well. Reviews of prescription medications in treating children with autism can be found in McDougle (1998).

In conclusion, any decision to use a medical treatment should be made with extreme caution by a physician experienced with children of similar age and condition. In general, behaviorally oriented treatments should be considered the primary treatment modality.

Concluding Comment

In the almost 60 years since autism was identified, and the 25 years that may be considered the modern era of autism research, tremendous progress has been made. Many cognitive theories stimulate research. A plethora of biological findings are awaiting interpretation and integration. Researchers have begun to understand the genetic contributions to autism. Perhaps most important to the children and their parents, professionals have developed interventions that greatly increase the chances for a positive outcome. It is to these interventions that the rest of the book is devoted.

References

American Psychiatric Association. (1994). *Diagnostic and statistical manual of mental disorders* (4th ed.). Washington, DC: Author.

Anderson, G. M., Freedman, D., Cohen, D., Volkmar, F., Hoder, E., McPhedran, P., Minderaa, R., Hansen, C., & Young, J. (1987). Whole blood serotonin in autistic and normal subjects. *Journal of Child Psychology and Psychiatry, 2,* 885–900.

Baron-Cohen, S., Leslie, A., & Frith, U. (1985). Does the autistic child have a "theory of mind"? *Cognition, 21,* 37–46.

Barth, C., Fein, D., & Waterhouse, L. (1995). Delayed match to sample performance in autistic children. *Developmental Neuropsychology, 11,* 53–69.

Bauman, N. M., & Kemper, T. (1985). Histoanatomic observations of the brain in early infantile autism. *Neurology, 35,* 866–874.

Bennetto, L., Pennington, B. F., & Rogers, S. (1996). Intact and impaired memory functions in autism. *Child Development, 67,* 1816–1835.

Boucher, J., & Warrington, E. (1976). Memory deficits in early infantile autism: Some similarities to the amnesic syndrome. *British Journal of Psychology, 67,* 73–87.

Burack, J., Ennis, J., Stauder, J., Mottron, L., & Randolph, B. (1997). Attention and autism: Behavioral and electrophysiological evidence. In D. Cohen & F. Volkmar (Eds.), *Handbook of autism and pervasive developmental disorders* (pp. 226–247). New York: Wiley.

Burd, L., Fisher, W., Kerbeshian, J., & Arnold, M. (1987). Is development of Tourette disorder a marker for improvement in patients with autism and other pervasive developmental disorders? *Journal of the American Academy of Child and Adolescent Psychiatry, 26,* 162–165.

Carpentieri, S. C., & Morgan, S. B. (1994). Brief report: A comparison of patterns of cognitive functioning of autistic and nonautistic retarded children on the Stanford-Binet–Fourth Edition. *Journal of Autism and Developmental Disorders, 24,* 215–223.

Ciaranello, R. D., VandenBerg, S. R., & Anders, T. F. (1982). Intrinsic and extrinsic determinants of normal development: Relation to infantile autism. *Journal of Autism and Developmental Disorders, 12,* 115–145.

Coleman, M., & Gillberg, C. (1985). *The biology of the autistic syndromes.* New York: Praeger.

Cook, E. (1998). Genetics of autism. *Mental Retardation and Developmental Disabilities Research Reviews, 42,* 113–120.

Courchesne, E. (1987). A neurophysiological view of autism. In E. Schopler & G. B. Mesibov (Eds.), *Neurobiological issues in autism* (pp. 285–324). New York: Plenum Press.

Courchesne, E., Courchesne, R., Hicks, G., & Lincoln, A. (1985). Functioning of the brainstem auditory pathway in non-retarded autistic individuals. *Electroencephalography and Clinical Neurophysiology, 61,* 491–501.

Courchesne, E., Townsend, J., Akshoomoff, N., Saitoh, O., Yeung-Courchesne, R., Lincoln, A. J., James, H. E., Haas, R. H., Schreibman, L., & Lau, L. (1994). Impairment in shifting attention in autistic and cerebellar patients. *Behavioral Neuroscience, 105,* 848–865.

Damasio, A., & Maurer, R. (1978). A neurological model of childhood autism. *Archives of Neurology, 35,* 777–786.

Dawson, G., Klinger, L., Panatiotides, H., Lewy, A., & Castelloe, P. (1995). Subgroups of autistic children based on social behavior display distinct patterns of brain activity. *Journal of Abnormal Child Psychology, 23,* 569–583.

Dawson, G., & Lewy, A. (1989). Reciprocal subcortical–cortical influences in autism. In G. Dawson (Ed.), *Autism: Nature, diagnosis and treatment* (pp. 144–173). New York: Guilford Press.

Delong, G. R. (1992). Autism, amnesia, hippocampus and learning. *Neuroscience Biobehavioral Review, 16,* 63–70.

Duncan, J. (1986). Disorganization of behavior after frontal lobe damage. *Cognitive Neuropsychology, 3,* 271–290.

Dunn, M., Gomes, H., & Sebastian, M. J. (1996). Prototypicality of responses of autistic, language disordered, and normal children in a word fluency task. *Child Neuropsychology, 2,* 99–108.

Dunn, M., & Vaughan, H. (1999). Electrophysiologic correlates of semantic classification in autistic and normal children. *Developmental Neuropsychology, 16,* 79–99.

Dunn, W., & Brown, C. (1997). Factor analysis on the Sensory Profile from a national sample of children without disabilities. *American Journal of Occupational Therapy, 51*(7), 490–495.

Ellaway, C., & Christodoulou, J. (1999). Rett syndrome: Clinical update and review of recent genetic advances. *Journal of Pediatric Child Health, 35*(5), 419–426.

Fein, D., Dunn, M., Allen, D., Aram, D., Hall, N., Morris, R., & Wilson, B. (1996). Neuropsychological and language data. In I. Rapin (Ed.), *Preschool children with inadequate communication* (pp. 123–155). London: MacKeith Press.

Fein, D., Humes, M., Kaplan, E., Lucci, D., & Waterhouse, L. (1984). The question of left hemisphere dysfunction in infantile autism. *Psychological Bulletin, 95,* 258–281.

Fein, D., Joy, S., Green, L., & Waterhouse, L. (1996). Autism and pervasive developmental disorders. In B. Fogel, R. Schiffer, & S. Rao (Eds.), *Neuropsychiatry* (pp. 571–614). Baltimore: Williams and Wilkins.

Fein, D., Lucci, D., Braverman, M., & Waterhouse, L. (1992). Comprehension of affect in context in children with pervasive developmental disorders. *Journal of Child Psychology and Psychiatry, 33,* 1157–1167.

Fein, D., Pennington, B., Markowitz, P., Braverman, M., & Waterhouse, L. (1986). Toward a neuropsychological model of infantile autism: Are the social deficits primary? *Journal of the American Academy of Child Psychiatry, 25,* 198–212.

Fein, D., Skoff, B., & Mirsky, A. F. (1981). Clinical correlates of brainstem dysfunction in autistic children. *Journal of Autism and Developmental Disorders, 11,* 303–315.

Fein, D., Stevens, M., Dunn, M., Waterhouse, L., Allen, D., Rapin, I., & Feinstein, C. (2000). Subtypes of pervasive developmental disorder: Clinical characteristics. *Child Neuropsychology, 39,* 346–352.

Fein, D., Tinder, P., & Waterhouse, L. (1979). Stimulus generalization in autistic and normal children. *Journal of Child Psychology and Child Psychiatry, 20,* 325–335.

Gaffney, G. R., Tsai, L. Y., Kuperman, S., & Minchin, S. (1987). Cerebellar structure in autism. *American Journal of the Disabled Child, 141,* 1330–1332.

Garretson, H., Fein, D., & Waterhouse, L. (1990). Sustained attention in children with autism. *Journal of Autism and Developmental Disorders, 20*(1), 101–114.

Gillberg, C. (1992). Autism and autistic-like conditions: Subclasses among disorders of empathy. *Journal of Child Psychology and Psychiatry, 33,* 813–842.

Gillberg, C., & Svennerholm, L. (1987). CSF monoamines in autistic syndromes and other pervasive developmental disorders. *British Journal of Psychiatry, 151,* 89–94.

Gillberg, C., Terenius, L., & Lonnerhold, G. (1985). Endorphin activity in childhood psychosis. *Archives of General Psychiatry, 42,* 780–783.

Grandin, T. (1995). How people with autism think. In E. Schopler & G. Mesibov (Eds.), *Learning and cognition in autism* (pp. 137–156). New York: Plenum Press.

Happe, F. G. E. (1994). Wechsler IQ profile and theory of mind in autism: A research note. *Journal of Child Psychology and Psychiatry, 35,* 1461–1471.

Hauck, M., Fein, D., Waterhouse, L., Feinstein, C., & Maltby, N. (1998). Memory for faces in autistic children. *Child Neuropsychology, 4,* 187–198.

Hobson, R. (1986). The autistic child's appraisal of emotion. *Journal of Child Psychology and Psychiatry, 27,* 321–342.

Hoon, A. H., & Reiss, A. (1992). The mesial temporal lobe and autism: Case report and review. *Developmental Medical Child Neurology, 34,* 252–265.

Hutt, S., Hutt, C., Lee, D., & Ounsted, D. (1965). A behavioral and electroencephalographic study of autistic children. *Journal of Psychiatric Research, 3,* 181–197.

Jarrold, C., Boucher, J., & Smith, P. (1994). Executive functioning deficits and the pretend play of children with autism: A research note. *Journal of Child Psychology and Psychiatry and Allied Disciplines, 35,* 1473–1482.

Kalat, J. W. (1978). Speculations on similarities between autism and opiate addiction [Letter to the editor]. *Journal of Autism and Childhood Schizophrenia, 8,* 447–497.

Kanner, L. (1943). Autistic disturbances of affective contact. *Nervous Child, 2,* 217–250.

Kinsbourne, M. (1987). Cerebral–brainstem relations in infantile autism. In E. Schopler & G. Mesibov (Eds.), *Neurobiological issues in autism* (pp. 107–125). New York: Plenum Press.

Kuperman, S., Beeghly, J., Burns, T., & Tsai, L. (1985). Serotonin relationships of autistic probands and their first-degree relatives. *Journal of the Academy of Child and Adolescent Psychiatry, 24,* 186–190.

Leaton, R., & Supple, W. R. (1986). Cerebellar vermis: Essential for long-term habituation of the acoustic startle response. *Science, 232,* 513–515.

Leboyer, M., Bouvard, M. P., Launay, J. M., Tabuteau, F., Waller, D., Dugas, M., Kerdelhue, B., Lensing, P., & Panksepp, J. (1992). A double-blind study of naltrexone in infantile autism. *Journal of Autism and Developmental Disorders, 22*(2), 309–319.

Lincoln, A., Dickstein, P., Courchesne, E., Elmasian, R., & Tallal, P. (1992). Auditory processing abilities in non-retarded adolescents and young adults with developmental receptive language disorder and autism. *Brain and Language, 43,* 613–622.

Liss, M., Fein, D., Bullard, S., Robins, S., & Waterhouse, L. (in press). Cognitive estimation in individuals of pervasive developmental disorders. *Journal of Autism and Developmental Disorders.*

Lord, C., & Paul, R. (1997). Language and communication. In D. Cohen & F. Volkmar (Eds.), *Handbook of autism and pervasive developmental disorders* (pp. 195–225). New York: Wiley.

Lovaas, O. I., Schreibman, L., Koegel, R., & Rehm, R. (1971). Selective responding by autistic children to multiple sensory input. *Journal of Abnormal Psychology, 77,* 211–222.

McDougle, C. J. (1998). Psychopharmacology. In F. Volkmar (Ed.), *Autism and pervasive developmental disorders* (pp. 169–194) (Cambridge Monographs in Child and Adolescent Psychiatry). Cambridge, England: Cambridge University Press.

McDougle, C., Holmes, J., Carlson, D., Pelton, G., Cohen, D., & Price, L. (1998). A double blind, placebo-controlled study of risperidone in adults with autistic disorder and other pervasive developmental disorder. *Archives of General Psychiatry, 55,* 633–641.

McEachin, J., Smith, T., & Lovaas, O. (1993). Long-term outcome for children with autism who received early intensive behavioral treatment. *American Journal of Mental Retardation, 97*(4), 359–372.

Minshew, N., & Goldstein, G. (1993). Is autism an amnesic disorder? Evidence from the California Verbal Learning Test. *Neuropsychologia, 7,* 209–216.

Minshew, N., Goldstein, G., Dombrowski, S., Panchalingam, K., & Pettegrew, J. (1993). A preliminary–3–1P MRS study of autism: Evidence for undersynthesis and increased degradation of brain membranes. *Biological Psychiatry, 33,* 762–773.

Modahl, C., Fein, D., Waterhouse, L., & Newton, N. (1992). Does oxytocin deficiency mediate social deficits in autism? [Letter to the editors]. *Journal of Autism and Developmental Disorders, 22,* 449–451.

Modahl, C., Green, L., Fein, D., Morris, M., Waterhouse, L., Feinstein, C., & Levin, H. (1998). Plasma oxytocin levels in autistic children. *Biological Psychiatry, 43,* 270–277.

Murakami, J. W., Courchesne, E., Press, G. A., Yeung-Courchesne, R., & Hesselink, J. R. (1989). Reduced cerebellar hemisphere size and its relationship to vermal hypoplasia in autism. *Archives of Neurology, 46,* 689–694.

O'Neill, M., & Jones, R. (1997). Sensory perceptual abnormalities in autism: A case for more research? *Journal of Autism and Developmental Disorders, 27*(3), 283–293.

Ornitz, E. (1985). Neurophysiology of infantile autism. *Journal of the American Academy of Child Psychiatry, 24,* 251–262.

Ornitz, E. (1988). Autism: A disorder of directed attention. *Brain Dysfunction, 1,* 309–322.

Ornitz, E., Atwell, C., Kaplan, A., & Westlake, J. (1985). Brainstem dysfunction in autism: Results of vestibular stimulation. *Archives of General Psychiatry, 42,* 1018–1025.

Ozonoff, S. (1995). Reliability and validity of the Wisconsin Card Sorting Test in studies of autism. *Neuropsychologia, 9,* 491–500.

Ozonoff, S., & McEvoy, R. (1994). A longitudinal study of executive function and theory of mind development in autism. *Development and Psychopathology, 6,* 415–431.

Ozonoff, S., Pennington, B., & Rogers, S. (1991). Executive function deficits in high-functioning autistic individuals: Relationship to theory of mind. *Journal of Child Psychology and Psychiatry, 32,* 1081–1105.

Ozonoff, S., Rogers, S., & Pennington, B. (1993). Can standard measures identify subclinical markers of autism? *Journal of Autism and Developmental Disorders, 23*(3), 429–441.

Ozonoff, S., Strayer, D. D., McMahon, W. M., & Filloux, F. (1994). Executive function abilities in autism and Tourette syndrome: An information processing approach. *Journal of Child Psychology and Psychiatry, 35,* 1015–1032.

Panksepp, J. (1979). A neurochemical theory of autism. *Trends in Neuroscience, 2,* 174–177.

Petty, L., Ornitz, E., Michelman, J., & Zimmerman, E. (1984). Autistic children who become schizophrenic. *Archives of General Psychiatry, 41,* 129–135.

Prior, M. R. (1979). Cognitive abilities and disabilities in infantile autism: A review. *Journal of Abnormal Child Psychology, 7,* 359–380.

Prior, M., Dahlstrom, B., & Squires, T. (1990). Autistic children's knowledge of thinking and feeling states in other people. *Journal of Child Psychology and Psychiatry, 31,* 587–601.

Prior, M., & Hoffmann, W. (1990). Brief report: Neuropsychological testing of autistic children through an exploration with frontal lobe tests. *Journal of Autism and Developmental Disorders, 20*(4), 581–590.

Rimland, B. (1964). *Infantile autism: The syndrome and its implications for a neural theory of behavior.* New York: Appleton-Century-Crofts.

Rimland, B., & Fein, D. (1988). Special talents of autistic savants. In L. Obler & D. Fein (Eds.), *The exceptional brain: Neuropsychology of talent and special abilities* (pp. 474–485). New York: Guilford Press.

Ritvo, E., Freeman, B., Pingree, C., Mason-Brothers, A., Jorde, L., Jenson, W. R., McMahon, W. M., Petersen, P., Mo, A., & Ritvo, A. (1989). The UCLA–University of Utah Epidemiologic Survey of Autism: Prevalence. *American Journal of Psychiatry, 146,* 194–199.

Ross, D., Klykylo, W., & Anderson, G. (1985). Cerebrospinal fluid indoleamine and monoamine effects of fenfluramine treatment of infantile autism. *Annals of Neurology, 15,* 394.

Rutter, M. (1968). Concepts of autism: A review of research. *Journal of Child Psychology and Child Psychiatry, 9,* 1–25.

Rutter, M., Greenfield, D., & Lockyer, L. (1967). A five to fifteen year followup of infantile psychosis: II. Social and behavioral outcome. *British Journal of Psychiatry, 113,* 1183–1199.

Sandberg, A. D., Nydern, A., Gillberg, C., & Hjelmquist, E. (1993). The cognitive profile in infantile autism: A study of 70 children and adolescents using the Griffiths Mental Development Scale. *British Journal of Psychology, 84,* 365–373.

Saulnier, C., & Liss, M. (2000, August). *Sensory disturbances in children with autism.* Paper presented at American Psychological Association, Washington, DC.

Skoff, B., Mirsky, A., & Turner, D. (1980). Prolonged brainstem transmission time in autism. *Psychiatry Research, 2,* 157–166.

Smalley, S., Asarnow, R., & Spence, A. (1988). Autism and genetics: A decade of research. *Archives of General Psychiatry, 45,* 953–961.

Smith, T. (1996). Are other treatments effective? In C. Maurice, G. Green, & S. C. Luce (Eds.), *Behavioral intervention for young children with* autism: A manual for parents and professionals (pp. 45–59). Austin, TX: PRO-ED.

Smith, T., Eikeseth, S., Klevstrand, M., & Lovaas, O. (1997). Intensive behavioral treatment for preschoolers with severe mental retardation and pervasive developmental disorder. *American Journal of Mental Retardation, 102*(3), 238–249.

Steffenburg, R., Gillberg, C., Hellgren, L., Andersson, I., Gillberg, I., Jacobsson, G., & Bohman, M. (1989). A twin study of autism in Denmark, Finland, Iceland, Norway, and Sweden. *Journal of Child Psychology and Psychiatry, 30,* 897–908.

Szatmari, P., & Jones, M. (1998). Genetic epidemiology. In F. Volkmar (Ed.), *Autism and pervasive developmental disorders* (pp. 109–129) (Cambridge Monographs in Child and Adolescent Psychiatry). Cambridge, England: Cambridge University Press.

Tager-Flusberg, H. (1985). The conceptual basis for referential word meaning in children with autism. *Child Development, 56,* 1167–1178.

Tager-Flusberg, H. (1991). Semantic processing in the free recall of autistic children: Further evidence for a cognitive deficit. *British Journal of Developmental Psychology, 9,* 417–430.

Tager-Flusberg, H., & Anderson, M. (1991). The development of contingent discourse ability in autistic children. *Journal of Child Psychology and Psychiatry, 32,* 1123–1134.

Tager-Flusberg, H., & Sullivan, K. (1994). A second look at second-order belief attribution in autism. *Journal of Autism and Developmental Disorders, 24,* 577–586.

Townsend, J., Courchesne, E., & Eggs, B. (1992). Visual attention deficits in autistic adults with cerebellar and partial abnormalities. *Society for Neuroscience Abstracts, 18,* 332.

Tuchman, R., Rapin, I., & Shinnar, S. (1991). Autistic and dysphasic children and epilepsy. *Pediatrics, 88,* 1219–1225.

Volkmar, F., Cohen, D., Bregman, J., Hooks, M., & Stevenson, J. (1989). An examination of social typologies found in autism. *Journal of the American Academy of Child and Adolescent Psychiatry, 28,* 82–86.

Waterhouse, L., & Fein, D. (1982). Language skills in developmentally disabled children. *Brain and Language, 15,* 307–333.

Waterhouse, L., Fein, D., & Modahl, C. (1996). Neurofunctional mechanisms in autism. *Psychological Review, 103,* 457–489.

Willemsen-Swinkels, S. H. N., Buitelaar, J. K., Nijhof, G. J., & van Engeland, H. (1995). Failure of naltrexone hydrochloride to reduce self-injurious and autistic behavior in mentally retarded adults: Double-blind placebo controlled studies. *Archives of General Psychiatry, 52,* 766–773.

Wing, L., & Atwood, A. (1987). Syndromes of autism and atypical development. In D. Cohen & A. Donnellan (Eds.), *Handbook of autism and pervasive developmental disorder* (pp. 3–19). New York: Wiley.

Wing, L., & Gould, J. (1979). Severe impairments of social interaction and associated abnormalities in children: Epidemiology and classification. *Journal of Autism and Developmental Disorders, 9,* 11–29.

Wong, V., & Wong, S. N. (1991). Brainstem auditory evoked potential study in children with autistic disorder. *Journal of Autism and Developmental Disorders, 21,* 329–340.

Yamaguchi, S., Tsuchiya, H., & Kobayashi, S. (1998). Visuospatial attention shift and motor responses in cerebellar disorders. *Journal of Cognitive Neuroscience, 10,* 95–107.

Young, J. G., Kavanagh, M. E., Anderson, G. M., Shaywitz, B. A., & Cohen, D. J. (1982). Clinical neurochemistry of autism and associated disorders. *Journal of Autism and Developmental Disorders, 12,* 147–165.

4

Prompts and Prompt-Fading Strategies for People with Autism

Gregory S. MacDuff, Patricia J. Krantz, and Lynn E. McClannahan

Learners with autism and related disabilities pose a number of challenges for those who are concerned about them. Many of the skills they need to live independently and happily are not in their repertoires, and they do not learn the skills through exposure to others. For example, many young children with autism do not respond to simple spoken requests such as "Come here" or "Play patty-cake," and they do not turn toward a speaker when their names are called or imitate what they see other people doing. Some skills may be present, but not used in functional ways. For example, responses such as naming objects or singing songs may occur, but not in typical, everyday situations, or at least not under circumstances that most people would consider appropriate.

Research and experience show that to develop useful skills, all learners—whether or not they have been diagnosed with autism—must practice skills frequently and receive some form of feedback about how they are doing. Therefore, the tasks facing parents and teachers of people with autism are not unlike the tasks that face all parents, educators, and trainers: helping learners display new responses and rewarding their efforts when they succeed. However, people with autism, unlike their typically developing peers, often do not learn from everyday events. Indeed, they may not respond to the kinds of cues that are immediately effective for nondisabled learners, such as spoken instructions or others' demonstrations.

The challenge for those involved in developing new skills for learners with autism, then, is to help them display new functional responses, provide frequent and immediate feedback, and arrange many opportunities for skills to be practiced under conditions in which they will eventually be used. All of this must be done in such a way as to ensure that the skills can be performed independently, without frequent extra cues from others. A great deal of research and practice in applied behavior analysis has been devoted to developing

techniques for accomplishing this. Most of those techniques have been derived from the principle of *stimulus control*, which means that behavior occurs in the presence of specific stimuli as a result of prior reinforcement. A common example of stimulus control is seen when a person answers a telephone. The ringing that precedes answering (an *antecedent stimulus*) has acquired stimulus control over the responses of picking up the receiver and saying "Hello." Stimulus control was established because, in the presence of ringing, picking up the receiver and saying hello was reinforced on many occasions in the past by the opportunity to talk to someone you really enjoy or by someone reporting interesting news. It is unlikely that you will pick up the receiver and say hello in the absence of the ring because that behavior has not resulted in reinforcement.

To recast some of our earlier comments in stimulus control terms, many types of antecedent stimuli that effectively control relevant behavior for typically developing learners—such as spoken requests, models, or printed words—are not effective for learners with autism, at least not without explicit and specialized training. For example, most typical youngsters quickly learn to respond appropriately when greeted; that is, naturally occurring stimuli such as the presence of another individual who says "Hello" readily come to control responses such as replying "Hi." That is not the case for many people with autism, who must be taught how to respond to (as well as to initiate) greetings. Research has shown that an effective way to help people with autism learn new skills is to provide them with extra cues, known as *prompts*.

Prompts are antecedent stimuli that are effective in getting responses to occur. Put another way, a prompt is a stimulus that controls a particular response (i.e., it is a *discriminative stimulus*). The prompt is added to a situation in which the naturally occurring stimulus does not yet control the response (i.e., it is not a discriminative stimulus for that response). For example, to teach a youngster with autism to respond when someone says "Hello," a parent might model saying "Hi" or instruct the youngster to "Say, 'Hi' " and then reinforce the child for responding "Hi." These additional antecedent stimuli are effective prompts (discriminative stimuli or S^{D}s) only if the youngster reliably imitates the modeled action or reliably follows the spoken instruction. If the response "Hi" is to be functional, however, it must occur in the presence of the relevant natural stimuli, not merely when prompts are provided. For many learners with autism, this is not likely to happen automatically; that is, it is rarely sufficient to prompt a few times and then simply discontinue prompting. Instead, it is usually necessary to withdraw prompts gradually, in small steps, over a series of learning opportunities, until no prompts are provided at all and the response occurs in the presence of the desired stimulus. In other words, stimulus control must be transferred from the prompt to the natural stimulus. Various techniques for transferring stimulus control—also known as *prompt fading*—are described in this chapter. They are illustrated with examples from experimental research and clinical experience. We conclude with some recommendations for selecting and using prompts and prompt-fading procedures.

Definitions of Prompts

Prompts are often defined as "auxiliary," "extra," or "artificial" stimuli that are presented immediately before or after the stimuli that will eventually cue the learner to display the behavior of interest at the appropriate time or in the relevant circumstances (e.g., Foxx, 1982). McClannahan and Krantz (1999) defined prompts as, "instructions, gestures, demonstrations, touches, or other things that we arrange or do to increase the likelihood that children will make correct responses" (p. 37). For example, the parent or instructor may provide a verbal model to increase the likelihood that a child will respond to the question, "What's your name?" Or, after giving the instruction, "Set the table," the parent or instructor may prompt by manually guiding the learner to correctly arrange plates, glasses, and silverware. Or, when teaching a child to imitate the sound "mm," the instructor may manually mold the learner's lips (the prompt) while simultaneously modeling the sound "mm" (the stimulus that will eventually control the youngster's verbal imitation). Of course, the teacher expects that later the child will respond to the verbal model alone, and the prompt will be unnecessary. In this chapter, we define prompting as an instructional technique used to help students make correct responses until they learn to respond to the stimuli that control the behavior of their typically developing peers.

Although prompting procedures can be classified in a number of ways, classification is mainly a matter of convenience. In practice, different prompting procedures are often combined into "packages."

Verbal Prompts

A review of 268 applied behavior analysis journal articles and book chapters revealed that verbal prompts are the most commonly reported auxiliary cues (G. S. MacDuff, 1999). Verbal prompts are words, instructions, or questions that are supposed to direct a person to engage in a target response. In one study, for example, teachers prompted preschoolers with autism to engage in social interactions with peers using verbal prompts such as, "Today I want you to play with John" (Odom & Strain, 1986). Typically, verbal prompts are used in conjunction with other prompts. When a mother gives her son a cookie and prompts, "Say, 'Thank you,' " she is using a verbal instruction ("Say") as well as a verbal model ("Thank you"). If the prompt is effectively faded (i.e., gradually removed), the child will respond "Thank you" in the absence of auxiliary cues when someone gives him something.

Modeling

G. S. MacDuff's (1999) review of the applied behavior analysis literature indicated that the second most commonly used prompting procedure is demonstrating or modeling a response. Like verbal prompts, models are usually used in conjunction with other prompts; no studies were found that used only modeling. In one investigation, peer models were used in conjunction with verbal instructions to teach 5- and 8-year-old boys with autism to check out library books, buy snacks, and cross the street (Blew, Schwartz, & Luce, 1985). In baseline, participants were taken to community settings and verbally instructed to complete target tasks. In the modeling condition, the peer tutors performed the tasks in close proximity to the children with autism, but did not help or reward them. None of the target skills was acquired in the modeling condition. During pretraining, the peers directed the children with autism to complete a variety of motor and discrimination tasks. This was designed to establish the peers as familiar persons; the peers provided instructions, redirected stereotypic behavior, and rewarded correct responses. In the final condition (peer tutoring), the peer models completed the assigned tasks in close proximity to the children with autism, and also prompted and rewarded completion of task components. During this condition, both students with autism acquired the target skills. The authors noted that the students' failure to display target responses in the first modeling condition was probably due to the absence of prompts and rewards for attending to the models.

In addition to live models, videotaped models are sometimes used to teach new skills. For example, videotaped models of a person making purchases were used to teach three young adults with autism to purchase food items in their high school cafeteria and in a convenience store, and to promote generalization of purchasing skills from training sessions (in which verbal and manual prompts as well as models were provided) to probe sessions in which none of these procedures was used (Haring, Kennedy, Adams, & Pitts-Conway, 1987). In another study, familiar adults modeled brief conversations on videotapes that were used to teach conversation skills to three 7- and 8-year-old boys with autism. All three youngsters acquired the target conversation skills after exposure to the modeling procedure. These skills generalized to untrained topics of conversation and maintained at a 15-month follow-up (Charlop & Milstein, 1989).

Some studies have suggested that modeling may be most effective when there is similarity between the learner and the model (Barry & Overman, 1977; Cooper, 1987b). For example, Egel, Richman, and Koegel (1981) reported that although 5- to 8-year-old children with autism did not master discrimination tasks that were taught by a therapist, their performance improved when typically developing peers (selected because they were approximately the same age as the participants) modeled correct responses on the same tasks.

Other investigators have achieved favorable behavior change using models who were dissimilar to the participants. In one study, four children with autism (ages 6 to 9) learned to answer "what," "why," and "how" questions when a teacher modeled the correct response, such as, "Why is he wearing a coat? Because it's cold" (Secan, Egel, & Tilley, 1989). Another investigation compared the effects of peer versus adult models on the development of question-answering skills by four boys with autism. The experimenter asked the peer or adult model a question and rewarded a correct response. The same question was then immediately presented to a child with autism. The boys learned to answer questions equally well when exposed to the 27-year-old adult and to the 9-year-old nondisabled peer (Ihrig & Wolchik, 1988).

Of course, people cannot benefit from modeling unless they have learned to imitate others' behavior. Some children and adults with autism may have learned to imitate certain actions or words, but they may not imitate other responses that have never been specifically taught and reinforced; that is, they do not display *generalized imitation* (Cooper, 1987b). Doing what the model does, whether or not that behavior was previously taught, is a necessary prerequisite skill; without it, people cannot benefit from modeling as a prompting procedure.

Manual Prompts

Manual or physical prompting is defined as physical contact from an instructor that is designed to help the learner display a behavior of interest. For example, an instructor may manually guide a youth's hands to the home row of a keyboard, or a parent may guide a young child who is learning to wash her hands to move from the sink to the towel rack. Manual prompts have been used to teach nonimitative children with autism to correctly form manual signs (Carr, Binkoff, Kologinsky, & Eddy, 1978), and parents have used manual guidance to help their children with autism complete photo-

graphic activity schedules (Krantz, MacDuff, & McClannahan, 1993; McClannahan & Krantz, 1999).

Only a few studies have used manual prompts exclusively. In one study, manual prompts were used to teach four youngsters with autism to independently complete hour-long activity schedules that included leisure and homework tasks such as puzzles and handwriting worksheets; no verbal instructions, praise, or tangible rewards were delivered. After training, the boys were on task during 80% to 100% of observations. This level of engagement maintained when the instructor was out of sight, when the pictures in activity schedules were resequenced, and when novel, untrained photographs were added to their schedules (G. S. MacDuff, Krantz, & McClannahan, 1993).

Gestural Prompts

Gestural prompts include pointing, motioning, or nodding toward students, materials, or activities to indicate an action to be performed. Although G. S. MacDuff's (1999) literature search revealed no examples of gestural prompts used in isolation, a number of studies used gestures as components of prompting packages. In one study, for example, three adults with severe mental retardation were taught a side-of-the-foot soccer pass using modeling, verbal prompts, manual prompts, and gestures, but a description of the gestures was not provided (Luyben, Funk, Morgan, Clark, & Delulio, 1986). Because most studies used gestures as components of prompting packages, it is difficult to determine the usefulness of gestures as prompts.

Photographs and Line Drawings

Pictures, photographs, and line drawings have been used to teach assembly tasks (Wacker & Berg, 1983, 1984), meal preparation (B. Johnson & Cuvo, 1981; Martin, Rusch, James, Decker, & Trtol, 1982; Robinson-Wilson, 1977), clerical and laundry tasks (Wacker, Berg, Berrie, & Swatta, 1985), self-care and daily living routines (Spellman, DeBriere, Jarboe, Campbell, & Harris, 1978; Thinesen & Bryan, 1981), time management (Sowers, Rusch, Connis, & Cummings, 1980; Sowers, Verdi, Bourbeau, & Sheehan, 1985), and computer use (Frank, Wacker, Berg, & McMahon, 1985). Most studies combined pictorial cues with other prompts, such as verbal instructions or video models.

One study measured the engagement of three boys with autism as they completed daily living activities, such as setting the table and getting dressed. Prompts included 4- by 6-inch color photographs, instructions, and modeling. In the teaching condition, on-task time increased and inappropriate behavior decreased. The boys remained engaged when the instructor was no longer visible and when the photographs in their picture albums were resequenced, and engagement generalized across tasks and settings (from clinic to home). But during follow-up, when the students were instructed to set the table and get dressed in the absence of photographs, all made errors (Pierce & Schreibman, 1994).

In clinical practice, we use photographs to cue students to complete lengthy response chains. For instance, many children and youths learn to prepare their school lunches using photographs. Pictures of bread, peanut butter, jelly, and a knife come to control sandwich making, and photographs of fruit, vegetables, snacks, and a napkin signal young people to place these items in a lunch bag. After these pictorial prompts are faded, students complete these sequences in response to a verbal or written cue to "make lunch," or lunch making may come under the stimulus control of time of day or the availability of lunch-making materials.

Textual Prompts

Textual prompts are written cues such as checklists, scripts, and written instructions. For example, a written checklist may be used to prompt a teenager to refill soap dispensers or to warm a frozen dinner in the microwave oven.

In one study, written task analyses (combined with praise, verbal feedback, and gestures) were used to teach adults with mild disabilities to clean the refrigerator and stove, and to do laundry. With the exception of cleaning the refrigerator, these home-maintenance skills were not acquired when textual prompts were presented alone (Cuvo, Davis, O'Reilly, Mooney, & Crowley, 1992).

Another study used written scripts and script fading to teach three young boys with autism to initiate and elaborate conversation with a teacher. The words "Look" and "Watch me" (which the learners had previously learned to read) were attached to pages of their photographic activity schedules. The boys were manually guided to point to a script, approach the teacher, and say the scripted words. When the students reliably said the scripts without prompts, the textual prompts "Look" and "Watch me" were faded by gradually cutting away portions of the cards on which they were displayed. In the third fading step, the cards and scripts were absent. Subsequently, all three boys displayed increases in unscripted interactions (defined as one or more understandable words uttered in the absence of a script) (Krantz & McClannahan, 1998).

Written scripts also were used to teach children with autism to engage in social interaction with peers during art activities in a classroom setting. In baseline, the instructions "Do your art" and "Talk a lot" were presented on a single sheet of paper. In the teaching condition, these instructions were followed by 10 written statements and questions such as "(Name), did you roller-skate outside today?" or "(Name), would you like to use one of my crayons?" Students were manually guided to pick up a pencil and move it along below the text. If a student did not say the script within 5 seconds, manual guidance was repeated. Script fading began after manual guidance was completely faded, and

scripts were faded from end to beginning by gradually and systematically deleting words in five steps. For example, the fading steps for the question "John, would you like some candy?" were (a) "John, would you like some"; (b) John, would you"; (c) "John, would"; (d) "J"; and (e) opening quotation marks ("). As scripts were faded, unscripted initiations (i.e., new combinations of previously taught scripts and novel, untaught utterances) increased. The authors noted that script fading reduces the involvement of teachers and parents during social interaction, thus decreasing the likelihood that learners' interactions will be dependent on prompts from other people (Krantz & McClannahan, 1993).

Other Types of Prompts

A few investigators have used tactile prompts such as letters and numbers drawn with glue and covered with sand (Berg & Wacker, 1989), tones and alarms (Lloyd, Bateman, Landrum, & Hallahan, 1989), and color cues (Dube, McDonald, McIlvane, & Mackay, 1991) to prompt target responses. For example, in one study, three children with autism learned to record their own behavior when their chronograph wristwatches signaled the end of a play interval (Stahmer & Schreibman, 1992).

How To Use Prompts Effectively

Prompts are useful initially in helping people display new, desirable behavior, but new skills are mastered (i.e., performed correctly and independently) only if prompts can be removed. Although many research articles fail to offer details about how prompts were faded, several prompting and prompt-fading procedures are described in the applied behavior analysis literature. Six of these are discussed in the following sections.

Increasing Assistance (Least-to-Most Prompts)

When using increasing assistance, the instructor provides a sequence of prompts that begins with minimal assistance and progresses to more assistance. Initially, the naturally occurring stimulus—that is, the stimulus that should ultimately control the behavior—may be presented without prompts. The teacher provides more help only if the student does not respond correctly within a specified time (often 5 to 10 seconds). Increasing assistance is provided until the student makes a correct response. A common least-to-most prompts system includes verbal prompts, gestures, modeling, and manual prompts.

Suppose a father wants to teach his daughter to put her cup in the dishwasher. On the first trial, the father presents the instruction, "Put your cup in the dishwasher." If the daughter does not respond, or makes an error, the father repeats the instruction, pauses, then points to the dishwasher. If this does not produce a correct response, the father repeats the instruction, pauses, and then models putting the cup in the dishwasher. If this fails to produce a correct response, the father gives the instruction again, pauses, and then manually guides her to put the cup in the dishwasher. This is a least-to-most, or increasing assistance, prompt hierarchy.

Less frequently, parents and professionals use hierarchies that include only verbal prompts or only manual prompts. Here is an illustration of a least-to-most system of verbal prompts to teach an adult with autism to respond to the question "What do you want?" by saying "I want _____." On the first trial the teacher asks, "What do you want?" and waits 5 seconds. If the individual makes an error or does not respond, the teacher repeats the question, pauses, then models "I." Increasingly complete verbal prompts ("I want," "I want soda") are provided until the person makes a correct response. Similarly, a least-to-most hierarchy of manual prompts could be used to teach an adolescent to sort silverware. If a light touch on the elbow does not produce sorting, the parent touches the forearm, then the wrist, and finally uses hand-over-hand guidance.

A frequently cited advantage of increasing assistance is that every trial provides an opportunity for the learner to make unprompted responses to relevant environmental stimuli (Cooper, 1987a; Risley & Cuvo, 1980). In our prior examples, the student may put the cup in the dishwasher or say "I want soda" before any prompts are delivered. This advantage may be overshadowed, however, by the fact that least-to-most prompt hierarchies reliably produce errors, may produce prompt dependence, and typically require more trials than delayed prompting procedures and modeling before students master the target behavior (Godby, Gast, & Wolery, 1987; Karsh, Repp, & Lenz, 1990; Repp, Karsh, & Lenz, 1990).

Decreasing Assistance (Most-to-Least Prompts)

In most-to-least prompt systems, learners receive whatever assistance (prompts) they need to successfully perform a new skill when instruction begins (Cooper, 1987a). Over successive teaching trials, the amount of assistance is gradually reduced until no prompts are provided. Most-to-least prompt systems often include complete physical guidance, partial physical guidance, modeling, gestural prompts, and verbal instructions (Berkowitz, 1990; Csapo, 1981; Goldstein & Cisar, 1992; Green, Reid, Canipe, & Gardner, 1991). When the goal of these procedures is to bring the target behavior under the control of a teacher's directions, each level of prompting is paired with a verbal instruction. Often, however, the goal is to have the learner perform an action or series of actions without instructions or cues, verbal or oth-

erwise, from adults. In these instances, verbal instructions are not used at all, because they can be very difficult to withdraw (fade) and their use can lead to overdependence on prompts.

Suppose a mother wants to teach an adolescent to put his laundry away, using a most-to-least prompts system. The mother begins by instructing, "Put your laundry away." Then she manually guides her son to remove the clean laundry from the basket and put items in drawers. After a specified number of correct responses, the mother gives the initial instruction and provides less and less physical guidance. In the next fading step, she gives the direction and models the correct response. If her son completes the task successfully with this type of prompt during a specified number of trials, she gives the direction and points toward the laundry basket. If he continues to correctly complete the task, his mother fades to the verbal instruction alone.

The majority of most-to-least prompt-fading procedures include several different types of prompts, but one study used only written stimuli to teach children with autism to initiate spoken comments and questions to classmates. Typed scripts were placed on each student's work space. In teaching, the written instruction "Do your art and talk a lot" was combined with a single manual prompt for the student to run his or her pencil under written scripts. Scripts were faded from complete sentences to single quotation marks by gradually removing words, starting with those at the ends of sentences. This fading procedure was effective in increasing unscripted peer initiations and in promoting generalization of conversation skills across settings (Krantz & McClannahan, 1993).

Although few data are available concerning error rates and instructional efficiency (the number of trials required to perform tasks to criterion), some researchers have noted that most-to-least prompt systems result in stable rates of correct responding (Luyben et al., 1986), and are preferred by instructors because they are easy to implement (McDonnell & Ferguson, 1989). In a review of prompting procedures, Demchak (1990) suggested that decreasing assistance is the most efficient prompt-fading procedure because it consistently produces fewer errors and more rapid skill acquisition than least-to-most prompting.

Delayed Prompts

Delayed prompting procedures fade prompts by imposing a brief period of time between the presentation of the naturally occurring stimulus that should ultimately control behavior and the delivery of a prompt (Oppenheimer, Saunders, & Spradlin, 1993). Researchers have repeatedly demonstrated that delayed prompting procedures can be effective, efficient ways to transfer stimulus control from prompts to appropriate environmental cues rapidly and with few errors (Gast, Ault, Wolery, Doyle, & Belanger, 1988; Handen & Zane, 1987; Jones-Ault, Wolery, Gast, Munson-Doyle, & Eizenstat, 1988; Touchette, 1971; Wolery et al., 1992). Suppose a mother decides to use a delayed prompting procedure with modeling prompts to teach her son to respond to the question "What's your name?" During the first 5 to 10 trials, the question "What's your name?" is followed immediately by the model prompt, "John," and the boy is rewarded for repeating "John." In subsequent trials, a 1-second delay is inserted between "What's your name?" and the model "John." If the child responds correctly, the delay is gradually increased (usually in 1-second increments) until he begins to respond before the prompt (model) is presented.

Delayed prompting can also be used to teach a child to point. For example, an instructor says "Point to blue" and simultaneously delivers a manual prompt, guiding the youngster to point. After a specified number of trials, a 1-second pause is inserted between the two stimuli (the instructor says "Point to blue," pauses for 1 second, and then manually guides the learner to point). In subsequent sessions, the delay between the instruction and the prompt is gradually increased in 1-second increments until the child responds before the prompt is delivered, and the prompt is no longer necessary.

Delayed prompt procedures can be effective for teaching new skills. They have one significant drawback, however: Learners with autism may simply wait for prompts rather than anticipating them (i.e., responding before a prompt is provided). In other words, these procedures can produce prompt dependence. In particular, gradually increasing the delay over successive trials can effectively shape waiting behavior, perhaps because the student learns that it is easier to wait for the prompt than to respond independently (Oppenheimer et al., 1993).

Graduated Guidance

In graduated guidance, the instructor provides manual prompts to complete an action, and then fades these prompts by changing their intensity or location. The instructor may begin by using complete hand-over-hand prompts, then use less forceful guidance, and then fade to prompts at the wrist, forearm, elbow, and shoulder (Cooper, 1987a). When prompts are faded to the shoulder, the next fading step may be shadowing, or following the learner's movements without making physical contact. For example, if a youngster is writing, the instructor may hold his or her hand above the child's hand without touching it.

The following is an example of a most-to-least prompt and prompt-fading sequence using graduated guidance: Parents wish to teach their son to push his chair in when he leaves the table. Initially, hand-over-hand prompts (usually light touches) are used to guide the child through the action of pushing his chair under the table. Later, the parents prompt at the wrist. In subsequent sessions, they deliver manual prompts at the forearm, then the elbow, then the shoulder. When the boy reliably pushes his chair under the

table with prompts at the shoulder, the parents no longer touch him, but instead stand behind him and follow his movements as he pushes his chair in. Gradually, they move farther away from the youngster, until he completes the task without prompts while they remain seated.

In many studies, graduated guidance has been used in conjunction with other prompting procedures. For example, procedures designed to teach 12- to 20-year-olds with autism to discriminate line drawings of household objects used graduated guidance in a prompting hierarchy that also included gestural prompts (Berkowitz, 1990). Other researchers combined graduated guidance with verbal prompts and modeling to teach children with autism and mental retardation to tie their shoes, brush their teeth, and dress (Matson, Taras, Sevin, Love, & Fridley, 1990). In these studies, it is impossible to assess the effectiveness of graduated guidance per se because it was one component of an instructional package with several components. In one study, however, graduated guidance was used exclusively to teach children with autism to independently complete hour-long photographic activity schedules that included leisure and homework tasks. Manual prompts were completely faded in 6 to 19 sessions. The authors noted that graduated guidance prevented errors and lengthy delays that might have impeded acquisition of the target skills (G. S. MacDuff et al., 1993).

Stimulus Fading

Stimulus-fading procedures exaggerate some physical dimension (e.g., color, size, intensity) of a relevant stimulus to help a person make a correct response. The exaggerated feature is the prompt, which is gradually faded or reduced in order to transfer stimulus control from the prompt to the stimulus that will ultimately control the behavior of interest (Cooper, 1987a; Etzel & LeBlanc, 1979; Fields, 1981; Groden & Mann, 1988). It is critical that the exaggerated cue emphasizes the dimension of the environmental stimulus that is ultimately expected to control responding (Etzel & LeBlanc, 1979). For example, if intensity is used as a prompt to teach color discrimination, both stimuli to be discriminated should be the same size and shape; for example, the instructor might use a blue circle and a red circle of exactly the same size, on the same background. On initial teaching trials, the color of the stimulus that is designated correct is presented at full intensity, while the color of the incorrect stimulus is very faint. Over successive trials, the correct stimulus is made gradually less intense, while the intensity of the incorrect stimulus is gradually increased until both colors are presented at the same intensity level. Their size and shape remain unchanged throughout teaching.

Many studies have demonstrated the importance of exaggerating the most salient elements of training stimuli. In a comparison of two stimulus-fading procedures, learners were exposed to (a) exaggerated aspects of a stimulus that were essential to making the final discrimination (criterion-related cues) and (b) other exaggerated aspects that were not part of the final, correct discrimination (non–criterion-related cues). The non–criterion-related prompting procedures were ineffective in teaching visual and auditory discriminations, but criterion-related fading procedures were effective for the majority of learners with autism. In addition, students who learned new discriminations using procedures that emphasized the critical dimensions of training stimuli later made errors when exposed to stimulus-fading procedures that did not exaggerate these key aspects (Schreibman, 1975).

In most stimulus-fading investigations, target behaviors are usually discrete responses (e.g., pointing to stimuli such as numbers, or naming colors) rather than lengthy response chains. However, one study designed to teach a bathing response chain to an adult with mental retardation used a stimulus-fading procedure. Applying colored liquid soap to the participant's body parts cued him to wash each soaped area without prompts from instructors. With the soap present, unprompted bathing was observed at a 3-month follow-up (Cameron, Ainsleigh, & Bird, 1992).

The small number of published examples of stimulus fading in teaching complex behavioral repertoires may be related to the difficulties of exaggerating relevant dimensions of stimuli that should eventually control desired responses. It is conceivable, however, that stimulus fading could be used in this context. For example, one could teach a child to vacuum and dust by making the carpet and furniture unusually or obviously "dirty" to begin with, and then gradually fading the amount of visible dirt over successive teaching trials. Alternatively, one could teach ironing by providing items with obvious wrinkles, and then gradually fading or diminishing the wrinkles.

Stimulus Shaping

In stimulus shaping, the physical characteristics of stimuli used in teaching are gradually changed (Etzel & LeBlanc, 1979). For example, a seven-step stimulus-shaping procedure was used to teach three youngsters with autism to state dollar amounts that included decimals. Initially, amounts were presented in writing as "$1 and 55" or "$4 and 67" which the youngsters could read. When the boys responded with 90% accuracy or better, the word "and" was reduced in size; then, during five stimulus-shaping steps, the word became increasingly "decimal-like" until eventually written amounts were presented as "$1.55" or "$4.67," and the youngsters read them accurately (e.g., by saying "one dollar and fifty-five cents") (J. L. MacDuff, MacDuff, McClannahan, Krantz, & MacDuff, 1996).

Although it can be a very effective and nearly errorless prompting and prompt-fading procedure (Mosk & Bucher, 1984; Schilmoeller, Schilmoeller, Etzel, & LeBlanc, 1979), stimulus shaping often requires extensive preparation of stimuli (Cooper, 1987a; Etzel, LeBlanc, Schilmoeller, & Stella, 1981) and may be difficult for many practitioners to implement (Lalli & Browder, 1993).

Prompt Dependence

In a discussion of teacher-training strategies, Koegel, Russo, Rincover, and Schreibman (1982) suggested that (a) a prompt is only a prompt if it works (i.e., it must produce a correct response), and if it does not work it should be replaced, and (b) prompts must be removed and the child or adult must respond to the relevant stimulus in the natural environment. Imagine that a parent decides to use manual (hand-over-hand) prompts to teach a teenager to get out of bed and begin dressing when her alarm clock rings. It is likely that constant use of these prompts will not teach the adolescent to independently respond to an alarm clock, but may increase her dependence on manual prompts.

Prompt dependence means that a person responds to prompts instead of responding to the cues that are expected to evoke the target behavior (Cameron et al., 1992). Suppose a youngster with autism is learning to ask, "How are you?" If the teacher's presence does not evoke the question "How are you?" the teacher may use an expectant look to prompt the response. If the student says, "How are you?" that response is reinforced. Over many trials, both the instructor's presence and the expectant look are correlated with reinforcement for asking "How are you?" Eventually, the response may occur when and only when the expectant look occurs, because the expectant look (not the presence of the instructor) signals an opportunity for reinforcement.

People with autism sometimes respond to irrelevant aspects of the environment. In part, this may be because many teaching procedures do not bring learners' behavior under the control of the key stimuli that control the behavior of most other people (Cuvo & Davis, 1983; Thorwarth-Bruey, 1989; Touchette & Howard, 1984). Consider the following description of discrete-trial teaching:

> The teacher gives an instruction or asks a question, and the learner attempts (or does not attempt) to follow the instruction, receives (or does not receive) a reward, and *waits* for the teacher to initiate the next trial. Thus, both passive waiting and adult instructions become discriminative for reinforcement. (McClannahan & Krantz, 1997, p. 271)

In other words, the learner may become dependent on adult-delivered prompts. Prompt dependence may be related to another widely discussed phenomenon, stimulus overselectivity. The stimulus overselectivity hypothesis suggests that when presented with a stimulus that has more than one component (e.g., a relevant cue and a prompt), people with autism often respond to only some of the components (Cook,

Anderson, & Rincover, 1982; Groden & Mann, 1988; Hoogeveen, Smeets, & Lancioni, 1989; Huguenin & Touchette, 1980; Koegel et al., 1982). Other studies, however, have shown that overselectivity is not unique to autism, and can be overcome by teaching learners to respond to multiple stimuli (e.g., Allen & Fuqua, 1985; Bailey, 1981; Dube, 1997; Dube & McIlvane, 1997; Huguenin, 1985; Litrownik, McInnis, Wetzel-Pritchard, & Filipelli, 1978).

Antecedent stimuli come to control responding because responding in their presence is reinforced frequently (Bailey, 1981; Bickel, Stella, & Etzel, 1984; Kirby & Bickel, 1988; Schneider & Salzberg, 1982). Sometimes prompting procedures cause people with autism to "attend to the teacher's prompt and learn nothing about the task" (Cameron et al., 1992, p. 329), or they "miscue learners and hence prevent them from responding to the critical stimuli" (Hoogeveen, Kouwenhoven, & Smeets, 1989, p. 344). That is, some prompting and reinforcement procedures may increase the likelihood that people with autism will attend to prompts and ignore relevant cues.

Rewarding Unprompted Responses

Although it may be necessary to reward prompted responses early in teaching, frequent reinforcement of prompted responses may inadvertently cause the response to occur *only* when it is prompted, because the prompt (and not the other stimuli that are present at the same time) reliably signals an opportunity for reinforcement. To illustrate, when teaching a child to follow directions, a teacher often uses spoken instructions ("Stand up," "Sit down"), manual guidance (prompts), and snacks (rewards). Initially, both prompted and unprompted responses are rewarded because the spoken instructions alone are not consistently effective—that is, they do not reliably control the specified responses. If the teacher continues to reward all prompted responses, however, the prompts, not the spoken instructions, may control direction following.

It appears necessary to reward prompted responses frequently in the early stages of teaching a new skill. What can teachers or parents do to help children respond to relevant stimuli other than prompts? One solution is to combine prompting and prompt fading with shaping, or rewarding unprompted approximations of desired responses (Litt & Schreibman, 1981). Suppose a father is teaching a youngster to put on her shoes by herself. The shoes next to her bed should be the stimuli that cue putting them on. Initially, the father puts the shoes on the floor next to the bed and prompts, "Put on your shoes." Because the presence of the shoes, not the instruction, should cue putting on shoes, the teaching and prompting procedures selected must make the presence of the shoes relevant. For several sessions, the father may physically guide his child to perform each of the several components in this skill, and reward each prompted response. Then, the

father may briefly withhold prompts and look for and reward components that are attempted without prompts. For example, the father might prompt one component (bending to pick up a shoe), then pause to give the child an opportunity to attempt the next response (moving the shoe toward her foot). If she does so, the father rewards that response and again pauses to observe whether she attempts the next component (putting the shoe on her foot). If she does not move the shoe toward her foot following the brief pause, her father physically guides her to complete that response, but does not deliver a reward. Over time, her father gradually increases the length of the pauses and continues to reward responses completed without prompts, until the youngster puts on her shoes independently. The father reinforces unprompted manipulation of the shoes to increase the likelihood that the presence of the shoes, not prompts from a parent or teacher, will ultimately control putting on shoes.

A 1980 study examined the effects of rewarding prompted and unprompted responses when teaching children with mental retardation to label pictures (Olenick & Pear, 1980). During prompted trials, the instructor presented a picture, asked the child "What's this?" and immediately prompted by naming the picture (e.g., "Apple"). During probe trials, the experimenter presented a picture and asked "What's this?" but did not prompt. In some teaching conditions, both prompted and unprompted labeling produced the same level of rewards; in other conditions, prompted responses produced fewer rewards than unprompted responses. The research demonstrated that providing more rewards for unprompted than prompted labeling resulted in more correct responses and more rapid learning.

Focusing Teaching on Relevant Environmental Cues

Shifting reinforcement from prompted to unprompted responses helps to avoid or diminish prompt dependence, but teachers must also ensure that their teaching strategies help people focus on the relevant aspects of teaching materials and social stimuli. If teachers want children, adolescents, and adults with autism to respond to the same environmental stimuli that control the behavior of people without disabilities, their prompting strategies must draw attention to the distinctive features of these stimuli (Etzel & LeBlanc, 1979; Etzel et al., 1981; Smeets, Hoogeveen, Striefel, & Lancioni, 1985; Smeets, Striefel, & Hoogeveen, 1990). Put another way, successful teaching means helping people respond to aspects of the environment that will continue to be present when teaching is completed (Zane, Handen, Mason, & Geffin, 1984; Zygmont, Lazar, Dube, & McIlvane, 1992). For example, when teaching a youngster with autism to discriminate red and blue, the relevant aspects of these stimuli are "redness" and "blueness." Other characteristics of the stimuli, such as size, shape, and texture, are not relevant in this context. To help students learn the relevant dimension, a teacher must design instruction to ensure that correct responses can be based only on color. The teacher might accomplish that by presenting two cars, two toothbrushes, or two gummy bears that are identical except for color, and reinforcing responses to the *color* that is designated correct on each trial, rather than responses to the larger, longer, or chewier stimulus.

Before designing instructional programs, it is often helpful to ask, "What stimuli should cue a person to engage in the target behavior?" In typical situations, greeting skills may be cued by a knock on the door, a ringing doorbell, or the approach of a familiar person. Hand washing may be cued by dirty hands, the presence of food, or flushing the toilet. To teach people to respond to all of the relevant stimuli, teachers must use teaching procedures that are likely to bring the target response under the control of environmental stimuli rather than prompts from other people. As a case in point, one might use a photographic activity schedule to teach a youngster to get dressed. In this instance, the schedule, not the presence of another person or prompts delivered by another person, should control dressing. The schedule might include pictures of each dressing skill (e.g., putting on undershirt, underpants, and socks). Manual prompts delivered from behind the boy would be used to teach him to (a) point to the picture in the schedule, (b) obtain the relevant materials, (c) complete that component of the activity, (d) return to the schedule, and (e) turn the page. During initial sessions, rewards would be delivered for *every* response, whether prompted or not, to establish the pictures as discriminative stimuli for dressing. Hand-over-hand prompts might continue for several sessions, but then would be faded by changing the location of the prompts (from hand-over-hand to prompts at the wrist, forearm, and shoulder) and by altering the intensity of the prompts (from a firm grasp to successively lighter touches). When prompt fading begins, reinforcement shifts from prompted to unprompted responses.

Because the boy has often completed the look-then-do sequence described above, he may now point to photographs or turn pages of his schedule book without prompts. Completing these steps without assistance will be followed by rewards, and eventually the teacher will shadow as the boy completes the schedule and continue to reward unprompted dressing. Finally, the teacher will gradually move farther away until the boy dresses independently. Now tangible rewards may be replaced by a photograph (e.g., breakfast). Prompts and rewards, delivered from behind the learner, increase the likelihood that the photographic activity schedule (not the teacher) acquires stimulus control over dressing (G. S. MacDuff et al., 1993; McClannahan & Krantz, 1999).

By ensuring that teaching procedures require and reward responses to relevant environmental stimuli, teachers decrease the likelihood of prompt dependence. Sometimes, however, despite best efforts, a child or adult continues to make errors when prompts are not provided, and does not independently perform the target responses.

Determining Effectiveness of Prompting Procedures

Research has shown that errors often interfere with acquisition, generalization, and maintenance of skills (Albin & Horner, 1988; Godby et al., 1987; Koegel et al., 1982) and may provoke disruptive and emotional responses (Carr & Durand, 1985; Smeets, Lancioni, & Striefel, 1987; Weeks & Gaylord-Ross, 1981). Errors also decrease the amount of time that students are available for instruction (C. M. Johnson, 1977; Lovaas, 1977) and increase the likelihood of further errors (Cooper, 1987a; Demchak, 1990; Richmond & Bell, 1986). Despite the potential side effects of errors, only a fraction of the studies G. S. MacDuff (1999) reviewed measured errors or conducted error analyses (Doyle, Wolery, Gast, Ault, & Wiley, 1990; McDonnell & McFarland, 1988; Stella & Etzel, 1986). Nonetheless, based on the research evidence, it appears important to use teaching procedures that produce few or no errors from the outset (Cameron et al., 1992; Etzel, Aangeenburg, Nelson-Burford, Holt, & Stella, 1982).

Comparisons of most-to-least prompting systems (e.g., decreasing assistance and stimulus fading) and least-to-most prompting systems (e.g., increasing assistance) indicate that least-to-most prompting consistently produces more errors (Gast et al., 1988; Godby et al., 1987; Jones-Ault et al., 1988; Munson-Doyle, Wolery, Gast, & Jones-Ault, 1990).

Another way to evaluate prompting and prompt-fading procedures is to examine their efficiency. Interventions that require fewer trials or less instructional time may be the procedures of choice because they enable learners to master tasks more rapidly. Most of the information available about the efficiency of prompting and prompt-fading procedures is the result of comparative studies. In a comparison of decreasing assistance and increasing assistance, adolescents with profound mental retardation learned to identify coins and kitchen utensils more rapidly when taught with decreasing assistance (Day, 1987). In another comparison, however, increasing assistance was found to be the more efficient means of teaching adolescents with severe handicaps a two-choice discrimination task (Csapo, 1981).

Other researchers have compared most-to-least and least-to-most prompts and delayed prompting procedures. Although both most-to-least prompts and delayed prompting resulted in acquisition and maintenance of banking skills (cashing checks and using an automatic teller) by adolescents with mental retardation, decreasing assistance required less training time (McDonnell & Ferguson, 1989). When compared with increasing assistance, delayed prompting has been deemed the more efficient method of teaching both discrete responses and chained responses (Bennett, Gast, Wolery, & Schuster, 1986; Demchak, 1990; Gast et al., 1988; McDonnell, 1987). As noted earlier, however, delayed prompting procedures may teach learners to wait for prompts (Oppenheimer et al., 1993).

In a comparison of the effects of delayed prompting and increasing assistance for teaching students with mental retardation and autism to respond to the instruction "Point to _____" by pointing to objects such as spoon, soap, or crayon, both procedures produced a desired behavior change, but delayed prompting required fewer sessions and fewer trials per session, and resulted in a smaller number of errors. The investigators suggested that if prompting procedures are equally effective, it is prudent to base the selection of procedures on the amount of instructional time required to produce a criterion performance (Godby et al., 1987).

Other factors that may influence the effectiveness and efficiency of prompting and prompt-fading procedures include (a) characteristics of learners, (b) characteristics of prompts, and (c) the difficulty of implementing procedures. Examining learner characteristics will likely produce useful guidelines; for example, if a person has not acquired generalized imitation skills, he or she is unlikely to correctly respond to model prompts. If an individual avoids or attempts to escape physical contact, manual guidance will probably hinder acquisition. If a child is apt to respond as soon as materials are presented and is unlikely to wait for prompts, delayed prompting may not be the procedure of choice. Effectiveness may also be influenced by a learner's prior history with prompting procedures (Demchak, 1990). For example, previous experience with a procedure may cause that intervention to be more effective than a novel procedure (Wolery, Ault, Doyle, & Gast, 1986).

Characteristics of prompts may affect instructional effectiveness and efficiency (Billingsley & Romer, 1983). One consideration is whether the natural cue (the stimulus that should ultimately control a behavior) and the prompt should be of the same sensory modality. For instance, will people with autism acquire visual discriminations more quickly and with fewer errors if visual prompts (e.g., models) are used rather than verbal prompts? Another consideration is how clearly prompts indicate the target behavior. Can people with autism more readily master response chains such as dressing, bed making, and table setting if separate responses are illustrated with photographs than with line drawings? These issues are yet to be addressed. Research in these areas would contribute to the development of guidelines for selecting the most effective and efficient prompting procedures.

Finally, the effectiveness and efficiency of prompting and prompt-fading procedures may be influenced by the ease or difficulty of implementation. A study that compared decreasing assistance and delayed prompting also included an assessment of teachers' preferences. Although delayed prompting was found to be more effective, decreasing assis-

tance was preferred by instructors because it was easier to implement (McDonnell & Ferguson, 1989). Perhaps less difficult procedures are more likely to be implemented and may therefore be more effective and efficient.

Selection of Prompting Procedures

Although prompts are an essential part of behavioral teaching technology, they must be used carefully to be effective. In his review of staff-training strategies, Jahr (1997) noted, "The fading of prompts is probably one of the more critical elements in the therapeutic process and lack of proficiency in such techniques may have very unfortunate effects on the client" (p. 81). Some of those unfortunate effects include prompt dependence, passivity, and the development of error patterns that can be very difficult to correct. These problems are greatly reduced when prompting and prompt-fading procedures are systematically planned and implemented, with careful, ongoing, direct assessment of learners' responses.

Although current research does not clearly indicate prompting procedures of choice for every learner under every circumstance, it does offer some practical guidelines:

- Prompts should be used judiciously; they should produce correct responses and opportunities for reinforcement when new skills are introduced, but should be faded as quickly as possible. Too many trials at one prompting level may reinforce dependence on prompts.

- On the other hand, prompts should not be faded too abruptly because this may result in errors that impede acquisition.

- Increasing assistance (least-to-most) procedures should be used to assess learners' current abilities to perform certain skills because this affords opportunities to determine what students can do independently or with minimal prompting, and what types or levels of prompts are necessary to the display of target responses.

- Decreasing assistance (most-to-least) procedures are preferred for teaching new skills because this approach produces more rapid skill acquisition, fewer errors, and less prompt dependence than least-to-most prompting procedures.

- When errors occur during teaching, it is usually desirable to return to the previous level of prompting (i.e., on the next learning opportunity, provide enough help to minimize the likelihood of additional errors). This also promotes skill acquisition because it decreases emotional responses that are frequently associated with errors.

- As quickly as possible, shift reinforcement from prompted responses to unprompted responses, because ongoing reinforcement of prompted behavior is likely to result in prompt dependence.

- Do not assume that the prompting and prompt-fading procedures that were effective for teaching one skill will be effective for teaching other skills, or for teaching other learners the same skill. Prompting and prompt-fading techniques should be selected through direct observation and measurement. Pretesting the effectiveness and efficiency of different prompting procedures in brief tryouts, and examining the data from these trials for evidence that one procedure results in more rapid acquisition or fewer errors than another, can help to identify prompting methods that are likely to be effective for instruction.

Summary

In this chapter, we defined prompts and examined several different types of prompts. We summarized several prompt-fading procedures (increasing assistance, decreasing assistance, delayed prompting, graduated guidance, stimulus fading, and stimulus shaping) and noted that fading procedures that help people acquire new skills in the fewest trials and with the fewest errors may be the most useful. We suggested that the likelihood of prompt dependence may be reduced by shifting reinforcement from prompted responses to unprompted responses as early as possible, and by fading prompts rapidly but carefully.

Finally, we underlined the importance of making careful decisions about the selection of prompting and prompt-fading procedures before teaching begins. Prompting procedures must enable learners to respond to relevant environmental stimuli. In our experience, prompting sequences such as verbal instructions that are faded to phrases, words, syllables, and then expectant looks can be very difficult to eliminate; when the expectant look is absent, the target response often fails to occur. Other prompt-fading strategies, such as graduated guidance delivered from behind children or adults, may be more effective than verbal prompts because throughout training the student responds to relevant environmental cues rather than to an instructor. For the same reasons, delayed prompt, stimulus-fading, and stimulus-shaping procedures may be useful for bringing the behavior of people with autism under the control of the same environmental stimuli that have an impact on the behavior of typical learners. We look forward to new investigations and new data on the effectiveness of prompting procedures. In the meantime,

thoughtful selection of prompting and prompt-fading procedures and careful assessment of their effects may help diminish the prompt dependence that is so often observed in young people with autism.

References

Albin, R. W., & Horner, R. H. (1988). Generalization with precision. In R. H. Horner, G. Dunlap, & R. L. Koegel (Eds.), *Generalization and maintenance: Life-style changes in applied settings* (pp. 99–120). Baltimore: Brookes.

Allen, K. D., & Fuqua, R. W. (1985). Eliminating selective stimulus control: A comparison of two procedures for teaching mentally retarded children to respond to compound stimuli. *Journal of Experimental Child Psychology, 39,* 55–71.

Bailey, S. L. (1981). Stimulus overselectivity in learning disabled children. *Journal of Applied Behavior Analysis, 14,* 239–248.

Barry, N. J., & Overman, P. B. (1977). Comparison of the effectiveness of adult and peer models with EMR children. *American Journal of Mental Deficiency, 82,* 33–36.

Bennett, D. L., Gast, D. L., Wolery, M., & Schuster, J. (1986). Time delay and system of least prompts: A comparison in teaching manual sign production. *Education and Training of the Mentally Retarded, 21,* 117–129.

Berg, W. K., & Wacker, D. P. (1989). Evaluation of tactile prompts with a student who is deaf, blind, and mentally retarded. *Journal of Applied Behavior Analysis, 22,* 93–99.

Berkowitz, S. (1990). A comparison of two methods of prompting in training discrimination of communication book pictures by autistic students. *Journal of Autism and Developmental Disorders, 20,* 255–262.

Bickel, W. K., Stella, M. E., & Etzel, B. C. (1984). A reevaluation of stimulus overselectivity: Restricted stimulus control or stimulus control hierarchies. *Journal of Autism and Developmental Disabilities, 14,* 137–157.

Billingsley, F. F., & Romer, L. T. (1983). Response prompting and the transfer of stimulus control: Methods, research, and a conceptual framework. *The Journal of the Association for the Severely Handicapped, 8,* 3–12.

Blew, P. A., Schwartz, I. S., & Luce, S. C. (1985). Teaching functional community skills to autistic children using nonhandicapped peer tutors. *Journal of Applied Behavior Analysis, 18,* 337–342.

Cameron, M. J., Ainsleigh, S. A., & Bird, F. L. (1992). The acquisition of stimulus control of compliance and participation during an AD routine. *Behavioral Residential Treatment, 7,* 327–340.

Carr, E. G., Binkoff, J. A., Kologinsky, E., & Eddy, M. (1978). Acquisition of sign language by autistic children: I. Expressive labeling. *Journal of Applied Behavior Analysis, 11,* 489–501.

Carr, E. G., & Durand, V. M. (1985). Reducing behavior problems through functional communication training. *Journal of Applied Behavior Analysis, 18,* 111–126.

Charlop, M. H., & Milstein, J. P. (1989). Teaching autistic children conversational speech using video modeling. *Journal of Applied Behavior Analysis, 22,* 275–285.

Cook, A. R., Anderson, N., & Rincover, A. (1982). Stimulus over-selectivity and stimulus control: Problems and strategies. In R. L. Koegel, A. Rincover, & A. L. Egel (Eds.), *Educating and understanding autistic children* (pp. 90–105). San Diego: College-Hill.

Cooper, J. O. (1987a). Stimulus control. In J. O. Cooper, T. E. Heron, & W. L. Heward (Eds.), *Applied behavior analysis* (pp. 299–326). Columbus, OH: Merrill.

Cooper, J. O. (1987b). Imitation. In J. O. Cooper, T. E. Heron, & W. L. Heward (Eds.), *Applied behavior analysis* (pp. 365–376). Columbus, OH: Merrill.

Csapo, M. (1981). Comparison of two prompting procedures to increase response fluency among severely handicapped learners. *Journal of the Association for the Severely Handicapped, 6,* 39–47.

Cuvo, A. J., & Davis, P. K. (1983). Methodological issues and future directions. In M. Hersen, V. B. Van Hasselt, & J. L. Matson (Eds.), *Behavior therapy for the developmentally and physically disabled* (pp. 374–380). New York: Academic Press.

Cuvo, A. J., Davis, P. K., O'Reilly, M. F., Mooney, B. M., & Crowley, R. (1992). Promoting stimulus control with textual prompts and performance feedback for persons with mild disabilities. *Journal of Applied Behavior Analysis, 25,* 477–489.

Day, H. M. (1987). Comparison of two prompting procedures to facilitate skill acquisition among severely mentally retarded adolescents. *American Journal of Mental Deficiency, 91,* 366–372.

Demchak, M. A. (1990). Response prompting and fading methods: A review. *American Journal on Mental Retardation, 96,* 603–615.

Doyle, P. M., Wolery, M., Gast, D. L., Ault, M. J., & Wiley, K. (1990). Comparison of constant time delay and the system of least prompts in teaching preschoolers with developmental delays. *Research in Developmental Disabilities, 11,* 1–22.

Dube, W. V. (1997). Restricted stimulus control and stimulus–reinforcer relations. *Experimental Analysis of Human Behavior Bulletin, 15,* 8–11.

Dube, W. V., McDonald, S. J., McIlvane, W. J., & Mackay, H. A. (1991). Constructed-response matching to sample and spelling instruction. *Journal of Applied Behavior Analysis, 24,* 305–317.

Dube, W. V., & McIlvane, W. J. (1997). Reinforcer frequency and restricted stimulus control. *Journal of the Experimental Analysis of Behavior, 68,* 303–316.

Egel, A. L., Richman, G. S., & Koegel, R. L. (1981). Normal peer models and autistic children's learning. *Journal of Applied Behavior Analysis, 14,* 3–12.

Etzel, B. C., Aangeenburg, M. H., Nelson-Burford, A. L., Holt, W. J., & Stella, M. E. (1982). Cognitive skill deficiencies: Behavioral assessment and intervention. In K. E. Allen & E. M. Goetz (Eds.), *Early childhood education: Special problems, special solutions* (pp. 253–307). Rockville, MD: Aspen.

Etzel, B. C., & LeBlanc, J. M. (1979). The simplest treatment alternative: The law of parsimony applied to choosing appropriate instructional control and errorless-learning procedures for the difficult-to-teach child. *Journal of Autism and Developmental Disorders, 9,* 361–382.

Etzel, B. C., LeBlanc, J. M., Schilmoeller, K. J., & Stella, M. E. (1981). Stimulus control procedures in the education of young children. In S. W. Bijou & R. Ruiz (Eds.), *Contributions of behavior modification to education* (pp. 3–37). Hillsdale, NJ: Erlbaum.

Fields, L. (1981). Early and late introduction of probes and stimulus control acquisition in fading. *Journal of Experimental Analysis of Behavior, 36,* 363–370.

Foxx, R. M. (1982). *Increasing behaviors of severely retarded and autistic individuals* (pp. 81–96). Champaign, IL: Research Press.

Frank, A. R., Wacker, D. P., Berg, W. K., & McMahon, C. M. (1985). Teaching selected microcomputer skills to retarded students via picture prompts. *Journal of Applied Behavior Analysis, 18,* 179–185.

Gast, D. L., Ault, M. J., Wolery, M., Doyle, P. M., & Belanger, S. (1988). Comparison of constant time delay and the system of least prompts in teaching sight word reading to students with moderate retardation. *Education and Training in Mental Retardation, 25,* 117–128.

Godby, S., Gast, D. L., & Wolery, M. (1987). A comparison of time delay and system of least prompts in teaching object identification. *Research in Developmental Disabilities, 8,* 283–306.

Goldstein, H., & Cisar, C. L. (1992). Prompting interaction during sociodramatic play: Teaching scripts to typical preschoolers and classmates with disabilities. *Journal of Applied Behavior Analysis, 25,* 265–280.

Green, C. W., Reid, D. H., Canipe, V. S., & Gardner, S. M. (1991). A comprehensive evaluation of reinforcer identification processes for persons with profound handicaps. *Journal of Applied Behavior Analysis, 24,* 537–552.

Groden, G., & Mann, L. (1988). Intellectual functioning and assessment. In G. Groden & M. G. Baron (Eds.), *Autism: Strategies for change* (pp. 81–82). New York: Gardner.

Handen, B. L., & Zane, T. (1987). Delayed prompting: A review of procedural variations and results. *Research in Developmental Disabilities, 8,* 307–330.

Haring, T. G., Kennedy, C. H., Adams, M. J., & Pitts-Conway, V. (1987). Teaching generalization of purchasing skills across community settings to autistic youth using videotape modeling. *Journal of Applied Behavior Analysis, 20,* 89–96.

Hoogeveen, F. R., Kouwenhoven, J. A., & Smeets, P. M. (1989). Establishing sound blending in moderately mentally retarded children: Implications of verbal instruction and pictorial prompting. *Research in Developmental Disabilities, 10,* 333–348.

Hoogeveen, F. R., Smeets, P. M., & Lancioni, G. E. (1989). Teaching moderately retarded children basic reading skills. *Research in Developmental Disabilities, 10,* 1–18.

Huguenin, N. H. (1985). Attention to multiple cues by severely mentally retarded adults: Effects of single-component pretraining. *Applied Research in Mental Retardation, 6,* 319–335.

Huguenin, N. H., & Touchette, P. E. (1980). Visual attention in retarded adults: Combining stimuli which control incompatible behavior. *Journal of the Experimental Analysis of Behavior, 33,* 77–86.

Ihrig, K., & Wolchik, S. A. (1988). Peer versus adult models and autistic children's learning: Acquisition, generalization, and maintenance. *Journal of Autism and Developmental Disabilities, 18,* 67–79.

Jahr, E. (1997). Current issues in staff training. *Research in Developmental Disabilities, 19,* 73–87.

Johnson, B., & Cuvo, A. J. (1981). Teaching mentally retarded adults to cook. *Behavior Modification, 5,* 187–202.

Johnson, C. M. (1977). Errorless learning in a multi-handicapped adolescent. *Education and Treatment of Children, 1,* 25–33.

Jones-Ault, M., Wolery, M., Gast, D. L., Munson-Doyle, P., & Eizenstat, V. (1988). Comparison of response prompting procedures in teaching numeral identification to autistic subjects. *Journal of Autism and Developmental Disorders, 18,* 627–636.

Karsh, K. G., Repp, A. C., & Lenz, M. W. (1990). A comparison of the task demonstration model and the standard prompting hierarchy in teaching word identification to persons with moderate retardation. *Research in Developmental Disabilities, 11,* 395–410.

Kirby, K. C., & Bickel, W. K. (1988). Toward an explicit analysis of generalization: A stimulus control interpretation. *Behavior Analyst, 11,* 115–129.

Koegel, R. L., Russo, D. C., Rincover, A., & Schreibman, L. (1982). Assessing and training teachers. In R. L. Koegel, A. Rincover, & A. L. Egel (Eds.), *Educating and understanding autistic children* (pp. 185–189). San Diego: College-Hill.

Krantz, P. J., MacDuff, M. T., & McClannahan, L. E. (1993). Programming participation in family activities for children with autism: Parents' use of photographic activity schedules. *Journal of Applied Behavior Analysis, 26,* 137–138.

Krantz, P. J., & McClannahan, L. E. (1993). Teaching children with autism to initiate to peers: Effects of a script-fading procedure. *Journal of Applied Behavior Analysis, 26,* 121–132.

Krantz, P. J., & McClannahan, L. E. (1998). Social interaction skills for children with autism: A script-fading procedure for beginning readers. *Journal of Applied Behavior Analysis, 31,* 191–202.

Lalli, J. S., & Browder, D. M. (1993). Comparison of sight word training procedures with validation of the most practical procedure in teaching reading for daily living. *Research in Developmental Disabilities, 14,* 107–127.

Litrownik, A. J., McInnis, E. T., Wetzel-Pritchard, A. M., & Filipelli, D. L. (1978). Restricted stimulus control and inferred attentional deficits in autistic and retarded children. *Journal of Abnormal Psychology, 87,* 554–562.

Litt, M. D., & Schreibman, L. (1981). Stimulus-specific reinforcement in the acquisition of receptive labels by autistic children. *Analysis and Intervention in Developmental Disabilities, 1,* 171–186.

Lloyd, J. W., Bateman, D. F., Landrum, T. J., & Hallahan, D. P. (1989). Self-recording of attention versus productivity. *Journal of Applied Behavior Analysis, 22,* 315–323.

Lovaas, O. I. (1977). *The autistic child: Language development through behavior modification.* New York: Irvington.

Luyben, P. D., Funk, D. M., Morgan, J. K., Clark, K. A., & Delulio, D. W. (1986). Team sports for the severely retarded: Learning a side-of-the-foot soccer pass using a maximum-to-minimum prompt reduction strategy. *Journal of Applied Behavior Analysis, 19,* 431–436.

MacDuff, G. S. (1999). *Prompts in intervention for people with developmental disabilities: A review.* Unpublished manuscript.

MacDuff, G. S., Krantz, P. J., & McClannahan, L. E. (1993). Teaching children with autism to use photographic activity schedules: Maintenance and generalization of complex response chains. *Journal of Applied Behavior Analysis, 26,* 89–95.

MacDuff, J. L., MacDuff, M. T., McClannahan, L. E., Krantz, P. J., & Mac-Duff, G. S. (1996). *Teaching students with autism to state decimals: The effects of a stimulus-shaping procedure.* Unpublished manuscript.

Martin, J., Rusch, F., James, V., Decker, P., & Trtol, K. (1982). The use of picture cues to establish self-control in the preparation of complex meals by mentally retarded adults. *Applied Research in Mental Retardation, 3,* 105–119.

Matson, J. L., Taras, M. E., Sevin, J. A., Love, S. R., & Fridley, D. (1990). Teaching self-help skills to autistic and mentally retarded children. *Research in Developmental Disabilities, 11,* 361–378.

McClannahan, L. E., & Krantz, P. J. (1997). In search of solutions to prompt dependence: Teaching children with autism to use photographic activity schedules. In D. M. Baer & E. M. Pinkston (Eds.), *Environment and behavior* (pp. 271–278). Boulder, CO: Westview.

McClannahan, L. E., & Krantz, P. J. (1999). *Activity schedules for children with autism: Teaching independent behavior.* Bethesda, MD: Woodbine.

McDonnell, J. (1987). The effects of time delay and increasing prompt hierarchy strategies on the acquisition of purchasing skills by students with severe handicaps. *The Journal of the Association for Persons with Severe Handicaps, 12,* 227–236.

McDonnell, J., & Ferguson, B. (1989). A comparison of time delay and decreasing prompt hierarchy strategies in teaching banking skills to students with moderate handicaps. *Journal of Applied Behavior Analysis, 22,* 85–91.

McDonnell, J., & McFarland, S. (1988). A comparison of forward and concurrent chaining strategies in teaching laundromat skills to students with severe handicaps. *Research in Developmental Disabilities, 9,* 177–194.

Mosk, M. D., & Bucher, B. (1984). Prompting and stimulus shaping procedures for teaching visual-motor skills to retarded children. *Journal of Applied Behavior Analysis, 17,* 23–34.

Munson-Doyle, P., Wolery, M., Gast, D. L., & Jones-Ault, M. (1990). Comparison of constant time delay and the system of least prompts in teaching preschoolers with developmental delays. *Research in Developmental Disabilities, 11,* 1–22.

Odom, S. L., & Strain, P. S. (1986). A comparison of peer-initiation and teacher-antecedent interventions for promoting reciprocal social interaction of autistic preschoolers. *Journal of Applied Behavior Analysis, 19,* 59–71.

Olenick, D. L., & Pear, J. J. (1980). Differential reinforcement of correct responses to probes and prompts in picture-name training with severely retarded children. *Journal of Applied Behavior Analysis, 13,* 77–89.

Oppenheimer, M., Saunders, R. R., & Spradlin, J. E. (1993). Investigating the generality of the delayed-prompt effect. *Research in Developmental Disabilities, 14,* 425–444.

Pierce, K. L., & Schreibman, L. (1994). Teaching daily living skills to children with autism in unsupervised settings through pictorial self-management. *Journal of Applied Behavior Analysis, 27,* 471–481.

Repp, A. C., Karsh, K. G., & Lenz, M. W. (1990). Discrimination training for persons with developmental disabilities: A comparison of the task demonstration model and the standard prompting hierarchy. *Journal of Applied Behavior Analysis, 23,* 43–52.

Richmond, G., & Bell, J. (1986). Comparison of trial-and-error and graduated stimulus change procedures across tasks. *Analysis and Intervention in Developmental Disabilities, 6,* 127–136.

Risley, R., & Cuvo, A. J. (1980). Training mentally retarded adults to make emergency telephone calls. *Behavior Modification, 4,* 513–525.

Robinson-Wilson, M. A. (1977). Picture recipe cards as an approach to teaching severely and profoundly retarded adults to cook. In M. E. Snell (Ed.), *Systematic instruction of the moderately and severely handicapped* (pp. 69–73). Columbus, OH: Merrill.

Schilmoeller, G. L., Schilmoeller, K. J., Etzel, B. C., & LeBlanc, J. M. (1979). Conditional discrimination after errorless and trial-and-error training. *Journal of the Experimental Analysis of Behavior, 31,* 405–420.

Schneider, H. C., & Salzberg, C. L. (1982). Stimulus over-selectivity in a match-to-sample paradigm by severely retarded youth. *Analysis and Intervention in Developmental Disabilities, 2,* 273–304.

Schreibman, L. (1975). Effects of within-stimulus and extra-stimulus prompting on discrimination learning in autistic children. *Journal of Applied Behavior Analysis, 8,* 91–112.

Secan, K. E., Egel, A. L., & Tilley, C. S. (1989). Acquisition, generalization, and maintenance of question-answering skills in autistic children. *Journal of Applied Behavior Analysis, 22,* 181–196.

Smeets, P. M., Hoogeveen, F. R., Striefel, S., & Lancioni, G. E. (1985). Stimulus overselectivity in TMR children: Establishing functional control of simultaneous multiple stimuli. *Analysis and Intervention in Developmental Disabilities, 5,* 247–267.

Smeets, P. M., Lancioni, G. E., & Striefel, S. (1987). Stimulus manipulation versus delayed feedback for teaching missing minuend problems to difficult-to-teach students. *Research in Developmental Disabilities, 8,* 261–282.

Smeets, P. M., Striefel, S., & Hoogeveen, F. R. (1990). Time-delay discrimination training: Replication with different stimuli and different populations. *Research in Developmental Disabilities, 11,* 217–240.

Sowers, J., Rusch, F., Connis, R., & Cummings, L. (1980). Teaching mentally retarded adults to time-manage in a vocational setting. *Journal of Applied Behavior Analysis, 13,* 119–128.

Sowers, J., Verdi, M., Bourbeau, P., & Sheehan, M. (1985). Teaching job independence and flexibility to mentally retarded students through the use of a self-control package. *Journal of Applied Behavior Analysis, 18,* 81–85.

Spellman, C., DeBriere, T., Jarboe, D., Campbell, S., & Harris, C. (1978). *Pictorial instructions: Training daily living skills.* Columbus, OH: Merrill.

Stahmer, A. C., & Schreibman, L. (1992). Teaching children with autism appropriate play in unsupervised environments using a self-management treatment package. *Journal of Applied Behavior Analysis, 25,* 447–459.

Stella, M. E., & Etzel, B. C. (1986). Stimulus control of eye orientations: Shaping S+ only versus shaping S– only. *Analysis and Intervention in Developmental Disabilities, 6,* 137–153.

Thinesen, P., & Bryan, A. (1981). The use of sequential picture cues in the initiation and maintenance of grooming behaviors with mentally retarded adults. *Mental Retardation, 19,* 246–250.

Thorwarth-Bruey, C. (1989). Daily life with your child. In M. D. Powers (Ed.), *Children with autism: A parents' guide* (pp. 90–91). Rockville, MD: Woodbine.

Touchette, P. E. (1971). Transfer of stimulus control: Measuring the moment of transfer. *Journal of the Experimental Analysis of Behavior, 15,* 347–354.

Touchette, P. E., & Howard, J. S. (1984). Errorless learning: Reinforcement contingencies and stimulus control transfer in delayed prompting. *Journal of Applied Behavior Analysis, 17,* 175–188.

Wacker, D. P., & Berg, W. K. (1983). Effects of picture prompts on the acquisition of complex vocational tasks by mentally retarded adolescents. *Journal of Applied Behavior Analysis, 16,* 417–433.

Wacker, D. P., & Berg, W. K. (1984). Training adolescents with severe handicaps to set up job tasks independently using picture prompts. *Analysis and Intervention in Developmental Disabilities, 4,* 353–365.

Wacker, D. P., Berg, W. K., Berrie, P., & Swatta, P. (1985). Generalization and maintenance of complex skills by severely handicapped adolescents following picture prompt training. *Journal of Applied Behavior Analysis, 18,* 329–336.

Weeks, M., & Gaylord-Ross, R. (1981). Task difficulty and aberrant behavior in severely handicapped students. *Journal of Applied Behavior Analysis, 14,* 449–463.

Wolery, M., Ault, M. J., Doyle, P. M., & Gast, D. L. (1986). *Comparison of instructional strategies: A literature review.* Unpublished manuscript, University of Kentucky, Lexington.

Wolery, M., Holcombe, A., Cybriwsky, C., Munson-Doyle, P., Schuster, J. W., & Jones-Ault, M. (1992). Constant time delay with discrete responses: A review of effectiveness and demographic, procedural, and methodological parameters. *Research in Developmental Disabilities, 13,* 239–266.

Zane, T., Handen, B. L., Mason, S. A., & Geffin, C. (1984). Teaching symbol identification: A comparison between standard prompting and intervening response procedures. *Analysis and Intervention in Developmental Disabilities, 4,* 367–377.

Zygmont, D. M., Lazar, R. M., Dube, W. V., & McIlvane, W. J. (1992). Teaching arbitrary matching via sample stimulus-control shaping to young children and mentally retarded individuals: A methodological note. *Journal of the Experimental Analysis of Behavior, 57,* 109–117.

♦ ♦ ♦ ♦ ♦ ♦ ♦ ♦ ♦ ♦ ♦ ♦ ♦ ♦ ♦ ♦ ♦

5

Help! My Son Eats Only Macaroni and Cheese: Dealing with Feeding Problems in Children with Autism

William H. Ahearn

The primary aim of this chapter is to describe feeding problems, how they develop, how they are assessed, and how they are treated. Although few researchers have published studies of the treatment of feeding difficulties of children with autism, many have described effective behavioral intervention strategies for a variety of feeding problems of children without autism.

Although feeding difficulties often develop from and involve physical or biological variables, the emphasis in this chapter is on the environmental variables that can lead to problematic eating and the behavioral interventions that can be used to treat them. Also discussed are some recommended strategies to assess eating, improve eating, and prevent feeding problems. Finally, circumstances that may necessitate professional assistance are discussed.

One of my first encounters of problematic eating in a child with autism was a boy who ate only macaroni and cheese. Not only would he refuse other foods, but he would eat only a particular brand of macaroni prepared in a specific manner. Since that time, I have met a number of children diagnosed with autism who had atypical eating habits. Some of these habits involved eating only fried foods, pureed food, starchy foods, or flavored milk. Many of these children would tantrum or display other disruptive behavior when nonpreferred foods were presented. In my experience, most children with severe feeding problems, both with and without autism, have required a great deal of time and patience to achieve acceptance of nonpreferred foods.

Incidence of Feeding Problems

Before discussing the causes of and treatments for feeding problems, it is useful to review the incidence of such difficulties. Feeding problems are typically encountered in young children with or without other disorders and in older persons with mental retardation. It has been estimated that over 30% of individuals with developmental disabilities have some form of feeding difficulty (Gouge & Ekvall, 1975; Palmer, Thompson, & Linscheid, 1975). Eighty percent of individuals functioning in the range of severe to profound retardation have been estimated to have feeding difficulties (Perske, Clifton, McClean, & Stein, 1977). Several studies also have estimated that up to 45% of typically developing children experience some form of mealtime problem during childhood (e.g., Bentovim, 1970; Dahl, 1987).

In addition to studies of children who are typically developing and children with developmental disabilities, there have been numerous reports of children with autism or pervasive developmental disorder–not otherwise specified who have had feeding problems. In fact, unusual patterns of food acceptance were once thought to be one of the clinical markers of autism (Ritvo & Freeman, 1978). Reports include children with autism who have food or texture selectivity, who refuse liquids, and who have unusual mealtime habits (Powell, Hecimovic, & Christensen, 1992). The majority of these accounts have been anecdotal, and little systematic incidental research has been conducted specifically with these children. However, one systematic survey of parents found that children diagnosed with autism were more likely than typically developing children to be reported as having mealtime problems (Archer, Rosenbaum, & Streiner, 1991). Another study surveyed parents of children with autism and over 90% who responded reported that their children had problems at mealtimes (DeMeyer, 1979).

A recent study assessed the patterns of food acceptance in children with autism by presenting a variety of foods across six meals (Ahearn, Castine, Nault, & Green, 2001). Half of the 30 participants exhibited selective acceptance of food. Although this confirms the reports of the tendency for children with autism to display selective eating, comparisons with the eating habits of typically developing children need to be made to determine whether children with autism are more susceptible than typically developing children to food selectivity.

How Feeding Skills Typically Develop

Eating is a complex repertoire of behavior, and several anatomical structures are involved in this activity. The structures of the oral cavity, specifically the teeth, jaw, and tongue, work in close coordination with the structures involved in breathing. Food is processed in the mouth, swallowed, and transported to the esophagus for further processing in the gastrointestinal system. The development of feeding skills over the first few years of life is dependent on the proper functioning of these anatomical structures and occurs as a result of central nervous system development and learning.

In addition to anatomy, the child's experience while eating contributes to the development of feeding skills. Specifically, the types and textures of food to which the child is exposed, the reactions the child has to eating those foods, and the reactions of the parent to the child during meals can all make substantial contributions. The infant comes to the world prepared to eat. At birth, the infant demonstrates reflexes such as the rooting reflex (moving the head toward the source of the stimulus that touches the cheek) and the suck–swallow reflex. These reflexes are important for the survival of the infant and have been shaped over time. These reflexes fade during the infant's first 3 to 4 months and are replaced with more mature feeding behaviors that have been shaped by the child's experience with food (Stevenson & Allaire, 1991). Around age 4 to 6 months, the child can take pureed food passively through spoon-feeding. With further experience, the child becomes more competent at this skill and eventually will actively take food off the spoon with the upper lip. After this skill has developed, munching or chewing patterns begin to emerge and crackerlike foods can be mouthed. Munching and chewing facilitates the eating of ground or mashed table food and the development of more

mature feeding skills. The eating of regular table food emerges with continued practice and exposure to different food textures and types. Any interruption of this process can contribute to or directly produce problematic feeding.

The development of mature oral-motor skills typically results from graduated exposure to food textures (pureed before mashed, mashed before chopped pieces of table food, etc.) during a period of neurological and anatomical development. Failure to experience these textures means that neurological and anatomical changes occur without the accompanying skill acquisition (Illingworth & Lister, 1964). Some indirect evidence supports this idea. Difficulties have been reported when reintroducing oral feedings to children who have required tube or other enteral (e.g., intravenous hydration) feedings prior to acquiring mature eating skills (Handen, Mandell, & Russo, 1986; Tuchman, 1988). Often attempts to initiate or reinitiate oral feedings are resisted by the child. Therefore, problems encountered in the development of appropriate feedings skills, particularly those that involve the failure to develop age-appropriate oral-motor skills, should be identified and assessed as early as possible.

Defining Feeding Problems

Although the approximate frequency of feeding difficulties encountered in children with and without developmental impairment is known, defining these problems presents a challenge. There are two widely used methods of defining feeding problems. One is by outcome. Failure to thrive refers to deficient weight and/or height that falls below the 5th percentile on the growth charts developed by the National Center for Health Statistics. A child could also be considered as failing to thrive if weight loss is evident across more than two major percentile groups. For example, suppose an 18-month-old is in the 50th percentile for weight. Then, when she is weighed and measured in 6 months, she is found to be just under the 10th percentile. For this child, a diagnosis of failure to thrive would be appropriate even though the child's weight is above the 5th percentile. Although the outcome of a feeding problem defines its severity, this form of classification is not particularly helpful in guiding treatment (Iwata, Riordan, Wohl, & Finney, 1982).

Another method of classifying problematic eating is by the child's pattern of behavior displayed during mealtimes. Specific definitions of feeding difficulties encompassing a wide variety of mealtime behaviors have been reported (e.g., O'Brien, Repp, Williams, & Christophersen, 1991; Palmer & Horn, 1978). These feeding problems can be grouped into particular categories according to common elements (see Table 5.1). For instance, one important class of problematic feeding involves patterns of *insufficient food intake*. Food refusal, refusal of liquids, food type selectivity (e.g., child eats only bread), food texture selectivity (e.g., child eats only

Table 5.1
Types of Feeding Problems

1. Insufficient Food Intake

Refusal

Selectivity for type or texture

Inadequate caloric intake

2. Skill Deficits

Chewing, sucking, and swallowing

Self-feeding

3. Disruptive Behavior

Crying

Spitting out food

Pushing away food

Knocking food off table

Out-of-seat

Aggression

Self-injury

pureed food when this is not developmentally appropriate), and inadequate caloric intake for weight gain and growth are feeding problems that describe a pattern of limited food consumption by the child over extended periods of time. These feeding problems are the most severe and can have a significant impact on the child's physical and cognitive development (Bithoney & Dubowitz, 1985; Christophersen & Hall, 1978; Howard & Cronk, 1983).

A second category of feeding problem consists of *skill deficits*. Oral-motor delays can affect the child's ability to chew, suck, or swallow. Fine motor delays can affect self-feeding. Both oral-motor and fine motor delays can be the result of physiological deficits or a lack of age-appropriate experience. In some cases, these oral-motor and fine motor skills are not developed because the child lacks the motivation to acquire them.

The last major class of feeding problems consists of *disruptive behavior* not directly related to the act of eating. Crying, spitting out food, knocking food off of the table, leaving the table, aggression, and self-injury are behaviors that can disrupt food consumption or the act of eating. If such behaviors occur frequently outside the context of eating and mealtimes, then they may have nothing to do with eating per se. When these problem behaviors occur across a child's day, their assessment should incorporate observation of all of the situations in which they take place (e.g., see Romanczyk, 1996). However, when these behaviors are encountered pri-

marily in the context of feeding, they should be assessed and treated within the feeding situation.

How Feeding Problems Develop

Prior to describing potential treatment for or prevention of problematic eating, it is necessary to review the etiology of eating problems. Just as there are many classes of feeding difficulties, there are many causes as well. Furthermore, the etiology of a feeding problem often dictates the intervention. In this section, I briefly describe the variables that can affect eating.

Gastrointestinal System

Research indicates that feeding problems are caused by physical or biological factors, environmental factors, or some combination of these factors. Various biological factors have been reported to be associated with feeding problems. Problems with the functioning of the gastrointestinal system can contribute significantly to or directly cause problematic eating. After the processing of food occurs in the mouth, further processing takes place in the gastrointestinal system. After food is swallowed, the esophagus transports food to the stomach via peristaltic waves. Once food is transported to the stomach, the muscles of the stomach grind the food and in combination with the stomach acids prepare the food for processing in the intestine. The nutrients of the food are absorbed in the intestine and the remaining matter is transported to the colon for expulsion from the body.

Many gastrointestinal problems have been noted in children who have feeding difficulties. One commonly encountered problem is gastroesophageal reflux, or GER, which is the movement of the substances in the stomach back into the esophagus. GER is a condition that results from the relaxation of a muscle at the end of the esophagus that functions to keep the stomach contents in the stomach. The environment of the stomach is acidic and the contact of these acidic stomach contents with the esophagus can be painful. Persistent GER in infants has been found to produce overt signs of pain, such as arching and crying, and has been associated with lack of weight gain and growth (Orenstein, 1992). In fact, eating that produces recurrent discomfort has been found to decrease a child's intake of food and is associated with difficult mealtimes (Mathisen, Worrall, Masel, Wall, & Shepard, 1999). Additionally, recurrent GER can produce damage to the lining of the esophagus, known as esophagitis. Esophagitis can result in discomfort from the passage of food down through the esophagus in addition to the discomfort that can accompany GER.

In addition to GER, gastric motility, the movement of food through the body, can also affect food intake. The movement of food through the gastrointestinal system occurs at a specific rate and speed. Though quite rare, food that passes too quickly results in less than optimal nutrient absorption. This can directly produce inadequate growth and other problems such as diarrhea. If food moves too slowly through the body, then vomiting, GER, constipation, and painful bowel movements can occur. Problems with motility sometimes impact eating because they can produce a reluctance to eat to avoid the side effects produced by this condition. Furthermore, constipation has been reported as a common problem in children with autism (Dalrymple & Ruble, 1992). Although many factors can contribute to constipation, it can be produced by selective eating. Moreover, intervention for this type of constipation should include an increased intake of fiber and fluids (Leung, Chan, & Cho, 1996).

Oral Cavity

Another variable that might affect eating is the ability to suck, chew, or swallow. Deficits in these skills can occur for a variety of reasons, some physical and some experiential, and can produce choking or aspiration of food. One physical aspect is the structure of the oral cavity. Some structural anomalies of the oral cavity, such as a cleft palate, can hinder eating. Another physical factor is the coordination of the oral structures. Disorders of neuromuscular dysfunction, such as cerebral palsy, may produce poorly coordinated chewing and swallowing (Eicher, 1997).

Furthermore, mature oral-motor functioning is influenced directly by experience. In general, more practice with eating a particular food texture facilitates competent processing of that texture. There are many ways in which proper practice with eating and the subsequent development of mature skill can be affected. Such a disruption can occur if a food texture is introduced before the child is prepared to eat it or if a food texture is introduced long after the child should have been exposed to it. To further explain, limited exposure to different food textures hinders skill acquisition, and limited exposure can happen for a variety of reasons. One obvious reason is the child's refusal to eat novel food textures.

In some situations, children should not be exposed to higher textured foods. Structural anomalies and neuromuscular dysfunction might necessitate limiting the food eaten to pureed food. Physical disease, particularly chronic illness, may preclude, interrupt, or otherwise affect eating. Life-threatening problems can even result in the use of supplemental feedings, such as intravenous tubes, nasogastric tubes, or surgically placed gastrostomy tubes.

Diet

The National Research Council's Food and Nutrition Board (1989) has published recommended daily allowances that suggest the calories and types of food substances required for typical weight gain and growth. An adequate diet would contain sufficient caloric intake and the nutritional composition for age-appropriate weight gain and growth. Feeding the child too little (or too much), or an inappropriate balance, results in an inadequate diet.

To summarize, the foods that parents present to children provide the selection from which their diet emerges. The resultant experience with these foods establishes those that are eaten and those that are not. Assuming that there is a core of items that are the bulk of a young child's diet, the diet expands through exposure to new items. When novel foods are presented to young children, a typical reaction is to reject them. A study conducted with typically developing children found that, at initial presentations, novel foods were usually not accepted (Birch & Marlin, 1982). However, with repeated presentations over time, these items were more likely to be sampled and less likely to be rejected. Those foods that are experienced repeatedly will not necessarily be eaten consistently, but *repeated exposure to novel foods* is important in helping to increase the variety of foods accepted by the child.

Diets or Vitamin Use as Treatment for Autism

Limiting the items presented to a child can have a profound impact on that child's eating. Dietary restrictions or fad diets (e.g., Feingold, 1975; Reiten, 1987) are popular forms of treatment for children with autism. The benefits of these diets are unproven (see New York State Department of Health Early Intervention Program [NYSDHEIP], 1999, for a summary). Therefore, given the restrictions these diets place on the foods presented to the child, these diets can lead to the worsening of eating problems or directly produce problematic feeding. However, for those children who have documented food allergies or intolerance, dietary restriction as directed by a pediatrician is appropriate.

A related topic is vitamin supplementation to diet. Supplementation to meet specific dietary needs is commonly recommended by primary care physicians and can be very important, particularly for the child with selective eating. However, vitamin therapy as treatment for autism has limited empirical support (NYSDHEIP, 1999). Aman and Singh (1988) stated that any substance given to an individual for the purpose of changing physical or mental functioning should be considered a drug. Based on this definition, the National Institute of Mental Health's Subcommittee on Vitamins (1995) proposed that the use of vitamin or mineral supplementation be considered similar to the administration of psychotropic medication. Furthermore, this panel found little benefit to the usage of these supplements as treatments for developmental impairments. In fact, the panel stated that the more scientifically sound an investigation into the effects of supplementation was, the less likely beneficial effects of vitamin therapy were to be found. Finally, because many high-dose vitamin and mineral supplements produce nausea, children undergoing vitamin therapy as a treatment for autism can be less motivated to eat.

The Effects of Consequences on Eating

To this point I have focused on physical and biological variables and their potential impact on eating. At several points during this discussion, I have alluded to the interaction between physical or biological factors and environmental variables. Iwata et al. (1982) stated that,

> although organic dysfunction such as motor impairment and metabolic imbalance can have detrimental effects on eating, abnormal eating patterns do not arise solely from physical variables, nor are they more cause than effect of clinical syndromes such as failure to thrive. (p. 301)

Although certain physical problems, such as recurrent gastroesophageal reflux and oral-motor dysfunction, can directly produce feeding problems, it is not typical for severe feeding problems to develop without significant contribution from environmental variables. Furthermore, when a child has a physical impairment, there is great potential for environmental variables to exacerbate the feeding problem (Palmer & Horn, 1978).

Feeding is a social interchange between the child and the parent. Moreover, the relationship between behavior and the environment can be complex. Behaviors that occur during meals can be produced by events that follow or precede mealtimes. The behavior that is affected can be the child's, the parent's, or both, and this behavior might also represent a more general pattern of behavior (Iwata et al., 1982). One of the ways that the behavior analyst evaluates a problem is by attempting to establish what contingencies or direct outcomes exist for the problem behavior. For example, a child who does not communicate might engage in self-injury frequently and in different situations. If this child engages in self-injury during meals and the behavior is taken as indicative of food dislike, a caregiver might provide other foods that the child has eaten in the past. This situation can lead the child to repeat self-injury in the future to gain access to preferred foods or to escape or avoid eating disliked food, although the original function of self-injury could have been established by some other consequence.

Three typical consequences or contingencies can produce problematic feeding: positive reinforcement of inappropriate behavior, negative reinforcement of inappropriate behavior, and punishment of appropriate behavior. Contingencies are relations between specific behaviors and the events that follow them. The events that follow a behavior in a contingency are what maintain that behavior. In the discussion that follows, I define these relations and provide some scenarios to illustrate how these contingencies can lead to feeding problems. Most of the examples focus on one aspect of the feeding situation; however, any individual's feeding problem might be influenced by several of these processes.

Positive Reinforcement of Inappropriate Behavior

One type of consequence or contingency that can lead to problematic feeding is positive reinforcement of inappropriate behavior. Positive reinforcement involves the presentation of some event (e.g., access to highly preferred food or social attention) contingent upon the occurrence of a behavior. Such reinforcers can increase the likelihood that comparable behavior will occur in future similar situations. For example, a parent who makes a negative comment such as "Don't do that" when a child spits out food can inadvertently positively reinforce the food expulsion. That is, the spitting out of food might be more likely to occur in the future *because* negative comments have followed food expulsion in the past. Such remarks or reprimands are not intended to reinforce inappropriate behavior; they are typically attempts to stop an ongoing behavior or to decrease the likelihood that the undesired behavior will recur. However, the intention of reprimands and the function that they serve are not always the same. Caregiver attention, whether supportive or critical, is not an uncommon cause of inappropriate behavior.

Providing access to preferred food when a child refuses to eat the items presented also can make food refusal more probable. If a child does not eat any food at a meal, does not eat as much as the caregiver would expect, or misbehaves during the meal, the caregiver might provide access to foods that the child has eaten in the past in an attempt to promote eating. This can result in more appropriate behavior in the short term (i.e., the child might eat at that meal), but the long-term effect could be more refusals at future meals. If a child is underweight, has growth problems, is sickly, or is otherwise impaired, the caregiver may be particularly anxious to find a way to get the child to eat. Although understandable, this type of reinforcement can result in persistent patterns of problem eating.

Negative Reinforcement of Inappropriate Behavior

Another contingency that sometimes maintains inappropriate behavior is negative reinforcement. A bit more complex than positive reinforcement, negative reinforcement is the removal of an unpleasant or aversive event contingent upon behavior. When something unpleasant occurs, an individual is likely to try to escape or avoid that aversive event. If eating, or some aspect of eating, is aversive to the child, then the child might engage in behavior as an attempt to escape from the meal. For example, a child who has recurrent GER, which causes discomfort and possibly vomiting, finds the results of eating aversive. Refusing to eat food would be negatively reinforced because that refusal makes it less likely that the child would experience the discomfort of GER. Stated another way, the discomfort of GER can be avoided by refusing to eat.

Another example is a child with poor oral-motor skills who finds the chewing and swallowing of food to be exceptionally challenging. When given higher textured food, the child might refuse to accept it, knock it off the table, or cry. If these behaviors result in the removal of the challenging event, then the inappropriate behavior is negatively reinforced. The child's behavior allows escape from the eating of food that is difficult to chew and swallow. Another contingency also may affect the child's behavior in this situation. If the parent presents the child with preferred food that is easier to chew and swallow after the child refuses the difficult-to-eat food, the parent is positively reinforcing the child's refusal of nonpreferred food. In this situation, both positive and negative reinforcement are contributing to the child's problematic eating.

Punishment of Appropriate Behavior

Punishment is similar to negative reinforcement in that something that is unpleasant to a person is involved. In fact, punishment is often confused with negative reinforcement because they both involve aversive events. However, behavior that is negatively reinforced removes or terminates an aversive event, whereas behavior that is punished is followed by an aversive event. For example, driving at the speed limit is negatively reinforced because it avoids a speeding ticket. Speeding, on the other hand, can result in a speeding ticket, a punishment for speeding. Stated differently, negative reinforcement consists of consequences that make behavior more likely to occur and punishment makes the behavior less likely to occur.

In common parlance, punishment often means that the perpetrator of a wrongful act is being made to pay for that act. Some form of penalty is paid or retribution is required. When a behavior analyst uses the term, it means that a behavior has led to a consequence and, because of that consequence, the behavior has become less likely to occur in the future. From this perspective, punishment is a technical term and the act in question is not judged as wrongful.

The child who is eating appropriately and experiences discomfort during or after eating (e.g., choking, aspiration of food, painful swallowing, GER, vomiting) might be less likely to eat, particularly the foods that he or she was eating during that meal. Most people have experienced discomfort or vomiting during or after eating, yet people still eat. They might even eat the foods they were eating when they felt discomfort or vomited. However, if discomfort or vomiting occurs frequently, it will be more likely to punish appropriate eating.

Evaluating a Child's Eating

To determine whether a child might have problematic eating, a concerned parent can take a few simple steps. First, the parent should evaluate caloric intake. Although selective eating is the most common problem for children with autism, adequate caloric consumption is the most important function of eating. The child's weight and height should be compared to the averages for other children at the same chronological age. Plotting weight and height on a growth chart with respect to chronological age gives a percentile score (Hamill et al., 1979). This percentile score gives an estimate of the percentage of the population at or below that score. For example, a score that falls on the 50th percentile is roughly equivalent to the "average" expected weight for that chronological age (see Figure 5.1). The child's pediatrician should have the child's growth history and can help determine whether weight and height are appropriate. If the child's weight and height fall between the 25th and 75th percentiles, then, unless there has been a notable drop in weight or a substantial period of time without linear growth (increase in length or height), it is likely that the amount of food the child currently consumes is adequate for growth and weight gain.

If a child's consumption seems inadequate, the parent should immediately discuss this with the child's doctor. If the doctor agrees that there is insufficient eating, further examination of the problem is warranted. However, the pediatrician may not be able to answer questions about food intake satisfactorily or may not agree with the parent's thinking. In either case, the parent may wish to obtain a second opinion from another physician.

In addition to evaluating intake, parents and practitioners need to examine the variety of food presented and consumed. Keeping a log of food items presented to and consumed by a child will provide useful information about the variety in the child's diet. The amount of food eaten can also be recorded. Figure 5.2 is an example of a food log. To provide an accurate depiction of current eating patterns when using a food log, the parent should present food in the typical manner; that is, the parent should continue to offer those foods that are usually presented and at the same times. This information should be collected for at least 2 weeks; however, to avoid an inaccurate sample of eating, the log should not be used when the child is sick or when there are other disruptions to the daily routines such as vacations, holidays, new care providers, starting a new school, and so on.

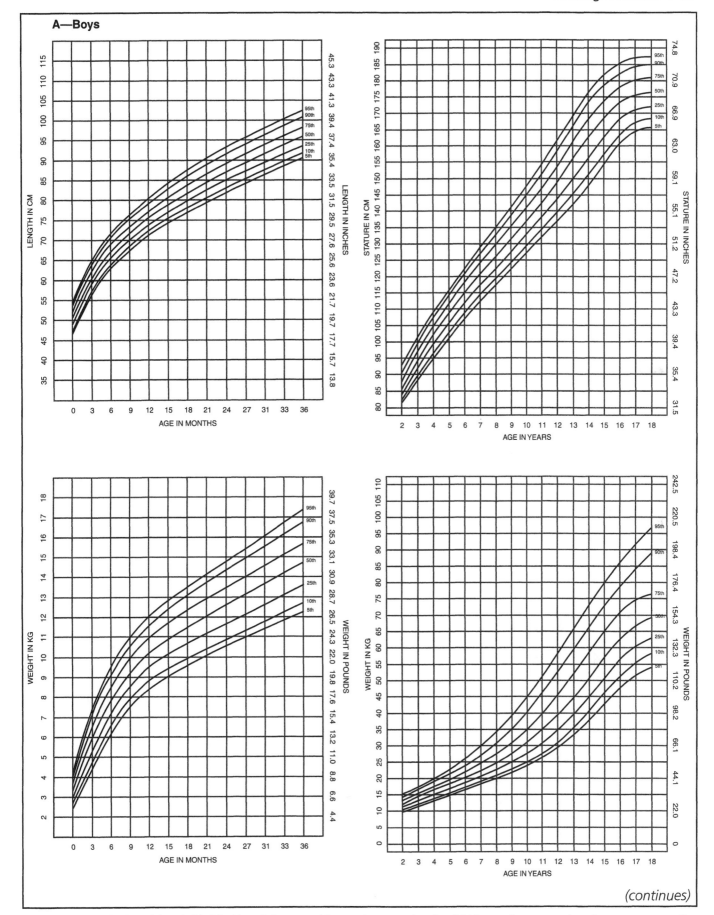

Figure 5.1. Charts for boys (A) and girls (B) of length (or stature) by age (top curves) and weight by age (lower curves), each curve corresponding to the indicated percentile level. *Note.* From "Physical Growth: National Center for Health Statistics Percentiles," by P. V. Hamill et al., 1979, *American Journal of Clinical Nutrition, 32*(3), p. 609. Copyright 1979 by the American Society for Clinical Nutrition. Reprinted with permission.

(continues)

B—Girls

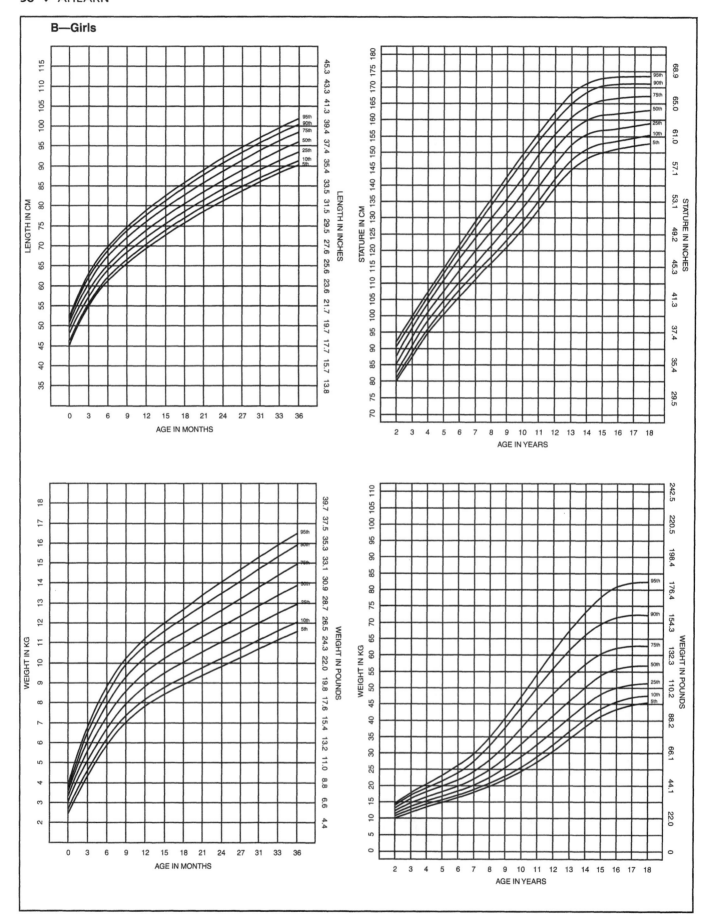

Figure 5.1. *Continued.*

Daily Food Intake Log

Date _____

Directions: *Record food or drink presented at any time during the day. Record each item presented on a separate row. Estimate as either cups presented (e.g., 1/4 cup of rice, 1/8 cup of peas), ounces presented (e.g., 4 oz yogurt, 8 oz apple juice), or number of items presented (e.g., 2 cookies, 1 hamburger, 6 chicken nuggets). Then record the percentage of the amount presented that was consumed. If you present more of one item, record the additional amount on a separate row.*

TIME	FOOD/AMOUNT PRESENTED	PERCENTAGE EATEN	DRINK/AMOUNT PRESENTED	PERCENTAGE DRUNK	NOTABLE EVENTS
	/		/		
	/		/		
	/		/		
	/		/		
	/		/		
	/		/		
	/		/		
	/		/		
	/		/		
	/		/		
	/		/		
	/		/		
	/		/		
	/		/		
	/		/		
	/		/		
	/		/		
	/		/		
	/		/		
	/		/		
	/		/		
	/		/		
	/		/		
	/		/		
	/		/		
	/		/		
	/		/		
	/		/		

Figure 5.2. Sample Daily Food Intake Log.

Once the logs have been filled out for a period of time, one can analyze what the child has eaten. Figure 5.3 provides a form for summarizing the intake logs. The items consumed should be grouped into categories, such as fruits (e.g., apple, banana, orange), vegetables (e.g., peas, corn, broccoli), proteins (e.g., chicken, beef, fish), starches (e.g., rice, potato, pasta), and snacks (e.g., cookies, candy, chips). It is not as important to have a large number of major food categories listed as it is to determine how many different items within categories are accepted by the child. In general, it is most desirable for the child to accept food from all categories and to accept a variety within each. However, if a child accepts food from only one category (regardless of the number of items accepted) or if food is accepted from only two categories with three or fewer items accepted from one or both, then the child's eating would be considered selective. Food acceptance that is overly selective is usually difficult to treat and the parent should seek assistance from a feeding specialist. However, when a child accepts food from two or more categories, he or she is less selective and hence there is a foundation upon which to expand the child's diet. Refusal of all foods from any food group may indicate an unbalanced diet, and eating items from each food group is a good goal.

Another potential cause for concern is when selectivity is developing over time. If the variety of foods a child accepts is becoming more limited over a period of months and no novel or previously rejected foods are being accepted, then this selectivity might be expected to worsen. When a child demonstrates selective acceptance, the parent should attempt the strategies for improving acceptance offered later in this chapter.

Although it is difficult to give general rules for determining when parents should be concerned about their child's eating, it is critical that the child consumes enough calories to gain weight and grow, has a balance of nutrients, and ingests adequate amounts of fiber and fluid. The diagnosis of failure to thrive, mentioned previously, is a gross indicator of deficient caloric consumption and should be considered problematic unless the child has been steadily gaining weight over a period of 6 months or more such that his or her growth and weight gain is accelerating. Also, if the child has always had weight and height below the 5th percentile but has been consistently gaining weight and growing during development, he or she might be following a pattern of growth consistent with genetic predisposition. Regardless, if a child is failing to thrive, a physician should be closely monitoring weight gain and growth.

Professional Feeding Assessment

Gathering accurate information regarding the individual's gastrointestinal system, oral structures, motor skills, and other related variables is necessary for treating a feeding problem. Because feeding problems potentially involve a number of biological and environmental variables, formal assessment should involve a thorough analysis of all possible contributing factors (see Kedesdy & Budd, 1998, for more detailed information). O'Brien et al. (1991) suggested that, in addition to a behavior analyst (with graduate-level training; see Shook & Favell, 1996), a physician, a nutritionist, and an occupational therapist should be involved in assessing feeding. The professional feeding assessment should provide a thorough analysis of a child's eating and will likely result in recommendations for the course of therapy should treatment be warranted.

Medical Assessment

Physicians are likely to be the first professionals to encounter a feeding problem. The pediatrician will typically have a record of weight and growth from the time of birth forward and documentation of the child's illnesses and chronic problems. The pediatrician should offer recommendations to parents of what foods to present to the child and when to present advanced textures. The doctor might also recommend testing for food allergies or suggest nutritional supplementation if there is a problem with weight gain or growth.

Typically, a pediatrician or family practitioner does not specialize in a specific body system and may need to refer a child to a physician who specializes in gastrointestinal medicine. This specialist could help determine any physical variables that might directly or indirectly affect eating. The records of all medical professionals who have seen the child should be reviewed by all clinicians involved in a feeding assessment.

Oral-Motor Assessment

One professional involved in the feeding assessment should have expertise in oral-motor functioning as it relates to feeding. This is usually an occupational therapist or speech pathologist who specializes in feeding. These professionals have training and experience with physiologically based swallowing difficulties. It is important to determine whether the child has the prerequisite skills for eating. If the child's oral-motor skills are not age appropriate, this will influence the nature of the treatment for the feeding problem. The assessment of oral-motor skills might, however, be complicated by the child's reluctance to eat food or participate in the oral-motor skill assessment.

Dietary Assessment

The role of a nutritionist in the feeding assessment is also important. The child's food intake needs to be assessed to determine whether adequate caloric intake is occurring. Additionally, the nutritionist should be able to provide recommendations about the types and quantity of food that the

Food Intake Log Summary Sheet

ITEM NAME	# OF TIMES PRESENTED	# OF TIMES EATEN	ITEM NAME	# OF TIMES PRESENTED	# OF TIMES EATEN
FRUIT			PROTEIN		
VEGETABLE			SNACK		
STARCH					

Figure 5.3. Sample Food Intake Log Summary Sheet.

child should consume. The nutritionist is often necessary to ensure that children with autism have a well-balanced diet given that many have selective intake. Nutritionists also might be able to manage tube-feeding requirements and hydration status.

Behavioral Assessment

Behavior analysts have devoted much time and energy to the development of assessment methodology, and these methods have resulted in significant improvement in the treatment of problem behaviors for individuals with disabilities (Bailey, Shook, Iwata, Reid, & Repp, 1987). Behavioral assessment begins with quantifiable measures of the presenting problem behaviors and should lead to quantifiable treatment goals (Barlow, Hayes, & Nelson, 1984). Table 5.2 lists some events that may be recorded during feeding assessment. Observation of the child being fed by the caregiver(s) is one critical tool for developing feeding treatment (Babbitt et al., 1994); during direct observation of a meal, the actions exhibited by the child and by the caregiver are typically recorded.

During mealtime assessment, the foods presented to the child should include those that the child usually accepts and some that are not typically accepted. It is important for the clinician to observe the child both accepting and refusing food. The events that occur during the examination of meals will provide information about the functions that these problem behaviors serve. Thus, assessment will help define and direct treatment for the feeding problem. It might be necessary for multiple meals to be conducted, because observation of one meal often does not provide an accurate representation of the child's typical pattern of eating (Munk & Repp, 1994).

Feeding Treatment

Up to this point, I have covered issues regarding the nature and causes of feeding difficulties. The previous section described the assessment of feeding and provided some guidelines for evaluating a child's eating. Ideally, when a child has a feeding problem, a professional or team of professionals should be consulted to direct treatment. Unfortunately, there are few such resources, and caregivers often must deal with these difficulties on their own.

In this section, I describe interventions that have been reported as effective for problematic feeding. However, a note of caution should be included whenever descriptions of treatment are made. Although these descriptions could be construed as recommendations for changing problematic behavior, feeding is different for each individual. Moreover, effective behavioral intervention requires attention to each person's unique situation. The information provided is based

Table 5.2
Definitions of Events Recorded During Meals

Acceptance—The child opens mouth and places (or allows placement of) food into the mouth.

Expulsion—Food appears past the outer edge of the lips after food has been accepted.

Disruption—The child interrupts food presentation (e.g., batting at spoon, knocking food off table, leaving table).

Presentations—Food is presented on a utensil or is otherwise put in front of the child.

Attention—The caregiver issues a verbal utterance directed to or about the child or the meal (e.g., "Take a bite," "Open up," "Nice job," "He won't eat that").

on research and is not reflective of the best strategy for any particular child.

The intervention for a feeding problem should address the specific hypothesized cause of the feeding problem. If a physical condition exists, then the intervention should focus on correcting or alleviating the physical problem. This form of therapy must be directed by a physician. A medical treatment, such as medication that affects the functioning of the gastrointestinal system, nutritional supplements for chronic illness or severely deficient caloric intake, or surgery that rectifies a structural anomaly, could correct or minimize the physical problem.

Although physiological functioning directly related to eating is most critical, it is also important to consider the child's general physical state. The child who has a chronic illness or who does not sleep adequately might be fatigued or agitated during meals. Addressing these issues also might result in better eating.

Feeding problems that have no readily identifiable physical cause or that do not improve after treatment tailored to the hypothesized physical cause of the problem will likely require changes in the conditions under which food is presented. One such approach involves alterations in the manner in which food is presented. Another involves providing a specific structure to mealtimes. These strategies can be effective. However, it is sometimes necessary to combine these strategies with positive reinforcement for appropriate eating. Positive reinforcement is discussed in a later section of this chapter.

Altering the Manner of Food Presentations

When a child demonstrates problems with eating, the manner of food presentations should be considered. Sometimes simple alterations in timing and structure of food presentations or texture of food presented can improve the child's eating. Another important consideration is the child's ability to self-feed.

Timing and Structure

There are many ways in which the feeding environment can be manipulated to improve eating. Food should be presented at consistent times each day for children who do not eat regularly (Bernal, 1972). Also, meals should be separated in time by several hours so that the motivation to eat is optimal when the next meal occurs. Children with autism often earn food for participating in teaching tasks. A child who "grazes," eating food between meals, is less motivated to eat during meals. If food is presented frequently through the day, then changing the schedule of food presentation by limiting treats for tasks completed might improve eating at mealtimes. On the other hand, if a child eats moderately sized meals but does not gain weight, then the opportunities to eat are too infrequent. Providing more chances to eat in the form of snacks, mini-meals, or increased use of food in behavioral programming may prove beneficial.

Having specific rules and guidelines is important whenever behavior is problematic. Minimizing distractions by turning off television or music focuses attention on eating. Determining when and how often during the meal to give prompts to eat is important. Even providing dessert or additional servings of food that has already been consumed only when the child has eaten a few bites of other foods on his or her plate will also contribute to structure. Another consideration is how long a meal should last. It might be useful to limit a meal to a specific time period, such as 30 minutes.

Texture

Another aspect of the feeding situation that can be altered is the texture in which food is presented. If a child does not have age-appropriate oral-motor skills and has not been offered regular table foods, then it would be appropriate, at least initially, to present pureed or mashed food. The child who has eaten only pureed food and exhibits age-appropriate oral-motor skills should be presented with higher textured foods, although this needs to occur in a slow, systematic manner. One means of introducing higher textured foods is called texture fading. This consists of gradually increasing the texture of the food presented at meals (Luiselli & Gleason, 1987; Shore, Babbitt, Williams, Coe, & Snyder, 1998). Changing the texture of the food presented to a child must be handled with great care when the child has an oral-motor skill deficit. In this situation, an experienced feeding therapist should supervise treatment. Additionally, if food is not accepted consistently or if chewing and swallowing require great effort, it might be necessary to positively reinforce eating prior to increasing the texture presented during meals.

Independent Feeding

Lack of independent feeding is a difficulty encountered by many parents of children with special needs. Some children do not eat enough or do not accept a variety when they feed themselves or refuse to self-feed. Lack of self-feeding can be related to food refusal; that is, children might not feed themselves as a form of refusing food. An initial approach for children who have occasionally fed themselves would be to establish a time limit for eating, with no snacks until the next meal occurs, and then to require the child to independently eat. If this is ineffective, the positive reinforcement strategies described later can be used to improve food acceptance prior to working on independent feeding.

Special attention is often required to teach the child who has not learned to independently eat. As long as the child eats readily when fed, the skills of self-feeding can be taught through task analysis. Task analysis involves breaking up the task of independent feeding into the chain of behaviors that make up this skill. Table 5.3 depicts one way of breaking up self-feeding. When the activity to be taught is task analyzed, a prompting strategy is selected for teaching the steps in the chain of behaviors. One study reported that a task-analyzed skill taught in a backward chain with graduated guidance prompting effectively taught self-feeding to a child with a disability (Luiselli, 1993). A more thorough description of task analysis and prompting techniques was written by Anderson, Taras, and Cannon (1996).

On the other hand, persistent food refusal or severe food selectivity may make it necessary or beneficial to feed the child. For example, when a child self-feeds and does not eat enough or will not eat foods targeted for acceptance, the child is required to do at least three things: pick up the food item, place it in the mouth, and chew and swallow the food. The caregiver presenting the child with food can eliminate one step in this chain to accelerate progress during treatment; that is, the caregiver can establish consistently acceptable levels of food consumption prior to attempting to give control of eating back to the child. It should be noted that feeding a child who already eats independently is a drastic

Table 5.3
Task Analysis for Self-Feeding Skills

1. Grasp utensil
2. Scoop food
3. Bring utensil toward mouth
4. Insert utensil into mouth
5. Deposit food into mouth
6. Remove utensil from mouth
7. Place spoon on plate or table
8. Repeat Steps 1 through 7 until meal is completed

step that should be taken with extreme caution. Still, the child should continue to practice self-feeding skills at times outside of feeding therapy unless it is necessary to restrict the child's access to food only to mealtimes.

Using Positive Reinforcement To Improve Eating

In this section, I describe the use of positive reinforcement of appropriate eating because this approach can be tried in the home. This technique involves delivering a preferred item or event contingent upon the child's accepting food, and if performed carefully and consistently, it can be very effective. More than one type of positive reinforcement–based intervention has been reported to produce food acceptance. One of these involves providing access to preferred events, such as playing with toys or watching videos, and social praise contingent upon food acceptance (e.g., Kerwin, Ahearn, Eicher, & Burd, 1995; Thompson & Palmer, 1974). Another effective technique is offering preferred food and social praise after the child has accepted nonpreferred foods (e.g., Bernal, 1972; Riordan, Iwata, Wohl, & Finney, 1980).

Identifying Potential Reinforcers

There are several critical components to positive reinforcement, but the most important is the selection of a reinforcer. Reinforcers offered for food acceptance must be highly preferred by the child. If the child is not motivated enough to earn the item being offered, then the intervention will not be effective. Consequently, these preferred items or events need to be systematically determined. One way to determine what might serve as a reinforcer is to conduct a preference assessment (e.g., Fisher et al., 1992). Each of the many procedures for identifying potential reinforcers consists of presenting an array of items or events, allowing the child to choose among the items, and then allowing access to the one chosen. Those items most consistently chosen are more likely to serve as effective reinforcers (for specific details on conducting preference assessments, see Luce & Dyer, 1996).

It is also important to ensure that the child is optimally motivated to earn that potential reinforcer. Therefore, if the reinforcer to be offered for eating is music, a video, or a toy, then the child should not have access to those items at any time except when he or she accepts food. If the item is a food, snack, or drink, the child should have no access to that item except after eating the food targeted for acceptance. Furthermore, the child should have no access to anything consumable for at least 30 minutes before and after the meal.

Positively Reinforcing Eating

Table 5.4 shows an example of a positive reinforcement procedure for attempting to increase food acceptance while self-

feeding (a similar program for increasing acceptance with a child who does not self-feed is included in Table 5.5, but is not directly discussed). In the initial stages of treatment, it is important to deliver reinforcement for *each* occurrence of the desired behavior (Step 3). Another critical aspect of positive reinforcement is the importance of delivering the preferred event *immediately* after the desired behavior. If a good deal of time elapses from the acceptance of food and the delivery of the preferred event, then the effectiveness of reinforcement is diminished. Also, other negative behaviors can occur during this time. What the caregiver does when the child does not accept the bite is equally important. Providing no interaction, including eye contact, when the child does not accept food will establish a contrast between the consequence for eating and the consequence for refusing to eat. Social interaction of any kind, whether it is a reprimand, a second prompt to take a bite, or a comment about what could be earned for eating, can make undesired mealtime behaviors more likely. In fact, when the child refuses food, it is best to remove the food when the child is quiet and not being disruptive (Table 5.4, Step 5). If food is removed as the child is disrupting food presentation or crying, then disruption or crying might be correlated with the food's being removed.

Disruption

Other aspects of the mealtime are often critical components of positive reinforcement–based interventions. Reinforcing appropriate behavior and ignoring all other responses is a typical approach; however, it can be challenging to reinforce eating if the child is disruptive during meals. Beyond ignoring such undesirable behavior, some clinicians have taken a proactive approach in attempting to prevent disruptive behavior (e.g., Ahearn, Kerwin, Eicher, Shantz, & Swearingin, 1996; Cooper et al., 1995). One such strategy involves using a seating arrangement that minimizes the likelihood of getting up (e.g., chair pulled up to table with arms of chair at or near table's edge). Prevention (Table 5.4, Step 8) can also be a physical response, such as directing the child's hands to his or her lap or side when the child attempts to push away food. Procedures that involve caregiver action should be done as unobtrusively and unemotionally as possible. Minimizing comments and maintaining a neutral facial expression are necessary in this situation to lessen the attention provided for the disruptive responding.

If disruption persists for more than 5 seconds during a food presentation and it is impossible to place the plate on the table, the caregiver should treat this instance as a refusal to accept (and follow Steps 4 through 6 in Table 5.4). If these disruptive responses persist and it is impossible to consistently present food on a plate, then it might be time to try another approach. One such tactic would be to teach the child to sit in a chair and to allow a plate to be placed on

Table 5.4
Positive Reinforcement for Food Acceptance for Self-Feeding Child

Feeder Action	Child Action
1. Present a small bite of food on a spoon from a plate and say, "Take a bite."	2. Child accepts bite.
3. Deliver brief praise (e.g., "Nice job") and deliver reinforcer (30 seconds access to toy or activity; 1 bite or small piece of favored edible).	
	4. Child does not accept bite.
5. Remove food when child is quiet (e.g., not crying or attempting to push food away), do not deliver reinforcer, do not interact or make eye contact for 30 seconds.	
6. Repeat Step 1 until all bites have been presented.	
	7. Child disrupts food presentation.
8. Neutrally block attempts to disrupt plate presentation.	
	9. Child expels food.
10. Neutrally remove expelled food item and remove reinforcer.	

Definitions: *Acceptance*—Child places food in mouth within 15 seconds of verbal prompt "Take a bite"; *Disruption*—Child knocks plate off table or demonstrates another behavior that disrupts the presentation of food; *Expulsion*—Food appears past the border of the lip after an acceptance of food (includes spitting food out of mouth or tipping head to allow food to fall out of mouth).

the table. At first the caregiver could place the plate on the table without food and reinforce the child for allowing the placement of the plate. This might result in the child's being less disruptive and then food could be reintroduced. If this strategy is not effective, the caregiver should seek professional help.

Food Expulsion

Another eating problem that sometimes needs to be addressed is the expulsion of accepted food. Expulsion is sometimes more difficult to manage than acceptance. From the child's viewpoint, spitting out food not only results in the food no longer being in the mouth, but often produces reactions, such as disapproving looks or remarks from others present during meals, which can reinforce expulsion. Food expulsion is sometimes related to oral-motor competency. The child with oral-motor skill deficits might expel food as part of the oral-motor pattern used to chew food. Regardless of the cause, if food expulsion is a persistent problem, a feeding specialist should be consulted.

Three types of interventions for expulsion have been reported: removing access to preferred events (e.g., Cooper et al., 1995), withholding preferred events until food has

been swallowed (e.g., Riordan et al., 1980), and re-presenting expelled food (Coe et al., 1997). Step 10 in Tables 5.4 and 5.5 is an example of the first strategy. The expelled food item is neutrally removed (i.e., without disapproving comments) and access to the reinforcer is terminated. This procedure is intended to provide the occasional expulsion of food with a clear consequence (termination of access to reinforcement). However, the child who expels frequently might respond better to the withholding of the reinforcer until food is kept in the mouth or swallowed. If this technique is used, the item to be delivered as a reinforcer can be withheld until the child starts to chew the food or swallows it. Food expulsion that persists despite these interventions might improve with re-presentation of the expelled food. Re-presentation involves immediately presenting the expelled item (or another piece of the same food) to the child. The repeated spitting out of food without chewing and swallowing produces the same result as food refusal—escape from consumption. Re-presenting food might prevent escape (if it is eventually eaten) but re-presentation that is not successful will still end in escape from food. Therefore, expelled food that is not accepted when re-presented should be removed when the child is calm. It is best to limit the number of times that an expelled item is re-presented. In these situations, some form

Table 5.5
Positive Reinforcement for Food Acceptance for Non–Self-Feeding Child

Feeder Action	Child Action
1. Present a small bite of food on a spoon at the middle of the lower lip and say "Open."	
	2. Child accepts bite.
3. Deliver brief praise (e.g., "Nice job") and deliver reinforcer (30 seconds access to toy or activity; 1 bite or small piece of favored edible).	
	4. Child does not accept bite.
5. Remove spoon when child is quiet (e.g., not crying or batting at the spoon), do not deliver reinforcer, do not interact or make eye contact for 30 seconds.	
6. Repeat Step 1 until all bites have been presented.	
	7. Child disrupts food presentation.
8. Block attempts to disrupt spoon presentation.	
	9. Child expels food.
10. Neutrally remove expelled food item and remove reinforcer.	

Definitions: Acceptance—Child opens mouth and allows placement of food in mouth within 10 seconds of verbal prompt "Open"; *Disruption*—Child bats at the spoon or demonstrates another behavior that disrupts the presentation of food; *Expulsion*—Food appears past the border of the lip after an acceptance of food (includes spitting food out of mouth or tipping head to allow food to fall out of mouth).

of escape prevention will likely be necessary to attain food acceptance without expulsion and a feeding specialist should direct this.

Some children play with food (i.e., manipulate food with their hands) after they have accepted it into their mouth. When this occurs, blocking the child's hands might be effective. This prevents expulsion and food play.

A response that can be related to expulsion is packing—that is, holding food in the mouth without chewing and swallowing. For the child with no oral-motor skill competency problems, withholding preferred events until food has been swallowed can be an effective strategy (e.g., Riordan et al., 1980). However, when oral-motor skills are immature or deficient, then manipulations such as using pureed foods instead of regularly textured food during meals might be more appropriate (e.g., Kerwin et al., 1995). Another approach that may be helpful is to perform an imitation task and reinforce swallowing. That is, the caregiver can place a piece of food in his or her mouth, chew, and swallow while having the child imitate the actions at each step. As with expulsion, packing can be difficult to treat and when this problem is encountered, a feeding specialist should be consulted.

Data Collection

Data collection during treatment is critical for evaluating the success of the program. Figures 5.4 and 5.5 are examples of a trial-by-trial data recording system that can be used for feeding. Prior to conducting a feeding session, the caregiver records the food items to be used for each trial. When the food has been presented and the child has either accepted or rejected the item (and after the reinforcer has been delivered, if appropriate), the caregiver records the response that occurred during the trial and places the next bite on the spoon for presentation. After the session has been completed, the caregiver summarizes the data collected during the meal in order to plan for the next session.

Establishing and Attaining Goals

Another critical aspect of intervention is establishing the desirable goals prior to initiating treatment. One should start with a general goal. For example, if eating is overly selective, the goal may be to have the child accept a wider variety of foods, whereas if the amount consumed is deficient, the goal may be for the child to eat enough to gain weight and grow.

Feeding Session Record for Self-Feeding Child

Directions: Enter the name of the food item for each trial of food presentation. Directly below the food name, circle each behavior exhibited at any time during that trial.

Key:
A = *Acceptance* — Child places food in mouth within 15 seconds of verbal prompt "Take a bite."
D = *Disruption* — Child bats at the spoon or demonstrates another behavior that disrupts the presentation of food.
E = *Expulsion* — Food appears past the border of the lip after an acceptance of food (includes spitting food out of mouth or tipping head to allow food to fall out of mouth).
T# = *Food item presented at that trial* — The name of the food item presented at a trial for which data are recorded directly below the name.

Meal # _____   Date _____   Time _____   Feeder initials _____

T1 =	T2 =	T3 =	T4 =	T5 =	Notes
A D E	A D E	A D E	A D E	A D E	
T6 =	T7 =	T8 =	T9 =	T10 =	
A D E	A D E	A D E	A D E	A D E	
T11 =	T12 =	T13 =	T14 =	T15 =	
A D E	A D E	A D E	A D E	A D E	
T16 =	T17 =	T18 =	T19 =	T20 =	
A D E	A D E	A D E	A D E	A D E	
T21 =	T22 =	T23 =	T24 =	T25 =	
A D E	A D E	A D E	A D E	A D E	
T26 =	T27 =	T28 =	T29 =	T30 =	
A D E	A D E	A D E	A D E	A D E	

Meal Summary

Food Item	Percentage of Bites Accepted
1	
2	
3	
4	

Figure 5.4. Sample Feeding Session Record for Self-Feeding Child.

Feeding Session Record for Non–Self-Feeding Child

Directions: Enter the name of the food item for each trial of food presentation. Directly below the food name, circle each behavior exhibited at any time during that trial.

Key:

A = *Acceptance* — Child opens mouth and allows placement of food within 15 seconds of verbal prompt "Open."

D = *Disruption* — Child bats at the spoon or demonstrates another behavior that disrupts the presentation of food.

E = *Expulsion* — Food appears past the border of the lip after an acceptance of food (includes spitting food out of mouth or tipping head to allow food to fall out of mouth).

T# = *Food item presented at that trial* — The name of the food item presented at a trial for which data are recorded directly below the name.

Meal # _____   Date _____   Time _____   Feeder initials _____

T1 =	T2 =	T3 =	T4 =	T5 =	Notes
A D E	A D E	A D E	A D E	A D E	
T6 =	T7 =	T8 =	T9 =	T10 =	
A D E	A D E	A D E	A D E	A D E	
T11 =	T12 =	T13 =	T14 =	T15 =	
A D E	A D E	A D E	A D E	A D E	
T16 =	T17 =	T18 =	T19 =	T20 =	
A D E	A D E	A D E	A D E	A D E	
T21 =	T22 =	T23 =	T24 =	T25 =	
A D E	A D E	A D E	A D E	A D E	
T26 =	T27 =	T28 =	T29 =	T30 =	
A D E	A D E	A D E	A D E	A D E	

Meal Summary

Food Item	Percentage of Bites Accepted
1	_____
2	_____
3	_____
4	_____

Figure 5.5. Sample Feeding Session Record for Non–Self-Feeding Child.

These general objectives then need to be broken into small initial steps. For attaining these goals, it is essential to set the child up to succeed. Attempting to move too quickly or expecting too much at the initial stages will likely produce insufficient progress. Starting with very small steps that are met with success will help build a positive experience for the caregiver and the child.

When working toward expanding the variety of foods accepted, getting the child to eat one bite of a previously rejected item is a good first goal. Once the initial objective is met, another step toward the general goal can be made. Again, I stress that each successive target needs to be an attainable goal and only one change should be involved in each step. For example, after achieving acceptance of one bite of apple, the next step should not entail one bite of apple and one bite of banana because this would entail two changes (another bite and another item). After the child eats one bite of a new food, eating two bites of that food is a better second step.

Finally, if the child does not achieve an objective, the caregiver should back up to a step where the goal was achieved and try to devise an intermediary step between the point where the child has been successful and the target that was not met.

Other Mealtime Considerations

Several fundamental aspects of a feeding program do not involve the consequences for eating. I discuss them in this section.

Choosing Food To Present

The items that the child does not accept can be numerous and he or she might not accept anything from more than one food category. It is important to establish acceptance as quickly as possible and to build a history of success where difficulties have occurred in the past. Beginning with a food the child accepts at least occasionally is a good starting point. However, if the child consistently accepts certain foods but reliably rejects all others, the caregiver should try presenting a novel food that is similar to an item that the child consistently eats. For example, if the child eats spaghetti, the caregiver can try a different but similar style of pasta (i.e., linguini). The child must accept food and have reinforcement delivered for this type of intervention to work. Furthermore, targeting one food item at a time for acceptance is a systematic approach and will allow easier evaluation of the effectiveness of positive reinforcement for that food.

Determining When To Implement Treatment

Implementing treatment during regular mealtimes is probably the most convenient and practical approach. However, chang-

ing any part of the feeding routine can have a detrimental impact on eating and some children might be more responsive to feeding sessions conducted outside of mealtimes. When using a feeding program during mealtimes, the caregiver should present the item targeted for acceptance at the beginning of the meal in order to maximize the child's motivation to eat. Additional food can be offered to the child afterward.

Determining Number of Bites

The number of bites of the food targeted for acceptance should be determined before a feeding session. At the beginning of treatment, the number of bites should be no more than two or three. More bites can be introduced once the child consistently accepts the item, although the increase should occur gradually (e.g., if the child accepts all three bites of linguini at one meal, four should be presented at the next meal).

Maintaining Acceptance of New Foods

Also, once acceptance of a food item has been achieved, it is important to *maintain* acceptance of that item while attempting to produce acceptance of other foods. Therefore, the caregiver should present previously targeted items at the beginning of the feeding session, followed by the newly targeted item (e.g., five bites of linguini, then three bites of ziti). Those foods that come to be consistently accepted might be readily incorporated into regular meals, although this should be done gradually. Food acceptance might be readily produced with positive reinforcement; however, if acceptance of the target item does not occur after a number of days, the item should be changed. If several different food items have been presented and acceptance has not been achieved or if the child starts refusing to eat when the regular meal is presented, then positive reinforcement might not be effective or appropriate positive reinforcement is not being used. At this point, seek professional help.

Addressing Limited Intake

The preceding suggestions pertain to improving the variety of food accepted. If the child has a problem of limited intake, then a somewhat different approach is warranted. If the child eats at meals but does not consume enough for weight gain and growth, the caregiver needs to address the volume consumed at meals. First and foremost, meals should be optimally spaced apart and the child should have minimal access to snacks outside of meals to optimize the child's motivation to eat. In addition, the reinforcement program depicted in Table 5.4 can be modified such that bites eaten during the meal are reinforced. To increase the volume consumed at a meal, the caregiver might reinforce a child who typically eats a small amount of food at a meal for eating additional bites after he or she has stopped accepting food for a few minutes. The child who eats at some meals but not others might be reinforced throughout each meal in an attempt to produce more consistent eating across meals. As stated earlier, each child will have his or her unique situation, and modification during treatment will likely be necessary. However, the program shown in Figure 5.4 in combination with the suggestions provided in this section can serve as a template for reinforcing appropriate eating.

Escape Prevention

Positively reinforcing appropriate eating is not always the most effective and best intervention for a child's problem. A feeding problem can be resistant to positive reinforcement because escape from or avoidance of eating may be the cause of the refusal to accept food (Ahearn et al., 1996; O'Brien et al., 1991; Riordan, Iwata, Finney, Wohl, & Stanley, 1984). If food acceptance has not been achieved through a well-developed and systematic attempt to implement positive reinforcement for accepting food, then the prevention of escape from food might be the appropriate treatment. However, escape prevention is intrusive, is labor intensive, can produce serious side effects, and if unsuccessful can make problem feeding worse. Therefore, *only trained professionals* should perform it or guide its implementation.

Two ways of preventing escape from eating have proven effective at producing food acceptance. One of these interventions, escape extinction, was described in a study conducted at the University of Iowa (Cooper et al., 1995). This treatment, which has also been referred to as nonremoval of the spoon (Ahearn et al., 1996), involves presenting food to the child and waiting for the food to be accepted. The other intervention, physical guidance, was documented in a study conducted at Johns Hopkins University School of Medicine (Iwata et al., 1982). In physical guidance, the professional presents food to the child and, if it is not accepted within some time limit, physically guides the child's mouth open and deposits food into the mouth. The most important component of both of these techniques is not allowing a meal to end without food consumption.

Both of these treatments are typically combined with positive reinforcement for food acceptance. In fact, one study referred to nonremoval of the spoon as "contingency contacting" (Hoch, Babbitt, Krell, & Hackbert, 1994). Hoch et al. hypothesized that a child who refuses food consistently has not come into contact with the contingencies that have been arranged to occur for food acceptance. Therefore, preventing escape from food forces food acceptance and, by doing this, provides access to preferred events when food is eaten. Once the appropriate behavior occurs and is reinforced, it should be more likely to occur again at future meals.

These two types of interventions, physical guidance and nonremoval of the spoon, are labor intensive and, more important, can produce undesirable side effects for the child,

such as crying, aggression, self-injury, and vomiting. One study compared the effectiveness and side effects of these two treatments and found that both treatments produced the desired level of food acceptance (Ahearn et al., 1996). It was also found that, in one child's treatment, nonremoval of the spoon produced more undesirable side effects (crying, self-injury, and disruption) and longer meals than physical guidance. Physical guidance, however, is more physically intrusive in that a therapist's hands are placed on the child. Behavioral interventions that involve escape prevention should be used only with the guidance of a qualified behavior analyst. Furthermore, one should embark on the use of such treatments after careful consideration of all possible alternatives to the procedure. If this type of intervention is going to be used, caregivers must be willing and able to personally implement the procedure with proper training and support from a behavior analyst.

Professionally Guided Feeding Treatment

Professionally guided therapy should occur after assessment of a child's problem eating and might be one of the initial recommendations following assessment. Feeding specialists typically provide services through outpatient consultation or inpatient admission and sometimes as day treatment. A severe problem can be best managed in a controlled setting. Inpatient and day treatment services provide feeding professionals the best possible situation in which to monitor the many variables that can impact a child's eating; however, these services are costly and not widely available. Typically outpatient consultation is attempted prior to moving to this intensity of service provision.

Outpatient treatment can help to provide specific guidelines and support to caregivers. This type of consultation requires that feeding treatment be implemented by the parent in the home. There are pros and cons to this approach. Advantages are that treatment conducted in the home is less costly and avoids the distress that children often display when treatment is conducted in an unfamiliar setting such as a hospital. Additionally, improvements in eating, if they occur, are taking place in the situation in which the child will be expected to eat and with the people who will be providing meals. Therefore, the treatment gains will not need to be generalized to the home setting. The obvious disadvantage is that meals are conducted without immediate professional supervision and progress may be slower than if a professional were available for each meal.

When feeding is seriously deficient or does not respond to in-home intervention, inpatient or day treatment services might be necessary. These settings offer one primary advantage: a team of professionals available at every step of the initial course of therapy. There also may be trained feeding therapists who will conduct treatment. These therapists will be familiar with the contingencies to be used and will have used these or similar strategies with other children. A therapist who has previously implemented feeding treatment can consistently use the prescribed protocol, whereas the child's caregiver would be learning these new guidelines while feeding meals. Also, the difficult caregiver–child feeding history can significantly influence treatment sessions. The feeding therapist begins anew with the child and the learning of new rules for eating might be easier for the child. The emotional impact of treatment on the caregiver is also an important consideration. Because feeding has been problematic in the past and some time might be required before progress occurs, it can be quite traumatic if a parent were to conduct the initial treatment sessions.

Regardless of the mode of treatment delivery, it should be conducted under the direction of experienced, qualified specialists. The individuals offering services should be able to (a) document the outcomes of other patients who have received treatment and (b) outline a child's feeding goals with explicit plans for reaching them, prior to the initiation of therapy. The advice and supervision of a behavior analyst when conducting any treatment for problem behavior improves the chances of success. Making appropriate changes in a feeding program is as difficult a task as designing one; however, a trained behavior analyst can help with this process.

Another individual who should be involved in any attempt to improve eating is a physician with experience in treating feeding difficulties. The physician needs to monitor the child's weight, caloric intake, and physiological status with respect to eating. If the child's weight is an issue, particular care must be taken to assure that enough calories are consumed to maintain or increase body weight. Additional food or other forms of supplementation can be offered after a feeding session or meal; however, this should be done so that the child is not given access to food shortly after refusing other food and so that it does not interfere with the child's motivation to consume food at subsequent feeding times.

Regardless of the setting for treatment, parents should be included in decision making from the beginning. It is imperative to the long-term improvement of eating for the parent to understand the rationale for using a treatment and to feel comfortable carrying out that treatment (Ahearn et al., 1996). Another important feature of initiating therapy is assuring the availability and thoroughness of training and follow-up provided to caregivers. It is likely that the feeding therapist will not be available for all feedings and the parents will be needed to conduct treatment. Regardless of whether trained individuals or caregivers conduct initial treatment sessions, the caregiver must receive systematic instruction in the feeding treatment to be used with the child (e.g., Ahearn et al., 1996; Thompson & Palmer, 1974). This should include written materials, reviewing the treatment, and roleplaying. Support, instruction, and feedback to parents are critical during the training process.

Optimizing the Feeding Environment

If the child's eating is adequate, there is no reason to expect problems to develop. Because children diagnosed with autism might be susceptible to selectivity, however, periodically noting the variety of foods consumed might help to identify minor feeding problems before they develop into major ones. Compiling a food log every 6 to 12 months, as described previously, will help caregivers to track the constituents of a child's diet.

If a child does not have a serious feeding problem and the caregiver is interested in maintaining or optimizing the child's current eating habits, the caregiver can do a few things to provide a supportive feeding environment. The extraneous activities should be limited immediately before and during meals. If the child does not eat a food presented to him or her, the caregiver should limit the number of times he or she asks the child to eat the food, and provide praise or access to preferred food when the child tries novel or previously rejected foods. It can be very distressing when a child does not eat at a meal, but the caregiver should try to avoid giving access to highly preferred foods when the foods presented to the child at a meal have been rejected. Doing so leads to further food refusals at later meals. When a child regularly refuses to eat at meals, it may be appropriate to seek an evaluation of the child's eating. If the caregiver feels compelled to give the child something he or she will eat, the caregiver should either provide a food that is not highly preferred or wait a while before giving a preferred food.

Final Comments

My goal in this chapter has been to provide an overview of pediatric feeding problems and the knowledge gained through clinical research. Though a great deal of information has been gathered, there is still much to learn. One area that has not received enough attention is early identification and prevention of feeding difficulties (Kedesdy & Budd, 1998). Because children with autism are prone to selective eating, particular consideration needs to be devoted to the variety present in the diets of these children. If a pattern of selective eating exists or starts to develop, then recognizing this early and establishing generalized acceptance can prevent what could become a daunting challenge. It might be a good practice to incorporate variety into as many aspects of the child's eating habits as possible. Presenting many different types of food and multiple forms of the same food (e.g., different varieties of apples; corn prepared in different ways; different varieties of pasta; chicken cooked differently; different brands of yogurt) will help to promote diversity as part of the child's mealtime routine.

The obstacles faced by the caregiver of a child with a feeding problem are many. The availability and accessibility of resources are limited in many ways. There are many children with these difficulties and not enough professionals to evaluate and assist in treating them. For those parents fortunate enough to live where such services exist, the most substantial hurdle can often be finding a means of financing assessment or treatment. It can be exceptionally difficult to obtain consent from insurance providers to pay for care, particularly when problematic eating is not life threatening. However, empirically valid and effective treatments have been developed for feeding problems that have physical or environmental causes. The guidelines and recommendations for practitioners and parents in this chapter, together with the research cited, should be viewed as a starting point in treating the feeding problems of children with autism.

References

Ahearn, W. H., Castine, T., Nault, K., & Green, G. (2001). *An assessment of food acceptance in children with autism or pervasive developmental disorder–not otherwise specified.* Manuscript submitted for publication.

Ahearn, W. H., Kerwin, M. E., Eicher, P. S., Shantz, J., & Swearingin, W. (1996). An alternating treatments comparison of two intensive interventions for food refusal. *Journal of Applied Behavior Analysis, 29,* 321–332.

Aman, M. G., & Singh, N. N. (1988). Patterns of drug use: Methodological considerations, measurement techniques, and future trends. In M. G. Aman & N. N. Singh (Eds.), *Psychopharmacology of the developmental disabilities* (pp. 1–28). New York: Springer-Verlag.

Anderson, S. R., Taras, M., & Cannon, B. O. (1996). Teaching new skills to young children with autism. In C. Maurice, G. Green, & S. C. Luce (Eds.), *Behavioral intervention for young children with autism: A manual for parents and professionals* (pp. 181–194). Austin, TX: PRO-ED.

Archer, L. A., Rosenbaum, P. L., & Streiner, D. L. (1991). The children's eating behavior inventory: Reliability and validity results. *Journal of Pediatric Psychology, 16*(5), 629–642.

Babbitt, R. L., Hoch, T. A., Coe, D. A., Cataldo, M. F., Kelly, K. J., Stackhouse, C., & Perman, J. A. (1994). Behavioral assessment and treatment of pediatric feeding disorders. *Journal of Developmental and Behavioral Pediatrics, 15,* 278–291.

Bailey, J. S., Shook, G. L., Iwata, B. A., Reid, D. H., & Repp, A. C. (1987). *Behavior analysis in developmental disabilities, 1968–1985* (Reprint series, Vol.1). Lawrence, KS: Society for the Experimental Analysis of Behavior.

Barlow, D. H., Hayes, S. C., & Nelson, R. O. (1984). *The scientist practitioner: Research and accountability in clinical and educational settings.* New York: Pergamon.

Bentovim, A. (1970). The clinical approach to feeding disorders of childhood. *Journal of Psychosomatic Research, 14,* 267–276.

Bernal, M. E. (1972). Behavioral treatment of a child's eating problem. *Journal of Behavior Therapy and Experimental Psychiatry, 3,* 43–50.

Birch, L. L., & Marlin, D. W. (1982). I don't like it; I never tried it: Effects of exposure on two-year-old children's food preferences. *Appetite, 3,* 353–360.

Bithoney, W. G., & Dubowitz, H. (1985). Organic concomitants of nonorganic failure to thrive: Implications for research. In D. Drotar (Ed.), *New directions in failure to thrive: Implications for research and practice* (pp. 47–68). New York: Plenum.

Christophersen, E., & Hall, C. L. (1978). Eating patterns and associated problems encountered in normal children. *Issues in Comprehensive Pediatric Nursing, 3,* 1–16.

Coe, D. A., Babbitt, R. L., Williams, K. E., Hajimihalis, C., Snyder, A. M., Ballard, C., & Efron, L. A. (1997). Use of extinction and reinforcement to increase food consumption and reduce expulsion. *Journal of Applied Behavior Analysis, 30,* 581–583.

Cooper, L. J., Wacker, D. P., McComas, J. J., Peck, S. M., Richman, D., Drew, J., Frischmeyer, P., Millard, T., & Brown, K. (1995). Use of component analyses to identify active variables in treatment packages for children with feeding disorders. *Journal of Applied Behavior Analysis, 28,* 139–154.

Dahl, M. (1987). Early feeding problems in an affluent society: III. Follow-up at two years: Natural course, health, behaviour, and development. *Acta Paediatrica Scandinavia, 76,* 872–880.

Dalrymple, N. J., & Ruble, L. A. (1992). Toilet training and behaviors of people with autism: Parent views. *Journal of Autism and Developmental Disorder, 22,* 265–275.

DeMeyer, M. K. (1979). *Parents and children in autism.* New York: Wiley.

Eicher, P. S. (1997). Feeding. In M. L. Batshaw (Ed.), *Children with disabilities* (pp. 620–642). Baltimore: Brookes.

Feingold, B. F. (1975). *Why your child is hyperactive.* New York: Random House.

Fisher, W., Piazza, C. C., Bowman, L. G., Hagopian, L. P., Owens, J. C., & Slevin, I. (1992). A comparison of two approaches for identifying reinforcers for persons with severe and profound disabilities. *Journal of Applied Behavior Analysis, 25,* 491–498.

Gouge, A. L., & Ekvall, S. W. (1975). Diets of handicapped children: Physical, psychological and socioeconomic correlations. *American Journal of Mental Deficiency, 80,* 149–157.

Hamill, P. V., Drizd, T. A., Johnson, C. L., Reed, R. B., Roche, A. F., & Moore, W. M. (1979). Physical growth: National Center for Health Statistics percentiles. *American Journal of Clinical Nutrition, 32*(3), 607–629.

Handen, B. L., Mandell, F., & Russo, D. C. (1986). Feeding induction in children who refuse to eat. *American Journal of Diseases of Children, 140,* 52–54.

Hoch, T. A., Babbitt, R. L., Krell, D. M., & Hackbert, L. (1994). Contingency contacting: Combining positive reinforcement and escape extinction procedures to treat persistent food refusal. *Behavior Modification, 18,* 106–128.

Howard, R. B., & Cronk, C. (1983). Nutrition and development. In M. D. Levine, W. B. Carey, A. C. Crocker, & R. T. Gross (Eds.), *Developmental–behavioral pediatrics* (pp. 412–426). Philadelphia: Saunders.

Illingworth, R. S., & Lister, J. (1964). The critical or sensitive period, with special reference to certain feeding problems in infants and children. *Journal of Pediatrics, 65,* 839–848.

Iwata, B. A., Riordan, M. M., Wohl, M. K., & Finney, J. W. (1982). Pediatric feeding disorders: Behavioral analysis and treatment. In P. J. Accardo (Ed.), *Failure to thrive in infancy and early childhood: A multidisciplinary approach* (pp. 297–329). Baltimore: University Park Press.

Kedesdy, J. H., & Budd, K. S. (1998). *Childhood feeding disorders: Biobehavioral assessment and intervention.* Baltimore: Brookes.

Kerwin, M. E., Ahearn, W. H., Eicher, P. S., & Burd, D. M. (1995). The costs of eating: A behavioral economic analysis of food refusal. *Journal of Applied Behavior Analysis, 28,* 245–260.

Leung, A. K., Chan, P. Y., & Cho, H. Y. (1996). Constipation in children. *American Family Physician, 54,* 611–618.

Luce, S. C., & Dyer, K. (1996). Answers to commonly asked questions. In C. Maurice, G. Green, & S. C. Luce (Eds.), *Behavioral intervention for young children with autism: A manual for parents and professionals* (pp. 345–358). Austin, TX: PRO-ED.

Luiselli, J. K. (1993). Training self-feeding skills in children who are deaf and blind. *Behavior Modification, 17,* 457–473.

Luiselli, J., & Gleason, D. J. (1987). Combining sensory reinforcement and texture fading procedure to overcome chronic food refusal. *Journal of Behavior Therapy and Experimental Psychiatry, 18,* 149–155.

Mathisen, B., Worrall, L., Masel, J., Wall, C., & Shepard, R. W. (1999). Feeding problems in infants with gastro-oesophageal reflux disease: A controlled study. *Journal of Paediatrics and Child Health, 35*(2), 163–169.

Munk, D. D., & Repp, A. C. (1994). Behavioral assessment of feeding problems of individuals with severe disabilities. *Journal of Applied Behavior Analysis, 27,* 241–250.

National Institute of Mental Health's Subcommittee on Vitamins. (1995). *Psychopharmacology Consensus Panel handbook: Vitamin, mineral, and dietary treatments for individuals with developmental disabilities.* Washington, DC: U.S. Government Printing Office.

National Research Council's Food and Nutrition Board. (1989). *Recommended daily allowances* (10th ed.). Washington, DC: National Academy Press.

New York State Department of Health Early Intervention Program. (1999). *Clinical practice guideline: Report of the recommendations. Autism/pervasive developmental disorders, assessment and intervention for young children (Age 0–3 Years)* (Publication No. 4215, pp. 163–194). Albany, NY: Author.

O'Brien, S., Repp, A. C., Williams, G. E., & Christophersen, E. R. (1991). Pediatric feeding disorders. *Behavior Modification, 15,* 394–418.

Orenstein, S. (1992). Gastroesophageal reflux. *Pediatrics in Review, 13,* 174–182.

Palmer, S., & Horn, S. (1978). Feeding problems in children. In S. Palmer & S. Ekval (Eds.), *Pediatric nutrition in developmental disorders* (pp. 107–129). Springfield, IL: Thomas.

Palmer, S., Thompson, R. J., & Linscheid, T. R. (1975). Applied behavior analysis in the treatment of childhood feeding problems. *Developmental Medicine and Child Neurology, 17,* 333–339.

Perske, R., Clifton, A., McClean, B. M., & Stein, J. I. (Eds.). (1977). *Mealtimes for severely and profoundly handicapped persons: New concepts and attitudes.* Baltimore: University Park Press.

Powell, T. H., Hecimovic, A., & Christensen, L. (1992). Meeting the unique needs of families. In D. E. Berkell (Ed.), *Autism: Identification, education and treatment* (pp. 187–224). Hillsdale, NJ: Erlbaum.

Reiten, D. J. (1987). Nutrition and developmental disabilities: Issues in chronic care. In E. Schopler & G. B. Mesibov (Eds.), *Neurobiological issues in autism* (pp. 373–388). New York: Plenum Press.

Riordan, M. M., Iwata, B. A., Finney, J. W., Wohl, M. K., & Stanley, A. E. (1984). Behavioral assessment and treatment of chronic food refusal in handicapped children. *Journal of Applied Behavior Analysis, 17,* 327–341.

Riordan, M. M., Iwata, B. A., Wohl, M. K., & Finney, J. W. (1980). Behavioral treatment of food refusal and selectivity in developmentally disabled children. *Applied Research in Mental Retardation, 1,* 95–112.

Ritvo, E. M., & Freeman, B. J. (1978). National Society for Autistic Children definition of the syndrome of autism. *Journal of Autism and Childhood Schizophrenia, 8,* 162–170.

Romanczyk, R. G. (1996). Behavior analysis and assessment: The cornerstone to effectiveness. In C. Maurice, G. Green, & S. C. Luce (Eds.), *Behavioral intervention for young children with autism: A manual for parents and professionals* (pp. 195–217). Austin, TX: PRO-ED.

Shook, G., & Favell, J. E. (1996). Identifying qualified professionals in behavior analysis. In C. Maurice, G. Green, & S. C. Luce (Eds.), *Behavioral intervention for young children with autism: A manual for parents and professionals* (pp. 181–194). Austin, TX: PRO-ED.

Shore, B. A., Babbitt, R. L., Williams, K. E., Coe, D. A., & Snyder, A. (1998). Use of texture fading in the treatment of food selectivity. *Journal of Applied Behavior Analysis, 31,* 621–633.

Stevenson, R. D., & Allaire, J. H. (1991). The development of normal feeding and swallowing. *Pediatric Clinics of North America, 38,* 1439–1453.

Thompson, R. J., & Palmer, S. (1974). Treatment of feeding problems: A behavioral approach. *Journal of Nutrition Education, 6,* 63–66.

Tuchman, D. N. (1988). Dysfunctional swallowing in the pediatric patient: Clinical considerations. *Dysphagia, 2,* 203.

6

♦ ♦ ♦ ♦ ♦ ♦ ♦ ♦ ♦ ♦ ♦ ♦ ♦ ♦ ♦ ♦ ♦ ♦

Incidental Teaching:
A Not–Discrete-Trial Teaching Procedure

Edward C. Fenske, Patricia J. Krantz, and Lynn E. McClannahan

Discrete-trial instruction is so widely used in autism treatment that many regard it as synonymous with behavioral intervention. However, applied behavior analysis is not defined by any single intervention procedure. Although discrete-trial training has been found effective in building language and other skills for young people with autism (Lovaas, 1977, 1981; Wolf, Risley, & Mees, 1964), it is only one of many science-based procedures that may be used to promote verbal and other behavior, and it has certain limitations. Indeed, the structured learning environment in which discrete-trial instruction typically occurs may fail to promote generalization of skills across situations (Anderson, Taras, & Cannon, 1996). Children may display better performances in the therapy room than in other locations, and their responses may be dependent upon prompts delivered by adults. Perhaps this occurs because, in typical discrete-trial training, the adult gives an instruction or asks a question, then the child responds or does not respond, receives or does not receive a reward, and waits for the adult to begin another trial. Waiting is part of a response chain that is repeatedly rewarded, thus diminishing the likelihood that youngsters will initiate social exchanges (McClannahan & Krantz, 1997). Researchers, however, have identified other behavioral procedures that promote generalization and spontaneous use of emerging skills, such as time-delay procedures (Charlop, Schreibman, & Thibodeau, 1985; Charlop & Walsh, 1986), video modeling (Charlop & Milstein, 1989; Krantz, MacDuff, Wadstrom, & McClannahan, 1991), scripting conversation and fading scripts (Krantz & McClannahan, 1993, 1998), and incidental teaching (Hart & Risley, 1968; McGee, Krantz, Mason, & McClannahan, 1983). This chapter focuses on the latter.

Incidental teaching has been part of the behavior analysis armamentarium for more than three decades. Hart and Risley (1968) found that traditional group language instruction failed to promote economically disadvantaged preschoolers' use of color–noun combinations (e.g., "yellow banana," "blue car") during free play, but when access to snacks and play materials was made contingent upon color naming, the children's spontaneous use of color descriptors and nouns increased. Significantly, the children's spontaneous use of color descriptors generalized to new color–noun combinations and maintained when access to materials was no longer contingent on their use. The investigators concluded that contingent access to snacks and play materials is a more powerful reward than the praise teachers delivered during traditional instruction, and that naturalistic consequences promoted generalization of new skills.

Definition of Incidental Teaching

In 1982, Hart and Risley wrote, "Incidental teaching is used to get elaborated language by waiting for another person to initiate conversation about a topic and then responding in ways that ask for more language from that person" (p. 5). The steps in incidental teaching include (1) arranging a setting that contains materials of interest to the child; (2) waiting for the child to initiate an interaction about an object of interest; (3) asking for more elaborate language, or approximations to speech; and (4) providing the object for which the child initiated.

Children's initiations reflect their current language repertoires. Children who have acquired productive language may initiate for items or activities with phrases ("Go car ride"), labels ("Video"), or approximations to words (e.g., saying "/m/" to signify "more"). However, even children who are not yet verbal can initiate by reaching for, pointing to, or gesturing toward activities or objects of interest, and are therefore candidates for incidental teaching. A toddler who has not yet acquired verbal imitation skills reaches for a toy, the adult models some sounds that are often heard when the youngster babbles, the child vocalizes, and the adult provides the toy. When a 2-year-old reaches for a bottle of juice, her father briefly holds her hand; provides a verbal model ("oo—juice"); after the youngster imitates "oo," the parent confirms that her response is correct by repeating "oo—juice"; and then provides the juice bottle. A preschooler who has learned to imitate words points to a cookie; the parent requests, "Say 'cookie' "; the child imitates; and the parent gives him the requested item.

Initially, use of incidental teaching for children with autism appeared limited by their severe language and social-skill deficits, but in 1983 McGee et al. demonstrated the effectiveness of a modified incidental-teaching procedure in teaching two youths with autism to receptively identify objects used during daily school lunch preparation. Because the participants had very limited expressive language skills, adults' requests for elaboration consisted of requests for specific items (e.g., "Give me relish"). The participants' new receptive language skills generalized to another room of their group home and to a different time of day.

In a comparison of incidental teaching and discrete-trial instruction, children with autism displayed more spontaneous use of prepositions taught through incidental teaching than through discrete-trial instruction, and incidental teaching promoted greater generalization from the classroom to a free-play setting (McGee, Krantz, & McClannahan, 1985). These studies demonstrated the effectiveness of incidental teaching in building new language skills for children with autism.

How Incidental Teaching Differs from Discrete-Trial Training

There are several procedural differences between discrete-trial instruction and incidental teaching. In discrete-trial instruction, the teacher or parent initiates teaching by asking a question or giving a direction (e.g., "What's this?" or "Point to the ball"). Incidental teaching begins with a child's initiation for materials, an activity, or a conversational topic that is, at that moment, highly preferred. Discrete-trial instruction typically occurs in a structured learning environment in which furniture and materials are carefully arranged to promote attending, whereas incidental teaching is conducted in the child's natural environment (e.g., in the kitchen, family room, car, or backyard). The instructional materials and rewards used in discrete-trial sessions are selected by the instructor, and may be unrelated to the learning activity; for example, a child may be given a cracker after correctly labeling a picture of a car. In incidental teaching,

the materials are selected by the child and the rewards are the materials for which he initiated; for example, the child initiates to go out by struggling to open the door, and after he responds to the request to say "Open please," the parent opens the door and allows access to the outside play area.

We do not suggest that discrete-trial instruction be abandoned in favor of incidental teaching. Insufficient attention has been given to the fact that these approaches teach different types of verbal behavior. Discrete-trial instruction typically teaches tacting, or labeling (e.g., answering questions such as "What is this?"), whereas incidental teaching usually addresses mand training, or requesting (e.g., "Help me" or "Turn on TV"). Research shows that both are effective for teaching expressive and receptive language skills to children with autism, and both are important components of a language curriculum (Reichle & Keogh, 1985; Sundberg & Partington, 1999).

How To Prepare for Incidental Teaching

Although incidental teaching begins with a child's initiation, advance planning can promote the development of new language skills. Preparation for incidental teaching includes identifying specific language targets, providing materials and activities that are of interest to the child, and arranging or manipulating materials in ways that attract the child's attention.

Identify Instructional Goals

When selecting target skills, it is important to consider a child's current language repertoire. Incidental teaching should help the child take the next steps, but must not request skills that are presently beyond his or her reach. Using incidental teaching, we have helped children acquire receptive object labels, approximations to expressive labels (i.e., initial sounds or phonemes), nouns, adjectives (e.g., color, size, shape, quantity), prepositions, pronouns, phrases and sentences, correct articulation, improved voice volume and prosody, question asking (e.g., "Where is my _____?"), skills in requesting assistance (e.g., "Help me open it"), responses to yes/no questions, and sight-word reading repertoires (McGee, Krantz, & McClannahan, 1986).

Teaching is more effective and children progress more rapidly if teachers or parent select one or only a few language skills at a time, rather than attempting to teach multiple responses. For example, a teacher might initially target the pronouns *I* and *you*, and reserve instruction on the use of other pronouns until the child masters these.

Children do not need any prerequisite skills to benefit from incidental teaching. The procedure is effective for shaping new language skills even before children learn to imitate verbal models or follow adults' directions. A child who initiates by pulling an adult toward the refrigerator, guiding a parent's hand toward a preferred object, or reaching for a favorite toy presents many opportunities for incidental teaching. An initial instructional goal might be a receptive label ("Point to the refrigerator") or an affirmative head nod ("Do you want _____?").

Arrange the Environment

Opportunities to conduct incidental teaching can be maximized through careful planning and arrangement of children's usual environments. Put favorite snacks, toys, books, videotapes, or games on high shelves, on countertops, or in tightly closed transparent containers where they are visible but out of reach or otherwise inaccessible to the child.

Promote Initiations

Children's initiations reflect their current language skills. Children with autism who have not yet acquired expressive language may initiate by pointing to or reaching for objects, attempting to open doors or containers, or taking an adult's hand and leading him or her to an object of interest. Children with limited verbal skills may initiate by vocalizing or approximating a word (e.g., saying "/m/" for *milk*), and those who have acquired more expressive language may initiate by labeling ("Milk") or by using phrases ("Want milk") or sentences ("I want milk").

Many children with autism initiate without any special training or environmental arrangements, but more teaching can be accomplished by displaying materials that interest the children and presenting them in ways that are likely to evoke initiations. For example, a father might give a youngster a small amount of a favorite snack food or a few construction toys, but control access to the main containers by putting foods or toys in transparent bins that she is unable to open, thus setting the occasion for her to initiate by attempting to open the tightly closed lids. Similarly, if a mother plays with her son's favorite computer game, he may initiate for a turn by climbing on his mother's lap or grabbing for the mouse. Many children enjoy repetitive play activities such as building block towers and watching them fall, or rolling marbles down a ramp. After the tower topples or the marble arrives at the bottom of the run, children may initiate by reaching for materials. The parent can also increase initiations by removing parts or temporarily disabling toys or games. A child who independently completes puzzles may initiate by asking for a piece that is not visible. If a child enjoys listening to music on a CD player, the parent might remove the battery to encourage a request for assistance. After the parent identifies activities that a child enjoys but never requests (e.g., making popcorn or roller skating) and makes available photographs of those activities, the child who has acquired picture–object correspondence skills may request activities although materials are absent, by pointing to or handing over pictures, or by asking for depicted toys or snacks. When playing a favorite song on the piano or blowing bubbles with a child, the parent can occasionally stop and provide an opportunity for the child to initiate for the continuation of the activity by reaching toward the keyboard or saying "More."

Parents who are busy with housekeeping and childcare often help with self-care tasks before children initiate. A parent might quickly tie the shoes of a typically developing preschooler so that he can run to the playground; however, for a child with autism, an initiation for help with shoe tying may be an opportunity to teach functional language. The parent can promote an initiation by momentarily detaining the child, glancing at her untied shoes, and giving her an expectant look. If she reaches for the parent's hand, the parent should ask, "What do you want?" and tie the child's shoes after she says "shoes" or responds to the verbal prompt (e.g., "Say, 'tie shoes' "). Mealtimes also provide regular opportunities for incidental teaching; moving the bowl of french fries closer but slightly beyond a child's outstretched arm is likely to gain the child's attention. If the parent waits, the child may initiate by saying "fries" and the parent will have an opportunity to teach by requesting the more elaborate response, "french fries, please."

We have suggested eight ways for adults to increase children's initiations: (1) control access to materials; (2) play with toys that are of special interest; (3) set up repetitive play situations; (4) withhold materials needed to pursue activities; (5) display photographs of preferred activities; (6) begin favorite activities, then pause; (7) glance at the materials, then look expectantly at the child; and (8) move the materials closer to the child. This list can be expanded, and we encourage caregivers and professionals to do so.

How To Do Incidental Teaching

It is exciting when new language skills emerge, and adults are especially pleased when young people with autism display spontaneous language. Use of the following procedures can help children attain this goal.

Wait for an Initiation

As previously mentioned, incidental teaching occurs only when children initiate for items or activities. Adults may arrange the environment and manipulate materials in ways that may evoke initiations; they may also promote initiations by making eye contact with the child and smiling with raised eyebrows (the "expectant look"). Ultimately, however, adults must wait for an initiation. Using verbal prompts (e.g., "What do you want?") quickly converts the activity to discrete-trial training.

Request Elaborated Language

After the child initiates, the adult's request for a more elaborate response should cue the child to display the language skill that has been identified as the goal of instruction. For example, when a child who is learning to imitate phonemes reaches for a ball, the teacher moves the ball beyond his reach, models the initial consonant /b/, and provides access to the ball only when the child imitates the target sound. Later, sounds can be combined to approximate labels (e.g., "Say, 'So-da' "), labels can be expanded to phrases (e.g., "Say, 'Coke please' "), and phrases expanded to sentences or questions (e.g., "Say, 'Can I have a drink?' "). If a child reliably makes requests, the adult can encourage a different language skill, such as using a possessive pronoun (e.g., "Whose shoes should I tie?").

Requests for elaboration are prompts. Some requests for elaboration, such as "What do you want?" or "Is something wrong?" are quite general, and do not indicate correct responses. If the child does not respond or responds incorrectly, the adult then provides a more specific request (prompt), such as "Say, 'I want the *big* cracker' " or "Say, 'Where are crayons?' " These are examples of a least-to-most prompt procedure, which is more likely to produce errors than a most-to-least prompt hierarchy, but less likely to provide assistance that the child does not need (see Chapter 4). In a most-to-least prompt sequence, the adult begins with a complete prompt or models exactly what the child should do or say (e.g., manually guides the child to point to a target object or requests, "Say, '_____' "), and only in later incidental teaching episodes are these very specific prompts replaced by more general requests for elaboration. The decision about whether to use most-to-least or least-to-most prompt procedures is based on the child's language repertoire and on data based on his or her performance.

Provide the Object for Which the Child Initiated

After an adult requests an elaboration (e.g., "What do you want?"), a child may (a) make the expected response, (b) give an incorrect or incomplete response, or (c) make no response. If a child provides a correct elaboration, the adult confirms that she is correct and immediately provides the object of interest (e.g., "Oh, you want milk. Here it is"). If the child does not respond correctly, the adult models the correct response (e.g., "Say, 'Milk, please' ") and delivers the item if the child imitates the verbal model. Incidental teaching occurs only if the adult provides the item for which the child initiated. If a youngster points to candy, responds to a request for elaboration, and is given raisins, incidental teaching has not occurred. Some examples of incidental teaching programs are shown in Table 6.1.

Collect Data

The most important data about the effects of incidental teaching are not what a youngster does during incidental teaching episodes, but whether the child uses the target language skills spontaneously, in relevant contexts, and in situations in which teaching has not occurred. After a parent has used incidental teaching to help a toddler say /m/ for *milk*, for example, it is important to observe whether she displays her new verbal approximation when the parent has not arranged the environment in any special way, when the parent is not providing teaching, and when the child encounters milk in new situations, such as at a restaurant or a grandmother's house.

We recently taught prepositions to several boys, ages 6 to 11, by arranging preferred snacks in relation to transparent plastic containers, and using elaboration requests such as "Where are the raisins? Say, 'The raisins are *on top of* the box.' " Then we gradually faded the request for elaboration ("Say, 'The Fig Newton is *beside* the box' ") in a most-to-least prompt-fading sequence. When our data about a child's performance in the specially arranged environment showed that he correctly responded to general requests for elaboration ("Where are the _____?"), we went to the classroom, put a pencil on top of, under, beside, and behind his notebook, and asked "Where is the pencil?" Some of the boys did not use correct prepositions when they encountered different target objects in a different environment. Subsequently, we taught prepositions in the classroom, placing preferred toys on, beside, under, and behind notebooks, desks, and bookcases. Later, we measured preposition use on the playground, where we placed Nerf balls, Frisbees, bikes, and soccer balls on, under, beside, and behind picnic table, slide, fence, tree, and so on, and asked, "Where is the _____?" When we collected data on the boys' responses to untrained stimuli on the playground, all scored 80% to 100% correct on each target preposition, and we concluded that we could now identify some new language goals to be addressed with incidental teaching. A specific incidental teaching program is completed when the data document that the child displays new language skills in contexts that were never used during teaching.

Find Alternatives for Problem Behaviors

If a child displays problem behavior during incidental teaching, the adult should interrupt instruction and direct the youngster to another activity, or use procedures that that have previously been effective for reducing inappropriate behavior, but should not provide the item for which the child initiated. A child who receives preferred snacks or toys while having a tantrum may learn that crying and screaming are effective ways to communicate with others. Incidental teaching is a set of procedures for teaching

Table 6.1
Examples of Incidental Teaching

Using Phonemes

Target response	Requesting preferred materials or activities with an initial sound or syllable.
Prerequisite skills	Initiates for objects or activities by reaching or pointing; imitates some sounds.
Environmental design	Make a list of the sounds the child imitates; then display favorite foods and activities that begin with those sounds (e.g., /m/ for milk, macaroni, movie, music).
Child's initiation	Reaches for, points or gestures to, or pulls an adult toward materials or activities.
Request for elaboration	Respond to his initiation with the question "What do you want?" If he does not respond or responds incorrectly, model the correct sound (e.g., "Say, '/m/.' ").
Provide the object for which the child initiated	When he responds with the correct sound, confirm that he is correct by stating the object label with emphasis on the target sound (e.g., "*m*ilk"), and give him the requested item.

Using Prepositions

Target response	Using one of the following prepositions or prepositional phrases: *in, on, under, next to, behind,* or *in front of.* (*Note:* You may want to begin with only two prepositions.)
Prerequisite skills	Uses sentences to request objects, imitates verbal models of 8 to 10 words.
Environmental design	Put high-interest toys or snacks in, on, under, or beside containers, and put containers on countertops, shelves, or tables in the kitchen, family room, or playroom. Use a variety of containers (e.g., shoeboxes, plastic food containers, food storage bags) to promote generalization. For example, put the child's favorite videotape in a bag, and put her stuffed bear behind a shoebox.
Child's initiation	The child requests food or play materials with a word, phrase, or sentence (e.g., "I want a cookie").
Request for elaboration	Respond to the child's initiation with a question that requires her to identify the location of the object in relation to a container, using a target preposition or prepositional phrase. For example, ask "Where is the videotape?" If the child makes an incorrect response or does not respond, provide a verbal model (e.g., "Say, 'I want the video that's *in* the bag' ").
Provide the object for which the child initiated	When the child uses a correct preposition or prepositional phrase in a sentence, confirm that her response is correct and immediately provide access to that item (e.g., "Oh, you want the videotape that is *in* the bag. Here it is").

Requesting Assistance

Target response	Requesting assistance to obtain an object that is not accessible (e.g., "Help me").
Prerequisite skills	Requests objects with a word or phrase; imitates verbal models.
Environmental design	Collect high-interest toys, activities, and snacks, and put them in view but out of the child's reach, on the top shelf of a bookcase, on top of the refrigerator, or on the back of the kitchen counter.
Child's initiation	The child requests an activity, snack, or play material, using a noun, phrase, or sentence (e.g., "I want popcorn").
Request for elaboration	Respond to the child's request with a comment that helps him locate the item, but also cues him to request assistance (e.g., "Sure, it's on top of the refrigerator"). If he does not request assistance, model a request (e.g., "Say, 'I can't reach it' " or "Say, 'Help me' ").
Provide the object for which the child initiated	After he requests assistance by saying "It's too high" or "I can't reach it," confirm that is response is correct and give him the requested item.

(continued)

Table 6.1
Examples of Incidental Teaching (*Continued*)

Requesting Missing Items

Target response	Asking for a missing item (e.g., "I can't find my ___" or "Where's the _____?").
Prerequisite skills	Requests objects with a noun or phrase. Imitates verbal models of three to five words.
Environmental design	Remove some of the materials needed to complete activities. For example, take the crayons out of the box, or the CD player out of the carrying case.
Child's initiation	The child searches through his desk drawer and says "Crayons."
Request for elaboration	Respond to the child's initiation with a question (e.g., "Is something wrong?") that calls for a description of the problem. If she does not respond, provide a verbal model of the target statement (e.g., "Say, 'Where are crayons?' ").
Provide the object for which the child initiated	After the child responds with the target statement, confirm that her response was correct (e.g., "Oh, you can't find your crayons. I'll help you look for them.") and produce the missing items.

functional language skills that are appropriate alternatives to tantrum behavior.

How To Teach Others To Do Incidental Teaching

Although research on incidental teaching has demonstrated its effectiveness in promoting generalization and spontaneous use of receptive and expressive language skills, parents and professionals often find that training materials are not readily available. Hart and Risley's (1982) monograph, *How To Use Incidental Teaching for Elaborating Language*, provides detailed instructions on how to do incidental teaching with typical children and children with language delays. It includes examples of incidental teaching episodes in home and school settings, and offers suggestions on how to respond when problems are encountered.

In 1988 MacDuff, Krantz, MacDuff, and McClannahan investigated a brief training procedure for group home staff who served children with autism. During five 30-minute training sessions, trainees received written materials consisting of (a) a list of the steps in incidental teaching, (b) written examples of incidental teaching episodes, (c) a form on which trainees wrote their own incidental teaching episodes, and (d) a description of ways to evoke child initiations. During training, the number of written examples of incidental teaching episodes systematically decreased and the number of episodes written by trainees increased. This time-effective training program increased the trainees' use of incidental teaching, and their skills generalized across materials, group home settings, children, and group size.

At the Princeton Child Development Institute, we deliver both didactic training and ongoing hands-on training to help staff members and parents acquire incidental teaching repertoires, and we assess staff members' skills using the procedures identified by MacDuff et al. (1988). Four components of incidental teaching are scored as present or absent (see Figure 6.1). An initiation is recorded if the child reaches for, points to, gestures toward, labels (or approximates a label), or verbally requests an item or activity. Observers record initiations by writing the name of the item or activity on the data sheet. A request for elaboration is scored if the instructor requests a verbal or nonverbal response (e.g., "What color is the M&M?" or "Point to the *yellow* M&M") that is contextually related to the item for which the child initiated. Repeated requests that are not separated by praise or verbal models, and instructions that address problem behavior (e.g., "Hands down") are not scored as requests for elaboration. Elaborations are scored as present if the child provides the requested response, either with or without the instructor's prompts. Providing the requested item is scored if the instructor gives the child the item for which he or she initiated (a) after the child makes a more elaborate response, (b) before the conversational topic changes, and (c) in the absence of stereotypy and disruptive behavior. An incidental teaching episode is defined by the presence of all four components.

Data on staff members' use of incidental teaching are collected during specified activities and times, and interobserver agreement between trainers or evaluators is typically at generally acceptable levels. Without specific training and regular evaluation, it is our experience that incidental teaching is rarely delivered by the majority of intervention personnel (McClannahan & Krantz, 1993).

Summary

Although highly structured discrete-trial training is unquestionably necessary for teaching children with autism to

Data Sheet: Assessing Instructors' Use of Incidental Teaching						
Component						
Item/activity for which the child initiated	Did the instructor prompt, model, or request an elaboration?		Did the child respond with more elaborate language?		Did the instructor provide access to the item or activity for which the child initiated?	
	Yes	No	Yes	No	Yes	No
_____	❏	❏	❏	❏	❏	❏
_____	❏	❏	❏	❏	❏	❏
_____	❏	❏	❏	❏	❏	❏
_____	❏	❏	❏	❏	❏	❏
_____	❏	❏	❏	❏	❏	❏

Figure 6.1. Data sheet used for assessing instructors' use of incidental teaching. *Note.* From "Providing Incidental Teaching for Autistic Children: A Rapid Training Procedure for Therapists," by G. S. MacDuff, P. J. Krantz, M. A. MacDuff, and L. E. McClannahan, 1988, *Education and Treatment of Children, 11,* pp. 205–217. Copyright 1988 by Gregory S. MacDuff. Reprinted with permission.

attend to teachers and materials, to follow instructions, to engage in verbal imitation, and to respond to questions, stimulus control of verbal behavior often fails to transfer from adult-presented instructions and prompts to people, objects, and activities in the natural environment. Incidental teaching, originally used with economically disadvantaged preschoolers, was modified to provide language instruction to children with autism, and research showed that these procedures promoted the generalization and spontaneous use of language. Some evidence indicates that incidental teaching reinforces social interaction responses beyond those specific skills that are the targets of teaching (Farmer-Dougan, 1994; McGee, Almeida, Sulzer-Azaroff, & Feldman, 1992) and contributes to overall increases in language use. Talking more appears to result in using more complex and elaborate language (Hart & Risley, 1980).

Although incidental teaching begins with a child's mand (e.g., a request for a preferred snack or toy), it can be used to teach a variety of language skills, such as use of articles ("Say, 'an apple' "; "Say, 'a book' "), use of adjectives ("Do you want spicy chips or salty chips?"), and question asking ("Say, 'Where is the truck?'"). The breadth of incidental teaching is related to careful identification of target responses, environmental arrangements that promote initiations and instruction, and advance specification of elaboration requests.

Adults who provide language instruction to children with autism must design learning environments and use teaching procedures that promote spontaneous use of emerging language, and that maintain verbal behavior through naturally occurring contingencies. Incidental teaching is helpful in achieving these goals, and we hope that the reader will put it into practice, thereby adding a powerful tool to behavioral intervention programs.

References

Anderson, S. R., Taras, M., & Cannon, B. O. (1996). Teaching new skills to young children with autism. In C. Maurice, G. Green, & S. C. Luce (Eds.), *Behavioral intervention for young children with autism: A manual for parents and professionals* (pp. 181–194). Austin, TX: PRO-ED.

Charlop, M. H., & Milstein, J. P. (1989). Teaching autistic children conversational speech using video modeling. *Journal of Applied Behavior Analysis, 22,* 275–285.

Charlop, M. H., Schreibman, L., & Thibodeau, M. G. (1985). Increasing spontaneous verbal responding in autistic children using a time delay procedure. *Journal of Applied Behavior Analysis, 18,* 155–166.

Charlop, M. H., & Walsh, M. E. (1986). Increasing autistic children's spontaneous verbalizations of affection: An assessment of time delay and peer modeling procedures. *Journal of Applied Behavior Analysis, 19,* 307–314.

Farmer-Dougan, V. (1994). Increasing requests by adults with developmental disabilities using incidental teaching by peers. *Journal of Applied Behavior Analysis, 27,* 533–544.

Hart, B., & Risley, T. R. (1968). Establishing use of descriptive adjectives in the spontaneous speech of disadvantaged preschool children. *Journal of Applied Behavior Analysis, 1,* 109–120.

Hart, B., & Risley, T. R. (1980). In vivo language instruction: Unanticipated general effects. *Journal of Applied Behavior Analysis, 13,* 407–432.

Hart, B. M., & Risley, T. R. (1982). *How to use incidental teaching for elaborating language.* Austin, TX: PRO-ED.

Krantz, P. J., MacDuff, G. S., Wadstrom, O., & McClannahan, L. E. (1991). Using video with developmentally disabled learners. In P. W. Dowrick (Ed.), *Practical guide to using video in the behavioral sciences* (pp. 256–266). New York: Wiley.

Krantz, P. J., & McClannahan, L. E. (1993). Teaching children with autism to initiate to peers: Effects of a script-fading procedure. *Journal of Applied Behavior Analysis, 26,* 121–132.

Krantz, P. J., & McClannahan, L. E. (1998). Social interaction skills for children with autism: A script-fading procedure for beginning readers. *Journal of Applied Behavior Analysis, 31,* 191–202.

Lovaas, O. I. (1977). *The autistic child: Language development through behavior modification.* New York: Irvington.

Lovaas, O. I. (1981). *Teaching developmentally disabled children: The ME book*. Baltimore: University Park Press.

MacDuff, G. S., Krantz, P. J., MacDuff, M. A., & McClannahan, L. E. (1988). Providing incidental teaching for autistic children: A rapid training procedure for therapists. *Education and Treatment of Children, 11*, 205–217.

McClannahan, L. E., & Krantz, P. J. (1993). On systems analysis in autism intervention programs. *Journal of Applied Behavior Analysis, 26*, 589–596.

McClannahan, L. E., & Krantz, P. J. (1997). In search of solutions to prompt dependence: Teaching children with autism to use photographic activity schedules. In D. M. Baer & E. M. Pinkston (Eds.), *Environment and behavior* (pp. 271–278). Boulder, CO: Westview Press.

McGee, G. G., Almeida, M. C., Sulzer-Azaroff, B., & Feldman, R. S. (1992). Promoting reciprocal interactions via peer incidental teaching. *Journal of Applied Behavior Analysis, 25*, 117–126.

McGee, G. G., Krantz, P. J., Mason, D., & McClannahan, L. E. (1983). A modified incidental teaching procedure for autistic youth: Acquisition and generalization of receptive object labels. *Journal of Applied Behavior Analysis, 16*, 329–338.

McGee, G. G., Krantz, P. J., & McClannahan, L. E. (1985). The facilitative effects of incidental teaching on preposition use by autistic children. *Journal of Applied Behavior Analysis, 18*, 17–31.

McGee, G. G., Krantz, P. J., & McClannahan, L. E. (1986). An extension of incidental teaching procedures to reading instruction for autistic children. *Journal of Applied Behavior Analysis, 19*, 147–157.

Reichle, J., & Keogh, W. J. (1985). Communication intervention: A selective review of what, when, and how to teach. In S. F. Warren & A. K. Rogers-Warren (Eds.), *Teaching functional language* (pp. 25–59). Baltimore: University Park Press.

Sundberg, M. L., & Partington, J. W. (1999). The need for both discrete trial and natural environment language training for children with autism. In P. M. Ghezzi, W. L. Williams, & J. Carr (Eds.), *Early childhood autism: Current theory and research* (pp. 139–156). Reno, NV: Context Press.

Wolf, M. M., Risley, T. R., & Mees, H. (1964). Application of operant conditioning procedures to the behavior problems of an autistic child. *Behavior Research and Therapy, 1*, 305–312.

◆　◆　◆　◆　◆　◆　◆　◆　◆　◆　◆　◆　◆　◆　◆　◆　◆　◆　◆

7

Teaching Peer Social Skills to Children with Autism

Bridget A. Taylor

Teaching children with autism to interact appropriately with their peers is an important component of a comprehensive behavioral program. Initial behavioral programming is typically conducted in a one-to-one format, with an adult and the child with autism (Green, 1996). As the child's skill repertoire increases (e.g., the child reliably follows directions from adults, imitates adult actions, plays with toys), he or she may benefit from instruction that addresses peer interaction skills. Involving peers in behavioral treatment sessions can provide opportunities to teach the child with autism to observe and learn from the behavior of other children, respond to social bids from peers, and initiate and sustain child-to-child interaction. Teaching children with autism to learn from and interact with peers, however, can be a challenging task. Researchers have documented that proximity alone is not sufficient to promote positive social interactions between children with autism and their peers; that is, most children with autism do not "become socialized" merely by spending time with typical children (Elliot & Gresham, 1993; Hauck, Fein, Waterhouse, & Feinstein, 1995; Hundert & Houghton, 1992; Mundschenk & Sasso, 1995; Pollard, 1998; Strain & Kohler, 1995). Rather, successful interactions depend on carefully planned instruction designed to teach children with autism, as well as typical children, how to interact with one another (Gaylord-Ross, Haring, Breen, & Pitts-Conway, 1984; Kohler et al., 1995; Odom & Watts, 1991; Strain & Odom, 1986).

The profound social and language deficits demonstrated by most children with autism, as well as their unique learning needs, necessitate specialized instruction if the children are to fully benefit from activities involving peers. Peer-related instruction requires individualization, both in the types of responses taught (e.g., initiating greetings or imitating a peer) and the instructional strategies used (e.g., modeling or verbal instruction). For example, a compliant child with good spoken communication skills may benefit from instruction designed to teach conversation skills in a play context, with adult modeling as the main instructional strategy. On the other hand, a nonspeaking child who follows a limited number of adult instructions may initially require fairly structured teaching sessions, using strategies that encourage responding to peers as opposed to initiating. Further, the types of social behavior that are deemed appropriate vary as a function of the child's age. During the preschool years, typical children are required to sustain peer interactions for fairly limited periods of time, mostly in the context of reciprocal play. As children move into the elementary school years, peer social interactions become more complex; they include playing games that incorporate multiple players and rules (e.g., tag, Red Rover, team sports) and sustaining conversation. Thus, effective instruction in peer interaction skills requires careful consideration of the objectives for the child with autism and the strategies that will be used to accomplish them.

This chapter provides an overview of research on teaching peer interaction skills to children with autism, procedures for teaching such skills, and suggested programs and activities for developing peer social skills in children with autism. The chapter is structured around some common concerns parents and professionals have about teaching children with autism to engage appropriately with other children.

Teaching Children with Autism To Interact with Peers: Research Findings

There has been considerable research documenting the benefits of peer social skills training for children with autism (e.g., Goldstein, Kaczmarek, Pennington, & Shafer, 1992; Kamps et al., 1992; McGee, Almeida, Sulzer-Azaroff,

& Feldman, 1992; Pierce & Schreibman, 1995; Strain & Odom, 1986; Strain, Shores, & Timm, 1977). Most studies have focused on four general areas: (1) teaching typical peers to engage in positive social interactions with children with autism (e.g., Haring & Breen, 1992; Hendrickson, Strain, Tremblay, & Shores, 1982; Odom, Chandler, Ostrosky, McConnell, & Reaney, 1992; Strain & Odom, 1986), (2) teaching children with autism to interact with typical peers (e.g., Gaylord-Ross et al., 1984; Taylor & Levin, 1998; Zanolli, Daggett, & Adams, 1996), (3) teaching children with autism to interact with their peers with autism (e.g., Hauck et al., 1995; Krantz & McClannahan, 1993), and (4) teaching both typical children and children with autism to engage in reciprocal interactions (e.g., Kamps et al., 1992; Odom & Strain, 1986; Oke & Schreibman, 1990). In these studies, peers have served several functions, such as being tutors or teachers for children with autism (Kamps, Locke, Delquadri, & Hall, 1989; Staub & Hunt, 1993), serving as recipients of social initiations from children with autism (Odom & Strain, 1986), and functioning as initiators or playmates for children with autism (Hendrickson et al., 1982; Pierce & Schreibman, 1995; Shafer, Egel, & Neef, 1984).

Although studies incorporating peers differed along a number of dimensions (e.g., age of individuals with autism, intervention used, target of the intervention), a number of general conclusions can be drawn from the existing research.

1. *Some form of teaching or training is necessary, directed either to the peer, the child with autism, or both.* In all the studies reviewed for this chapter, specific procedures were required to promote social interactions. Baseline data in most studies indicated that prior to or in the absence of specific intervention, social interaction between children with autism and their peers was minimal (e.g., Hendrickson et al., 1982; Krantz & McClannahan, 1993; Mundschenk & Sasso, 1995; Odom, Hoyson, Jamieson, & Strain, 1985). For example, Gonzalez-Lopez and Kamps (1997) demonstrated that social interaction was limited prior to teaching typical peers to give easy instructions, prompt responses, ignore disruptive behavior, and praise appropriate behavior. Social skills training for both groups of children, combined with reinforcement procedures, led to increased rates and longer durations of social interactions for the four children with autism. When treatment was removed, however, social interactions decreased, then increased again when treatment was reimplemented.

In general, then, research indicates that the development of specific goals and the implementation of carefully planned behavioral intervention are necessary to teach functional peer social skills to children with autism. Otherwise, social engagement between children with autism and their peers will be limited.

2. *Typical children benefit from learning specific skills for interacting with children with autism.* In several studies incorporating typical peers, interactions increased when peers were taught specific strategies to use during play sessions with children with autism (Odom et al., 1985; Pierce & Schreibman, 1995). The work of Strain and colleagues demonstrated that teaching typical children such skills as sharing, organizing play, assisting, persisting, requesting shares, and getting attention, substantially increased rates of social interactions between the typical peers and the children with autism (Hendrickson et al., 1982; Strain, 1977; Strain & Kohler, 1999; Strain & Odom, 1986). For example, one study documented that typical children could be taught to use a self-evaluation procedure to engage in a set of initiation skills (i.e., getting attention, organizing play, sharing, responding to the target child) during play sessions with children with autism. Use of these skills resulted in increased rates of initiations by the typical peers and socially relevant responses by the children with autism (Sainato, Goldstein, & Strain, 1992).

The amount of training required for the typical peer is likely to vary as a function of the skills of the child with autism. For example, if the child with autism has significantly limited spoken language and social skills, the typical peer may require substantial training to engage successfully with him or her. On the other hand, if the child with autism has developed relatively good social skills (e.g., engages in play conversation, shares toys readily), the typical peer may not require as much specific training. Nevertheless, it is recommended that typical children be taught specific skills that will enable them to interact productively with their peers with autism.

3. *Specific reinforcement procedures are required to encourage interaction.* In most studies, reinforcement procedures were used to teach and maintain specific social behaviors (e.g., Gonzalez-Lopez & Kamps, 1997; Kohler et al., 1995; Oke & Schreibman, 1990; Zanolli & Daggett, 1998). Reinforcers, such as access to preferred toys, teacher praise, tokens, and edibles, have been used to increase and maintain the use of initiation strategies by typical peers and to encourage children with autism to engage in social interactions. For instance, one study demonstrated that a group reinforcement procedure was effective for increasing play interactions between typical peers and children with autism. Children were taught a number of socially relevant responses (e.g., sharing and requesting assistance), and were taught to provide supportive comments encouraging other children in the play group to use the social responses (e.g., "Ask Billy to share the toy with us"). Before each play session, the teacher reminded the group of children that they could earn "happy faces" if they engaged in the social responses and that the whole "Happy Face Chart" had to be filled in order to earn a prize. This training led to an increase in social interactions

between the typical peers and the children with autism, as well as an increase in supportive prompts by the typical peers toward one another (Kohler et al., 1995). Similarly, another study found that frequency and duration of interactions were greater when stickers were placed on cards for engaging in social interactions (Gonzalez-Lopez & Kamps, 1997).

Typical peers and children with autism may initially require individualized reinforcement systems in order to learn and maintain social responses. Because most children with autism are not automatically motivated to engage in social interactions, reinforcers should be paired with naturally occurring social consequences in order for those consequences to gain reinforcing value. For example, each time a child with autism is prompted to respond positively to a peer's overture to play, the peer could be prompted to reward the response of the child with autism by providing praise. Likewise, peers may not initially experience interacting with children with autism as rewarding; therefore, extrinsic rewards may be necessary to encourage their participation.

4. *Additional strategies may be needed to generalize or maintain interactions.* A number of studies have documented that, unless specific training or generalization procedures were used, children with autism and their peers failed to engage in social interactions with novel peers in novel settings, and sometimes did not maintain responses in the absence of intervention (e.g., Hendrickson et al., 1982; Hundert & Houghton, 1992; Mundschenk & Sasso, 1995; Odom et al., 1985). Generalization of social skills can be promoted by involving multiple peers in training, conducting training in settings where the behavior is most likely to occur (e.g., the playground, recess), using materials that resemble those found in the natural environment, teaching many examples of social responses, and using procedures that ensure that the social behaviors of children with autism and peers will contact naturally occurring reinforcers (Stokes & Bear, 1977; Stokes & Osnes, 1988). For example, typical peers could ask the child with autism to play with a toy that the child with autism enjoys, thereby increasing the likelihood that the child with autism will respond favorably to the initiation and perhaps respond more favorably to other initiations in the future. Also, peer social skills training can be conducted in the child's home in the environment where the child is likely to play with friends.

5. *Specific procedures are required to reduce and eliminate adult prompts.* Studies have documented that when adult prompts are removed, peer interactions tend to decrease (e.g., Odom et al., 1985). To avoid this undesirable outcome, adult prompts should be faded systematically and quickly from peer social skills instruction. It is not uncommon for adults to use verbal instructions (e.g., "Ask Billy if you can play") to encourage children with autism to engage with other children. Such instructions, however, are likely to promote reliance on adult prompts by children with autism, with the result that their social interactions do not persist in the absence of adult instruction. Interventions that do not include adults in peer social interactions (e.g., photographic prompts, written scripts, audiotaped prompts) may reduce the likelihood that the peers and children with autism will rely on adults to engage in the interaction (Jolly, Test, & Spooner, 1993; Krantz & McClannahan, 1993; Taylor & Levin, 1998).

One set of investigators found that displaying pictures of social responses to which typical peers could refer during play sessions assisted in the transfer from teacher instructions to natural stimuli and reinforcers. The picture system allowed peers to monitor their use of sharing responses, organizing play statements, and requesting assistance. Adult verbal prompts and the visual display of responses were eventually faded until peers were monitoring their interactions in the absence any adult-delivered cues (Odom et al., 1992).

When designing procedures to teach social interactions, practitioners should recognize that children tend to rely on adults to sustain interaction. Procedures to teach social interaction skills to children with autism should be designed accordingly. Without careful planning and use of strategies that minimize and eventually eliminate adult prompts, parents and teachers are likely to find that children continue to require adults to negotiate their peer interactions.

6. *Interactions between typical peers and children with autism are more likely to occur when both are taught the necessary skills.* Several researchers have documented that children with autism do not necessarily learn to initiate interactions with other children simply as a result of receiving initiations from those children (e.g., Odom & Strain, 1986; Oke & Schreibman, 1990). For example, although typical peers were taught to engage in a high rate of social initiations toward children with autism, the children with autism responded to but did not initiate interactions at a higher rate (Sainato et al., 1992). On the other hand, when a child with autism was taught the same initiation skills as typical peers, rates of initiations by the child with autism increased and disruptive behavior decreased (Oke & Schreibman, 1990). Similarly, social initiations and responses of children with autism increased when teachers prompted the child with autism to engage in initiations with typical peers who were trained to respond to the initiations (Odom & Strain, 1986).

In summary, the impaired social behavior of children with autism often means that they do not respond to and may actively reject bids for social interaction from other children. Thus, although peers may be taught to engage with a child with autism, those attempts may not be reinforced by the child with autism. Therefore, equal emphasis should be placed on teaching children with autism to respond as well as to initiate interactions with peers.

7. *It is difficult to ascertain which children with autism will benefit from which types of instructional techniques (e.g., peer-mediated vs. adult-mediated interventions).* A variety of techniques to increase peer social interactions in children with autism have

been explored. Some of these procedures have focused on adult prompting and reinforcement, whereas others have focused on teaching typical peers the skills to sustain and increase interaction. In addition, some interventions appeared to have taken place within fairly structured contexts, whereas others occurred during more "naturalistic" play contexts. Although most studies documented changes in rates of social interaction, little information is available about how to match strategies to children's existing skills. It seems logical that children with significant challenges in understanding language and in behaving appropriately in unstructured contexts will require fairly systematic adult-directed instruction in nondistracting environments to learn peer social skills, at least initially. A careful assessment of the strengths and skill deficits of the child with autism should precede selection of instructional strategies, and every effort should be made to match the procedures used, as well as the instructional objectives, to the child's current skills.

Determining Readiness for Peer Social Skills Instruction

Research does not yet provide any specific guidelines for determining when a child with autism is ready to begin learning to interact with peers. Some researchers have suggested that children with autism need certain prerequisite skills to benefit fully from peer interaction training (e.g., Breen & Haring, 1990; Ladd & Hart, 1992). For example, Hauck et al. (1995) observed that the quality and quantity of social interactions by children with autism varied with the setting and the child's cognitive and verbal abilities. This suggests that children with autism need to have specific skills to benefit from activities with peers.

Some of these skills can be deduced from careful consideration of the components of peer social interactions. The child with autism who can imitate the behavior of other children, follow adult instructions, and play appropriately with a number of toys likely will find it easier to learn to interact with peers than will a child who lacks those skills. Conversely, a child with autism who has not yet learned to follow a variety of simple instructions may not readily learn to respond to peers' verbal overtures to play. Further, peers will likely experience interactions more favorably if the child with autism is compliant and does not engage in highly disruptive behavior.

To determine if a child with autism is ready to learn peer interaction skills, the professional or parent should evaluate the current capabilities of the child as well as the expected outcomes of the instruction. If the child is lacking critical prerequisites, time would be better spent teaching those skills first rather than trying to teach them in the context of peer activities. In short, peer social skills training will be more productive if the child with autism has already mastered a number of relevant skills, such as following direc-

tions, identifying and labeling objects and people, looking at adults, imitating a variety of actions, playing with toys appropriately, and maintaining near-zero rates of disruptive and stereotypic behavior.

Identifying Peers

Identifying appropriate peers requires a degree of networking on the part of families or treatment team members. Peers can be children in the neighborhood, siblings or other relatives (e.g., cousins), other children with autism, siblings of other children with autism, or children from the school the child attends. Some families offer free baby-sitting or quality supervised play dates as incentives for families to have a child participate in instructional sessions with a child with autism. It is best to inform the parents of the purpose of the sessions.

Peer Characteristics

Although research to date does not clearly indicate the characteristics of peers that lead to successful peer instruction with children with autism, children who are outgoing and like to be leaders may serve as effective peers. In general, when considering a peer, parents and professionals should keep the following in mind:

- It may be helpful for the peer to be a little older than the child with autism. This will increase the likelihood that the peer will model appropriate social, language, and play behavior for the child with autism.

- Because the peer will be asked to engage in many types of activities, he or she should be flexible and cooperative in following adult directions.

- A peer who enjoys directing the play of other children or is assertive in play sessions will likely persist in getting the child with autism to respond to him or her, which is important if the child with autism is to have sufficient opportunities to practice his or her new skills. A child who gives up easily or who is shy may not be as insistent in getting a response from the child with autism.

- The peer should be capable of sustaining attention to activities. He or she may be asked to engage in activities for long periods of time, and to repeat certain activities so the child with autism has ample opportunity to practice social skills.

- The peer should be socially competent (e.g., use polite language, engage in a high rate of initiations, share appropriately with peers, offer assistance) to serve as an appropriate model for the child with autism.

- In general, the peer should demonstrate an interest in helping the child with autism by participating in the sessions.

Number of Peers

Some research suggests that the use of multiple peers in social skills training can facilitate generalization (e.g., Belchic & Harris, 1994; Mundschenk & Sasso, 1995). For example, one study found that reciprocal interactions occurred with greater frequency when multiple peer initiators were present during play periods with peers (Mundschenk & Sasso, 1995). Involving several peers also precludes the possibility that a single peer will become bored with the activities or find the instructional sessions too demanding. The number of peers incorporated will depend on their availability, as well as the goals of instruction and the frequency of sessions. Initially, a limited number of peers who can participate at regular intervals should be involved. This will make it easier to ensure that peers are consistent in the way they interact with the child with autism. It will also maximize opportunities for both the peer and the child with autism to practice the targeted skills.

Siblings as Peers

Several researchers have demonstrated that siblings can be taught to serve as peer instructors for their sibling with autism (Celiberti & Harris, 1993; Schreibman, O'Neill, & Koegel, 1983; Taylor, Levin, & Jasper, 1999). Celiberti and Harris (1993), for example, taught three siblings of children with autism to deliver play-related commands, prompts if the sibling failed to respond correctly, and praise for correct responses during play sessions. Modeling, role playing, verbal instructions, and praise were effective in increasing these skills in the siblings as well as appropriate responses by the children with autism. Taylor et al. (1999) taught children with autism to make play-related comments to their siblings by using video modeling. Siblings participated in the video modeling sessions and subsequent play sessions with their siblings with autism. Both the siblings and the children with autism learned to engage in play-related dialogue during the play sessions.

Siblings often express an interest in or a curiosity about their brother's or sister's participation in behavioral programming and may be eager to help. It is recommended that they always be given a choice to participate so they do not experience the play sessions as too demanding. Efforts also should be made to make the sessions as enjoyable as possible for the siblings, for example, by having them choose the activities and assist in determining goals (e.g., by requesting that their sibling learn to play a particular game).

Use of Peers with Autism

A number of studies have shown that children with autism can be taught to interact with their peers with autism. For example, conversation among youths with autism was increased via a script fading procedure (Krantz & McClannahan, 1993). Behavioral school programs often teach children with autism to interact with one another as part of their daily instruction. For example, Taylor and Holberton (1998) taught two students with autism to engage in conversation during snack time by teaching them to self-monitor their use of questions and comments about various topics (e.g., sports, music, vacation). The youths were taught to check off on an index card each time they asked a question or made a comment about a topic to their peer. Once they completely filled out their index card, they chose a preferred activity. This self-monitoring procedure increased the rate of socially appropriate questions and comments for both boys.

The programs provided in this chapter can be taught with a peer with autism. However, when two children with autism are involved instead of one typical child and one with autism, more intensive direct instruction (e.g., physical prompting, textual prompts, extrinsic reinforcement systems) and the availability of another adult may be required.

Social Skills Instruction for Nonspeaking Children

Few researchers have specifically taught nonspeaking children with autism to engage in socially relevant responses with peers, although a few have documented that nonverbal peer interactions can be taught (e.g., Coe, Matson, Fee, Manikam, & Linarello, 1990; Jasper, 1996; Jolly et al., 1993). Jasper (1996) demonstrated that a nonspeaking child with autism could be taught to use an electronic communication device to initiate social interactions with a peer with autism. The child was taught to type into the device sentences consisting of peer initiation statements, approach a designated peer, activate the device (which produced the initiation statement), and play with the peer. Teacher prompts were eventually faded until the child used the device independently to make a variety of play-related initiations toward peers with autism.

Even though a child with autism does not have functional vocal speech, he or she can still participate in some peer social skills instruction. For example, the child can be taught to respond to peers as opposed to initiating (e.g., following directions from a peer, imitating a peer, responding to play initiation statements). Alternatively, nonspeaking children with autism can be taught a variety of initiations that do not necessarily involve speaking, such as taking a toy to a peer, tapping the peer on the shoulder, or pointing to preferred play activities. Additionally, augmentative communication systems (e.g., picture systems, sentence strips, electronic systems) can be used by the student with autism to engage in socially relevant responses (Schwartz, Garfinkle, & Bauer, 1998).

If the child with autism uses an augmentative communication system, it is important to establish that the peer understands the system. For example, the peer may not readily understand the picture icons used in a picture communication system. A communication system that provides auditory feedback to the peer, such as a voice output device, may make peer interactions flow more smoothly. In other words, pictures or printed word communication systems that do not include voice output may be cumbersome in peer social skills instruction because the peer may have difficulty interpreting the communications without specific training in how to do so.

Helpful Skills for Typical Peers

As previously mentioned, when typical peers are taught specific skills, social interactions with children with autism are enhanced. A number of researchers (e.g., Odom & Strain, 1986; Strain, 1977; Strain & Kohler, 1999) have documented that peers benefit from learning the following skills:

- *Sharing*—Teach the peer to offer toys or activities to the child with autism (e.g., peer hands a toy to child with autism and says, "Here, you can play with this truck").

- *Requesting shares*—Teach the peer to request items or to request a turn with an activity (e.g., peer says, "Can I play with that truck?").

- *Organizing play*—Teach the peer to suggest play activities or to organize the play activity (e.g., peer says to child with autism, "Let's play with the blocks" or "You be the bad guy and I'll be the policeman").

- *Offering assistance*—Teach the peer to offer assistance to the child with autism (e.g., peer observes child with autism struggling to take the top off the bubbles and peer says, "I'll open it for you").

- *Requesting assistance*—Teach the peer to request assistance from the child with autism (e.g., peer says to child with autism, "Help me take this puzzle apart").

- *Making complimentary statements*—Teach the peer to compliment the child with autism (e.g., peer and child with autism are drawing together and peer says, "I like your picture").

- *Making overtures of affection*—Teach the peer to be affectionate toward the child with autism (e.g., peer holds hand of child with autism while walking to the block area).

- *Providing supportive comments to other peers*—If more than one peer is available during the

instructional sessions, teach the peer to provide prompts to the other typical peer to initiate social interaction (e.g., peer says to another typical peer, "Ask Billy if he wants to play with the block too").

Others have documented additional skills (e.g., Celiberti & Harris, 1993; Gonzalez-Lopez & Kamps, 1997; Pierce & Schreibman, 1995):

- *Getting attention*—Teach the peer to state the name of the child with autism, or make sure the child with autism is looking before giving instructions (e.g., peer says, "John, give me that block").

- *Responding to initiations*—Teach the peer to respond when the child with autism initiates toward him or her (e.g., when child with autism says, "Do you want to play ball?" peer says "Okay").

- *Greetings*—Teach the peer to greet the child with autism (e.g., peer says, "Hi, Michael").

- *Asking questions of peer*—Teach the peer to ask the child with autism questions about the play activities (e.g., while playing with blocks, peer says to child with autism, "What are you building?").

- *Providing choices of activities to peer*—Teach the peer to provide the child with autism a choice of activities throughout the play session (e.g., peer holds up two toys and says, "Do you want the red ball or this green truck?").

- *Commenting on play activities*—Teach the peer to comment about play activities (e.g., while drawing with child with autism, peer says, "I'm making a house" or "I like to draw").

- *Withholding preferred activities until child makes a verbal initiation*—Teach the peer to wait until the child with autism says something to get a preferred activity (e.g., peer holds up a toy and says to child with autism, "What do you want?" but waits to give the toy until peer with autism says what he or she wants).

- *Giving easy instructions*—Teach the peer to provide instructions in simple sentences that are likely to get a response (e.g., peer says to child with autism, "Put the man in the truck").

- *Demonstrating responses*—Teach the peer to demonstrate the action for the child with autism (e.g., in the above example, peer shows child with autism the response by placing the man in the truck).

- *Providing physical prompts*—Teach the peer to guide the child's hand to perform the response (e.g., peer takes hand of child with autism and places it on the man to place in the truck).

- *Providing praise statements for good behavior*—Teach the peer to provide verbal praise for socially appropriate behavior (e.g., peer says to child with autism, "Thanks for sharing!").

- *Ignoring disruptive behavior*—Teach the peer to ignore disruptive behavior displayed by the child with autism (e.g., child with autism knocks toys over and peer continues with the play activity).

- *Persisting until a response is obtained*—Teach the peer to be persistent with the child with autism until he or she gets a response (e.g., peer says to child with autism, "Give me the ball"; if the child with autism does not respond, the peer repeats the instruction and prompts the child to respond).

Strategies To Teach Skills to Typical Peers

A number of strategies have been used to teach these skills to peers. These include the following:

- *Preteaching of responses*—During preteaching sessions, the target responses are taught to the peer, who is provided an opportunity to practice the responses with an adult first, then the child with autism. Verbal praise or some other reinforcer is provided for demonstrating the response with the adult and then with the child with autism.

- *Role playing*—During role-play exercises, an adult performs the role of the child with autism and the peer practices the response with the adult. Role playing continues until the peer is able to demonstrate the response with accuracy.

- *Reinforcement procedures*—Usually during the training sessions, verbal praise or access to tangible reinforcers is provided for demonstrating the responses (e.g., after peer shares a toy, adult says, "I like when you share with Billy!"). Reinforcement systems such as a token system, a star chart, or a happy face chart can be used to successfully maintain responses during play sessions with peers.

- *Use of visual aids*—Drawings or photographs can be used during the teaching sessions to illustrate specific skills (e.g., a picture of a child handing a toy to another child to demonstrate a sharing response). These visual aids can be used during instructional sessions and play activities with peers to serve as prompts for the typical peer to remember the responses.

- *Video demonstrations*—Videotapes can be used to show the peer how to perform the response (e.g., a tape is made of an adult making play initiations toward a child with autism). Typically, the peer observes the response on the videotape, then is provided with opportunities to practice the response with the child with autism.

- *In vivo prompting*—Prompts for target responses can be provided directly during the teaching sessions (e.g., while two children are playing with blocks, teacher models verbal initiations for peer to make toward child with autism). Verbal prompts, while common, are challenging to fade and often make peers reliant on adult prompts to initiate and sustain interactions. It is better to use prompts that do not require adult mediation, such as photographs or written instructions that tell the peer what to do.

- *Self-monitoring*—Peers can be taught to keep track of how often they are using target skills with the child with autism. For example, peers can be taught to check off on an index card whether they did or did not use a specific strategy.

- *Group contingencies*—Peers can be taught as a group to increase interactions with children with autism and everyone in the group earns reinforcers for social responses. If the entire group makes a certain number of social responses, then all peers in the group earn the reinforcer.

- *Peer-to-peer prompting*—Peers can be taught to provide prompts to other peers to engage socially with the child with autism. For example, a peer is taught not only to display social responses with the child with autism, but also to prompt his or her friends to do so.

In general, the training needs of the typical peer will depend on the current capabilities and goals for the child with autism. If the goal is to have the child with autism respond to play initiation statements from the peer, then the peer will require training to make frequent initiations toward the child with autism. The peer may not require as much training if the child with autism already demonstrates a fair number of socially relevant responses.

Informing Typical Peers About Autism

Decisions to tell peers about the learning needs of the child with autism should be individualized based on the profile of the learner with autism, the age of the peer, and the purpose of the instructional sessions. For example, preschool peers will not necessarily need to know the child has autism, but they may benefit from being told that their friend needs extra help learning how to play and how to talk. Peers who will be involved in instructional sessions with children with autism who have severe learning and behavioral deficits may require more information about the nature of autism to interact successfully. On the other hand, for more capable children with autism, telling their typical peers they have autism may actually stigmatize the child with autism and result in reduced participation on the part of the typical peer.

Teaching Strategies for the Child with Autism

Effective strategies for teaching social skills to children with autism are grounded in the principles and methods of applied behavior analysis (e.g., positive reinforcement, shaping, modeling, prompting and prompt fading, incidental teaching, discrimination training). Teaching strategies, like instructional objectives, should be individualized to each child's current skills and characteristics. For example, if the child with autism responds well to written cues, then written instructions can be used to teach social initiation skills. On the other hand, if the child learns readily through imitation, then modeling may function as an effective prompt. A number of techniques have been validated through research; the teaching programs outlined in Chapter 8 incorporate a number of them.

Verbal Modeling with Contingent Reinforcement

In one study, students with moderate handicaps were taught via verbal modeling and positive reinforcement to initiate and expand on conversational topics (Haring, Roger, Lee, Breen, & Gaylord-Ross, 1986). Typically, when using a verbal model, an adult demonstrates for the child the appropriate verbalization to make and reinforces the child's response of imitating the model. The adult eventually fades the model over time. Verbal modeling can be used in a variety of ways to teach social skills. For example, to teach a child with autism to respond affirmatively to a play initiation from a peer (e.g., peer says to Mary, "Mary, let's go down the slide"), a verbal model of the affirmative statement can be provided by an adult (e.g., the adult says, "Say, 'Okay'"). When the child with autism imitates the model, the adult provides praise (e.g., "Great job, saying 'Okay'") and a preferred edible. Over subsequent learning opportunities, this verbal model is reduced or faded (e.g., "Say, 'O'" then just a pause) until reinforcement is provided only for responses that occur in the absence of a prompt from an adult.

Time-Delay Prompting

A number of researchers have shown that time-delay prompt and fading procedures can be effective for teaching social responses (Charlop & Walsh, 1986; Ingenmey & Houten, 1991; Matson, Sevin, Box, Francis, & Sevin, 1993; Taylor & Harris, 1995). One variation of time-delay procedures is a progressive time delay. This involves initially providing a prompt (e.g., a verbal model) immediately upon the presentation of a particular stimulus (e.g., a question), then, over successive trials, delaying the presentation of the prompt for brief but gradually increasing intervals (e.g., 1 second, 3 seconds, 5 seconds) until the child is performing the response prior to the prompt. For example, to teach a child with autism to say "Hi" when his friend enters the room, the child is first prompted to say "Hi" as soon as his friend enters the room (e.g., immediately upon Brian's entering into the room, the adult models "Hi, Brian" for the child with autism to repeat). Once the child repeats the greeting reliably for several trials, the prompt is delayed briefly after Brian enters to give the child the opportunity to produce the response before the prompt. Reinforcers are provided initially for imitating the prompt and then for responding in the absence of the prompt.

Textual Prompts

Textual prompts are written or typed stimuli that function to prompt the child with autism to engage in a response (Krantz & McClannahan, 1993; Sarakoff, Taylor, & Poulson, in press). For example, Krantz and McClannahan (1993) taught teenagers with autism to engage in conversational exchanges by teaching them to read a script. The script was gradually faded, and the youths continued to make the conversational statements. Textual stimuli are often faded by gradually removing components, such as the last letter in a word, then the second-to-last letter or the last word in the script, then the second-to-last word, and so on, until no prompt is visible. For example, to teach a child with autism to make an appropriate play initiation statement toward a peer, an initiation statement (e.g., "Let's play with the blocks") could be written or typed on a card for the child with autism to read when she approaches the peer. Once the child reliably makes the statement with all of the script present, words are removed systematically across successive learning opportunities (e.g., "Let's play with the" to "Let's play with" to "Let's play" to "Let's" to no text). For textual prompts to be effective, the child with autism must be able to read and carry out the prescribed actions. These skills are best taught directly by an adult before they are to be used in the context of peer interactions.

Photographic Prompts

Photographs also have been used as prompts for learners with autism. For instance, researchers at the Princeton Child Development Institute have demonstrated that children with autism can learn to engage independently in appropriate play and leisure activities by following photographic activity schedules (e.g., Krantz, MacDuff, & McClannahan, 1993). Photos can also be used during peer social skills training. For example, a child could be taught to follow a schedule in which pictures serve as cues for the child with autism to obtain specific toys, approach peers, and ask to play. Children are typically taught to follow photo activity schedules by being guided from behind to point to a picture in a notebook representing an activity, get the materials for the activity, approach a peer, engage in the activity with the peer, return to the book, turn the page, point to the next photo representing another activity, and so on. Reinforcers (usually in the form of edibles) are provided for independent and accurate responding (McClannahan & Krantz, 1999). Usually a child is taught how to follow photo activity schedules during individual treatment sessions before they are used to teach peer social interaction skills.

Tactile Prompts

One set of researchers showed that a vibrating pager could serve as a prompt for a child with autism to make conversational statements to peers (Taylor & Levin, 1998). Another study found that a similar device could be used to prompt a preschooler with autism to make play-related comments to peers in play activities with his brother and in his preschool class with peers (Holberton, Taylor, & Levin, 1998). In these studies, the children with autism were first taught to state initiations with adults when the device was activated before introducing the device into activities with peers. First, the child's hand was placed on the device, and when it was activated, the adult modeled an initiation for the child to imitate and then reinforced the response. Once the child independently produced appropriate verbalizations when the device was activated, the device was placed in the child's pocket and he was taught to put his hand on his pocket. Over successive teaching sessions, the child was no longer required to keep his hand on the device.

Tactile prompts such as vibrating pagers can be used to prompt a number of peer interactions, such as play comments (e.g., "I have a green truck"), play initiation statements (e.g., "Do you want to play ball?"), or conversational statements (e.g., "I like popcorn too"). Once the child with autism reliably produces statements in response to the device's vibration during specific activities with peers, the device should be placed in his or her pocket but not activated to determine if the prompt is still needed. Holberton et al. (1998) found that spontaneous play comments, independent of the tactile prompt, increased during play sessions with the vibrating beeper simply placed in the child's pocket, suggesting that the tactile prompt was no longer required.

Incidental Teaching Procedures

Incidental teaching procedures (Hart & Risley, 1982) have been shown to be effective for increasing language use in children with autism (e.g., Farmer-Dougan, 1994; McGee et al., 1992). Incidental teaching requires that an adult arrange the environment in such a manner as to entice initiations from

the child with autism. For example, preferred items may be placed in view but out of reach of the child. When the child shows interest in the item (e.g., points toward a ball on the shelf), the adult prompts a verbal response (e.g., by saying, "Say, 'I want the ball'"). When the child imitates the verbal model, the response is reinforced with access to the item of interest (e.g., the ball). Over successive teaching opportunities, the prompt is faded gradually until the child makes the statement spontaneously and independently.

Incidental teaching procedures can be used in a variety of ways. In one study, typically developing preschool students were taught to implement incidental teaching procedures with three preschool children with autism. The typical children were taught to wait for the child with autism to show interest in a toy (e.g., reach for a toy), to ask the child with autism to label the toy (e.g., "Say ball"), to give the toy to the child, and then to praise him or her. With this procedure, reciprocal social interactions among the typical children and children with autism increased (McGee et al., 1992).

Incidental teaching procedures can also be used to encourage play initiations by children with autism. For example, if the child with autism expresses interest in an item or activity (e.g., by asking an adult, "Can I have the trains?"), the child can be prompted to ask a peer to play in order to access the activity. For instance, the adult might guide the child with autism to the peer and model "Let's ask if we can play with the trains." When the child with autism imitates the verbal model, the response is reinforced by obtaining access to the activity: The adult says, "Great asking Billy to play; here are the trains" and hands the items to the children.

Audiotaped Prompts

Audiotaped prompts presented via Language Masters (see Appendix 7A, which is a resource guide) have been used to teach spontaneous language to children with autism (Stevenson, Krantz, & McClannahan, 2000; Taylor, 1999). These are machines that play prerecorded audiotaped prompts. A statement or a question (e.g., "Hi, Billy") is recorded onto a card, which is then run through the Language Master machine to play the recorded message. Such messages can serve as models for the child with autism to imitate (e.g., the child repeats "Hi, Billy" after listening to the message); thus the messages can serve as model prompts. The prompts are faded by recording messages that systematically remove parts of the message (e.g., the last word of the model is removed, then the next to last, and so on, until nothing is recorded on the card). Probes can also be conducted by running the card through the machine with the audiotaped prompt blocked (the Language Master is equipped with a blocking mechanism). To illustrate, to teach a child with autism to direct the play of another child, the directions (e.g., "Get the ball") might be recorded onto Language Master cards. The child is taught to run the card through the machine, or an adult may stand behind the child and run the card through the machine. The child repeats the audiotaped model (e.g., says "Get the ball"), and the adult reinforces the response. Over subsequent teaching sessions, the audiotaped prompt is faded gradually by removing one word at a time (e.g., "Get the," to "Get," to nothing on the card), or all at once by running the card through the machine with the blocking feature on so that the model is not audible.

Typically, children are taught to imitate models from the Language Master before this prompting method is used to teach peer interaction skills. Additional training sessions may be required to teach the child with autism to listen to the prompt, approach the peer, and then state the verbalization. Although verbal models can be provided by adults or even other children instead of the Language Master, use of the Language Master makes it possible to fade the prompts very systematically, precisely, and consistently. It can also preclude prompts from adults.

Video Modeling Procedures

Peer social skills can be taught via video modeling procedures (Charlop & Milstein, 1989; Taylor et al., 1999). A videotape is made of the responses such as conversational exchanges. Usually an adult depicts the desired responses on the tape, although another child could just as easily serve as the model. The child with autism views the tape several times and is then provided with opportunities to practice the responses, either with an adult or a peer. For example, to teach a child with autism to engage in conversation about play activities with a peer, a videotape could be made depicting two people (e.g., two adults, two children, or an adult and a child) engaged in conversation about the play activities. The child with autism might view the tape several times. Then the play materials shown on the tape are provided and the adult or peer states his or her portion of the dialogue. If the child with autism states any portion of the dialogue viewed on the tape, the adult provides reinforcement. After a number of teaching sessions, the child with autism might be presented with the opportunity to engage in the play activity in the absence of videotape viewing.

Video modeling can be used in a variety of ways. For example, videotapes can be used to provide feedback to children with autism about their performance during play sessions. Videotapes can be made of play sessions between a peer and the child with autism. The child with autism can then view the tape with an adult, who points out appropriate responses and responses that could be performed differently during the next play session, and perhaps also provides reinforcement and corrective feedback. Follow-up tapes can be made and reviewed to help the child see his or her progress. For this type of intervention to be effective, the child with autism must be capable of discriminating and talking about his or her own behavior and modifying behavior based on verbal feedback.

Self-Monitoring

In self-monitoring, "an individual systematically [observes] his own behavior and [responds] to the occurrence or non-occurrence of a specified target response" (Cooper, Heron, & Heward, 1987, p. 524). Children with autism can be taught to self-monitor their social interactions by discriminating and recording their own behavior, and accessing reinforcement for appropriate social responses. For example, Taylor and Holberton (1998) taught two boys with autism to self-monitor their use of comments and questions toward one another about a variety of topics. The children were taught to display the responses of asking questions and making comments and to check off on an index card whenever they displayed these responses with one another. If the children made comments and questions accurately and checked off on the index card each time they did so, they were able to choose a preferred activity at the end of the conversational interaction. When the self-monitoring system was introduced during a snack time, both boys engaged in significantly higher rates of questions and comments about a variety of topics. Eventually, the self-monitoring system (i.e, the cards and the writing utensils) was no longer needed and both boys continued to ask questions and make comments.

Time Allocated to Peer Social Skills Instruction

All children with autism should have programming goals to develop and increase their peer interaction skills. The amount of time that should be devoted to peer social skills instruction, however, depends on the skill level and goals for the learner with autism. For example, if the child is preparing for participation in a regular education class and has the necessary component skills, then peer social skills training should be a priority. On the other hand, if the child is just beginning programming, engages in high rates of stereotypic and disruptive responses, does not reliably imitate others, and has little functional speech, then programming time is better spent addressing those skills.

Length of Teaching Sessions

The length of teaching sessions depends on the goals of the instruction, the skills of the child with autism, and the interest of the peer. Beginning with brief, focused teaching sessions designed so that the peer and the child with autism experience immediate success will increase the likelihood that they will want to continue to participate in the training.

Arrangement of Teaching Environment

Children with autism may engage in more social interactions if the instruction occurs in a context with preferred items and activities (Koegel, Dyer, & Bell, 1987). Using play materials that interest both the child with autism and the peer may enhance their participation in the activities. If the child with autism requires highly systematic instruction, it may be necessary to begin social skills instruction in a setting that minimizes distractions for both children. Arrange the environment according to the goals of instruction and the behavioral profile of the child. For example, if the goal is to teach play initiations in a free-play context, then toys will need to be arranged around the room to simulate free play.

Determining Skills To Teach

The skills taught at any given point in time will depend on the goals for each child. The programs outlined in Chapter 8 encompass some skills that have been found, through research and experience, to enhance peer interactions. They do not include all of the skills children with autism need to be perceived as socially competent. These programs should be modified as needed, and social skills instruction should be preceded by a careful assessment of each child's current skills.

Appendix 7A
Resources

Communication Systems

Attainment Company
Options Catalog
P.O. Box 930160
Verona, WI 53593-0160
Phone: 800/327-4269
Fax: 800/942-3865

Crestwood Company
Communication Aids for Children and Adults
6625 North Sidney Place
Milwaukee, WI 53209-3259
Phone: 414/352-5678

DynaVox, DynaMyte Systems
Sentient Systems Technology, Inc.
2100 Wharton Street
Pittsburgh, PA 15203
Phone: 888/697-7332
Fax: 412/381-5241

Mayer-Johnson Company
P.O. Box 1579
Solana Beach, CA 92075-7579
Phone: 619/550-0084
Fax: 619/550-0449

Speaking Language Master Special Edition
Franklin Electronic Publishers
One Franklin Plaza
Burlington, NJ 08016-4907
Phone: 800/266-5626
Fax: 609/239-5950

Language Masters

EIKI International, Inc.
26794 Vista Terrace Drive
Lake Forest, CA 92630
Phone: 800/242-3454

Highsmith, Inc.
West 5527 Highway 106
P.O. Box 800
Fort Atkinson, WI 53838-0800
Phone: 800/558-3899
Fax: 800/835-2329

Tactile Prompts
JTECH, Inc.
Premise Pager Systems
6413 Congress Avenue, Suite 150
Boca Raton, FL 33487
Phone: 800/321-6221
Fax: 407/997-0773

WatchMinder
PMB #278
5405 Alton Parkway #5A
Irvine, CA 92604-3718
Phone: 800/961-0023

References

Belchic, J. K., & Harris, S. L. (1994). The use of multiple peer exemplars to enhance the generalization of play skills to siblings of children with autism. *Child and Family Behavior Therapy, 16,* 1–25.

Breen, C. G., & Haring, T. G. (1990). Effects of contextual competence on social initiations. *Journal of Applied Behavior Analysis, 24,* 337–347.

Celiberti, D. A., & Harris, S. L. (1993). Behavioral intervention for siblings of children with autism: A focus on skills to enhance play. *Behavior Therapy, 24,* 573–599.

Charlop, M. H., & Milstein, J. P. (1989). Teaching autistic children conversational speech using video modeling. *Journal of Applied Behavior Analysis, 23,* 275–285.

Charlop, M. H., & Walsh, M. E. (1986). Increasing autistic children's spontaneous verbalizations of affection: An assessment of time delay and peer modeling procedures. *Journal of Applied Behavior Analysis, 19,* 307–314.

Coe, D., Matson, J., Fee, V., Manikam, R., & Linarello, C. (1990). Training nonverbal and verbal play skills to mentally retarded and autistic children. *Journal of Autism and Developmental Disorders, 20* (2), 177–187.

Cooper, J. O., Heron, T. E., & Heward, W. L. (1987). *Applied behavior analysis.* New York: Macmillan.

Elliot, N. E., & Gresham, F. M. (1993). Social skills interventions for children. *Behavior Modification, 17*(3), 287–313.

Farmer-Dougan, V. (1994). Increasing requests by adults with developmental disabilities using incidental teaching by peers. *Journal of Applied Behavior Analysis, 27,* 533–544.

Gaylord-Ross, R. J., Haring, T. G., Breen, C., & Pitts-Conway, V. (1984). The training and generalization of social skills with autistic youth. *Journal of Applied Behavior Analysis, 17,* 229–247.

Goldstein, H., Kaczmarek, L., Pennington, R., & Shafer, K. (1992). Peer-mediated intervention: Attending to, commenting on, and acknowledging the behavior of preschoolers with autism. *Journal of Applied Behavior Analysis, 25,* 289–305.

Gonzalez-Lopez, A., & Kamps, D. M. (1997). Social skills training to increase social interactions between children with autism and their typical peers. *Focus on Autism and Other Developmental Disabilities, 12,* 2–14.

Green, G. (1996). Early behavioral intervention for autism. In C. Maurice, G. Green, & R. Fox (Eds.), *Behavioral intervention for young children with autism: A manual for parents and professionals* (pp. 29–44). Austin, TX: PRO-ED.

Haring, T. G., & Breen, C. G. (1992). A peer mediated social network intervention to enhance the social integration of persons with severe disabilities. *Journal of Applied Behavior Analysis, 25,* 319–333.

Haring, T. G., Roger, B., Lee, M., Breen, C., & Gaylord-Ross, R. (1986). Teaching social language to moderately handicapped students. *Journal of Applied Behavior Analysis, 19,* 159–171.

Hart, B., & Risley, T. R. (1982). *How to use incidental teaching for elaborating language.* Austin, TX: PRO-ED.

Hauck, M., Fein, D., Waterhouse, L., & Feinstein, C. (1995). Social initiations by autistic children to adults and other children. *Journal of Autism and Developmental Disorders, 25,* 579–595.

Hendrickson, J. M., Strain, P. S., Tremblay, A., & Shores, R. E. (1982). Interactions of behaviorally handicapped children: Functional effects of peer social initiations. *Behavior Modification, 6,* 323–353.

Holberton, L., Taylor, B. A., & Levin, L. (1998, October). *The use of a tactile prompt with a child with autism to increase play related comments to peers.* Symposium presented at the New York Association for Behavior Analysts Conference, Saratoga.

Hundert, J., & Houghton, A. (1992). Promoting social interaction of children with disabilities in integrated schools: A failure to generalize. *Exceptional Children, 58,* 311–320.

Ingenmey, R., & Houten, V. R. (1991). Using time delay to promote spontaneous speech in an autistic child. *Journal of Applied Behavior Analysis, 24,* 591–596.

Jasper, S. P. (1996). *Teaching social initiations to children with autism.* Unpublished master's thesis, William Paterson University, Wayne, NJ.

Jolly, A. C., Test, D. W., & Spooner, F. (1993). Using badges to increase initiations of children with severe disabilities in a play setting. *Journal of the Association for Persons with Severe Handicaps, 18* (1), 46–51.

Kamps, D. M., Leonard, B. R., Vernon, S., Dugan, E. P., Delquadri, J. C., Gershon, B., Wade, L., & Folk, L. (1992). Teaching social skills to students with autism to increase peer interactions in an integrated first-grade classroom. *Journal of Applied Behavior Analysis, 25,* 281–288.

Kamps, D., Locke, P., Delquadri, J., & Hall, R. V. (1989). Increasing academic skills of students with autism using fifth grade peers as tutors. *Education and Treatment of Children, 12,* 38–51.

Koegel, R. L., Dyer, K., & Bell, L. K. (1987). The influence of child-preferred activities on autistic children's social behavior. *Journal of Applied Behavior Analysis, 20* (3), 243–252.

Kohler, F. W., Strain, P. S., Hoyson, M., Davis, L., Donina, W. M., & Rapp, N. (1995). Using a group-oriented contingency to increase social interactions between children with autism and their peers. *Behavior Modification, 19,* 10–32.

Krantz, P. J., MacDuff, M. T., & McClannahan, L. E. (1993). Programming participation in family activities for children with autism: Parents' use of photographic schedules. *Journal of Applied Behavior Analysis, 26,* 137–138.

Krantz, P. J., & McClannahan, L. E. (1993). Teaching children with autism to initiate to peers: Effects of a script fading procedure. *Journal of Applied Behavior Analysis, 26,* 121–132.

Ladd, G. W., & Hart, C. H. (1992). Creating informal play opportunities: Are parents' and preschoolers' initiation related to children's competence with peers? *Developmental Psychology, 28*(6), 1179–1187.

Matson, J. L., Sevin, J. A., Box, M. L., Francis, K. L., & Sevin, B. M. (1993). An evaluation of two methods for increasing self-initiated verbalizations in autistic children. *Journal of Applied Behavior Analysis, 26,* 389–398.

McClannahan, L. E., & Krantz, P. J. (1999). *Activity schedules for children with autism: Teaching independent behavior.* Bethesda, MD: Woodbine House.

McGee, G. G., Almeida, M. C., Sulzer-Azaroff, B., & Feldman, R. S. (1992). Promoting reciprocal interactions via peer incidental teaching. *Journal of Applied Behavior Analysis, 25,* 515–524.

Mundschenk, N. S., & Sasso, G. S. (1995). Assessing sufficient social exemplars for students with autism. *Behavior Disorders, 21,* 62–78.

Odom, S. L., Chandler, L. K., Ostrosky, M., McConnell, S. R., & Reaney, S. (1992). Fading teacher prompts from peer-initiation interventions for young children with disabilities. *Journal of Applied Behavior Analysis, 25*(2), 307–317.

Odom, S. L., Hoyson, M., Jamieson, B., & Strain, P. S. (1985). Increasing handicapped preschoolers' peer social interactions: Cross-setting and component analysis. *Journal of Applied Behavior Analysis, 18*(1), 3–16.

Odom, S. L., & Strain, P. S. (1986). A comparison of peer-initiation and teacher-antecedent interventions for promoting reciprocal social interaction of autistic preschoolers. *Journal of Applied Behavior Analysis, 19*(1), 59–71.

Odom, S. L., & Watts, E. (1991). Reducing teacher prompts in peer-mediated interventions for young children with autism. *The Journal of Special Education, 25,* 26–43.

Oke, N. J., & Schreibman, L. (1990). Training social initiations to a high-functioning autistic child: Assessment of collateral behavior change and generalization in a case study. *Journal of Autism and Developmental Disorders, 20,* 479–497.

Pierce, K., & Schreibman, L. (1995). Increasing complex social behaviors in children with autism: Effects of a peer mediated pivotal response training. *Journal of Applied Behavior Analysis, 28,* 285–295.

Pollard, N. L. (1998). Development of social interaction skills in preschool children with autism: A review of the literature. *Child and Family Behavior Therapy, 20,* 1–16.

Sainato, D. M., Goldstein, H., & Strain, P. S. (1992). Effects of self-evaluation on preschool children's use of social interaction strategies with their classmates with autism. *Journal of Applied Behavior Analysis, 25,* 127–141.

Sarakoff, R. A., Taylor, B. A., & Poulson, C. L. (in press). Teaching children with autism to engage in conversational exchanges: Script-fading with embedded textual stimuli. *Journal of Applied Behavior Analysis.*

Schreibman, L., O'Neill, R. E., & Koegel, R. L. (1983). Behavioral training for siblings of children with autism. *Journal of Applied Behavior Analysis, 16,* 129–138.

Schwartz, I. S., Garfinkle, A. N., & Bauer, J. (1998). The picture exchange communication system: Communicative outcomes for young children with disabilities. *Topics in Early Childhood Special Education, 18,* 144–159.

Shafer, M. S., Egel, A. L., & Neef, N. A. (1984). Training mildly handicapped peers to facilitate changes in social interaction skills of autistic children. *Journal of Applied Behavior Analysis, 17,* 461–477.

Staub, D., & Hunt, P. (1993). The effects of social interaction training on High School Peer Tutors of Schoolmates with Severe Disabilities. *Exceptional Children, 60,* 41–57.

Stevenson, C. L., Krantz, J. P., & McClannahan, L. E. (2000). Social interaction skills for children with autism: A script-fading procedure for nonreaders. *Behavioral Interventions, 15,* 1–20.

Stokes, T. F., & Bear, D. M. (1977). An implicit technology of generalization. *Journal of Applied Behavior Analysis, 10,* 349–367.

Stokes, T. F., & Osnes, P. G. (1988). The developing applied technology of generalization and maintenance. In R. Horner, G. Dunlap, & R. Koegel (Eds.), *Generalization and maintenance: Life style changes in applied settings* (pp. 5–19). Baltimore: Brookes.

Strain, P. S. (1977). An experimental analysis of peer social initiations on the behavior of withdrawn preschool children: Some training and generalization effects. *Journal of Abnormal Child Psychology, 5,* 445–455.

Strain, P. S., & Kohler, F. W. (1995). Analyzing predictors of daily social skill performance. *Behavior Disorders, 21,* 79–88.

Strain, P. S., & Kohler, F. W. (1999). Peer mediated intervention for young children with autism: A 20-year retrospective. In P. M. Ghezzi, W. L. Williams, & J. E. Carr (Eds.), *Autism: Behavior-analytic perspectives* (pp. 189–211). Reno, NV: Context Press.

Strain, P. S., & Odom, S. L. (1986). Peer social initiations: Effective intervention for social skills development of exceptional children. *Exceptional Children, 52,* 543–552.

Strain, P. S., Shores, R. E., & Timm, M. A. (1977). Effects of peer social initiations on the behavior of withdrawn preschool children. *Journal of Applied Behavior Analysis, 10,* 289–298.

Taylor, B. A. (1999). *Teaching children with autism to make conversational statements about preferred activities: Combining incidental teaching and the systematic fading of audiotaped prompts.* Unpublished manuscript.

Taylor, B. A., & Harris, S. L. (1995). Teaching children with autism to seek information: Acquisition of novel information and generalization of responding. *Journal of Applied Behavior Analysis, 28,* 3–14.

Taylor, B. A., & Holberton, A. (1998). *Teaching two youths with autism to self-monitor their conversational interactions.* Unpublished manuscript.

Taylor, B. A., & Levin, L. (1998). Teaching a student with autism to make verbal initiations: Effects of a "tactile prompt." *Journal of Applied Behavior Analysis, 31,* 651–654.

Taylor, B. A., Levin, L., & Jasper, S. (1999). Increasing play-related statements in children with autism toward their siblings: Effects of video modeling. *Journal of Developmental and Physical Disabilities, 11,* 253–264.

Zanolli, K., & Daggett, J. (1998). The effects of reinforcement rate on the spontaneous social initiations of socially withdrawn preschoolers. *Journal of Applied Behavior Analysis, 31,* 117–125.

Zanolli, K., Daggett, J., & Adams, T. (1996). Teaching preschool age autistic children to make spontaneous initiations to peers using priming. *Journal of Autism and Developmental Disorders, 26,* 407–422.

8

♦ ♦ ♦ ♦ ♦ ♦ ♦ ♦ ♦ ♦ ♦ ♦ ♦ ♦ ♦ ♦ ♦ ♦ ♦ ♦

Teaching Programs To Increase Peer Interaction

Bridget A. Taylor and Suzanne Jasper

The programs outlined in this chapter have been found (through research and experience) to improve the social behavior of children with autism and increase positive interactions between children with autism and their peers. Some are specific skills to increase the social competence of the child with autism (e.g., Imitates Peer's Verbalizations), whereas others are activities that lead to reciprocal social interaction (e.g., Initiates Topic for Conversation). Several of the programs recommend specific prompting procedures. These procedures are discussed in the previous chapter. When choosing programs, it is important to individualize the prompting and reinforcement procedures for the responses of the child with autism and the peer. Each program listed in Table 8.1 is outlined in detail in the form of a program sheet. In the program sheets, the child with autism is referred to as "the child"; the peer who interacts is referred to as "the peer."

Authors' Note: Some of the programs listed in this chapter were developed at the Alpine Learning Group. The authors are grateful to the teaching staff and administration of Alpine for allowing us to share some of their creative ideas.

Table 8.1
Program List

Beginning Programs

1. Looks at peer when instructed by adult
2. Establishes eye contact when name is called by peer
3. Reciprocates greetings
4. Initiates greetings
5. Imitates peer's actions
6. Imitates peer's actions when instructed by adult
7. Imitates peer's verbalizations
8. Follows instructions presented by peer
9. Follows instructions to play with peer
10. Takes turn with toy or activity
11. Answers social questions presented by peer
12. Reciprocates social questions
13. Initiates social questions
14. Follows play initiations stated by peer
15. Reciprocates comments about objects
16. Reciprocates social information (Beginning, Intermediate, and Advanced)
17. Makes play initiation statements
18. Shows toy items to peer
19. Requests preferred items
20. Gives items requested by peer
21. Attends to items when requested by peer
22. Plays games with peer

Intermediate Programs

1. Responds to and initiates parting statements
2. Directs play task
3. Follows play-related directions
4. Asks question following reciprocation statement
5. Initiates comments about objects
6. Asks to join play activity
7. Learns new responses by observing peer (verbal)
8. Learns new responses by observing peer (nonverbal)
9. Responds to and reciprocates compliments
10. Responds affirmatively to peer's requests
11. Requests assistance from peer
12. Offers assistance to peer
13. Pretends to be teacher or student
14. Plays pretend games
15. Initiates pretend play with peer
16. Uses assertive language
17. Relates experiences to peer
18. Offers personal information
19. Invites peer to join play activity

Table 8.1 (*Continued*)
Program List

Intermediate Programs (Continued)

20. Delivers messages stated by peer
21. Comments about play activities

Advanced Programs

1. Asks questions to gain information
2. Comments about play behavior of peer
3. Asks permission of peer to play with peer's toys
4. Responds to refusals
5. Responds to peer's gestures
6. Differentiates when to ask question and when to reciprocate information
7. Initiates topic for conversation
8. Demonstrates appropriate nonverbal behavior when listening or speaking to peer
9. Responds to peer's comments about personal states
10. Expresses empathy
11. Offers alternative play activity
12. Acknowledges similarities or differences between self and peer
13. Makes subtle comments to peer's statements
14. Plays guessing game
15. Defends peer
16. Joins conversation
17. Responds to changes in conversational topic
18. Responds to nonverbal cues of listener

Looks at Peer When Instructed by Adult   Beginning Program 1

Procedure
Seat the child and the peer facing one another. Present the instruction, "Look at (peer's name)" (e.g., Jill). Prompt the child to look toward the peer by gesturing (e.g., pointing at peer) or guiding the child (e.g., gently turning the child's face in the direction of the peer). When the response is demonstrated, provide a tangible reinforcer (e.g., an edible or a preferred toy) and praise (e.g., "Good job, you looked at Jill!"). Fade prompts over subsequent teaching trials and differentially reinforce responses demonstrated with the lowest level of prompting. Eventually, reinforce only correct, unprompted responses. Vary the location of the child and the peer across trials (e.g., seat the peer next to the child rather than across from the child). As the child meets criterion on simply looking in the direction of the peer, change the criterion to making eye contact with the peer.

Suggested Prerequisites
Child establishes eye contact with adult when asked, follows simple directions, and responds to gestural and physical prompts.

Prompting Suggestions
Point toward the peer or turn the child toward the peer.

Specific Instructions for Peer
Tell the peer the child is going to practice looking at him or her. Provide social praise and tangible reinforcers to peer for sitting nicely and waiting. Encourage the peer to provide praise and tangible reinforcers when the child looks.

Instruction	Response	Date Introduced	Date Mastered
"Look at ____ (peer's name)"	1. Looks in direction of peer while seated across from peer	_____	_____
	2. Looks in direction of peer with peer seated in various locations	_____	_____
	3. Looks in direction of peer with peer engaged in a variety of activities	_____	_____
	4. Makes eye contact with peer	_____	_____

Helpful Hint: It may be difficult to determine that the child with autism is actually making eye contact with the peer. Role playing the program with the adult can help the peer to discriminate looking from not looking. The peer may have to report if the child actually makes eye contact with him or her. If necessary the peer can be taught to prompt for eye contact by holding a preferred item at eye level when the adult provides the instruction. Have the peer provide the child with a highly preferred toy or food item when the child looks at him or her.

Establishes Eye Contact When Name Is Called by Peer

Beginning Program 2

Procedure
Seat the child and the peer facing one another. Provide prompts (verbal, textual, or auditory) to the peer to state the child's name. When the peer states the child's name, prompt the child to look at the peer (e.g., point to the peer or turn the child toward the peer), or teach the peer to prompt the response (e.g., teach the peer to gently guide the child's face toward him or her or to bring a preferred edible or toy to eye level). When the child demonstrates the response, provide a tangible reinforcer (e.g., an edible) and praise (e.g., "Great, you looked at John!"), or teach the peer to provide reinforcers. Fade prompts over subsequent teaching trials and differentially reinforce responses demonstrated with the lowest level of prompting. Eventually, reinforce only correct, unprompted responses.

Suggested Prerequisites
Child establishes eye contact with adult when instructed, follows simple directions, and looks at peer when instructed by adult.

Prompting Suggestions
Point toward the peer, turn the child toward the peer, have the peer gently guide the child's face toward him or her, or have the peer hold up a desired item at his or her eye level to prompt the child to look.

Specific Instructions for Peer
Tell the peer that the child is going to learn to look at him or her when the peer states the child's name. Role-play the program with the peer before introducing the child with autism, so the peer can discriminate looking correctly (i.e., making eye contact) from looking incorrectly. Provide social praise and tangible reinforcers to the peer when he or she states the child's name. Audiotaped prompts or textual prompts can be used to prompt the peer to say the child's name. Encourage the peer to provide praise and tangible reinforcers when the child looks.

Instruction	Response	Date Introduced	Date Mastered
Peer states child's name	1. Looks at peer	_____	_____
	2. Makes eye contact with peer	_____	_____
	3. Makes eye contact with peer from varied locations	_____	_____
	4. Makes eye contact with peer when engaged in an activity	_____	_____

Helpful Hint: Have the peer provide a highly preferred toy to the child when the child looks at him or her. Once the response is reliable, have the peer ask a question of the child. For example, the peer says, "John" and when John looks, the peer says, "Do you want this toy?"

Reciprocates Greetings Beginning Program 3

Procedure

Provide prompts (verbal, textual, or auditory) to the peer to greet the child (e.g., peer is told to say, "Hi, [child's name]" to the child). When the peer states the greeting, prompt the child to reciprocate the greeting (e.g., provide a model, "Hi, [peer's name]"). When the child demonstrates the response, provide a tangible reinforcer (e.g., an edible) and praise (e.g., "Great, you said hi to Lily!"). Fade prompts over subsequent teaching trials and differentially reinforce responses demonstrated with the lowest level of prompting. Eventually, reinforce only correct, unprompted responses.

Suggested Prerequisites

Child reciprocates greetings with adults, imitates vocal models.

Prompting Suggestions

Use a time delay procedure (see description of procedure in Chapter 7). If the child can read, a textual prompt could be presented for the child to read.

Specific Instructions for Peer

Tell the peer that the child is going to learn to say "Hi" after a greeting. Provide social praise and tangible reinforcers to the peer for greeting the child. Encourage the peer to provide praise and tangible reinforcers when the child says "Hi."

Instruction	Response	Date Introduced	Date Mastered
Peer says, "Hi" or "Hi, ____ (child's name)"	Child states, "Hi" or "Hi, ____ (peer's name)"		
	1. Responds to greeting seated face to face	_____	_____
	2. Responds to greeting when peer approaches child	_____	_____
	3. Responds to greeting when peer enters room	_____	_____
	4. Responds to greeting from various locations around room	_____	_____

Helpful Hint: Encourage eye contact when the child reciprocates the greeting. Once the response is established in one location, change rooms and the location of where the peer presents the greeting. If the child does not speak, waving can be taught instead of a verbal response to the greeting.

Initiates Greetings   **Beginning Program 4**

Procedure
Prompt the child to greet the peer (e.g., provide a model "Hi, [peer's name]"). When the child demonstrates the response, provide a tangible reinforcer (e.g., an edible) and praise (e.g., "Great, you said hi to Amir!"). Fade prompts over subsequent teaching trials and differentially reinforce responses demonstrated with the lowest level of prompting. Eventually, reinforce only correct, unprompted responses.

Suggested Prerequisites
Child reciprocates greetings with peers, imitates vocal models.

Prompting Suggestions
Use a time-delay procedure. If the child can read, a textual prompt could be presented for the child to read.

Specific Instructions for Peer
Tell the peer that the child is going to learn to initiate saying "Hi." Provide social praise and tangible reinforcers to the peer for reciprocating the greeting. Encourage the peer to provide praise and tangible reinforcers when the child greets him or her.

Discriminative Stimulus	Response	Date Introduced	Date Mastered
The presence of peer	Child states, "Hi" or "Hi, ___ (peer's name)"		
	1. Initiates greeting as soon as peer enters room	_____	_____
	2. Initiates greeting when child enters room	_____	_____
	3. Initiates greeting when peer or child is playing with an activity and peer or child approaches activity ·	_____	_____
	4. Initiates greeting when child passes peer in hallway	_____	_____

Helpful Hint: Encourage eye contact when the child initiates the greeting. Once the response is established in one location, change rooms and the location of where the peer presents the greeting. Nonspeaking children can be taught to use an augmentative device to say the greeting (see Attainment Company in Appendix 7A).

Imitates Peer's Actions   **Beginning Program 5**

Procedure
Seat the child and the peer facing one another. Provide prompts (verbal, photographic, or textual) to the peer to demonstrate a gross motor action and to say the verbal instruction, "Do this." Physically prompt the child from behind to imitate the action. When the child demonstrates the response, reinforce the response. Fade prompts over subsequent trials and differentially reinforce responses demonstrated with the lowest level of prompting. Eventually, reinforce only correct, unprompted responses.

Suggested Prerequisites
Child establishes eye contact when name is called by peer, follows simple instructions, and imitates generalized gross motor movements of adult.

Prompting Suggestion
Physically prompt the child to imitate the action.

Specific Instructions for Peer
Tell the peer that the child is going to learn to imitate him or her. Role-play the program with the peer prior to introducing the child with autism. When the peer can accurately demonstrate actions with you, introduce the child with autism. If necessary, prompt the peer to model an action by either whispering in the peer's ear or by providing photographs of the actions for the peer to demonstrate. Once the peer has the general idea, he or she should be encouraged to come up with his own actions in addition to those suggested by the adult.

Instruction	Response	Date Introduced	Date Mastered
"Do this"	Child imitates the movement		
	1. Simple movements (e.g., clapping, touching nose, stomping feet)	_____	_____
	2. Actions with objects (e.g., ringing bell, pushing car)	_____	_____
	3. Gross motor movements out of the chair (e.g., marching, jumping, running)	_____	_____

Helpful Hint: Make the actions with objects play related (e.g., pushing car). Encourage the peer to reinforce the child's imitation of the action. Make this fun by playing "Simon Says."

Imitates Peer's Actions When Instructed by Adult

Beginning Program 6

Procedure

Prompt the peer to engage in an action (e.g., ask the peer to jump on the trampoline). Present the instruction, "Do what ___ (peer's name) is doing." Prompt the child to engage in the same action as the peer (e.g., guide the child to the trampoline to jump with the peer). When the child demonstrates the response, reinforce the response. Fade prompts over subsequent trials and differentially reinforce the response demonstrated with the lowest level of prompting. Eventually, reinforce only correct unprompted responses. Vary actions across each teaching trial.

Suggested Prerequisites

Child imitates adult's actions, follows adult's directions.

Prompting Suggestion

Physically prompt the child to imitate the action.

Specific Instructions for Peer

Tell the peer that the child is going to learn to imitate him or her. Provide social praise to the peer for demonstrating actions for the child. Encourage the peer to provide social praise when the child imitates the action.

Instruction	Response	Date Introduced	Date Mastered
"Do what ___ (peer's name) is doing"	Child does what the peer is doing		
	1. Simple gross motor actions (e.g., clapping, stomping)	_____	_____
	2. Actions with objects (e.g., rolling a ball, pushing a car)	_____	_____
	3. Play-related actions (e.g., completing a puzzle, building with blocks)	_____	_____

Helpful Hint: Make the actions related to fun activities that both children might enjoy.

Imitates Peer's Verbalizations   Beginning Program 7

Procedure
Prompt the peer (e.g., use auditory prompts or whispered instructions into the peer's ear) to model verbalizations for the child to imitate. When the peer states the instruction (e.g., "Say, 'Ball' "), prompt the child to imitate the peer's verbalization. When the child demonstrates the response, reinforce the response. Fade prompts over subsequent trials and differentially reinforce responses demonstrated with the lowest level of prompting. Eventually, reinforce only correct unprompted responses. Vary verbalizations across each teaching trial.

Suggested Prerequisites
Child imitates actions of peers, imitates adult's verbal models.

Prompting Suggestions
Have the peer repeat the model several times. If necessary, model the verbalization for the child after the peer states the verbalization.

Specific Instructions for Peer
Tell the peer that the child is going to learn to say words. Role-play the procedure with the peer before introducing the child with autism. Provide social praise to the peer for asking the child to talk. Encourage the peer to provide social praise when the child imitates the verbalization.

Instruction	Response	Date Introduced	Date Mastered
Peer says, "Say ___ (verbalization)"	Child imitates verbalization		
	1. Simple sounds and words	_____	_____
	2. Simple sentences	_____	_____
	3. More complex sentences	_____	_____

Helpful Hint: Pair the verbalization with a preferred item. For example, have the peer (a) hold up a cookie, and (b) ask the child to say "Cookie." When the child says "Cookie," have the peer provide the cookie to the child.

Follows Instructions Presented by Peer   **Beginning Program 8**

Procedure
Prompt the peer (e.g., use auditory prompts, textual prompts, or whisper instructions into the peer's ear) to provide instructions to the child (e.g., prompt the peer to provide the instruction "Stand up" to the child). Prompt the child to follow the instruction (e.g., physically guide the child from behind to stand up) or teach the peer to prompt the child to respond correctly. When the child demonstrates the response, reinforce the response or teach the peer to reinforce the response. Fade prompts over subsequent trials and differentially reinforce responses demonstrated with the lowest level of prompting. Eventually, reinforce only correct, unprompted responses.

Suggested Prerequisites
Child imitates actions of peers, follows instructions presented by adults.

Prompting Suggestion
Provide physical guidance to the child to follow the instruction.

Specific Instructions for Peer
Tell the peer that he or she is going to help the child with autism follow instructions. Role-play the program with the peer before introducing the child with autism. If the peer can read, the instructions he or she will present to the child with autism can be written, or audiotaped prompts can be provided via Language Master cards (see Appendix 7A). Provide social praise to the peer for helping the child follow directions. Encourage the peer to provide social praise when the child follows the direction.

Instruction	Response	Date Introduced	Date Mastered
Peer says "(Instruction)"	Child follows instruction		
	1. Simple one-step instructions (e.g., "Stand up," "Clap hands")	_____	_____
	2. Simple object-related instructions (e.g., "Get the ball," "Push the truck")	_____	_____
	3. More complex instructions within a play context (e.g., "Get the car and put it on the track")	_____	_____

Helpful Hint: Be sure the child is looking at the peer when the peer provides the instruction. Vary instructions across trials. Quickly move to play-related instructions.

Follows Instructions To Play with Peer   Beginning Program 9

Procedure
Place a variety of activities that both children enjoy around the room. Tell the peer to choose something to play with (e.g., looking at books). Provide the instruction, "Play with ___ (peer's name)" to the child. Prompt the child to go to the activity that the peer is playing and engage in the same activity alongside the peer. When the child demonstrates the response, reinforce the response. Fade prompts over subsequent trials and differentially reinforce responses demonstrated with the lowest level of prompting. Eventually, reinforce only correct, unprompted responses.

Suggested Prerequisite
Child imitates peer's actions when instructed by adult.

Prompting Suggestion
Provide physical guidance to the child to engage in activity alongside the peer.

Specific Instructions for Peer
Tell the peer that the child is going to learn to play with him or her. Allow the peer to choose activities that he or she wants to do.

Instruction.	Response	Date Introduced	Date Mastered
"Play with ___ (peer's name)"	Child goes to where peer is playing and engages in activity alongside peer		
	1. Simple play activities structured at a table	_____	_____
	2. Simple play activities in play area on the floor	_____	_____

Helpful Hint: Provide preferred edibles for engaging in the play activity. Prompt the peer to provide a socially appropriate play comment or a sharing response when the child approaches the peer's activity (e.g., "Here you can play with this"). Choose activities that both peers would like to play with.

Takes Turn with Toy or Activity Beginning Program 10

Procedure
Seat the peer and the child on the floor in a play area. Present them with a toy or an activity. Give one child a turn initially. Following a short period of time (e.g., 30 seconds), prompt the child or the peer to provide a turn to the other (e.g., say, "Kerri [child], it's Tommy's [peer] turn"). Provide physical prompting to the child to hand the toy to the peer. Reinforce the response. Fade prompts over subsequent trials and differentially reinforce responses demonstrated with the lowest level of prompting. Eventually, reinforce only correct, unprompted responses.

Suggested Prerequisites
Child engages in parallel play, follows adult's instructions.

Prompting Suggestions
Physically guide the child to hand the toy to the peer. A timer can be used to help cue both children when their turn is over. Eventually, fade the use of the timer.

Specific Instructions for Peer
Tell the peer that the child with autism is going to learn to share toys. Provide praise to the peer for sharing.

Instruction	Response	Date Introduced	Date Mastered
"It's ____ (peer's name) turn"	Child hands toy to peer		
	1. Engages in turn taking with set group of toy items	_____	_____
	2. Engages in turn taking with variety of toy items	_____	_____
	3. Engages in turn taking when peer asks for turn	_____	_____

Helpful Hint: Let the children take turns choosing activities. Vary toys often. If the child has language, prompt him or her to say "It's your turn" when handing the toy to the peer. Eventually, teach the child to hand the toy to the peer when the peer says "It's my turn" or asks "Can I have a turn?"

Answers Social Questions Presented by Peer   Beginning Program 11

Procedure
Prompt the peer (e.g., use audiotaped prompts, textual prompts, or whispered prompts into the peer's ear) to direct social questions to the child (e.g., prompt the peer to ask the question "What's your name?"). Prompt the child to answer the question (e.g., provide a model of the answer or repeat the question stated by the peer). When the child demonstrates the response, reinforce the response. Fade prompts over subsequent trials and differentially reinforce responses demonstrated with the lowest level of prompting. Eventually, reinforce only correct, unprompted responses.

Suggested Prerequisites
Child follows peer's instructions, answers social questions presented by adult.

Prompting Suggestions
Allow the peer to repeat the questions several times before providing a prompt. If repetitions are required over subsequent trials, use a time-delay procedure to prompt for the response immediately upon presentation of the question.

Specific Instructions for Peer
Tell the peer that the child is going to learn to answer questions. Role-play the program with the peer before introducing the child with autism. If the peer can read, questions can be written for the peer to read to the child, or audiotaped prompts can be provided via Language Master cards (see Appendix 7A). If Language Master cards are used, the peer should wear headphones so the child does not hear the prompt being presented to the peer. Provide social praise to the peer for helping the child answer questions. Encourage the peer to provide social praise to the child for answering questions.

Instruction	Response	Date Introduced	Date Mastered
Peer provides questions to child	Child answers questions		
	1. Simple social questions (e.g., name, age, where do you live)	_____	_____
	2. More complex personal information (e.g., favorite snack, favorite toy)	_____	_____

Helpful Hint: Be sure the child is attending to the peer when the peer asks the question. Prompt the peer to respond by reciprocating relevant information about himself or herself (e.g., After the child answers "What's your name?" the peer states "My name is _____").

Reciprocates Social Questions

Beginning Program 12

Procedure

Prompt the peer (e.g., use audiotaped prompts, textual prompts, or whispered prompts into the peer's ear) to direct social questions to the child (e.g., prompt the peer to ask the question "What's your name?"). Prompt the child to answer the question and to ask the same question of the peer (e.g., "Emily, what's your name?"). The peer should then answer the question. When the child demonstrates the response, reinforce the response. Fade prompts over subsequent trials and differentially reinforce responses demonstrated with the lowest level of prompting. Eventually, reinforce only correct, unprompted responses.

Suggested Prerequisites

Child follows peer's instructions, answers social questions presented by peer.

Prompting Suggestion

Audiotaped prompts can be provided of the correct answer and question.

Specific Instructions for Peer

Tell the peer that the child is going to learn to answer and ask questions. If the peer can read, the questions can be written for the peer, or audiotaped prompts can be provided via Language Master cards (see Appendix 7A). If Language Master prompts are used, the peer should wear headphones so the child does not hear the prompt. Provide social praise to the peer for helping the child answer questions. Encourage the peer to provide social praise to the child for answering questions.

Instruction	Response	Date Introduced	Date Mastered
Peer provides question to child	Child answers question and then asks peer the same question		
	1. Simple social questions (e.g., name, age, where do you live)	_____	_____
	2. More complex personal information (e.g., favorite snack, favorite toy)	_____	_____

Helpful Hint: Be sure the child is attending to the peer when the peer asks the question. If both children can read, write out the questions on cards and make a game out of practicing questions and answers. They can take turns choosing cards to ask questions of each other.

Initiates Social Questions **Beginning Program 13**

Procedure
Seat both children across from each other. Present the instruction, "Ask ___ (peer's name) some questions." Prompt the child (e.g., use textual or audiotaped prompts) to ask a question of the peer (e.g., "How old are you?"). The peer should then answer the question. When the child demonstrates the response, reinforce the response. Fade prompts over subsequent trials and differentially reinforce responses demonstrated with the lowest level of prompting. Eventually, reinforce only correct, unprompted responses.

Suggested Prerequisites
Child follows peer's instructions, answers social questions presented by peer.

Prompting Suggestion
Audiotaped prompts can be provided of the questions that the child is to ask of the peer.

Specific Instructions for Peer
Tell the peer that the child is going to practice asking questions. Provide social praise to the peer for answering the child's questions.

Instruction	Response	Date Introduced	Date Mastered
"Ask ___ (peer's name) some questions"	Child asks questions		
	1. Simple social questions (e.g., name, age, where do you live)	_____	_____
	2. More complex personal information (e.g., favorite snack, favorite toy)	_____	_____

Helpful Hint: Be sure the child is attending to the peer when he or she asks the question. If both children can read, write the questions on cards and make a game out of practicing questions. They can take turns choosing cards to ask questions of each other.

Follows Play Initiations Stated by Peer   **Beginning Program 14**

Procedure

Set up around the room a number of preferred play activities (e.g., cars, puzzles, blocks, trains). Seat the child in a chair and prompt the peer (e.g., model for the peer or provide the peer with instructions) to approach the child and state a play initiation statement (e.g., "Let's play with the blocks"). Prompt the child to say "Okay" (if he or she can speak) and to go with the peer to the play activity and engage in the activity. Following several minutes of playing with the activity, prompt the peer to present another play initiation to the child (e.g., "Let's go play with the trains"). Prompt the child to respond affirmatively (e.g., "Okay") and to go.to the activity. Reinforce the response. Fade prompts over subsequent trials and differentially reinforce responses demonstrated with the lowest level of prompting. Eventually, reinforce only correct, unprompted responses.

Suggested Prerequisites

Child imitates actions of peers, follows instructions presented by peer.

Prompting Suggestions

Have the peer prompt the child by taking the child's hand and leading the child to the activity. Provide a verbal model of the affirmative statement.

Specific Instructions for Peer

Tell the peer that you want him or her to help the child learn to play with a variety of toys. Role-play the program with the peer before introducing the child with autism. Teach the peer to be persistent in prompting the child to go with him or her to the play activity. Provide social praise and tangible reinforcers to the peer for helping the child play. Encourage the peer to provide social praise when the child follows and plays with him or her. Allow the peer to choose the play activities.

Instruction	Response	Date Introduced	Date Mastered
Peer presents play initiation statement	Child states an affirmative response and engages in activity with peer		
	1. Simple initiations (e.g., "Let's jump," "Let's race," "Catch the ball")	_____	_____
	2. More complex initiations (e.g., "Come play with the blocks")	_____	_____
	3. Initiations involving roles (e.g., "Let's play house")	_____	_____

Helpful Hint: Choose activities that both children are likely to enjoy. Nonverbal children can be taught to nod and go with the peer to engage in the activity.

Reciprocates Comments About Objects Beginning Program 15

Procedure
Seat the children on the floor facing each other. Place a box of motivating play items in front of the students. Prompt the peer (e.g., model for the peer or provide direct instruction) to pick a toy out of the box and to state the label or a comment about the item (e.g., "I have a ball"). Prompt the child to pick a toy out of the box and to state a comment that is related to the peer's comment (e.g., "I have a car"). Fade prompts over subsequent trials. Differentially reinforce responses demonstrated with the lowest level of prompting. Eventually, reinforce only correct, unprompted responses. Over teaching opportunities, increase the number of comments for the child to reciprocate about the object (e.g., label, color, attribute).

Suggested Prerequisites
Child reciprocates information to adult, follows instructions from peer.

Prompting Suggestions
Provide physical guidance to choose an object, and a verbal model or audiotaped prompt of the target statements.

Specific Instructions for Peer
Tell the peer that the child is going to learn to talk about objects. Role-play the program with the peer before introducing the child with autism. Provide verbal praise for making comments about the objects. Audiotaped prompts can be used to prompt the peer to say a variety of things about the objects.

Instruction	Response	Date Introduced	Date Mastered
Peer chooses item and states comments about the item	Child chooses item and reciprocates relevant information about the item		
	1. Reciprocates name of item (e.g., "I have a cat")	_____	_____
	2. Reciprocates an attribute about the item (e.g., "This cat is yellow")	_____	_____
	3. Reciprocates an action related to the item (e.g., "The cat is eating")	_____	_____
	4. Reciprocates additional comments (e.g., "The cat says meow")	_____	_____

Helpful Hint: Make sure the child is looking at the peer when the peer talks about his or her object. Prompt the child to hold the item up to display it when talking about his or her object.

Reciprocates Social Information (Beginning, Intermediate, and Advanced)

Beginning Program 16

Procedure

Seat the children on the floor facing each other. Prompt the peer (e.g., use audiotaped or textual prompts) to state a socially relevant statement (e.g., "My name is ___ [peer's name]"). Prompt the child to reciprocate relevant information (e.g., "My name is ___ [child's name]"). Fade prompts over subsequent trials. Differentially reinforce responses demonstrated with the lowest level of prompting. Eventually, reinforce only correct, unprompted responses.

Suggested Prerequisites

Child reciprocates information to adult, follows instructions from peer, reciprocates information about objects.

Prompting Suggestions

Provide verbal models or audiotaped prompts.

Specific Instructions for Peer

Tell the peer that the child is going to learn to talk about himself or herself. Role-play the program with the peer before introducing the child with autism. Audiotaped prompts can be used to prompt the peer to say a variety of things. If audiotaped prompts are used, use headphones so the child does not hear the prompt being presented to the peer. Provide verbal praise for making socially relevant statements.

Instruction	Response	Date Introduced	Date Mastered
Peer makes a social statement	Child reciprocates a socially relevant comment		
	1. Reciprocates basic information (e.g., name, age, address, sibling's name)	_____	_____
	2. Reciprocates intermediate information (e.g., favorite game, what he or she likes to eat)	_____	_____
	3. Reciprocates advanced information (e.g., what he or she likes to do at the park, who is in his or her family, what he or she likes to do on vacation)	_____	_____

Helpful Hint: Make sure the child is looking at the peer when the peer makes the comment and when the child reciprocates.

Makes Play Initiation Statements   **Beginning Program 17**

Procedure

Set up around the room a number of preferred play activities (e.g., cars, puzzles, blocks, trains). Seat the peer in a chair and prompt the child (e.g., use audiotaped prompts or verbal models) to approach the peer and state a play initiation statement (e.g., "Let's play with the blocks"). Prompt the peer to say "Okay" and to go with the child to the play activity and engage in the activity. Following several minutes of playing with the activity, prompt the child to present another play initiation to the peer (e.g., "Let's go play with the trains"). Prompt the peer to respond affirmatively and to go to the activity. Reinforce the response. Fade prompts over subsequent trials and differentially reinforce responses demonstrated with the lowest level of prompting. Eventually, reinforce only correct, unprompted responses.

Suggested Prerequisites

Child imitates actions of peer, follows instructions presented by peer, requests preferred items from peer.

Prompting Suggestions

Use audiotaped prompts of the play initiation statements presented via Language Master cards (see Appendix 7A). Prompt the child to take the peer's hand and lead the peer to the activity.

Specific Instructions for Peer

Tell the peer that you want him or her to help the child learn to initiate play activities with him or her. Role-play with the peer prior to introducing the child with autism. Teach the peer to respond affirmatively to the child's initiation statement. Provide social praise and tangible reinforcers to the peer for playing with the child.

Discriminative Stimulus	Response	Date Introduced	Date Mastered
Presence of peer or photographs of peer and activity	Child asks peer to play		
	1. Simple initiations (e.g., "Let's jump," "Let's race," "Catch the ball")	_____	_____
	2. More complex initiations (e.g., "Come play with the blocks")	_____	_____
	3. Initiations involving roles (e.g., "Let's play house")	_____	_____

Helpful Hint: Choose activities that both children are likely to enjoy. Nonspeaking children can be taught to use an augmentative device to provide the initiation statement. Photographs of activities to initiate can be provided in a book in the form of an initiation schedule. The child can be prompted to point to a picture of an activity, get the activity, bring it to the peer, and state the initiation. These photographic prompts can be faded over time.

Shows Toy Items to Peer   **Beginning Program 18**

Procedure

Place enticing items in a box. Prompt the peer to sit on the floor and to play with some toys. Hand the box of enticing items to the child and provide the instruction, "Talk to your friend about your toys." Prompt the child to take one item from the box, walk over to the peer, and state an introductory comment about the object (e.g., "Look at this funny Slinky!"). Prompt the peer to make a comment about the object (e.g., "It's really long!") and to engage in the activity with the child. Following several minutes of playing with the activity, or until it appears the children are no longer interested in the activity, prompt the child to return to the box to choose another item to show to the peer. Fade prompts over subsequent trials and differentially reinforce responses demonstrated with the lowest level of prompting. Eventually, reinforce only correct, unprompted responses. Over teaching sessions, fade the verbal instruction "Talk to your friend about your toys," and just present the box.

Suggested Prerequisites

Child reciprocates comments about objects, takes turns with activity.

Prompting Suggestion

Use audiotaped prompts of the initiation presented via Language Master cards (see Appendix 7A).

Specific Instructions for Peer

Tell the peer that you want him or her to help the child learn to initiate play activities with him or her. Role-play with the peer prior to introducing the child with autism. Teach the peer to comment about the object when the peer shows him or her the toy. Provide social praise and tangible reinforcers to the peer for playing with the child.

Instruction	Response	Date Introduced	Date Mastered
Hand box of enticing items to child and say, "Talk to your friend about your toys"	Child takes out a toy, approaches peer, shows the item to peer, and states a comment about the object		
	1. Simple introductory comments (e.g., "Look, bubbles!")	_____	_____
	2. More complex introductory comments (e.g., "Want to see my bubbles?")	_____	_____
	3. More sophisticated introductory comments (e.g., "Look at this scary monster. It has big eyes!")	_____	_____

Helpful Hint: Make sure the child displays the item when showing the item to the peer. Choose items that are likely to evoke interest on the part of both peer and child.

Requests Preferred Items   Beginning Program 19

Procedure
Seat the children at a table across from each other or on the floor in a play area. Place a variety of the child's preferred items on the peer's side of the table or near the peer. Have the peer manipulate or hold up one of the child's preferred items and wait for the child to initiate, by reaching, pointing, or naming the item. Prompt the child or teach the peer to prompt the child to ask him or her for the item (e.g., models for the child, "Say, 'Billy, can I have a chip?'"). Once the child makes an appropriate request for the item, prompt the peer to provide the item to the child (e.g., prompt the peer to hand the chip to the child). Fade prompts over subsequent trials. Differentially reinforce responses demonstrated with the lowest level of prompting.

Suggested Prerequisites
Child establishes eye contact, requests items from adults, imitates vocal models.

Prompting Suggestions
Provide verbal models of the request or model for the child how to request an item from the peer.

Specific Instructions for Peer
Tell the peer that the child is going to learn how to ask for things. Role-play the program with the peer before introducing the child with autism. Teach the peer how to manipulate the child's preferred items or to hold the items in view. Teach the peer to wait until the child initiates before he or she gives the item to the peer.

Discriminative Stimulus	Response	Date Introduced	Date Mastered
Peer manipulates preferred item in front of child or holds item in view	Child requests the item (e.g., says to peer, "Can I have the Slinky, please?")		
	1. Requests preferred items while seated at a table across from peer	_____	_____
	2. Requests preferred play-related items while seated on the floor across from peer	_____	_____
	3. Requests preferred items by approaching peer from across the room	_____	_____

Helpful Hint: Have the peer and the child take turns requesting items from one another. Vary items across teaching opportunities to increase interest.

Gives Items Requested by Peer　　　　　　**Beginning Program 20**

Procedure

Seat the child and the peer at a table across from each other or on the floor in a play area. Place a variety of the peer's preferred items on the child's side of the table or near the child. Prompt the peer to ask the child for a preferred item (e.g., "John, can I have a chip?"). Once the peer asks for the item, prompt the child to hand the item to the peer. If the child can speak, prompt the child to state an affirmative statement (e.g., "Okay" or "Sure"). Fade prompts over subsequent trials. Differentially reinforce responses demonstrated with the lowest level of prompting. Eventually, reinforce only correct, unprompted responses.

Suggested Prerequisites

Child establishes eye contact, follows instructions from a peer.

Prompting Suggestions

Provide verbal models of the affirmative statements and physical guidance to hand the item to the peer.

Specific Instructions for Peer

Tell the peer that the child is going to learn how to give things that the peer requests. Over teaching opportunities, teach the peer to provide the prompt to the child.

Instruction	Response	Date Introduced	Date Mastered
Peer asks for a preferred item	Child states an affirmative statement and hands item to peer		
	1. Gives preferred food items while seated at table across from peer	_____	_____
	2. Gives preferred play-related items while seated on the floor	_____	_____
	3. Gives preferred items requested by peer from across the room	_____	_____

Helpful Hint: Have the child and the peer take turns requesting items from each other.

Attends to Items When Requested by Peer   Beginning Program 21

Procedure
Place enticing items on the table and around the room. Prompt the peer (e.g., provide a verbal instruction or model for the peer) to point to one of the items around the room and say, "Look at that ___ (name of item)." Prompt the child to look at the item that the peer pointed to. When the child demonstrates the response, reinforce the response. Fade prompts over subsequent teaching trials and differentially reinforce responses demonstrated with the lowest level of prompting. Eventually, reinforce only correct, unprompted responses.

Suggested Prerequisite
Child follows instructions stated by peer.

Prompting Suggestion
Physically guide the child to look toward the object.

Specific Instructions for Peer
Tell the peer that you want him or her to help the child learn to look at things he or she is talking about. Role-play the program with the peer before introducing the child with autism. Provide tangible reinforcers to the peer for each item he or she points out and for varying the comments made about the item.

Instruction	Response	Date Introduced	Date Mastered
Peer points to an object and says, "Look at the ___ (name of item)"	Child looks in direction of the item		
	1. Looks at indicated items on the table	_____	_____
	2. Looks at indicated items around the room	_____	_____
	3. Looks at indicated items outside	_____	_____

Helpful Hint: Use enticing, motivating items that both children would find of interest. Have children take turns pointing things out to look at. Once the child is reliably looking in the direction of the item, teach the child to make a comment about the item. For example, the peer says, "Look at the tiger!" and points to it. The child then looks and makes a comment about the item (e.g., "That's a big tiger!").

Plays Games with Peer   **Beginning Program 22**

Procedure
Prompt the peer and the child with autism to play age-appropriate games. Fade prompts over teaching opportunities. Differentially reinforce responses demonstrated with the least amount of prompting.

Suggested Prerequisites
Child imitates actions of peers, follows instructions presented by adults, plays with toys.

Prompting Suggestions
Provide verbal prompts and physical guidance to the child to participate in the game.

Specific Instructions for Peer
Tell the peer that he or she is going to help the child learn to play specific games. Role-play the games with the peer before introducing the child with autism. Provide social praise to the peer and the child for playing the games.

Suggested Games	Date Introduced	Date Mastered
1. Simon Says		
2. Follow the leader		
3. Hide and seek		
4. Tag		
5. Board games		
6. Hot potato		
7. Telephone		
8. Hopscotch		
9. Red light/green light		
10. Tug of war		
11. Round the world		
12. Charades		

Helpful Hint: Teach the peer to teach the child with autism how to play the game.

Responds to and Initiates Parting Statements   Intermediate Program 1

Procedure
When the peer is leaving or when the child is finished talking to the peer, prompt the child to make an appropriate parting statement (e.g., provide a verbal model for the child to imitate, such as "Bye, see you later"). Or when the peer makes an appropriate parting statement (e.g., the peer says to the child, "I'm going home now"), prompt the child to respond with an appropriate parting statement (e.g., "See you tomorrow"). Reinforce the response. Fade prompts over subsequent teaching opportunities. Differentially reinforce responses demonstrated with the lowest level of prompting. Eventually, reinforce only correct, unprompted responses.

Suggested Prerequisites
Child reciprocates greetings with peers, imitates vocal models.

Prompting Suggestions
Use a time-delay procedure (see Chapter 7). If the child can read, a textual prompt of the response could be presented.

Specific Instructions for Peer
Tell the peer that the child is going to learn to practice saying "Goodbye." Provide social praise and tangible reinforcers to the peer for initiating parting statements and waiting for the peer to reciprocate the parting statement.

Instruction	Response	Date Introduced	Date Mastered
Peer indicates he or she is leaving	Child states an appropriate parting statement		
	1. States parting statement in response to peer's parting statement	_____	_____
	2. Initiates parting statement when leaving	_____	_____
	3. Initiates parting statement at the end of a play activity	_____	_____
	4. Initiates parting statement at the end of a conversational interaction	_____	_____

Helpful Hint: Teach a variety of parting statements (e.g., "Bye," "See you later," "See you tomorrow," "I had fun today!").

Directs Play Task   Intermediate Program 2

Procedure

Seat the child and the peer facing one another. Place a play task that has component parts (e.g., Mr. Potato Head) on the table between the two children. Present the instruction "Play _____ (name of activity) with _____ (name of peer)." Provide textual prompts, audiotaped prompts, or picture prompts for the child to direct the play behavior of the peer. For example, record directions onto Language Master cards (see Appendix 7A). Each phrase on the card should provide a direction for the child to state to the peer (e.g., "Let's play Mr. Potato Head," "Put his eyes on," "Now put on his nose"). Have the child wear headphones so the peer does not hear the prompt being provided to the child. Stand behind the child and run the card through the machine. The child should repeat the model (e.g., child says to peer, "Put his hat on") and the peer should follow the child's direction (e.g., peer places hat on Mr. Potato Head). When the child repeats the model, provide a tangible reinforcer (e.g., an edible). Fade audiotaped prompts over teaching sessions. Differentially reinforce directions stated with the lowest level of prompting. Eventually, reinforce only correct, unprompted responses.

Suggested Prerequisites

Child requests preferred items from peer, makes play initiation statements.

Prompting Suggestions

Provide audiotaped prompts, textual stimuli, pictorial stimuli (e.g., pictures of the component parts or steps to be stated to the peer), or verbal models.

Specific Instructions for Peer

Tell the peer that the child is going to play with him or her and that the child will practice giving play instructions. Role-play the program with the peer before introducing the child with autism. Provide tangible reinforcers for waiting and responding accurately to the child's instruction. Let the peer choose the play activities.

Discriminative Stimuli	Response	Date Introduced	Date Mastered
The activity, the peer, and the teacher's instruction "Play with _____ (name of activity)"	Child presents instructions to the peer to complete a play task		
	1. Directs simple completion and assembly activities (e.g., Mr. Potato Head, puzzles, buildings)	_____	_____
	2. Directs play involving doll figures (e.g., "Put the girl in the car")	_____	_____
	3. Directs play involving roles (e.g., "Let's play house," "You be the Daddy")	_____	_____

Helpful Hint: Vary play tasks often to avoid boredom. Vary the order of the presentation of directions so the peer does not anticipate the direction that will be coming next.

Follows Play-Related Directions   Intermediate Program 3

Procedure

Seat the child and the peer facing one another. Place a play task that has component parts (e.g., Mr. Potato Head) on the table between the two children. Present the instruction "Play _____ (name of activity) with _____ (name of child)" to the peer. Provide prompts (e.g., audiotaped prompts or pictures) to the peer to provide directions to the child to complete the play task (e.g., peer says to child, "Let's play Mr. Potato Head," "Put his hat on"). Prompt the child to follow the directions presented by the peer (e.g., child places hat on Mr. Potato Head). When the child follows the instruction, provide a tangible reinforcer (e.g., an edible). Fade prompts over subsequent teaching sessions. Differentially reinforce responses demonstrated with the lowest level of prompting. Eventually, reinforce only correct, unprompted responses.

Suggested Prerequisites

Child responds to play initiation statements, follows instructions of peer.

Prompting Suggestion

Physically prompt the child to complete the direction.

Specific Instructions for Peer

Tell the peer that the child is going to play with him or her and that the child will practice following his or her play instructions. Role-play the program with the peer before introducing the child with autism. Give the peer tangible reinforcers for providing the play directions.

Instruction	Response	Date Introduced	Date Mastered
Peer presents directions to the child to complete the play task	Child will follow directions to complete the play task		
	1. Follows directions for simple completion and assembly activities (e.g., Mr. Potato Head, puzzles, buildings)	_____	_____
	2. Follows directions for play involving doll figures (e.g., "Put the girl in the car")	_____	_____
	3. Follows directions for play involving roles (e.g., "Let's play house," "You be the Daddy")	_____	_____

Helpful Hint: Vary play tasks often to avoid boredom. Vary the order of the presentation of directions so the child does not anticipate the direction that will be coming next.

Asks Question Following Reciprocation Statement

Intermediate Program 4

Procedure
Seat the child across from the peer. Prompt the peer (e.g., use textual stimuli, verbal models, or audiotaped prompts) to state a social comment (e.g., "I like playing with dinosaurs"). Prompt the child (e.g., use textual stimuli, verbal models, or audiotaped prompts) to reciprocate the comment and ask a question of the peer (e.g., "I like playing with trains. Do you like trains?"). The peer should be prompted to answer the question. Reinforce the peer's and child's responses. Fade prompts over subsequent teaching trials. Differentially reinforce responses demonstrated with the lowest level of prompting. Eventually, reinforce only correct, unprompted responses. Vary social comments across trials and prompt for a variety of questions (e.g., "I like playing with Legos. Have you ever played with Legos?").

Suggested Prerequisites
Child reciprocates comments about objects, asks social questions, reciprocates social questions.

Prompting Suggestions
Use textual stimuli, or audiotaped or verbal models.

Specific Instructions for Peer
Tell the peer that the child is going to learn to reciprocate information and ask questions. Role-play the program with the peer before introducing the child with autism. Provide tangible reinforcers for providing social comments and answering the questions.

Instruction	Response	Date Introduced	Date Mastered
Peer states a comment (e.g., "I like to eat chips")	Child reciprocates the comment and asks a question (e.g., "I like to eat pretzels. What do you like to eat?")		
	1. Reciprocates and asks about basic interests (e.g., favorite snacks, drinks, toys, movies)	_____	_____
	2. Reciprocates and asks about more complex information (e.g., what peer likes to do at the park, things at peer's school, games peer plays with friends)	_____	_____

Helpful Hint: Assure that child learns a variety of questions to ask after reciprocating.

Initiates Comments About Objects Intermediate Program 5

Procedure
Place enticing items on the table and around the room. Seat the children across from each other. After providing a model (e.g., "Billy, look at that tiger"), prompt the child to point to an item and say, "_____ (peer's name), look at that ___ (name of item)." When the child demonstrates the response, reinforce the response. Prompt the peer to look at the item that the child pointed to and to provide a follow-up comment (e.g., "It's scary"). Fade prompts over subsequent teaching trials and differentially reinforce responses demonstrated with the lowest level of prompting. Eventually, reinforce only correct, unprompted responses.

Suggested Prerequisites
Child reciprocates comments about objects, makes simple play initiation statements.

Prompting Suggestions
Physically guide the child to point at the object, and provide a verbal model, textual prompt, or audiotaped prompt of the comment.

Specific Instructions for Peer
Tell the peer that you want him or her to help the child learn to point to things around the room and talk about what he or she sees. Teach the peer to comment after the child points to the item. Role-play the program with the peer before introducing the child with autism. Provide the peer with social praise and tangible reinforcers for looking at the item that the child is referring to, and for providing a follow-up comment.

Instruction	Response	Date Introduced	Date Mastered
Enticing objects located around the room	Child looks in direction of the item		
	1. Points to and comments about items located on the table	_____	_____
	2. Points to and comments about items located around the room	_____	_____
	3. Points to and comments about items located outside	_____	_____

Helpful Hint: Use enticing items that both children would find of interest. Have children take turns pointing to items and commenting. Once the child is reliably pointing out items and making a comment, teach him or her to make another comment following the peer's comment. For example, the child points to a lion and says, "Look John it's a lion." The peer then says, "It's scary." The child could then be prompted to say another comment (e.g., "It's got a big mane.").

Procedure

Set up the peer with an activity (e.g., prompt the peer to build with blocks). Prompt the child to approach the peer and ask if he or she can also play with the activity (e.g., guide the child over to the blocks and provide a verbal model or audiotaped prompt of the statement, such as "Austin, can I play blocks with you?"). When the child demonstrates the response, provide a tangible reinforcer (e.g., an edible) and praise (e.g., "Good for you, you asked Austin to play!"). The peer should be encouraged to provide an affirmative response ("Okay") and hand the child a toy. Fade prompts over subsequent teaching trials and differentially reinforce responses demonstrated with the lowest level of prompting. Eventually, reinforce only correct, unprompted responses. Allow the children to play with the activity for a period of time and then prompt the peer to play with a different activity so the child can practice asking to join additional activities.

Suggested Prerequisites

Child makes play initiation statements, requests preferred items from peer.

Prompting Suggestions

Physically guide the child to approach the peer and provide a verbal model or auditory prompt of the initiation. Provide photographs of the peer in an activity schedule to cue the child to approach the peer to ask to play.

Specific Instructions for Peer

Tell the peer the child is going to practice asking to join his or her play activities. Role-play the program with the peer before introducing the child with autism. Allow the peer to choose the activities. Provide social praise and tangible reinforcers for making affirmative statements and for including the child.

Discriminative Stimulus	Response	Date Introduced	Date Mastered
Peer playing with enticing activity	Child approaches peer and asks to join play activity (e.g., "Can I play with the cars with you?")		
	1. Asks to join activities that have multiple items to share (e.g., cars, blocks, puzzles)	_____	_____
	2. Asks to join activities that require turn taking with the item (e.g., bubbles, pogo stick, handheld video game)	_____	_____
	3. Asks to join activities that require cooperation to complete the activity (e.g., building a structure, drawing a scene)	_____	_____
	4. Asks to join activities that require role playing (e.g., playing house, playing with figures)	_____	_____

Helpful Hint: Use highly motivating activities to encourage the child's interest. Change activities regularly. Initially, teach the child to respond to the instruction, "Ask _____ (peer's name) if you can play with the _____ (activity)." Eventually, fade the instruction so that the child independently asks to join in playing with an enticing item.

Learns New (Verbal) Responses by Observing Peer

Intermediate Program 7

Procedure
Seat the children in chairs or on the floor in a circle. Present to the child a question whose answer he or she does not know (e.g., ask the child about the peer, "How old is Sara?"). Because the child does not know the answer, he or she should state, "I don't know." After the child states "I don't know," turn to the peer and ask the peer the question (e.g., turn to Sara and say, "How old are you, Sara?"). When Sara answers, reinforce Sara's response ("Wow, you're a big girl!"). Turn to the child and ask the question again (e.g., "How old is Sara?"). The child should say the correct answer (e.g., "She's five years old"). Reinforce the response. If the child does not say the correct answer, re-present the question to the peer and prompt the child to look at the peer when the peer answers. Fade prompts over subsequent teaching opportunities. Differentially reinforce responses demonstrated with the lowest level of prompting. Eventually, reinforce only correct, unprompted responses.

Suggested Prerequisites
Child imitates peer's verbal models, looks at peer when instructed by adult, states "I don't know" to novel questions.

Prompting Suggestions
Guide the child to visually attend to the peer when the question is presented to the peer. Re-present the question to the peer until the child gets the correct response.

Specific Instructions for Peer
Tell the peer the child is going to practice answering questions and learning answers to questions. Provide social praise and tangible reinforcers for answering questions accurately.

Instruction	Response	Date Introduced	Date Mastered
A question whose answer is unknown to the child; peer models answer	Child states "I don't know" to novel question, observes peer answering question correctly, and imitates peer's answer when asked the question again		
	1. Answers novel question correctly, immediately following peer's model	_____	_____
	2. Answers novel question correctly following peer's model and after several known distractor questions are presented	_____	_____
	3. Answers novel questions correctly following peer's model and after several known and novel questions are presented	_____	_____

Helpful Hint: Use questions related to items (e.g., labels of pictures) and social questions related to the peer.

Learns New (Nonverbal) Responses by Observing Peer

Intermediate Program 8

Procedure

Seat the children in chairs or on the floor. Present a direction to the child that he or she cannot perform (e.g., ask the child to get an item whose label is unknown to the child, such as "Go get the spatula") or present a toy that the child cannot operate (e.g., hand the child a portable CD player to operate). The child should ask for clarification or state that he or she does not know how to perform the response (e.g., child says to the adult, "How does this work?"). Following the response, present the direction or the toy to the peer (be sure the peer can perform the response correctly prior to the lesson) so he or she can demonstrate the response for the child. Following the peer's response (e.g., the peer opens the CD player, inserts the disk, and presses play), re-present the direction or toy to the child to try again. The child should perform the response correctly, having observed the peer model the correct response. Reinforce the response. If the child does not perform the response correctly, have the peer model the response again. Fade prompts over subsequent teaching opportunities. Differentially reinforce responses demonstrated with the lowest level of prompting. Eventually, reinforce only correct, unprompted responses.

Suggested Prerequisites

Child imitates peer's responses and follows peer's instructions.

Prompting Suggestions

Guide the child to visually attend to the peer when the peer models the response. Re-present the direction or toy to the peer until the child performs the response correctly.

Specific Instructions for Peer

Tell the peer that he or she is going to help the child learn to play with some new toys and to follow directions. Role-play the program with the peer before introducing the child with autism. Provide social praise and tangible reinforcers for modeling correct responses for the child.

Instruction	Response	Date Introduced	Date Mastered
Present a direction the child cannot follow or a toy the child cannot operate; peer models correct response	Child states that he or she does not know how to perform the response, observes peer demonstrating the response correctly, and imitates peer's response	_____	_____
	1. Performs novel instructions correctly, immediately following peer's model	_____	_____
	2. Performs novel instructions correctly following peer's model and after several known directions are presented	_____	_____
	3. Follows novel instructions correctly following peer's model and after several known and novel instructions are presented	_____	_____

Helpful Hint: Choose fun play-related instructions. Choose enticing toys the child cannot operate.

Responds to and Reciprocates Compliments   Intermediate Program 9

Procedure
Prompt the peer to provide a compliment to the child (e.g., provide a verbal model, textual prompt, or auditory prompt of a contextually relevant compliment for the peer to state to the child, such as "I like your picture"). Prompt the peer to say "Thank you" and to reciprocate a compliment (e.g., "I like yours too") Reinforce the response. Fade prompts over subsequent teaching opportunities. Differentially reinforce responses demonstrated with the lowest level of prompting. Eventually, reinforce only correct, unprompted responses.

Suggested Prerequisites
Child reciprocates greetings with peers, imitates vocal models.

Prompting Suggestions
Use a time-delay procedure. If the child can read, a textual prompt could be presented for the child to read.

Specific Instructions for Peer
Tell the peer that the child is going to learn to practice saying "Thank you" when complimented. Role-play the program with the peer before introducing the child with autism. Teach the child to provide a variety of compliments in a variety of settings. Provide social praise and tangible reinforcers to the peer for providing compliments.

Discriminative Stimulus	Response	Date Introduced	Date Mastered
Peer states a compliment	Child states "Thank you" and reciprocates a compliment		
	1. Responds to compliments related to play activities (e.g., "That's a cool tower!")	_____	_____
	2. Responds to compliments related to gross motor activities (e.g., "You run fast!")	_____	_____
	3. Responds to compliments related to personal belongings (e.g., "I like your hat!")	_____	_____

Helpful Hint: Once the child is responding to compliments, teach him or her to initiate compliments to the peer in similar contexts.

Responds Affirmatively to Peer's Requests   Intermediate Program 10

Procedure
Prompt the peer to ask the child to follow a direction (e.g., "Can you get that block for me?"), or wait until the peer presents a direction naturally during play activities. Prompt the child to state an affirmative statement (e.g., "Okay" or "Sure") prior to following the direction. When the child demonstrates the response, reinforce the response. Fade prompts over subsequent teaching opportunities and differentially reinforce responses demonstrated with the lowest level of prompting. Eventually, reinforce only correct, unprompted responses.

Suggested Prerequisite
Child follows instructions presented by peer.

Prompting Suggestion
Provide a verbal model.

Specific Instructions for Peer
Tell the peer that the child is going to practice following instructions. Encourage the peer to provide play-related directions during play activities. Provide social praise and tangible reinforcers to the peer for asking the child to follow directions.

Instruction	Response	Date Introduced	Date Mastered
Peer asks child to perform an instruction	Child responds affirmatively (e.g., "Okay" or "Sure")		
	1. Child responds affirmatively to directions presented in a structured context	_____	_____
	2. Child responds affirmatively to directions presented in a play context	_____	_____

Helpful Hint: Have the peer present directions that are play related (e.g., "Go get that ball so we can play with it").

Requests Assistance from Peer

Intermediate Program 11

Procedure
Present the child with a toy or activity that requires assistance from the peer (e.g., provide the child with a toy that he or she cannot operate but that the peer can). When the child demonstrates difficulty with the task or asks you for assistance, prompt the child to approach the peer and ask the peer for assistance with the activity. Encourage the peer to respond affirmatively and to provide assistance. When the child demonstrates the response, reinforce the response. Fade prompts over subsequent teaching opportunities and differentially reinforce responses demonstrated with the lowest level of prompting. Eventually, reinforce only correct, unprompted responses.

Suggested Prerequisite
Child requests items from peer.

Prompting Suggestion
Provide verbal model.

Specific Instructions for Peer
Tell the peer that the child is going to practice asking for help. Role-play the program with the peer before introducing the child. Encourage the peer to provide assistance when the child asks. Provide social praise and tangible reinforcers to the peer for providing assistance.

Discriminative Stimulus	Response	Date Introduced	Date Mastered
Child is presented with toy or activity that requires assistance from peer	Child approaches peer and asks for assistance with play-related activities		

Helpful Hint: Present challenging activities that are likely to encourage interest of both children (e.g., a box filled with fun toys that only the peer knows how to open).

Offers Assistance to Peer   Intermediate Program 12

Procedure

Present the peer with a toy or activity that requires assistance from the child (e.g., a toy that the peer cannot operate but that the child can). Prompt the peer to make a statement that indicates that he or she needs help (e.g., prompt the peer to say, "I can't do this" or "How does this work?"). Prompt the child to approach the peer and ask the peer if he or she needs assistance with the activity or offer to help (e.g., the child says, "Can I help you?" or "I'll show you how to do it"). Encourage the peer to respond affirmatively (e.g., peer says, "Okay, thanks"). When the child offers assistance, reinforce the response. Fade prompts over subsequent teaching opportunities and differentially reinforce responses demonstrated with the lowest level of prompting. Eventually, reinforce only correct, unprompted responses.

Suggested Prerequisites

Child follows directions of peer, imitates peer responses, imitates verbal models.

Prompting Suggestions

Provide verbal models and physical guidance to manipulate the activity.

Specific Instructions for Peer

Tell the peer that the child is going to practice offering assistance and helping. Role-play the program with the peer prior to introducing the child with autism. Encourage the peer to request assistance even if he or she does not need it in order to increase the number of teaching opportunities. Provide social praise and tangible reinforcers to the peer for requesting assistance.

Discriminative Stimulus	Response	Date Introduced	Date Mastered
Peer manipulates a toy or item in front of child and presents a statement indicating a need for assistance (e.g., "I can't reach this")	Child offers assistance and assists with the task (e.g., child says, "I'll get it for you," and gets the item)		
	1. Offers assistance when specific statements are made by peer (e.g., "I can't reach this toy")	_____	_____
	2. Offers assistance to general statements made by peer (e.g., "There are so many toys to clean up!")	_____	_____

Helpful Hint: Suggested statements for peer to make: "I don't know how this works," "I can't reach this," "This is too heavy," "I can't fix this."

Pretends To Be Teacher or Student   Intermediate Program 13

Procedure

Set up materials to simulate school (e.g., blackboard, desk, chair). Provide the instruction "Play school." Prompt the child to assume either the role of teacher (e.g., stand in front of the class and present instructions for the peer to follow) or the role of student (e.g., visually attends to peer and follows peer's instructions). Reinforce the responses. Fade prompts over subsequent opportunities. Differentially reinforce responses demonstrated with lowest level of prompting.

Suggested Prerequisites

Child follows instructions presented by peer, presents instructions to peer.

Prompting Suggestion

Provide verbal models.

Specific Instructions for Peer

Tell the peer that the child is going to learn to play school. Role-play with the peer the directions to present to the child. Provide social praise to the peer for providing instructions to the child and for following the child's instructions. Encourage the peer to provide social praise when the child follows instructions.

Instruction	Response	Date Introduced	Date Mastered
Present the instruction "Play school"	Child provides instructions in role of teacher and follows peer's instructions in role of student		
	1. Performs role of teacher	_____	_____
	2. Performs role of student	_____	_____

Helpful Hint: Encourage both children to provide praise to one another for following directions and answering questions correctly.

Plays Pretend Games   Intermediate Program 14

Procedure

Make cards with written stimulus words or photographs of animals, characters, or actions to pretend. Sit in a circle with the children. Place the pile of cards face down on the floor in the middle of the circle. Present the instruction, "Play the pretend game." Prompt the child to (a) pick up a card, (b) read or look at the picture, (c) say to the peer "Guess what I am," and (d) pretend to act out the action or to be the character or animal on the card (e.g., the child looks at a picture of a bird, stands up, and pretends to be a bird). Prompt the peer to guess what the child is pretending (e.g., peer calls out, "You're pretending to be a bird"). After the peer guesses, prompt the peer to pick a card and take a turn pretending. Prompt the child to guess what the peer is pretending. Fade prompts over subsequent teaching opportunities. Differentially reinforce responses demonstrated with the lowest level of prompting. Eventually fade your prompts so that the children are playing the game without your assistance.

Suggested Prerequisites

Child uses gestures, responds to gestures, plays simple games.

Prompting Suggestions

Provide verbal modeling with contingent reinforcement and physical guidance to the child to engage in the pretending response.

Specific Instructions for Peer

Tell the peer that the child is going to learn to pretend. Role-play the program with the peer before introducing the child. Provide social praise to the peer for participating in the game. Encourage the peer to provide social praise when the child guesses correctly.

Instruction	Response	Date Introduced	Date Mastered
Present the material and the instruction "Play the pretend game"	Child chooses card from pile, says "Guess what I am" or "Guess what I am doing," and pretends to perform action or to be animal or character depicted on the card; or child guesses what peer is pretending		
	1. Pretends and guesses simple actions (e.g., drinking, eating, sleeping)	_____	_____
	2. Pretends and guesses animals (e.g., bird, dog, cat)	_____	_____
	3. Pretends and guesses characters or community helpers (e.g., firefighter, doctor, dentist)	_____	_____

Helpful Hint: Encourage both children to provide praise to one another for guessing correctly.

Initiates Pretend Play with Peer   Intermediate Program 15

Procedure

Set up a number of pretend play activities (e.g., play kitchen materials, dress-up materials). Prompt the peer to play with some of the activities. Prompt the child (e.g., use verbal models, audiotaped prompts, textual prompts) to approach the peer and initiate pretend play (e.g., "Let's pretend to play house"). Reinforce the response, and prompt the peer to say "Okay" and to engage in the activity with the child. Prompt the child for additional verbal statements for the designated pretend play activity (e.g., prompt the child to say, "I'll be the mommy"). Reinforce the responses. Fade prompts over subsequent opportunities and differentially reinforce responses demonstrated with the lowest level of prompting.

Suggested Prerequisites

Child plays the pretend game, makes simple play initiations.

Prompting Suggestions

Use verbal models, audiotaped prompts, or textual prompts.

Specific Instructions for Peer

Tell the peer that the child is going to learn how to initiate pretend play. Prompt the peer to respond affirmatively to the child's request. Reinforce affirmative responses and play interactions with social praise.

Discriminative Stimuli	Response	Date Introduced	Date Mastered
Peer present in the play area with representational play materials (e.g., dress-up materials)	Child makes an initiation to engage in pretend play		
	1. Makes simple initiations with specific props (e.g., says, "Let's make a hamburger")	_____	_____
	2. Makes more complex initiations with props (e.g., says, "Let's play house")	_____	_____
	3. Makes initiations that do not necessarily involve specific props (e.g., says, "Let's pretend to drive the car")	_____	_____

Helpful Hint: Choose activities that both children are likely to enjoy. Photographs of activities to initiate can be provided in a book in the form of an initiation schedule. The child can be prompted to point to a picture of the activity, get the activity, bring it to the peer, and state the initiation. These photographic prompts can be faded over time.

Uses Assertive Language
Intermediate Program 16

Procedure
Set the children up with some play activities. Prompt the peer to behave in a manner that would cause the child to use assertive language (e.g., have the peer take one of the child's toys). Prompt the child to make an assertive statement to the peer (e.g., "Hey, that's my toy!"). When the child demonstrates the response, prompt the peer to give the toy back and reinforce the responses of both children. Fade prompts over subsequent teaching opportunities and differentially reinforce responses demonstrated with the lowest level of prompting. Eventually, reinforce only correct, unprompted responses.

Suggested Prerequisite
Child requests items from peer.

Prompting Suggestion
Provide verbal models.

Specific Instructions for Peer
Tell the peer that the child is going to practice being assertive. Be sure the peer understands that they are practicing so as not to encourage provocative behavior on the part of the peer at other times. Role-play the program with the peer before introducing the child. Provide reinforcement when the peer responds appropriately to the child's response (e.g., gives the toy back when asked).

Discriminative Stimuli	Response	Date Introduced	Date Mastered
Peer behaves in a manner that causes child to respond assertively	Child responds with an assertive statement		
1. Peer disrupts play behavior of child (e.g., knocks over child's toys)	Child says, "Don't do that!" or "Hey, stop that!"	_____	_____
2. Peer asks child to do something inappropriate (e.g., "Go stand on the table")	Child says, "No way!"	_____	_____

Helpful Hint: The peer should be encouraged to respond assertively if the child engages in a behavior that would cause the peer to be assertive.

Relates Experiences to Peer Intermediate Program 17

Procedure

Prompt the child to engage in a short-duration activity (e.g., take the child outside and let him or her go down the slide). When the child to returns to the room, prompt him or her to approach the peer and relate what he or she just did (e.g., "Guess what? I just went down the slide!"). Prompt the peer to engage in a follow-up question (e.g., "Was it fun?"). When the child demonstrates a response, reinforce the response. Fade prompts over subsequent trials and differentially reinforce responses demonstrated with the lowest level of prompting. Eventually, reinforce only correct, unprompted responses. Vary experiences across trials.

Suggested Prerequisites

Child makes play initiations, answers questions directed by peer.

Prompting Suggestions

Use audiotaped prompts. Prompt the child to engage in the activity, return to the playroom, run a Language Master card containing the audiotaped prompt through the machine, and approach the peer to state the experience. Fade the audiotaped prompts across teaching opportunities.

Specific Instructions for Peer

Tell the peer that the child is going to learn to tell him or her about activities. Role-play the program with the peer before introducing the child with autism. Prompt the peer to ask the child a follow-up question or to comment about the activity to the child (e.g., "Going down the slide is fun"). Provide social praise to the peer for responding to the child.

Instruction	Response	Date Introduced	Date Mastered
Child is prompted to engage in an activity	Following activity, child approaches and tells peer what he or she just did		
	1. Relates immediate experiences (e.g., "I just jumped on the trampoline!")	_____	_____
	2. Relates past experiences (e.g., "This morning I went to the park")	_____	_____
	3. Relates past events with increasing delays (e.g., "Yesterday, I went to the circus with my dad")	_____	_____

Helpful Hint: Once the child is relating the experience, teach the child to make follow-up exchanges (e.g., "I went down the slide. It was fun!").

Offers Personal Information   Intermediate Program 18

Procedure
Seat the child and the peer across from one another. Present the instruction, "Tell _____ (peer's name) about yourself." Prompt the child (using audiotaped or textual prompts) to make personal statements about himself or herself (e.g., "My name is ____"). Reinforce the response and prompt the peer to reciprocate the information (e.g., peer says, "My name is ____."). Fade prompts over subsequent teaching opportunities and differentially reinforce responses demonstrated with the lowest level of prompting. Eventually, reinforce only correct, unprompted responses.

Suggested Prerequisite
Child reciprocates social information.

Prompting Suggestions
Use verbal models or audiotaped prompts.

Specific Instructions for Peer
Tell the peer that the child is going to practice talking about himself or herself. Role-play the program with the peer before introducing the child. Provide reinforcement when the peer responds appropriately to the child's response (e.g., reciprocates relevant information).

Instruction	Response	Date Introduced	Date Mastered
"Tell ___ about yourself"	Child makes statements about himself or herself		
	Suggested statements:		
	Name	_____	_____
	Age	_____	_____
	Sibling's name	_____	_____
	Favorite toy	_____	_____
	Favorite food	_____	_____
	Favorite movie	_____	_____
	Activity at park	_____	_____
	Name of school	_____	_____
	Pet's name	_____	_____
	Favorite sport	_____	_____

Helpful Hint: Be sure the child visually attends to the peer when speaking. Once the child is making the statements reliably, teach the child to ask the peer questions related to the peer's response (e.g., if the child says "I love to eat chips" and the peer responds "I love to eat cookies," the child can be taught to ask "What kind of cookies?").

Invites Peer To Join Play Activity   Intermediate Program 19

Procedure
Set the child up with an activity (e.g., prompt the child to build with blocks) and the peer with a different activity. Prompt the child to call to the peer and ask if the peer wants to play with him or her (e.g., provide a verbal model, textual prompt, or audiotaped prompt of "Hey, _____ [peer's name], do you want to play blocks with me?"). When the child demonstrates the response, provide a tangible reinforcer (e.g., an edible) and praise (e.g., "Good for you, you asked Gerome to play!"). The peer should be encouraged to provide an affirmative response (e.g., "Okay") and to join the activity. Fade prompts over subsequent teaching trials and differentially reinforce responses demonstrated with the lowest level of prompting. Eventually, reinforce only unprompted responses.

Suggested Prerequisites
Child makes play initiation statements, requests preferred items from peer.

Prompting Suggestions
Provide verbal models, audiotaped prompts, or textual prompts.

Specific Instructions for Peer
Tell the peer that the child is going to practice asking him or her to join in play activities. Role-play the program with the peer before introducing the child. Provide the peer with social praise and tangible reinforcers for making affirmative statements to the child's request.

Discriminative Stimulus	Response	Date Introduced	Date Mastered
Peer plays with one toy and child plays with another	Child calls to and asks peer to join play activity (e.g., "Hey, Tommy, do you want to play with the cars?")		
	1. Asks peer to join activities that have multiple items to share (e.g., cars, puzzles)	_____	_____
	2. Asks peer to join activities that require taking turns with the item (e.g., blowing bubbles, using a pogo stick, using handheld video game)	_____	_____
	3. Asks peer to join activities that require cooperation to complete (e.g., building a structure, drawing a scene)	_____	_____
	4. Asks peer to join activities that require role playing (e.g., playing house, playing with figures)	_____	_____

Helpful Hint: Use highly motivating activities to encourage interest of both children. Change activities regularly. Initially, teach the child to respond to the instruction, "Ask _____ (peer's name) to play with you."

Delivers Messages Stated by Peer   **Intermediate Program 20**

Procedure
Prompt the peer (e.g., use audiotaped prompts, textual prompts, or whispered prompts into the peer's ear) to state a message to the child that requires transmission to an adult (e.g., prompt the peer to say to the child, "Go ask Ms. Smith if we can play with the cars"). Prompt the child to respond with an affirmative statement (e.g., "Okay"), approach the adult, and deliver the message ("Can we play with the cars?"). When the child demonstrates the response, reinforce the response. Fade prompts over subsequent trials and differentially reinforce responses demonstrated with the lowest level of prompting. Eventually, reinforce only correct, unprompted responses.

Suggested Prerequisites
Child follows peer's instructions, requests items of peer, imitates peer's verbal model.

Prompting Suggestions
Have the peer repeat the message if the child does not get the message correct. If necessary, the adult should provide a verbal model of the message.

Specific Instructions for Peer
Tell the peer that the child is going to learn to deliver messages. Role-play the program with the peer before introducing the child. If the peer can read, the messages can be written for the peer to read to the child, or audiotaped prompts can be provided via Language Master cards (see Appendix 7A). If Language Master cards are used, use headphones so the child does not hear the prompt being presented to the peer. Provide social praise to the peer for asking the child to deliver messages. Encourage the peer to provide social praise to the child for delivering the message (e.g., "Thanks for asking Ms. Smith for me!").

Instruction	Response	Date Introduced	Date Mastered
Peer tells child to say something to an adult (e.g., "Go tell Ms. Smith we want to go outside")	Child delivers messages to adult when asked by peer		
	1. Delivers messages involving requests for desired items (e.g., "Can we play with the trains now?")	_____	_____
	2. Delivers messages involving personal information (e.g., "Ms. Smith, Billy said he's tired")	_____	_____

Helpful Hint: Set up activities that will require the children to ask an adult for items or assistance. The peer can be prompted to ask the child to deliver messages related to the activity (e.g., "Tell Ms. Smith we need some batteries").

Comments About Play Activities   Intermediate Program 21

Procedure

Seat the children on the floor facing each other and present play activities about which the children can make verbal comments (e.g., dollhouse figures with props). Provide the instruction "Play with the _____ (activity)." Prompt the child (use verbal models, audiotaped prompts, video modeling prompts) to comment about the play activity (e.g., prompt the child to put the doll in the car and say, "He's going for a ride"). Provide the peer with a turn to comment (e.g., prompt the peer to manipulate the doll and say, "He is going up the stairs"). Reinforce comments. Fade prompts over subsequent trials. Differentially reinforce responses demonstrated with the lowest level of prompting. Eventually, reinforce only unprompted responses.

Suggested Prerequisite

Child reciprocates comments about objects.

Prompting Suggestions

Use video modeling procedures as discussed in Chapter 7, verbal models, or audiotaped prompts. Initially, teach specific comments related to specific activities and then program for generalization to novel play activities. Teach a variety of comments.

Specific Instructions for Peer

Tell the peer that the child is going to learn to talk about play activities. Role-play the program with the peer before introducing the child. Initially, prompts (e.g., audiotaped prompts) may be needed to cue the peer to comment about the play activities. Provide verbal praise to the peer for making comments and acknowledging the comments made by the child.

Instruction	Response	Date Introduced	Date Mastered
"Play with _____ (activity)"	Child takes turn manipulating toy and makes comment about the toy (e.g., child pushes car and says, "The car is going fast!")		

Helpful Hint: Encourage a variety of comments. Teach both children to respond to one another's comments. Allow the children to choose activities. Change activities often. Suggested activities: dollhouse with props and play figures, color forms, action figures, play kitchen with props, and farm with animals.

Asks Questions To Gain Information   **Advanced Program 1**

Procedure
Prompt the peer (using verbal models, audiotaped prompts, or textual prompts) to present a statement that occasions a question of the child (e.g., peer says, "I went somewhere last night"). Prompt the child (using verbal models, audiotaped prompts, or textual prompts) to ask a relevant question (e.g., "Where did you go?"). Prompt the peer to answer the question (e.g., "I went to the movies."). When the child demonstrates the response, reinforce the response. Fade prompts over subsequent trials and differentially reinforce responses demonstrated with the lowest level of prompting. Eventually, reinforce only correct, unprompted responses.

Suggested Prerequisites
Child reciprocates comments, initiates social questions, and asks a question following social reciprocation.

Prompting Suggestion
Audiotaped prompts can be provided of the questions to ask.

Specific Instructions for Peer
Tell the peer that the child is going to practice asking questions. Role-play the program with the peer before introducing the child with autism. Prompt the peer, using verbal models or audiotaped prompts, to present statements to the child that occasion questions. Provide social praise to the peer for providing the statements to the child.

Discriminative Stimulus	Response	Date Introduced	Date Mastered
Peer presents a statement that occasions a question	Child asks an appropriate question		
1. Verbal statements that evoke "what" questions (e.g., "Guess what?" "Do you know what?" "I have something." "I did something yesterday." "Later, I'm doing something really fun.")	Child asks an appropriate question	_____	_____
2. Verbal statements that evoke "where" questions (e.g., "I went somewhere." "I'm going somewhere fun after school." "On Thursday my Dad is taking me somewhere.")	Child asks an appropriate question	_____	_____
3. Verbal statements that evoke "who" questions (e.g., "Someone is coming over today." "I saw someone at the park." "Someone went with me to the movies.")	Child asks an appropriate question	_____	_____

(continues)

Asks Questions To Gain Information (*Continued*)   Advanced Program 1

Discriminative Stimulus	Response	Date Introduced	Date Mastered
4. Verbal statements that evoke "when" questions (e.g., "I'm going to the beach." "We're going to have pizza." "I'm going to Billy's house.")	Child asks an appropriate question	_____	_____
5. Verbal statements that evoke "why" "or "how come" questions (e.g., "I had to go to the doctor." "I didn't get to go to the park." "We can't play with the cars today.")	Child asks an appropriate question	_____	_____

Helpful Hint: Prompt the peer to come up with statements that actually pertain to the peer's life. Once the peer has the hang of this, he or she should be able to provide statements without adult prompting. Prompt the peer to provide statements that are logically linked to one another (e.g., "I went somewhere." "Where?" "To the park. Someone came with me." "Who?" "My friend Danny. We played lots of fun games." "What games?").

Comments About Play Behavior of Peer   Advanced Program 2

Procedure
Seat the children on the floor facing each other and present a play activity. Initially, prompt the child to sit and observe the peer perform a play-related response (e.g., peer builds a tower). Prompt the child (e.g., use verbal models, audiotaped prompts, or textual prompts) to make a comment about the play behavior of the peer (e.g., "Wow, that's a tall building!"). Prompt the peer to say, "Thanks!" Reinforce comments. Fade prompts over subsequent trials and differentially reinforce responses demonstrated with the lowest level of prompting. Eventually, reinforce only unprompted comments.

Suggested Prerequisites
Child reciprocates comments about objects, and comments about play activities.

Prompting Suggestions
Use verbal models, audiotaped prompts, or textual prompts. Initially, teach comments related to specific responses of the peer and then program for generalization to novel play activities. Teach a variety of comments about each activity simultaneously.

Specific Instructions for Peer
Tell the peer that the child is going to learn to comment about his or her play behavior. Prompt the peer to acknowledge the comment made by the child. Provide verbal praise for acknowledging the comments made by the child.

Discriminative Stimulus	Response	Date Introduced	Date Mastered
Peer performs a play-related response (e.g., jumps on the trampoline)	Child makes a comment about the peer's response (e.g., "Wow, you jump high!")		
	1. Makes comments about peer's play responses when observing peer perform specific play responses (e.g., shooting basket into the net)	_____	_____
	2. Makes comments about peer's play responses while simultaneously playing with the same activity (e.g., both children are building with blocks)	_____	_____

Helpful Hint: Teach a variety of comments about each play response (e.g., if the peer is shooting baskets, you can prompt the child to say, "That was a good shot" or "You almost got that one in").

Asks Permission of Peer To Play with Peer's Toys   Advanced Program 3

Procedure
Place several of the peer's toys around the play area. When the child initiates toward an item (e.g., asks you for an item or takes an item), prompt the child (using verbal models) to ask the peer if he or she can play with the toy (e.g., prompt the child to approach the peer and say, "Can I play with your car?"). Prompt the peer to respond affirmatively and to give the child access to the item. Reinforce the child's response of asking permission from the peer. Fade prompts over subsequent trials and differentially reinforce responses demonstrated with the lowest level of prompting. Eventually, reinforce only correct, unprompted responses.

Suggested Prerequisites
Child requests preferred items from peer, makes play initiation statements.

Prompting Suggestion
Provide verbal models.

Specific Instructions for Peer
Tell the peer that the child is going to learn to ask permission to play with his or her toys. The peer should be asked to bring some of his or her toys to the play session. Initially, prompt the peer to respond affirmatively to all of the child's requests. Reinforce the peer for sharing toys.

Discriminative Stimulus	Response	Date Introduced	Date Mastered
Peer's toys or activities are in view	Child asks peer for permission to play with one of the toys or to engage in one of the activities	_____	_____

Helpful Hint: Have the peer bring toys and activities that the child may be interested in. Once the child is reliably asking permission to play with the peer's toys, teach the child to respond appropriately when the peer does not allow permission to play with a toy (see Responds to Refusals, Advanced Program 4).

Responds to Refusals

Advanced Program 4

Procedure

Prompt the child to ask the peer to play with a particular item (e.g., "Do you want to play with the castle?") (see Makes Play Initiation Statements, Beginning Program 17). When the child states initiations, prompt the peer to make a refusal statement to some of the child's initiations (e.g., "No thanks"). (The peer is told in advance to provide refusal statements every so often, so the child can practice the relevant response.) Prompt the child (using verbal models) to respond appropriately to the refusal statement (e.g., say "Okay, how about the trains?" or say "Okay" and walk away). When the child demonstrates the response, reinforce the response. Fade prompts over subsequent trials and differentially reinforce responses demonstrated with the lowest level of prompting. Eventually, reinforce only correct, unprompted responses.

Suggested Prerequisites

Child follows instructions presented by peer, asks permission to play with peer's toys, makes simple play initiations.

Prompting Suggestion

Provide verbal models.

Specific Instructions for Peer

Tell the peer that the child is going to learn to respond when the peer does not want to play a particular game. Role-play refusal responses with the peer in advance. Explain to the peer that this is only practice, so as not to encourage refusal statements at other times. Prompt the peer to respond affirmatively to some of the initiations and to respond sometimes with a refusal statement. Reinforce the peer for responding appropriately if the child provides an alternative statement (e.g., if the child says "Okay, how about the trains?" the peer should be prompted to say "That's a good idea" and play with the trains).

Discriminative Stimulus	Response	Date Introduced	Date Mastered
Peer presents a refusal statement to the child's initiation (e.g., child says "Do you want to play with the trucks?" and the peer says "No thanks.")	Child responds to the refusal statement (e.g., child says "Okay" and walks away or says "Okay. Do you want to play trains instead?")		
	1. Child acknowledges refusal statement and walks away	_____	_____
	2. Child acknowledges refusal statement and offers an alternative (e.g., "Okay, how about playing with the race car?")	_____	_____
	3. Child acknowledges refusal statements and asks to join play of peer (e.g., "Okay, can I play with the airplanes too?")	_____	_____

Helpful Hint: Peer should be prompted to vary whether he or she refuses to play or agrees to play. To promote generalization of the child's responses, prompt the peer to make a variety of verbal statements to indicate refusal (e.g., "No," "Not now," "No thanks," "Maybe later," "I'm playing with this toy").

Responds to Peer's Gestures Advanced Program 5

Procedure
Have the peer and the child sit across from each other several feet apart. Prompt the peer to present a gesture for the child to follow (e.g., prompt the peer to motion with his or her hand for the child to come over to him or her, without using a verbal direction), or present the child with an instruction that occasions a response from the peer (e.g., tell the child to ask the peer if he or she wants a particular toy; when the peer shakes his or her head "No," the child should return to the adult and report that the peer does not want the toy). When the child follows the gesture (e.g., walks over to peer, or interprets the gesture), reinforce the response. Fade prompts over subsequent trials and differentially reinforce responses demonstrated with the lowest level of prompting. Eventually, reinforce only correct, unprompted responses.

Suggested Prerequisite
Child follows instructions presented by peer.

Prompting Suggestion
Provide physical guidance to the child to follow the instruction.

Specific Instructions for Peer
Tell the peer that the child is going to learn to follow gestures. Role-play with the peer the gestures to present to the child. Provide social praise to the peer for using gestures. Encourage the peer to provide social praise when the child follows the gesture.

Discriminative Stimulus	Response	Date Introduced	Date Mastered
Peer presents a gesture for the child to follow or adult presents direction to occasion a gesture by the peer	Child follows the gesture		
	1. Follows gestures for "Come here" (e.g., hand motion or finger motion)	_____	_____
	2. Follows gesture for "No" (e.g., head shake)	_____	_____
	3. Follows gesture for "Yes" (e.g., head nod)	_____	_____
	4. Follows gesture for "Stop" (e.g., hand held up)	_____	_____
	5. Follows gesture for "I don't know" (e.g., shoulder shrug)	_____	_____
	6. Follows "pointing" gesture (e.g., pointing of index finger toward object)	_____	_____

Helpful Hint: Make a game out of this program. Have the children provide directions to one another using only gestures rather than verbal directions.

Differentiates When To Ask Question and When To Reciprocate Information

Advanced Program 6

Procedure
Prompt the peer (using verbal models, audiotaped prompts, or textual prompts) to present a statement that occasions a question from the child (e.g., peer says, "I went somewhere last night") or to provide a socially relevant comment ("My favorite thing to do at the park is to go down the slide"). Prompt the child (using verbal models, audiotaped prompts, or textual prompts) to ask a relevant question (e.g., "Where did you go?") or to reciprocate with a relevant comment (e.g., "My favorite thing is to go on the monkey bars"). When the child demonstrates the response, reinforce the response. Fade prompts over subsequent trials and differentially reinforce responses demonstrated with the lowest level of prompting. Eventually, reinforce only correct, unprompted responses.

Suggested Prerequisites
Child reciprocates comments, asks questions to gain information.

Prompting Suggestions
Audiotaped prompts of the questions and comments can be presented.

Specific Instructions for Peer
Tell the peer that the child is going to practice asking questions and making verbal comments. Role-play the program with the peer before introducing the child with autism. If necessary, prompt the peer, using verbal models or audiotaped prompts, to present statements or questions to the child. Provide social praise to the peer for providing the statements and questions.

Discriminative Stimulus	Response	Date Introduced	Date Mastered
Peer presents a statement that occasions a question (e.g., "I went somewhere") or a socially relevant comment that occasions a comment (e.g., "I love to eat french fries at McDonald's")	Child asks an appropriate question (e.g., "Where did you go?") or reciprocates a socially relevant comment (e.g., "I love Big Macs")		
	1. Asks appropriate questions	_____	_____
	2. Reciprocates relevant comments	_____	_____

Helpful Hint: Prompt the peer to provide statements that are logically linked to one another (e.g., "I went somewhere." "Where?" "To the park." "I love to go down the slide." "I love to swing." "I saw someone at the park." "Who?" "My friend Billy. Billy is my best friend." "Mark is my best friend.").

■ Initiates Topic for Conversation   Advanced Program 7

Procedure
Present the instruction "Talk to _____ (peer's name) about _____ (topic, e.g., sports)." Prompt the child to approach the peer and to initiate a conversation about the topic (e.g., use textual prompts, audiotaped prompts, or verbal models) (e.g., "Billy, my favorite basketball team is the Knicks"). Prompt the peer to respond with a socially appropriate comment or question (e.g., "Do you like the _____ [another team]?"). When the child demonstrates the response, reinforce the response. Fade prompts over subsequent trials and differentially reinforce responses demonstrated with the lowest level of prompting. Eventually, reinforce only correct, unprompted responses. Over teaching sessions, fade the verbal instruction of the suggested topic to "Talk to _____ (peer's name)."

Suggested Prerequisites
Child reciprocates comments, initiates social comments, offers information.

Prompting Suggestions
Provide audiotaped prompts or written scripts of the initiation statements or written scripts of the conversation content.

Specific Instructions for Peer
Tell the peer that the child is going to practice having a conversation. Prompt the peer, using verbal models or audiotaped prompts, to ask a question or make a comment to the child about what the child stated. Provide social praise to the peer for engaging in the conversation with the child.

Instruction	Response	Date Introduced	Date Mastered
a. "Talk to _____ (peer's name) about _____ (topic)"	Child approaches peer and initiates a topic for a conversation (e.g., "Do you know what? I'm going to Disney World in March")		
b. "Talk to _____ (peer's name)"	1. Makes initiation statement	_____	_____
c. No explicit instruction presented (provide prompt of the initiation statement during play activities)	2. Makes initiation statement and participates in follow-up statements (e.g., "My favorite ride at Disney World is the roller coaster")	_____	_____

Helpful Hint: Prompt the peer to make statements that will serve as models for the child. For example, the peer can use phrases the child may say at another time (e.g., "The roller coaster is the coolest ride!"). Reinforce any spontaneous comments the child makes toward the peer about the topic. Choose topics that the child has an interest in. Over time, require that the children engage in a number of exchanges about the topic. The statements about the topic can be taught separately with an adult before introducing the topic in the conversation program.

Demonstrates Appropriate Nonverbal Behavior When Listening or Speaking to Peer   Advanced Program 8

Procedure
Prompt the peer (using verbal models, textual prompts, or audiotaped prompts) to talk to the child about a topic (e.g., "On Saturday I went to the aquarium. I saw a really big shark!") or prompt the child to engage in a conversation with the peer (see Initiates Topic for Conversation, Advanced Program 7). Prompt the child (using physical guidance or verbal prompts) to engage in appropriate nonverbal responses while listening to or talking to the peer (e.g., the child maintains appropriate physical distance to the peer, stands still, sustains eye contact, and nods head when appropriate). Reinforce the responses with tangible reinforcers (e.g., edibles) and social praise ("Good, you're looking at Brianna when she is talking to you!"). Fade prompts over subsequent trials and differentially reinforce responses demonstrated with the lowest level of prompting. Eventually, reinforce only correct, unprompted responses.

Suggested Prerequisites
Child responds to peer instructions, initiates topics for conversation.

Prompting Suggestions
Provide physical guidance or verbal reminders prior to the conversation (e.g., before the child talks to the peer, tell the child, "Look at _____ [peer's name] when she is talking to you" or "Look at _____ [peer's name] when you talk to her"). For teaching appropriate distance, a marker can be placed on the floor (e.g., a piece of paper) to serve as a prompt for the child to know the appropriate distance to stand in relation to the peer.

Specific Instructions for Peer
Tell the peer that the child is going to learn to stand still and look while talking to him or her. The peer can be taught to stop talking when the child looks away to serve as a prompt for the child to look back at the peer. When the child looks back, the peer should begin talking again. Role-play this procedure with the peer. Teach the peer to reinforce the child's responses of looking and standing still.

Discriminative Stimulus	Response	Date Introduced	Date Mastered
Peer talks to child about a topic or child talks to peer about a topic	Child engages in appropriate nonverbal behavior while listening or talking		
	Responses to teach:		
	1. Makes consistent eye contact	_____	_____
	2. Stands at appropriate distance	_____	_____
	3. Stands still	_____	_____
	4. Nods head at appropriate times	_____	_____
	5. Uses appropriate gestures when talking or keeps hands to his or her side	_____	_____

Helpful Hint: Shape these responses while teaching other programs (e.g., while teaching a child to reciprocate comments about objects, be sure the child is looking at the peer when the peer describes an object).

Responds to Peer's Comments About Personal States

Advanced Program 9

Procedure
Prompt the peer (using verbal models, textual prompts, or audiotaped prompts) to make a contextually relevant comment about himself or herself (e.g., "I'm tired of this game" or "I'm hungry"). Prompt the child (using verbal models) to respond verbally to the peer's comment (e.g., "Okay, let's play with something else" or "Let's ask Mr. Gonzales if we can have a snack"). Reinforce the response. Fade prompts over subsequent trials and differentially reinforce responses demonstrated with the lowest level of prompting. Eventually, reinforce only correct, unprompted responses.

Suggested Prerequisites
Child comments on play behavior of peer, offers information, asks questions of peer.

Prompting Suggestions
Provide verbal models, auditory prompts, or textual prompts.

Specific Instructions for Peer
Tell the peer that the child is going to learn to respond to his or her personal comments. Role-play with the peer the statements he or she should present to the child. Provide social praise to the peer for making the comments. Encourage the peer to respond affirmatively to the child's response (e.g., "Yeah, let's ask Mr. Gonzales for some cookies").

Discriminative Stimulus	Response	Date Introduced	Date Mastered
Peer presents a comment about a personal state (e.g., "I'm thirsty")	Child responds with a socially appropriate solution (e.g., "Let's go get a drink")		
Sample comments for peer to state:	Sample responses for child to state:		
1. "I'm hungry."	"Let's ask for a snack."	_____	_____
2. "I'm thirsty."	"Do you want something to drink?"	_____	_____
3. "This game is boring."	"Let's play with something else."	_____	_____
4. "It's cold in here."	"Do you want a sweater?"	_____	_____
5. "I'm tired of playing this."	"Okay, what should we play with?"	_____	_____

Helpful Hint: Prompt the peer to make contextually relevant comments (e.g., when the peer has had enough of a particular game, prompt the peer to say to the child, "I'm tired of this game.").

Expresses Empathy Advanced Program 10

Procedure

Prompt the peer (using verbal models, textual prompts, or audiotaped prompts) to make a statement or to gesture to indicate an emotional state (e.g., while playing, the peer says "Ouch!" and holds an arm). Prompt the child (using verbal models) to respond verbally to the peer's comment (e.g., child says, "Are you all right?"). Reinforce the response. Fade prompts over subsequent trials and differentially reinforce responses demonstrated with the lowest level of prompting. Eventually, reinforce only correct, unprompted responses.

Suggested Prerequisites

Child comments on play behavior of peer, asks questions of peer.

Prompting Suggestion

Provide verbal models.

Specific Instructions for Peer

Tell the peer that the child is going to learn to respond to his or her statements of emotion. Role-play with the peer the statements he or she should present in specific contexts to the child. Provide social praise to the peer for making the comments. Encourage the peer to respond to the child's response (e.g., "I hurt my arm, but I'll be okay. Thanks.").

Discriminative Stimulus	Response	Date Introduced	Date Mastered
Peer presents a statement and a gesture indicating an emotional state	Child responds with a socially appropriate comment or question to express empathy		
Sample statements for peer to make:	Sample responses for child to make:		
1. Statements or gestures to indicate pain or illness (e.g., "Ouch," "I don't feel good," "I feel sick," holding stomach and groaning)	Responses or questions that indicate empathy (e.g., "Are you okay?" "Does your belly hurt?" "Do you want to go home?" "Do you need a Band-Aid?"), or an offer of a hug or comfort	_____	_____
2. Statements indicating sadness (e.g., peer pretends to cry, peer makes sad face, peer says, "I'm sad")	"Why are you crying?" "It will be okay." "Don't cry." or child offers peer a toy or comfort	_____	_____
3. Statements indicating frustration or disappointment (e.g., blocks fall over: "Oh!"; peer can't get a toy to work: "I can't do this!"; peer loses a game: "Oh shucks!")	"That's okay." "I'll help you." "Better luck next time!"	_____	_____

(continues)

Expresses Empathy (*Continued*)   Advanced Program 10

Discriminative Stimulus	Response	Date Introduced	Date Mastered
4. Statements indicating anger (e.g., another child takes peer's toy: "Oh, I hate it when he takes my toys like that!")	Offers solution (e.g., "Yeah, that's not nice. Here, take this toy.")		

Helpful Hint: Role-play these interactions with the children so they can practice these statements under contrived contexts. Assess if child uses the responses appropriately in real-life situations.

Offers Alternative Play Activity   Advanced Program 11

Procedure

Prompt the child to engage in a preferred play activity. Prompt the peer to approach the child and ask him or her to play a particular game or activity that you have identified as nonpreferred by the child. When the peer makes an initiation to the child to engage in the less preferred activity, if the child indicates a negative response through gesture (e.g., pushes toy away or shakes head no), prompt the child (using verbal models) to make an appropriate refusal statement (e.g., "No thanks") and to state an alternative activity (e.g., "Do you want to play with the race cars instead?"). Reinforce the response. Fade prompts over subsequent teaching opportunities and differentially reinforce responses demonstrated with the lowest level of prompting. Eventually, reinforce only correct, unprompted responses.

Suggested Prerequisites

Child responds to play initiation statements and makes play initiation statements.

Prompting Suggestion

Provide verbal models with contingent reinforcement.

Specific Instructions for Peer

Tell the peer that the child is going to learn to respond appropriately when asked to play a game or activity that he or she does not want to play. Prompt the peer to respond affirmatively to the alternative activity or toy that the child offers. Reinforce the peer for responding appropriately if the child provides an alternative activity.

Discriminative Stimulus	Response	Date Introduced	Date Mastered
Peer invites child to play a particular activity that has been designated as nonpreferred	Child responds with appropriate refusal statement and offers an alternative (e.g., "No thanks. Do you want to play a board game instead?")		
	1. Responds in structured play sessions while seated at a table	_____	_____
	2. Responds in less structured play sessions while playing with toys on the floor	_____	_____

Helpful Hint: Prompt the peer to vary the initiations between the child's preferred and nonpreferred activities, so the child has an opportunity to respond affirmatively to some initiations.

Acknowledges Similarities or Differences
Between Self and Peer

Procedure

Prompt the peer (using verbal models, textual prompts, or audiotaped prompts) to make a statement to the child (e.g., "I have a cat") or provide the peer with an item that the child also has at home (e.g., peer is given a toy to play with that the child has at home). Prompt the child (using verbal models, textual prompts, or auditory prompts) to acknowledge the similarities or differences between the peer and himself or herself (e.g., "I don't have a cat, but I have a dog" or "Hey, I have that toy at home!"). When the child demonstrates the response, reinforce the response. Fade prompts over subsequent trials and differentially reinforce responses demonstrated with the lowest level of prompting. Eventually, reinforce only correct, unprompted responses.

Suggested Prerequisites

Child comments on play behavior of peer, reciprocates comments, asks questions of peer.

Prompting Suggestions

Provide verbal models or audiotaped prompts.

Specifics Instructions for Peer

Tell the peer that the child is going to learn to identify similarities and differences between them. Role-play with the peer the statements he or she should present to the child. Provide social praise to the peer for making the comments. Encourage the peer to respond to the child's response (e.g., "Really, what's your dog's name?").

Discriminative Stimulus	Response	Date Introduced	Date Mastered
Peer presents a statement or shows an item to child	Child responds by acknowledging the similarity or difference between peer and self		
1. Peer presents verbal statements to which child acknowledges similarity (e.g., "My brother's name is Sammy," "I have this toy at my house!" "I love french fries!")	Responds "Really? So is mine." "I do too!" "Me too!" "So do I!"	_____	_____
2. Peer presents verbal statements to which child acknowledges dissimilarity (e.g., "I love pickles")	Responds "I don't! They taste yucky!"	_____	_____
3. Peer has an item to which child acknowledges similarity (e.g., peer is provided with toy that is same as child has at home, peer is provided with clothing item that child has)	Responds "I have that toy at home," "Hey, that looks like my toy!" "I have the same hat!"	_____	_____

Helpful Hint: Identify real similarities and differences between the children and incorporate these into the program.

Makes Age-Appropriate Slang Comments to Peer's Statements

Advanced Program 13

Procedure
Prompt the peer (using verbal models, textual prompts, or audiotaped prompts) to talk to the child about a topic (e.g., "On Saturday I went to the aquarium. I saw a really big shark!"). Prompt the child (using verbal models, textual prompts, or audiotaped prompts) to make age-appropriate slang comments in response to the peer's statements (e.g., "Really?" "Wow!" "That's cool!"). Reinforce the response. Fade prompts over subsequent trials and differentially reinforce responses demonstrated with the lowest level of prompting. Eventually, reinforce only correct, unprompted responses.

Suggested Prerequisites
Child comments on play behavior of peer, reciprocates comments, asks questions of peer.

Prompting Suggestions
Provide verbal models or auditory prompts.

Specific Instructions for Peer
Tell the peer that the child is going to learn to make responses when the peer talks to the child about a topic. Role-play with the peer the statements he or she should present to the child. Provide social praise to the peer for making the comments. Prompt for a variety of conversational statements to be made by the peer.

Discriminative Stimulus	Response	Date Introduced	Date Mastered
Peer talks to the child about a topic (e.g., peer describes a movie)	Child responds by making slang comments to demonstrate attention and interest as the peer is talking (e.g., "Wow!" "That's cool!" "Uh-huh" "Really?" "Oh")	_____	_____

Helpful Hint: The peer should be prompted to describe things that are of interest to both children.

Plays Guessing Game   Advanced Program 14

Procedure
Seat the children across from each other. Place a barrier between the child and the peer so that each cannot see what the other is holding. Provide picture cards to each of them. Present the instruction, "Play the guessing game." Prompt the child to pick up a card and describe the card without naming what the card depicts (e.g., "It's yellow, it's in the sky, and it's hot"). Prompt the peer to guess what picture the child is holding (e.g., peer calls out, "The sun!"). After the peer guesses, prompt the child to acknowledge the peer's response (e.g., "You're right!"). Prompt the peer to take a turn describing a card. Prompt the child to name what the peer is describing. Reinforce the response. Fade prompts over subsequent teaching opportunities and differentially reinforce responses demonstrated with the lowest level of prompting. Eventually, fade prompts so that the children are playing the game without your assistance.

Suggested Prerequisite
Child plays the pretend game.

Prompting Suggestion
Provide verbal models.

Specific Instructions for Peer
Tell the peer that the child is going to learn to describe pictures and to guess what the peer describes. Provide social praise to the peer for participating in the game. Encourage the peer to provide social praise when the child guesses correctly.

Instruction	Response	Date Introduced	Date Mastered
Present the material and the instruction, "Play the guessing game"	Child describes a picture for the peer to guess and guesses item peer is describing		
	1. Describes and guesses simple nouns	_____	_____
	2. Describes and guesses places	_____	_____
	3. Describes and guesses familiar people	_____	_____

Helpful Hint: Encourage both children to provide praise to one another for guessing correctly. Use motivating stimuli that include many attributes for description.

Defends Peer

Advanced Program 15

Procedure

This program requires more than one peer. While the child and a peer are playing, prompt a second peer to disrupt the play (e.g., the "interfering" peer knocks over a tower that was built by the first peer). Prompt the child (using verbal models) to defend the peer (e.g., prompt the child to say, "Hey, that's not nice!"). Reinforce the response and prompt the second peer to apologize (e.g., say, "I'm sorry"). Fade prompts over subsequent teaching opportunities and differentially reinforce responses demonstrated with the lowest level of prompting. Eventually, reinforce only correct, unprompted responses.

Suggested Prerequisite

Child makes empathy statements.

Prompting Suggestion

Provide verbal models with contingent reinforcement.

Specific Instructions for Peer

Tell the peer(s) that the child is going to learn to defend a peer when a second peer does something naughty. Role-play these activities with peers and explain to them that this is only practice. Prompt the peer to provide social praise to the child when he or she defends him or her.

Discriminative Stimulus	Response	Date Introduced	Date Mastered
A second peer disrupts the play of peer and child	Child responds with a statement that defends the peer		
Examples of disruptions:	Examples of responses:		
1. Peer knocks over other peer's toys	1. "Hey, that's not nice!"		
2. Peer takes a toy away from other peer	2. "Hey, that's his. Give it back!"		
3. Peer teases other peer	3. "Stop it! That's not nice!"		

Helpful Hint: Watch for opportunities for the child to defend the peer in play contexts.

Joins Conversation Advanced Program 16

Procedure

Seat two peers facing each other (or, if a second peer is not available, an adult can participate). Prompt the peers to engage in a conversation about a topic (e.g., tell the peers to talk about their favorite movie). As the two peers are talking, prompt the child to sit with the peers and, at an appropriate time, prompt the child to make a statement to join the conversation (e.g., use verbal models, auditory prompts, or textual prompts for the child to say, "I saw that movie too"). When the child demonstrates the response, reinforce the response. Encourage the peers to acknowledge the statement and to include the child in the conversation (e.g., peers say, "You did? What was your favorite part?"). Fade prompts over subsequent opportunities and differentially reinforce responses demonstrated with the lowest level of prompting. Eventually, reinforce only correct, unprompted responses.

Suggested Prerequisites

Child reciprocates comments, initiates social comments, and initiates topics for a conversation.

Prompting Suggestions

Provide verbal models, auditory prompts, or textual prompts.

Specific Instructions for Peer

Tell the peer(s) that the child is going to practice joining a conversation. Prompt the peer(s), using verbal models or auditory prompts, to engage in a conversation about a topic. Role-play the conversation with the peer(s) prior to introducing the child into the conversation. Provide social praise to the peer(s) for acknowledging the child's statement and including him or her in the conversation.

Discriminative Stimulus	Response	Date Introduced	Date Mastered
Two peers or an adult and a peer are engaged in a conversation	Child makes an appropriate statement to join the conversation		

Helpful Hint: Have the peers talk about topics that are of interest to the child so that the child is more likely to join the conversation.

Responds to Changes in Conversational Topic   Advanced Program 17

Procedure
Prompt the peer to engage in a conversation with the child. At variable intervals, prompt the peer (use textual prompts, audiotaped prompts, or verbal instructions) to change the topic of conversation (e.g., both children are talking about sports; at an appropriate moment, prompt the peer to change the subject to gym activities). When the peer changes the subject, prompt the child to change responses according to the new topic. When the child demonstrates the response, reinforce the response. Fade prompts over subsequent trials and differentially reinforce responses demonstrated with the lowest level of prompting. Eventually, reinforce only correct, unprompted responses.

Suggested Prerequisites
Child reciprocates comments, initiates social comments, offers information.

Prompting Suggestion
Provide verbal models.

Specific Instructions for Peer
Tell the peer that the child is going to practice having a conversation. Role-play with the peer ways to change topics. Provide social praise to the peer for engaging in the conversation with the child.

Discriminative Stimulus	Response	Date Introduced	Date Mastered
Peer changes topic of conversation	Child makes verbal comments or asks questions related to new topic		

Helpful Hint: Teach the peer to change topics at appropriate times during the conversation.

Procedure
Tell the child, "Talk to _____ (peer's name) about _____ (topic, e.g., sports)." Prompt the child to approach the peer and to initiate a conversation about the topic (e.g., use textual prompts, audiotaped prompts, or verbal models) (e.g., "Billy, my favorite basketball team is the Knicks"). Prompt the peer to respond with socially appropriate comments or questions (e.g., "Do you like the _____ [another team]?"). During the conversation, prompt the peer to indicate disinterest in the conversation by looking away, talking to someone else, picking up something to look at, looking behind the child, or not responding. When the peer indicates that he or she is no longer interested, the child should be prompted to respond appropriately (e.g., to make an appropriate departing statement such as "Okay, see you later," look in the direction the peer is looking, and ask "What are you looking at?" or make an appropriate verbal response such as "Are you busy?"). When the child demonstrates the response, reinforce the response. Fade prompts over subsequent trials and differentially reinforce responses demonstrated with the lowest level of prompting. Eventually, reinforce only correct, unprompted responses.

Suggested Prerequisites
Child reciprocates comments, initiates social comments, offers information.

Prompting Suggestions
Provide verbal models and physical guidance.

Specific Instructions for Peer
Tell the peer that the child is going to practice having a conversation with the peer and reacting appropriately when the peer indicates loss of interest. Role-play the program with the peer before introducing the child. Be sure to inform the peer that this is only for practice and his or her disinterest should only be demonstrated to help the child learn how to respond. Provide social praise to the peer for engaging in the conversation with the child.

Discriminative Stimuli	Response	Date Introduced	Date Mastered
Peer demonstrates disinterest in the child's conversation	Child makes an appropriate parting statement		
Responses for peer to demonstrate:			
1. Looks away when child is talking	Child looks in direction peer is looking and either comments about what peer is looking at or makes an appropriate parting statement	_____	_____
2. Peer starts talking to someone else	Child either joins their conversation or makes an appropriate parting statement	_____	_____
3. Peer starts manipulating a toy	Child either comments about what peer is playing with or makes a parting statement	_____	_____
4. Peer does not respond	Child asks, "Are you busy?"	_____	_____

Helpful Hint: Have the child practice this with an adult first so that the adult can exaggerate the responses for the child.

9

Notes from the Speech Pathologist's Office

Margery F. Rappaport

Many parents of children with autistic spectrum disorders are highly motivated to improve their children's communication skills. Parents and caregivers routinely ask questions and seek ideas concerning ways to enhance their children's speech and language. This chapter contains questions taken from the speech pathology files of children with autism and pervasive developmental disorders. The questions and answers focus on individuals of all ages who have passed the early, just-emerging levels of language development and who are now speaking in multiword utterances. Although there may be remaining deficiencies in vocabulary and grammar, limitations in the *use of language in social context*—that is, using language with other people—predominate. Four important areas of social or pragmatic language usage should be evaluated:

1. *Communicative acts* may be restricted, so that language is not used for a wide variety of purposes.

2. *Conversational skills* may be limited.

3. There may be difficulty in *adapting to listeners' needs*.

4. There may be an inability to cope with *communication breakdowns*.

I have been guided by two principles in working with families with autistic spectrum disorders. The first principle involves having a respectful attitude toward the individual with autism, who may be exhibiting unusual behaviors such as hand flapping or twirling. The child may be trying to communicate to the best of his or her ability in whatever form that may take. This respect is continually combined with parental action seeking to help the child behave and present himself or herself more and more in the manner of his or her peers. When presented with a stimulating toy, for example, a child may begin to flap his arms. My goal is to replace unusual behaviors with more conventional verbal responses. A parent might gently guide the child's hands down, while modeling an appropriate comment such as "I'm so excited" or "I like this toy," so that the child may learn to express excitement in a more conventional manner.

The second guiding principle is that I view the parent as the child's primary teacher and as my partner in therapy. A speech pathologist can train a parent in communication-enhancing techniques, while the parent conveys expertise regarding his or her individual child to the therapist. The parent is the indispensable bridge carrying over and integrating goals from the therapy sessions into and throughout the child's day. An effective parent pulls it all together. By prompting, reinforcing, and reminding, the parent can fill the need for a high level of consistency in expectation of skills. Common sense would dictate that children will do well when parents work in partnership and open communication with all professionals.

Following are often-asked speech, language, and communication questions. For each question asked, I suggest a strategy or two that may prove helpful for some children. The questions and answers are intended for individuals who have a fair amount of language and are at the intermediate and above stages of language development. If you find a strategy that appears to hold some promise, remember that it will be important to repeat it many times in many different circumstances in order for generalization to take place.

> ▶ Can you describe a good way to speak with children who have language disorders?

By changing the way that you speak to a child with a language disorder, it is sometimes possible to improve the child's level of communicating. I recommend that you try the following ideas.

Minimize a Directive Style of Talking

A directive style of talking involves issuing commands and asking questions. Do as little of this as possible. Constant questions become prompts upon which children become dependent.

They learn to wait for the question before speaking. Although it will not be possible to eliminate questions entirely, reducing the number of questions and adjusting the types of questions can be helpful. For example, children can get by with only one- or two-word responses to the following questions:

ADULT: What's this?

CHILD: A fish.

ADULT: Where are we going?

CHILD: Home.

ADULT: Where are we?

CHILD: New York City.

ADULT: What do we call this?

CHILD: A comb.

Adopt a Facilitative Style

Here are six ways to accomplish a more facilitative style of talking.

1. Use less adult talking; *encourage turn taking* instead. Here is an example of an adult doing too much talking:

ADULT: Nat, I hear something outside. I think I know what it is. It must be Dad's car! I think he's home now. Put your toys away. Come on. Let's go see if it's Dad.

Here is an example of an adult doing less talking and encouraging turn taking.

ADULT: Nat, I hear something (pause).

NAT: I hear it.

ADULT: I wonder what it is (pause).

NAT: I don't know.

ADULT: It might be Dad (pause).

NAT: Oh, Dad's home now.

ADULT: Let's go see (pause).

NAT: Let's go. Let's see Dad.

2. A facilitative style also involves less adult questioning for single-word responses. Instead *ask thought-provoking questions* such as the following:

- How did that happen?
- Why do you think he said that?

- How do you know that . . . ?
- What would happen if . . . ?

These kinds of questions offer practice in thinking and talking, and could be posed throughout the day.

3. *Expand the child's utterances* to help facilitate language, as in these examples:

CHILD: I want a blue one.

ADULT: A blue one *next*.

CHILD: I want a blue one next.

CHILD: I don't have it.

ADULT: I *still* don't have it.

CHILD: I still don't have it.

4. *Speak in shorter sentences*, as appropriate. For example, instead of saying "Please get me the red sweater; maybe it's on the big chair in the living room," try "Please get my red sweater (pause). Look in the living room (pause). It's on the big chair."

5. *Follow your child's leads and interests.* When your child is engrossed in an activity such as playing with the family dog, rather than changing her focus to something *you* would like to talk about, try commenting on what *the child* is doing, as in the following example:

Father enters the room and sees his son playing ball with the dog.

FATHER: Max likes it when you roll the ball. Look!

CHILD: He likes it. Here Max. Get the ball.

6. *Increase your responsiveness* to your child's communicative attempts in order to reward him or her for communicating. Even if you are busy and focused on something else or if your child's message was not completely clear, acknowledge that you heard and that the message was received. You may then go on either to request clarity or to model a better response.

Shift the Communicative Responsibility to the Child

Expect the child to

1. Initiate communication
2. Hold up his or her end of the conversation by

- Being clear
- Maintaining the conversational flow

Parents of children with language disorders often assume the entire burden of the conversation—initiating, interpreting, and maintaining. Parents often interpret what their child meant to say rather than taking the time to go back and encourage linguistic clarity. Although this may be expedient, it is not helpful in the long run. Here is an example of an adult taking all the conversational responsibility:

ADULT: Oh, no. What happened to your new dress?

CHILD: Dirty.

ADULT: You got all dirty. You spilled paint on it. Take it off and we'll clean it.

In the following example, the adult encourages the child to bear more of the communicative responsibility.

ADULT: Oh, no! Look at your new dress.

CHILD: Dirty.

ADULT: I don't understand. Tell me more.

CHILD: It's paint. Spilled paint in school.

ADULT: Oh. That's okay. What could we do?

CHILD: Clean paint.

ADULT: (Pause and look expectant)

CHILD: Clean dress in laundry, Mom.

ADULT: Good idea, honey.

In the second example, the adult took the time to encourage the child to hold up her end of the conversation using the following strategies. The parent

- Signaled lack of understanding

- Requested more information and language

- Encouraged using language to problem solve

- Used waiting as a minimal prompt, which allows the child to figure out for herself that more is needed and specifically *what* is needed

- Reinforced good problem solving

In summary, you may be able to enhance your child's communication skills by restructuring your exchanges using the three main strategies described:

1. Minimize commands and questions

2. Use the more facilitative language style

3. Take the time to encourage your child to hold up his or her end of the conversation

▶ How can I improve my son's language skills when he is not in therapy? I understand that it is important to work on his communication skills throughout the day. I would like some ideas as to how to accomplish this.

It is gratifying to know that you appreciate the importance of working on your child's language skills throughout the day. *It is a mistake to think that experts alone will fix a language disorder in therapy.* There is evidence that early intensive intervention may yield a better outcome, and therefore a significant, ongoing effort is required by the adults in your child's life. You must make a commitment to use the out-of-therapy time advantageously by learning and utilizing language-enhancing strategies. Without this commitment, the rate of improvement and the level of the eventual outcome may be decreased. To effectuate language goals, parents and therapists should work as partners. This will increase the probability of generalization and reinforcement of similar goals. Remember that therapy sessions alone are not enough to accomplish communication goals.

You can do various things to improve your son's language and communication skills throughout his day. I discuss three ideas that you might try.

Look for or Invent Communicative Moments

Communication occurs in the context of interpersonal relationships and daily events or routines, such as doing dishes together or folding laundry. Language learning should be associated with fun. You may set up a daily routine and attempt to invite your child's participation in the routine. The following are examples of activities in which the child can take part:

- Mealtime or meal preparation

- Preparing snacks: making popcorn, brownies, or cupcakes

- Shopping

- Laundry

- Cleanup

- Sports

- Bath time

- Play activities

- Turn-taking games

- Wrapping presents

- Picnic or party preparations

- Pet care: bathing the dog, cleaning the hamster's cage

Use More Facilitative Language Input

Think to yourself, "How can I make this a communicative moment?" Pose questions and statements that will provide opportunities for your child to use language for various pragmatic purposes, such as the following:

- Problem solving
- Predicting
- Explaining
- Comparing
- Contrasting
- Planning
- Discussing feelings
- Joking
- Rationalizing

When, for example, something that you and your child are using breaks, use the opportunity to work on using language *to offer explanations*. Ask "How did that happen?" or "How can we fix it?" Be a great actor and avoid using an academic tone that makes your child think, "Oh, no, Mom's enhancing language skills again!" Instead, act as if you are really stumped and need help.

If you are preparing a salad for dinner, pick up two vegetables and help your child to use language *to compare and contrast* by asking "How are these the same?" "How are these different?" or "Which do you like better? Why?"

As you are watching television or videos together, ask a probing question so that your child can practice using language *to make predictions*. Ask "What will happen next, do you think?" and "What do you think he will say?" You may also use television or videos *to discuss feelings*, as in "How did that make the boy feel? Did you ever feel that way? When?"

As you are assembling something, play dumb and ask "How does this go together?" encouraging the child to use language *to problem solve* while showing you and explaining how to assemble the object. If the child requests something from a high shelf, say that it's too high and you can't reach it, then pause. If the child doesn't say anything to solve the problem, point to a nearby chair and prompt "You can climb on the chair."

As you are packing and preparing for a picnic or a party, encourage using language *to plan*, asking "What will we need?" and "What else should we get?"

In responding to these thought-provoking kinds of questions, your child may experience difficulty in achieving a coherent sentence. Help the child by using the *scaffolding technique*. Scaffolding means supporting a child's language by tossing out an appropriate word or phrase when you realize that the child is stuck or getting confused. Say the word softly, as you listen to the child. Hopefully, the child will use the words and move smoothly through the explanation. Here is an example of a parent using the scaffolding technique.

PARENT: How does this work?

CHILD: Um, some popcorn first and . . .

PARENT: First measure . . .

CHILD: First measure some popcorn and then, um . . .

PARENT: Then pour

CHILD: And then pour it in the machine so, ah . . .

PARENT: Pour it in the machine and then turn on . . .

CHILD: Turn on the switch and it pops.

PARENT: What?

CHILD: And then turn on the switch and it pops.

Note the parent's last question "What?" This is an important part of the scaffolding technique. The parent is pretending not to have heard but in fact is actually providing an opportunity for the child to say the whole sentence again for fluency and without support (without the scaffolding). You can say "What?" or "Hmm?" I think it is better to pretend that you didn't hear than to use the annoying "Say it again, dear."

Keep Child's Current Therapy Goals in Mind

Mastery of a specific therapy goal will take place faster if it is brought into a fun context during the child's day, such as during mealtime or washing the family pet. Parents can serve as a bridge to promote the rapid generalization of the language targets from the sessions into the child's spontaneous daily usage.

Therapy goals that you are trying to generalize may be as specific as, for example, the use of prepositions. The goals may also be broad, such as the pragmatic skills of using language to predict or to relate past events. Some examples of therapy goals follow.

Prepositions. You may work on receptive and expressive prepositions by integrating them into any physical task. When doing the laundry, for example, you can work on understanding prepositions by telling your child "Please get the soap. It is *above* the sink" or "The sweater fell *next to* the washing machine. Would you get it?" or "The bleach is *behind* the door." You can work on expressing prepositions by saying "I don't see the basket. Where is it?" When setting the table for dinner, you may ask "Where should we put the glasses?" "Where do the forks go?" or "Where do the knives go?"

Predictions. Using language to make predictions can be practiced while reading aloud together. After reading a paragraph, you can stop and ask "Now what do you think he will say to her?" "What will they do now?" or "Where should they go after this?"

Storytelling. If your child has been learning how to tell a story in therapy, help him to relate coherently the story of some real-life events that he has experienced, such as a vacation, holiday, family event, or play activity. To narrate effectively, one must organize the following:

- Setting
- Exposition
- Characters
- Events
- Consequences
- Resolution
- Correct grammar
- Vocabulary

Start by prompting the child to use the basic storytelling strategies taught in therapy: exposition, action, and resolution. Say, for example, "Tell me what happened when you rode your bike" or "Tell about your fishing trip with Dad." Here is a sample of a basic storytelling structure:

I. *Exposition/description*
Tell something he was *doing* or tell *where* he was (e.g., "I was riding on my bike" or "We were fishing in the country").

II. *Action*
Tell what *happened*; at first tell only one specific thing (e.g., "I bumped into a log" or "I caught a fish in my net").

III. *Resolution/Conclusion*
Tell the ending (e.g., "So I ran home to Mom" or "But Dad threw it back in the water").

Following are some more ideas for working on telling stories.

1. To make the task concrete, start by using three numbered photos depicting each part of an event, then fade the photos (slowly eliminate each one), and finally fade the numbers too. Discourage nonessential details. Reward the child for making points succinctly, without rambling, in order to hold the listener's attention. Teach conversational openers such as these:

Listen to this.
Do you know what happened to me?
Do you want to hear something?
Hey, guess what happened to me.

When the basics are mastered, add meaningful or interpretative detail such as

- Cohesive language elements (e.g., *and so, but, because, and then*)

- Setting

- Other people

- Feelings

- The weather

2. Use small albums with photographs depicting events in your child's life (e.g., visits to the zoo, the grocery store, the park, or a birthday party) that the child can carry around and use to practice telling stories.

3. You can also practice storytelling and sequencing using the comics section of Sunday newspapers.

In summary, the key to working on language throughout a child's day is to keep asking yourself, "How can I make this a communicative moment?" thereby giving your child as many opportunities as possible to stretch his language skills within the rich, affective context of real-life events and his relationship with you.

▶ How can I get my daughter to initiate more language on her own? She has acquired quite a bit of language which she uses in therapy, but she does not talk very much in real-life situations, unless I draw language out of her by constantly asking questions.

Although thought-provoking questions are useful, constantly asking questions to elicit language is not an ideal approach because it tends to cause prompt dependency. The child learns to wait for the question before talking, rather than self-initiating. Our goal is child-initiated verbal interactions. Try, instead, using the four-way prompt, which can be a productive strategy for encouraging language. The four-way prompt involves using

1. Heightened affect
2. Gesture
3. First-sound prompt
4. Silent signaling

Gradually diminish the prompt by fading each of the four parts as soon as possible. Heightened affect and facial expression, called *affective prompting*, are used to call attention to a person or event that you would like your daughter to talk about. Through appropriate, even exaggerated facial expressions and body language, communicate emotions such as these:

- Delight
- Surprise
- Confusion
- Fear
- Shock
- Sorrow
- Disappointment

Affective prompting serves four important functions:

1. To secure the child's attention

2. To focus awareness on your words

3. To stabilize the message (because spoken words quickly disappear)

4. To reinforce meaning

Affective prompting emphasizes and helps to convey the meaning of the message. You may include an *attention-getting word* such as "Wow!" or a *gesture* such as a point toward the person or thing you want your child to talk about.

If necessary, also prompt the *first sound of the word* that you expect her to say, as in this example:

CHILD: More soup.

PARENT: Gi–

CHILD: Give me more soup, please.

Sound prompts will work only in cases where your child actually knows what word to say, but does not habitually use the word.

Use *silent signaling* to communicate that you are waiting for and expecting your child to say something in response. Silent signaling means that you look at your child expectantly in the following manner:

- Establish eye contact
- Hold lips slightly apart
- Raise eyebrows
- Lean head and body in slightly toward child
- Wait

The following is an example of an exchange in which several strategies were used together to encourage a boy named Teddy to offer comments and questions. Teddy had much more language than he habitually used. Many children with autism, like Teddy, are too passive verbally; that is, they are *capable* of using better language than they *habitually* use. The goal was to get Teddy to use the language that he had. We played with Play-Doh, which he enjoyed very much. To capture a child's attention and motivation, it is crucial to try to find an activity that the child enjoys and not waste your time on materials that are not motivating.

ADULT: We've got Play-Doh today. I want to make a dog (points to child's ball of Play-Doh). I (silent signal) . . .

TEDDY: I want to make a snowman (works silently).

ADULT: Oh (affective prompting in a sad voice). Look (pointing). H– (silent signal) . . .

TEDDY: His arm is broken.

ADULT: Oh. Too bad (affective prompting; shrug gesture as if to say "What can we do?").

TEDDY: I can fix it.

ADULT: Good (point to jar of Play-Doh; silent signal).

TEDDY: Can I have some more Play-Doh?

ADULT: Sure (knock Play-Doh off table). Oops (silent signal).

TEDDY: I'll get it for you.

ADULT: Thank you.

In this example, the strategies used to encourage Teddy to initiate language were:

- Affective prompting
- Gesture
- Initial-sound prompting
- Silent signaling
- Minimal adult talking
- Commenting
- Minimal direct questions
- Choosing a motivating activity

▶ Although we have no trouble understanding what my son is saying, there is something different, even odd, about the sound of his speech. What could be causing this? How can we help him to overcome it?

Your son may sound stilted or artificial when he speaks because of his speech articulation pattern or because of the way in which he uses language.

Speech Articulation Pattern

There may be true articulation errors or there may be inconsistent affectations or peculiarities of pronunciation. Schedule a thorough speech evaluation if you suspect his articulation.

If your son's speech is mechanical or repetitive sounding, it may be helpful to work on pitch, stress, rhythm, or melody. These intonational features are referred to as *vocal prosody*, meaning the emphasis of key words or emotions through the melodic line of a sentence. Prosodic errors might involve the following:

- A lack of rising inflection for questions

- A lack of falling inflection for statements

- Flat, unmodulated intonation

- Use of the same repetitive intonation for every utterance

Even when sentences are correct from every other standpoint, aberrant prosody will mark an individual as sounding different. Much of spoken language is conveyed not only through words, but by the communication features that accompany the words, such as vocal inflection and tone of voice. If I asked "*Open* the door?" I would mean "Oh, you want me to open, not close it?" But, using the same words, if I said "Open the *door*?" I might mean, "Oh, you want me to open the door, not the window?"

In addition to intonation, other paralinguistic features—that is, components of communication that enhance words—include

- Facial expression
- Body posture
- Gesture
- Body orientation
- Eye contact
- Volume (loudness level)

The following is a program for working on vocal prosody.

1. Listen as the child speaks. Note the melodic line or contour of his sentences. You may note a monotonous, singsong, or mechanical sound reflecting problems with emphasis, rhythm, or pitch modulation. He may be speaking out of the expected pitch range—that is, his pitch may be too low or too high—which would also mark him as sounding unusual.

2. Begin by targeting single words. Model a downward inflection and appropriate pitch and ask your son questions to which the response will be the single word "yes." Think of some silly questions to make the work entertaining. This can be fun when you are engaged in another activity such as riding in the car, taking a walk, or preparing dinner. It would go like this:

PARENT: Do you like ice cream?

CHILD: Yes (firm, downward intonation).

PARENT: Do you have a nose?

CHILD: Yes.

PARENT: Is your name David?

CHILD: Yes.

3. For rapid generalization, in addition to reinforcement and praise, you might insert an unrelated question (use your best acting skills and a very casual tone, as if you just thought of it), for example, "Oh, would you like a drink?" See if he uses the lower pitch and downward inflection. Do this several times throughout the program.

4. When he begins using a more natural intonation on "yes" in the program, introduce the *key word concept*, which may also help to achieve generalization. The key word will be a frequently used word that must now be produced with good prosody absolutely every time, all day long. To begin, choose "yes" as your child's first key word. He can tell the whole family to remind him to use his key word the new way. Use a reward system to achieve success; for example, "If I

hear you say 'yes' the new way six times today (spontaneously and unprompted), you get a _____" (previously determine prize or ticket collected toward a specific treat at the end of the week).

5. Once he has mastered saying "yes" the new way, have him practice new single key words using good prosody and pitch. Then, first in drill only, move on to two-word phrases, such as "I'm hungry," and then to sentences, such as "I like your hat." Model the way you expect him to say the phrase or sentence.

6. In spontaneous conversation, soon you will be able to use only a cue, such as "Say it lower" or "Say it better," if he speaks the old way. Interestingly, parents have often reported that their children's speech sounds the most normal, that is, the prosody is best, when their child is angry. For this reason, some families use the cue "Say it like you mean it" or "Say it stronger," which sometimes produces better prosody and pitch.

In addition to having trouble using prosodic features in their own speech, children with significant language disorders often have difficulty in comprehending the meaning expressed by prosodic features in other people's speech. This subtle aspect of verbal comprehension should be evaluated because, as explained, a slight change in tone, emphasis, or inflection, without changing a word in a sentence, can signal radically different meaning. Individuals may have difficulty following conversation, not because they do not understand the vocabulary or grammar, but because they do not understand the meaning carried by the prosodic features.

Another way to work on both expressing and understanding the emotional message of a sentence as expressed by prosodic features is by playing theatrical games in which you and your child express different emotions while counting to 10 or repeating the same simple sentence. If your child can read, write the names of various emotions (e.g., angry, sad, happy, frightened) on index cards. If, for example, your child draws the "angry" card, he will count to 10 or say "It is a nice day" as if he is angry while you try to guess which emotion he is expressing. Then switch roles, choose a different card, and let him guess which emotion you are expressing. It is best to play this game behind some sort of a screen so that one concentrates on what the voice alone is conveying.

Use of Language

It may be the language that your son is using that is causing him to sound different. Some children use *pedantic vocabulary* and sound like little professors. If he is doing this, you may wish to point this out to him and explain why his peers may not like it (makes him sound different; makes him sound as if he is showing off).

Sometimes children who have learned language through therapy, rather than as typical children do, will use *full-sentence responses*, which may cause their language to sound stilted or odd. If asked "What would you like for dinner tonight?" most often one would respond with a single-word or a short reply, not a full sentence (e.g., "Spaghetti" or "Maybe, spaghetti"). A full-sentence response (e.g., "I would like spaghetti for dinner") is usually expected in the case where the speaker wishes to convey special emphasis. If your son often answers in complete sentences, model shorter, more conversational responses. Practice by asking questions and facilitating a short response. The expression "stepping on one's line" is used in the theater to mean not allowing someone to finish their line of dialogue before beginning your own. Step on his line if he starts to give the stilted, whole sentence reply and model the one-word response with a little snap of the head to get his attention and to indicate that the one word is the whole response. Here are two examples of stiff, full-sentence replies, often called *mitigated echolalia*:

ADULT: Do you want a sandwich?

CHILD: I want a sandwich.

ADULT: Do you want to go home?

CHILD: I want to go home.

Here is an example of a parent targeting a more conversational tone by stepping on the child's line.

ADULT: What would you like for dinner?

CHILD: I would like spa–

ADULT: Spaghetti, please!

CHILD: Spaghetti, please.

▶ My daughter often misinterprets what is said to her. She does not get jokes or realize when she is being teased. How can we help her?

An *overly concrete* interpretation of words can elicit the difficulties you have described. The following three areas of comprehension should be evaluated.

Word Meaning

Does your daughter have a narrow understanding of word meaning, functioning as if a word can have only one meaning? A narrow interpretation of words will interfere with daily functioning, sabotaging comprehension of nonliteral uses of language such as colloquial expressions, riddles, jokes, slang, sarcasm, teasing, metaphors, and idioms.

Social problems may develop because the interpretation of jokes and riddles told by peers is dependent upon knowledge of the multiple meanings of words. You may help your daughter to develop a richer, more flexible understanding of

word meanings by purchasing materials for understanding the multiple meanings of words from the semantic language sections of commercial speech–language catalogs, a list of which appears at the end of this chapter.

You may also work on telling and explaining jokes and riddles. In explaining a joke, as with any other task, break it down, explaining that a word can have two meanings, illustrating them, and explaining that word usage is what makes the joke funny. If the joke is "What is black and white and red (read) all over?" explain that the word *red* (*read*) has two meanings (the color and what we did with a newspaper) and that is why the joke is funny. If the riddle is "When is a door a jar?" explain that there are two meanings to *a jar* (*ajar*) and that one first thinks of "a jar" as in "container." The humor is that it is the other, less common meaning (*ajar*) that is being used. On the topic of how to tell a joke, be sure to teach how one introduces the joke into the conversation. One 8-year-old entered my office for the first time and, wanting to make a connection with me, decided to tell a joke about raccoons. When I said, "Hello, Adam," the first thing he said was, "Are there any raccoons in here?" It seemed like an irrelevant question. He needed to work on greetings, such as, "Hello, Margery. How are you?" and then on how to introduce a new topic, "Hey, I know a funny joke. Would you like to hear it?"

Implied Meanings and Inferences

Does your daughter notice implied meanings, using contextual cues to draw inferences? Implied or hidden meanings are often lost on a person who is overly literal. When asked "Do you know the time?" an overly literal person might respond "Yes" instead of giving the time. People who do not infer implied meanings miss unspoken questions. In response to "You are wearing your fish shirt *again*?" a boy named Ivan responded "Yes," unaware of the implied question, "*Why* are you wearing your fish shirt again?"

As previously discussed, parents tend to shoulder the responsibility in discourse with their children by using an overly directive language style. Outside the home, children will be expected to understand language without an inordinate amount of extra cues. I suggest that you shift the burden of interpretation of meaning to your child and offer her practice in inferencing. Here are some ideas to try.

1. You can make statements with implied meanings, then wait and silently signal that something is expected. If necessary, go back and ask the implied question overtly, then repeat the original statement and prompt, as in the following example of Ivan and the fish shirt.

FATHER: You are wearing your fish shirt *again*?

IVAN: Yes.

FATHER: *Why* are you wearing your fish shirt again? (makes the implied question overt)

IVAN: Because it's my favorite.

FATHER: Oh, I see. *(pause)* You are wearing your fish shirt *again* (pause)? Be—

IVAN: Because it's my favorite.

FATHER: I like it too.

2. Minimize use of direct instructions such as "Please shut the door." Instead, pose statements and pause. If necessary, gesture in order to help with inferencing. From minimal statements such as "Sara, the door," using the contextual clue that the door is ajar, one could infer the meaning "You left the door open. Please close it."

3. Target the child's comprehension of and appropriate responses to slang, idioms, and common expressions, such as "What's up?" "What's happening?" and "Chill out." To be accepted by peers, teenagers and middle schoolers need to understand that words can mean the opposite of what they say, such as "a bad hat" might mean a very good hat. Keep a special notebook for identifying and explaining the meaning of these expressions as well as idioms such as the following:

- Taking turns
- Pulling my leg
- Change your mind
- The grass is greener
- Put your foot in your mouth
- On the fence

4. A higher functioning individual should be able to explain the inferences she was able to make using both verbal and contextual cues by answering questions such as "How do you know the girl does not like her sandwich?" or "How do you know that the boy misses his dog?" Pose these questions at any time, but particularly as you read or watch television or videos together. When you are reading a picture book together, for example, you might ask your child "How do you know the girl does not like her sandwich?" Prompt "Because I see that . . ." and then silently point to the parts of the pictures (e.g., a sour facial expression) that illustrate the answers. In another example, you may ask, "How do you know the boy misses his dog?" Prompt "Because he said he feels sad."

Prosodic Features

Is your daughter able to derive meaning from prosodic features and other paralinguistic cues, such as facial expression? As discussed in the earlier question on prosody, overly concrete interpretations also result from difficulty in understanding the significance of prosodic changes. These changes can cause a sentence to mean the opposite of what the words

say. It may be helpful to teach the interpretation of these nonverbal communication signals. Your daughter may be oblivious to, for example, the humor, sarcasm, or teasing that these features signal. For example, "Oh, right!" is an expression that is often used both literally and sarcastically. You may demonstrate the two ways the expression can be said. Ask her what she observes and discuss what is different about each. Point out that when the speaker smiles and uses a flat vocal inflection, the expression is meant literally. If uttered with the mouth in a grimace and an exaggerated vocal inflection, it is probably meant sarcastically.

You can teach your daughter to attend to facial expressions and intonational changes in order to figure out a speaker's intent. Attention to intonational changes and facial expressions will also help her learn how to recognize when she is being teased. Practice strategies for responding to teasing as well. For example, agreeing with the person or a simple "So?" can deflate a teaser when it is repeated after each jibe.

▶ It is difficult for a listener to follow my son as he speaks because he omits vital pieces of information. It is often left up to me to interpret his meaning for others. How can I help him with this?

It may be helpful to teach your son to learn how to *take the listener's perspective or needs* into consideration when he speaks. Listeners require certain background information in order to understand a speaker. If, for example, a speaker used an unidentified name or an unreferenced pronoun, he would not be understood by his listener. If a boy named Sam is mentioned, the speaker must consider whether the listener knows who Sam is. To know what information must be made explicit, an individual must be able to shift from his own perspective to the listener's. Passive speakers tend to depend on others to do the work of interpretation and often do not practice making themselves clear. Because they share the same frame of reference, adults who live with children with language disorders may be in the habit of deciphering their children's meaning, rather than relying upon the words that have actually been said. The following are ideas for working on perspective taking and considering listeners' needs.

1. If your child is using vague language during a conversation, you might feign misunderstanding, even when you do know what he means, so that he has the opportunity to practice being explicit. If an unknown name is mentioned, you might ask, "Do I know Sam?"

2. You can work on perspective taking or listener needs via the Naive Listener technique. A child and another person, perhaps his mother, engage in an activity such as an art project or playing a board game. After a period of time, a

third person enters the room. The child must explain to the new person what he and his mother were doing. If the child is not being clear, the listener should state that he does not understand and the child should try to make himself understood. The parent can assist using modeling, scaffolding (as described in Question 2), or probing questions.

3. Other ways to work on perspective taking include pausing during reading or watching TV and videos together, and posing questions such as "What do you think the boy might say to her?" "How do you think she will answer him?" "How do you think the Dad feels?" These thought-provoking questions will require your child to shift to the character's perspective in his answer.

4. Puppets, flannel board cutouts, or toy figurines may be used to act out stories in which the characters' dialogue will be created. Use dialogue that will communicate what characters are feeling and thinking. Keep it very simple to begin with by using only a few characters and props. At first you might act out the story yourself to give your child the idea of talking about feelings and plans. The first few times, he can imitate your story. After a while give him some new figures and encourage him to make up his own story and dialogue.

5. Barrier Games can be very effective in teaching children to consider listeners' needs. Players give commands and use descriptive language while working on achieving linguistic clarity by taking the listener's perspective. Various materials may be used in Barrier Games. Colorform kits or dollhouse furniture are two examples. Purchase two of the same kits because each player should have the same board and pieces. Each sits on the opposite side of a barrier so that he cannot see the other person's board and must rely only on what is said, not seen. The barrier could be a piece of cardboard or a briefcase. The first player tells the other player which piece to select and where to put it on the board as he places the same piece on his own board. They then compare boards to see if they have both done the same thing and the communication has been successful. When describing a piece to select, the player must consider what the other player needs to know in order to select the correct piece and to place it in the correct location. If there is more than one boy figure, for example, the player may say "Take the tall boy with black hair." Accurate, discriminating clues must be used so that the speaker is very clear and the listener knows which of similar pieces to select. Barrier Games also call for players to make *repairs* when there are *communication breakdowns*.

As mentioned in the beginning of this chapter, difficulty in coping with communication breakdowns is one of the main language problems of children who are functioning at the higher range of the autistic spectrum. It may be useful to start noticing if your child realizes when listeners signal that they do not understand him and whether your child pur-posefully signals other people when *he* does not understand *them*. Breakdowns may occur when language is too vague or complex or when noise or other distractions interfere. Effectively coping with communication breakdowns within a conversation involves three skills.

The first of these skills is *being able to express lack of understanding*, that is, to signal others when a clarification is needed. Individuals with language disorders tend to be passive conversationalists, allowing language that they do not understand to pass them by. This is a significant and common problem. You can see if your child is doing this by purposely using a vocabulary word that you are quite sure he does not understand, to see if he asks for clarification. You might ask him, for example, what *beverage* he would like with his dinner. If he does not ask *"What does beverage mean?"* you can work on teaching him to request repairs. You might also try the following ideas:

- *Whispering strategies*—As you are talking, whisper part of a sentence or say "Tell Harry to . . ." and then say in his ear "whisper whisper whisper." If he looks at you quizzically, teach him to seek a repair by saying "Say that again," "What did you say?" or "I don't understand."

- *Naming unknown objects*—You can teach your child to seek clarification by giving him a pile of objects or small toys whose names he probably does not know, such as *dromedary* or *finial*. Have him drop the objects in a box after you name them. Say, "Put the finial in the box." Help him to request clarification by asking, for instance, "What's a finial?" when he does not recognize the word.

- *Use new vocabulary words*—Give your child a special jar for collecting a nickel a or dime when he asks "What does that word mean?" When the jar is full, he can buy a treat for himself.

The second skill involved in coping with communication breakdowns is *recognizing that a repair has been requested* by one's conversational partner. A speaker must first *notice* that a breakdown has occurred, that is, interpret his partner's distress signals indicating that his listener does not understand him. Many children with language disorders miss this crucial first step. The request for repair may be an overt statement such as "I don't understand what you are saying" or the request may be nonverbal. Children may need practice in tuning into nonverbal cues, such as tone of voice, facial expression, and body language, that signal lack of understanding. If, for example, the listener makes a confused face, the speaker must recognize that some kind of repair strategy is needed. If the listener begins to show signs of boredom by, for instance, looking away or yawning, the child can be taught to be aware of these signals.

The third skill involved in coping with communication breakdowns is *knowing various strategies to repair a communication breakdown* once it has been signaled. The following are some strategies for making repairs:

- Repetition
- Rewording
- Adding more information
- Increased volume
- Improved eye contact
- Corrected body position facing the listener
- Using emphasis
- Abbreviating stories that go on too long

Provide practice in using repair strategies by putting a desired item whose name is unknown to the child out of reach. If he requests the item in a vague manner, use a quizzical expression and tell him, "I don't understand." If he repeats the same statement but does not succeed in repairing the communication breakdown, be more directive by asking for a description of the item. Say, for example, "What else can you tell me? Tell me the color (shape, size)." Next time try just "What else could you say?" or "I need more information" and see if he adds useful information or uses some other repair strategy. He should learn that "Tell me more" or "I need more information" means that he has to say it in some other way. Eventually he should learn to make a repair based solely on his partner's visual or more subtle verbal expression of lack of comprehension, such as "What?" or "Huh?" or just a confused look. A speaker must also reevaluate after each attempt to repair to see if his attempt has been effective and, if not, try a different strategy.

▶ My daughter rambles on and on when she talks. How can I help her come to a specific point? Often when responding to questions or in explaining things, she talks too much and seems to get lost.

Children with language disorders may demonstrate different kinds of *overtalking*. Some children, on an agenda of their own, converse in monologues, ignoring their listeners' signals of boredom, annoyance, or confusion. These children require practice in reading nonverbal signals. Other children overtalk when they have trouble organizing their language. They become entangled in a verbal maze in which they lose both themselves and their listener. Not sure if they have "hit the mark," they keep talking, hoping that some of what they say will be correct. You may be able to help a child with this kind of overtalking by using both top–down and bottom–up approaches.

In a *top–down approach*, the adult uses, along with an appropriate facial expression, a hand signal in a Stop! position, flat palm facing the speaker, indicating that the speaker has gone off the track and gone on too long. This signal should foster a pause for reflection and regrouping. Prompt-ing or scaffolding, as explained earlier in the chapter, may help to get her back on target. In time, the hand signal is faded and, as in typical conversation, the child can be taught to pay attention to and read the listener's facial expression which indicates confusion.

The *bottom–up approach* involves solidifying the child's word-finding skills, knowledge of grammar, and ability to stay on topic. When your daughter overtalks, analyze her errors so that you know what needs to be worked on in order to help her.

1. *Is she word searching?* Circumlocuting all around a word may indicate verbal retrieval problems. You know she "knows" the appropriate word, because you have heard her use it previously in an appropriate context, but she cannot think of it at the moment. Substituting the wrong word may also indicate a retrieval error. Children with verbal retrieval difficulties may have different underlying weaknesses and therefore may respond to different compensatory strategies. Children may find that rhyming words, associative words, or visual cues (picturing the object and its associated environment) will improve their particular verbal retrieval problem.

2. *Is she demonstrating difficulty with a grammatical form?* There may be grammatical knowledge that she needs to learn. You may want to have her range of grammatic and syntactic knowledge formally evaluated.

3. *Does she veer off topic?* Keep refocusing her back to the topic at hand by promoting self-monitoring. Ask her "What were we talking about?" "What did I ask you?" "What did you say?"

Note the types of errors that she makes and try to work on them. As she strengthens her knowledge of the basic tools of language, vocabulary, and grammar, the overtalking may improve as her confidence in her ability to express herself increases.

Your daughter's language may become more specific and concise if you keep presenting opportunities for her to practice higher level language functions while you continue the work on syntax and semantics. As you work on language structure, practice using language to

- Explain
- Predict
- Compare
- Rationalize
- Negotiate
- Problem solve

Interject thought-provoking questions as you play, work, and converse, facilitating the use of these language functions within the goals of specificity and brevity.

Barrier Games, described previously in reference to learning to meet listeners' needs, are also effective in working on overtalking because relevant versus irrelevant information is targeted. If, in a Barrier Game, there is only one couch, for example, and the child describes "the big, blue couch with green flowers on it," you can explain why all the modifiers are unnecessary.

> ► How can I help my son to have a real conversation? He converses by asking one question after another. He will ask a question, receive an answer, and then ask a new, usually unrelated question.

Children with autism, who may have well-developed vocabulary and grammar, often lag behind in their knowledge of the rules of the art of conversation, which are complex and based on one's knowledge of the social world. One is usually not aware that conversation has rules until they are violated, at which point the speaker will sound odd. If, for example, a person was sharing a sad occurrence and his listener abruptly changed the topic or said he had to go now, that could be considered a violation of the conversational rules of topic maintenance or topic termination. It would also indicate a lack of other attributes that make a good conversationalist, such as using empathetic statements. Basic conversational rules include knowledge of

- Initiating a conversation

- Terminating a conversation

- Topic management: initiation, maintenance, shifting, terminating

- Repairing conversational breakdowns

A sophisticated conversationalist, however, using advanced social knowledge, will demonstrate more complex conversational rule knowledge, such as the rules of logic, courtesy, knowing how and when to interrupt a speaker, and so on, which many typical adults find hard to master. Constant question asking has a perseverative, inappropriate quality to it.

Topic Maintenance

As your son habitually changes topics by asking new questions directly after his questions are answered, I would begin by introducing the rule of topic maintenance. A conversational topic, like a tennis ball, is served and then volleyed back and forth before the topic is terminated (the ball is dropped) and a new topic is established. The following are some ways in which you can help your son to maintain conversational topics.

1. Watch conversations together in movies or homemade videos. Point out to your son that one person initiates the topic and then the speakers converse back and forth on the established topic. Use the rewind button to replay the conversations.

2. With a third person, have your child begin a conversation and you whisper appropriate responses into his ear.

3. Print individual sentences on index cards to use as prompts for conversing, as follows.

   - To respond to her partner: "That was funny"

   - To maintain a topic: "That's interesting," "Oh, really?" or "Tell me more about that."

4. It may be helpful to explain the meaning of the word *topic* or *subject* to your child. You may write a specific topic, such as "School" or "Christmas," on a card, or you could show your child a picture of a school or Christmas scene. As you converse, you will then be able to point to the topic card, indicating that he changed the topic. If necessary, say "What were we talking about? Say something about that." The following is an example of an adult redirecting a child to stay on topic as they converse:

ADULT: Let's have a chat. What shall we talk about? (Present two topic choice cards.)

CHILD: Let's talk about movies.

ADULT: Yes, let's talk about movies. The topic is movies.

CHILD: Do you like trains?

ADULT: (Holds up topic card)

CHILD: Oh, movies. I like movies.

ADULT: Me too. Ask me what movies I like.

CHILD: What movies do you like?

ADULT: I like scary movies. I bet you do too.

CHILD: I like funny movies. Do you like elevators?

ADULT: (Points to topic card)

CHILD: Movies. I liked the movie *101 Dalmatians*. Do you like—Did you see *101 Dalmatians*?

ADULT: Good. You stayed on the topic. No, I didn't see that movie. I bet it was good (pause). Can you tell me what it was about?

In this example, the adult keeps redirecting the child back to the topic and also models how the child can maintain the topic using a related question or a comment.

5. A useful prop for working on topic maintenance is a basket of different looking balls, each of which represents a topic. You pass a ball to the other person without dropping it when it is his turn to respond on topic. The idea is to keep *increasing the number of turns* on one topic by passing the same ball back and forth. Picking up a different ball indicates a change of topic.

6. Your child should learn to analyze statements by telling when a topic was changed abruptly and what might have been said. Sometimes kids like calling off-topic statements "off-the-wall" and enjoy pointing them out in this way.

Conventional Opening Statements

As your son only initiates conversations by asking questions, he could benefit from learning conventional opening statements. Although questions, if appropriate, can be good for initiating conversation, he needs to be more flexible, using other strategies as well. Engaging in conversation by *sharing information* is a good strategy, as in, "I had my birthday party yesterday. We went to Sea World." Children also initiate conversation by *showing off things*, asking the peer "Do you want to see what I have?" Caregivers can get a notebook and eavesdrop at the playground, listening for age-appropriate conversational openers that are used in their neighborhood and then practicing them at home with their child.

Shifting Topics and Ending Conversations

Learning expressions to use in order to shift topics smoothly such as "That reminds me . . ." or "Speaking of . . ." is important, as is knowing how to end a conversation. Notice how many "volleys" are made the next time you are coming to the end of a telephone conversation, as opposed to abruptly hanging up, as in this example:

PERSON 1: Well, it sure was good speaking with you.

PERSON 2: Oh, it was good to speak to you too.

PERSON 1: I hope we can get to see each other soon.

PERSON 2: Me too. Maybe we could have lunch next week.

PERSON 1: That would be fun. I'll give you a call.

PERSON 2: Great. Take care.

PERSON 1: You too.

PERSON 2: Bye.

PERSON 1: Bye-bye now.

Although a very young child would not be expected to demonstrate this much finesse, by middle school, this conversational skill has begun to develop. Appropriately initiating conversations, maintaining topics, shifting topics smoothly, and terminating conversations are some of the basic skills used by competent conversationalists.

▶ My daughter often talks to herself. It makes her seem different from her peers. How can we minimize or eliminate this?

Talking to oneself is not uncommon in individuals with autistic spectrum disorders and is referred to variously as delayed echolalia, self-talk, or undirected conversation. Your daughter may be repeating dialogue from a favorite video or book or attempting to regulate her own behavior by repeating to herself instructions that have been given to her such as "everybody clean up now." You may notice that this self-talk increases in new situations or when she shows signs of being anxious. Some strategies for responding to children's self-talking are as follows:

1. Redirect the child to another activity when this behavior occurs.

2. Use the verbal cue "We're not talking about that now" or the visual prompt of a "Shhh" signal, with a finger on the lips. This may also be followed by redirection.

3. Teach that it is important not to talk to oneself when others are around.

4. If self-talking escalates in new and unfamiliar situations, try to prepare the individual for what to expect with words, pictures, objects, or enactment of what will take place.

5. If it appears that your child is trying to regulate her behavior by reminding herself or cuing herself, cue her with "Think it. Don't say it."

6. If self-talk escalates during a listening task, such as circle time at school, she might not be understanding the language. Request the teacher to

   • Lower the language level

   • Increase the visual supports

   • Obtain an aide for the child

   • Send home prep work the night before to preview the topic and language

7. Respond to self-talking by asking "What are you talking about?" If the child learns to respond appropriately, as in "Oh, nothing" or "I'm talking about a Disney movie," the self-talk becomes more acceptable.

As children become more competent language users and more tuned into the world, self-talking may decrease.

> ▶ I have seen other kids look at my son in a strange way when he tells them the same thing two times or more. We would like some ideas to help him to refrain from doing this.

Children who are in the habit of repeating themselves may benefit from the "One time" prompt. Use the verbal cue "One time" with your arm straight out in front and your index finger indicating "one" as an accompanying visual cue. You can easily fade the verbal and leave the visual prompt.

If you suspect that your son repeats things when he does not understand what is being said and does not know how else to respond, teach him to use sentences such as the following:

- I am not sure what you mean.
- I need to think about that.
- I don't understand.
- Can you say that again?

Repeating statements is related to a common problem of perseverating on favorite topics. The facts of a known topic, such as state capitals or train schedules, rarely change, in contrast to social discourse, which is far less predictable and therefore more confusing. When a child is stumped and does not know how to respond, he may switch to a favorite, familiar topic. Various strategies may be tried:

- Redirect to another topic.
- Use the prompt "We're not talking about that now" and redirect.
- Set boundaries by saying "We can talk about trains again after breakfast. I'd like to talk about something else now."
- Ask if he has anything *new* to say on a topic; if not, it is time to stop talking about it.

> ▶ How do you suggest I handle it when my daughter abruptly changes the topic or responds to a question as if I had said something completely different?

Off-topic responding may occur when your daughter

- Does not comprehend what was said to her because of complex grammar, unknown vocabulary, lack of inferencing on her part, or a sentence that is too long for her to process.
- Understands but does not know how to respond.
- Loses attention.
- Prefers to pursue her own agenda.

Sometimes, children misunderstand the intent or meaning of an entire sentence and respond to only one word, often the last word in the sentence. Their irrelevant comments may be merely word associations. If you feel your daughter goes off topic because of a lack of comprehension, as discussed in the previous question, you can teach her to take some control of the conversation by learning to say things such as "I'm confused" or "I don't understand."

It may be hard to determine if your daughter responds off topic because her attention drifts or she prefers to pursue her own agenda. In either case, you will want to promote self-monitoring by asking her to repeat what you just asked her or asking "What did you say when I asked you that?" The nuisance of being asked such questions may help her to stay tuned in or to notice when her responses do not make sense. As described earlier, introduce and explain the notion of *topic* so that you can ask her what the topic was whenever she strays. Ask her what she could say about the topic you were talking about. Once children get the topic idea, they sometimes will tell you, amusingly, that they do not *want* to talk about *your* topic. Then it is time to talk about the rules of conversation.

> ▶ My son is able to speak in sentences, but he will often speak only in single words, naming objects that he sees. On another day, he will do the same thing again with the same objects. What would be more appropriate?

I would suggest that you work on helping your son to express comments and opinions about the things he sees instead of just labeling them. The goal would be to use more social language, that is, sharing his enjoyment of the objects with another person. Instead of "It's a clock," a comment such as "I like your clock" with a nice, social smile and a gaze shift from object to person and back to the object again might be modeled. As he moves on to another object, interrupt the labeling with the prompt "I like this . . ." or "Nice clock!" You might model questions such as "Where did you get that clock?" By modeling comments or questions, he may get the idea of another way to talk about things that he is interested in.

> ▶ Recently my daughter received a speech–language reevaluation in school. To our surprise, all her scores were at age level or above, and therapy was not recommended. How can this be? I know that she still has problems with language. What can be done to have her speech services resumed?

Standardized language tests usually evaluate individual aspects of language, such as word knowledge or grammar, in an isolated, out-of-context state, and in most cases do not evaluate a child's use of language, that is, what speech–language pathologists term the pragmatics of language. The separation of language function, form, and meaning is an artificial one because in real life they overlap. By testing the individual aspects of language in this manner, children who have progressed in semantics and grammar, but who still have difficulty in using language in a social context, are often misdiagnosed. If you feel your child has language weaknesses despite good standardized test scores, her pragmatic skills may be deficient. In order for professionals to view the larger picture, you can suggest that they include an observational session with analysis of the following:

- Conversation
- Narrative skill
- A range of pragmatic skills (speech acts)
- Nonverbal communication

▶ Sometimes my son sounds bossy and even abrasive when he speaks. This tends to alienate his peers and others as well. People think of him as rude. How can I help him with this?

Because of poor pragmatics, children with superficially well-developed language skills, meaning reasonably good vocabulary and grammar, may be misinterpreted as rude, impatient, or tactless. Effective speakers are able to modulate their language based on the needs of the situation, using politeness, directness, brevity, or comprehensiveness. Changes in language and tone depending upon context are called changes in *register*. Often individuals do not wish to appear rude but end up appearing so because of an inability to modify their register. One would not address a school principal, for example, in the same way as one would speak to the family dog. One speaks differently to a job interviewer than to a sibling. When your son sounds rude, you can help him to understand how he may sound to a listener. The following strategies may be helpful:

1. Try telling him "It hurts my feelings when you talk like that" because he may not realize this.

2. Model "softeners," that is, language with a more friendly tone, such as *please, would you,* and *Do you mind* . . . , as well as using questions instead of demands, such as, "Can I have a toy car?" rather than "I want a toy car." One little boy made all his requests with a demanding "I want the . . ." After each demand, I prompted, "Marg–," whereupon he would sweetly ask "Margery, can I have the . . . ?" Soon he learned to do this spontaneously and his parents were delighted at how much more pleasant he sounded.

3. Ask him "Can you say it another way?" "Can you say it nicer?" or "Can you ask me nicely?"

4. You might contrast saying or asking for things in rude and polite ways for different situations. Practice, for example, different ways that he might respond if he left his school books at a friend's house.

Children with pragmatic language disorders are often interpreted as rude when using the telephone. Good telephone manners involve learning what words to say when answering the phone or making a call, such as "Hello this is _____. May I speak with _____?" When asked if a person is there, a concrete language user might reply "No" if the person is in another room of the house or might not make polite inquiries, such as "Oh, Richard, how are you?" after the caller identifies himself. Problems with using brutal honesty, such as proclaiming "She's so fat" on the bus, may also have to be explained.

Another example of a problematic conversational style is speaking in one-sided monologues. Problematic styles may improve by working on understanding listeners' needs and the fact that other people may have differing points of view. You might directly tell the individual who is on his own agenda, for example, that now it is your turn to talk about something and his turn to listen. As discussed previously, a skill such as this would be considered "high level." Many typical adults interrupt, engage in monologues, or have other conversational style difficulties.

▶ Our daughter is able to engage in simple conversations, but she lags behind her siblings, even the younger ones, who are able to have more mature conversations. What higher level skills does she need to help her to become a better conversationalist?

Besides the conversational basics discussed previously, there are many higher level, subtle conversational skills that are based on an understanding of social complexities. Some examples of these conversational rules, which might also be called social norms or conventions, follow. You might actively teach your child to be aware of such underlying conventional norms. Competent conversationalists

1. *Know rules for interrupting* conversation, such as waiting for a pause or pitch change, waiting for the end of a topic, or watching body language and eye contact.

2. *Are aware of rules for quantity of conversation.* Speakers must know when they are being overly terse or verbose. Teach your child to monitor the length of her stories, jokes, and so on.

3. *Use graceful ways of shifting conversational topic.* For this your child might need to learn expressions such as "Oh, that reminds me of . . ." or "Speaking of . . . ."

4. *Follow rules concerning relevancy;* for example, initiating an interaction on the playground by asking another child if she knows all the train station stops from here to Albany might seem irrelevant, as would attempting to make friends with a new neighbor by informing him of the

exact street addresses of one's relatives. Although these topics might be of great interest to the speaker, by learning to take a listener's perspective, the speaker might consider whether the topics might also be interesting to another person. More appropriate opening statements, depending on the age of the child, might be "Hi, my name is _____. Do you want to play with me?" or "Do you want to be my friend?" or "Do you want to see what I found?"

5. *Comment on others' experiences*, offering sympathy and compliments. They use empathetic comments such as "Oh, that's too bad," "I am sorry to hear that," "Congratulations!" or "That's great news." If your child makes comments like Boy 2 in the first dialogue, work on changing them to more empathetic comments, as in the second dialogue:

BOY 1:   My brother won the race.

BOY 2:   Oh.

BOY 1:   My brother won the race.

BOY 2:   That's great. Congratulations.

6. *Know how to make their own topic interesting*, using emphasis, relevant details, and suspense. You might teach your child to use emphasis, such as saying the key word in a sentence louder and slower as in "My brother *won* the race!" She could be taught to offer a relevant detail to garner her listener's interest, as in "He won in only 52 seconds!" Suspense can be captured by asking leading questions, such as "And do you know what the coach said?" or "Do you know what happened next?"

7. *Understand that if one violates a rule, the violation will be acceptable if awareness of the violation is communicated to the listener.* If, for example, an extremely personal question is being asked, one can communicate that one understands this by using a few words to excuse the question before or after it is asked. If a speaker asks how old a person is, he could ask "May I ask you a personal question?" first. In this case, it might be helpful to discuss what a "personal question" is and give examples such as "How much do you weigh?" or "How much did this cost?" If, in another example, a speaker is talking a great deal, this may be more acceptable if he says "I know I am talking a lot, but I am so excited about this!"

8. *Are responsive to other people's opinions*, using expressions such as "I don't think so" or "I don't agree with that" or "Yes, that's true." If, for example, a child says "I don't like it when the teacher gives homework on weekends," it would be important to respond either in agreement ("Neither do I") or disagreement ("Oh, I don't mind it so much").

Many people with autistic spectrum disorders do not learn these rules and expressions by themselves because the rules are based on an understanding of the complexity of social interaction. Children with autism may have grown up less attentive to social cues, so conversational rules may have to be specifically taught by using modeling, prompting, or practicing scripts. *Social skills groups*, where several peers meet with a facilitator and play games or act out situations in order to learn appropriate social and language behavior, can be good opportunities to practice these rules. *Video modeling*, where typical peers are filmed while engaging in verbal interactions, is an excellent way to teach higher level conversational skills because video watching is often appealing to children. In addition, the videos can be viewed repeatedly, with a parent or teacher pointing out and explaining the key features.

▶ Since my child can read, can you give me examples of how to use this skill to improve his language?

Knowledge of visual–spatial symbols, such as letters and numbers, and the ability to read may be strengths for some children with autism. The ability to read offers the opportunity to work on a deficit area, verbal language, while relying on what may be an area of strength, reading. Capitalize on a child's attraction to the written word by using printed cue cards which can be faded over time. The following are some ideas.

1. You can print short phrases for your child to learn to say (e.g., "My turn") in order to teach turn taking in playing board games.

2. You may print longer sequences that are hard to master when taught aurally. For example, use of complex sentences, such as "The big boy who is sitting in the brown car is my brother," can be written out using different colored markers and different sized print to emphasize specific words that are hard to remember. The idea is to get the child to verbally reproduce what he is capable of understanding in a written form.

3. When trying to facilitate the verbal use of more complex grammar, such as dependent clauses, you can print and hold up a single word that is frequently omitted, such as "so" or "that." In working on causality, one boy was having difficulty remembering to say "and so." I printed these words

on a card which I placed between each of two cause–effect pictures obtained through a speech–language catalog (e.g., "The boy ate too much chocolate" AND SO "he had a stomachache").

4. You can use cue cards for teaching conversational skills by writing and prompting, for example, a topic to talk about. Have two children sit down and attempt to engage in conversation. If there is a lull, you might hold up a cue card with the word "Pets" written on it, to prompt the child to extend the conversation by asking if his partner has any pets or sharing information about his own pet. You can write appropriate conversational questions on individual cue cards, such as "What did you do today?" "What is your favorite TV show?" as well as conversational extenders such as "Do you know what else?" and hold them up at appropriate moments during the conversation.

5. You can also point to a printed cue hanging on the wall, such as "Look at Speaker."

A child may learn specific verbal behaviors faster if the adult points to a written cue rather than always relying on spoken prompts. Write the cards in front of the child to increase interest and motivation. Single words or short written sentences have been used successfully with children who are prereaders. Children are often motivated by the written word and quickly memorize what is on the cards.

▶ My daughter is unable to tell me about her day in school or most past events. Is there some way I can help her with this?

Immature language users tend to be mired in the here and now. Being able to convey information about past and future events takes skill and is an important part of being an effective language user. The following are some suggestions.

1. It may help to have a special notebook that goes back and forth from home to school each day. You may ask your daughter's classroom teacher to place pictures, photos, objects, or words into the book that can be used as prompts to talk about her day once she gets home. Also use the book to prompt her to share special home events with her classmates at school.

2. You may ask the teacher to leave a short message on your answering machine about something interesting that happened during the day.

3. Children who read can use fill-in worksheets to help exchange information between home and school.

4. Small, separate photo albums of special events can be used for retelling the events.

5. Practice having your child tell someone, using objects as prompts, what she was doing in another place. If she and Dad were raking leaves in the yard, for example, Dad should have her practice saying what they are doing and then say, "Let's go and tell Mom what we were doing." Give her a leaf to hold as a cue and send her back into the house. Mother asks, "What were you doing with Dad?" If there is no response, Dad may point to the leaf as a prompt.

6. It will be important to structure the teaching of talking about past events in small steps by beginning with the very recent past and slowly building up to more distant past events. You might begin with something very immediate. For example, as soon as you are finished building a tower with blocks, ask her "What did we do?" and facilitate "We built a very tall tower." The next step might be to tell a toy animal or doll in the room what you did. The next step would be to go into another room and tell it to Mom. Gradually increase the time and space between the event and her telling of it. Encourage her to tell a neighbor or the doorman as she leaves the building, tell someone as soon as she gets home, tell Dad when he comes home from work at dinnertime, tell Grandma later in the evening, and so on.

7. Relating past events well involves taking the listener's perspective into account. For more ways to work on this, see the Naive Listener strategy and Barrier Games discussed earlier in the chapter.

In relating past events, children often need to be actively taught the past tense of a few verbs. They may begin to generalize this skill over time.

▶ My son's language is at its best when he is with his brother. He seems to be strongly motivated to sustain his brother's attention. How can I encourage him to speak at this level with other people instead of resorting to the constant "I don't know," which brings conversations to a full stop?

Parents often bring siblings into my office to demonstrate how much better a child speaks when with a sibling. Earning points for good responding while riding in the car or eating dinner may keep motivation up, as in this example:

MOTHER: I bet you had fun at Grandma's house this morning.

CHILD: Yep. We baked chocolate chip cookies and ate them.

MOTHER: That was a great answer. You get one point.

One mother I know has her boys compete for points for Nintendo time, which they receive for good answering during dinnertime conversation. Each point equals another minute of time playing Nintendo. This system might be set up in other situations as well, for example, when visiting, eating out with friends, or playing at the playground. The caregiver can eavesdrop and the point system can be covert if appropriate. For example, if peers are present, you may not wish to embarrass your child by commenting on his language out loud. In this case it would be important to tell him ahead of time, "I'm going to be listening as you talk to Steven. I won't say them out loud, but I will be giving you points for good talking and extra minutes to stay up late tonight."

When I get too many "I don't know" responses, I write the sentence "I don't know" with a red line through it and hang it on a wall nearby. I point to it to remind the child that that response is discouraged. If the child is a nonreader, I tell her what it says.

Many children use better language when speaking at home with familiar family members than when speaking to strangers. Role enactment and short scripts may be helpful in learning how to speak in specific situations outside the home. You can write scripts for your child to act out with friends. I have seen many children start out with scripts and learn to improvise and elaborate when their social confidence increases. Social communication groups with peers are useful for enacting scripts as well as for practicing appropriate conversation while involved in activities such as board games or crafts. Depending on a child's age, it might be appropriate to practice scripts involving

- Answering a telephone
- Making a purchase at a store
- Ordering at a restaurant
- Requesting directions
- Borrowing a book from the library
- Asking a friend out on a date
- Trying on new shoes
- Inviting a friend over for a sleepover

▶ Where can I find materials to help my child improve communication skills?

Appendix 9A offers a list of companies that produce materials for working on communication skills. Check their catalogs for sections for working on

- Word knowledge (may be listed as semantics)

- Grammar (may be listed as syntax or morphology)

- Pragmatics (using language in social context)

- Speech (if your child has an articulation disorder, you will find board games and workbooks listed under speech or phonological skills)

Appendix 9A
Resources

Academic Communication Associates
Publications Center, Department 20F
4149 Avenida de la Plata, P.O. Box 4279
Oceanside, CA 92052-4279
760/758-9593

Communication Skill Builders
P.O. Box 839954
San Antonio, TX 78283
800/211-8378

Different Roads To Learning
12 West Street, Suite 3 East
New York, NY 10011
800/853-1057

Imaginart
307 Arizona Street
Bisbee, AZ 85603
800/828-1376

Janelle Publications
P.O. Box 811
1189 Twombley Road
De Kalb, IL 60115
800/888-8834

LinguaSystems
3100 4th Avenue
East Moline, IL 61244-9700
800/776-4332

PRO-ED
8700 Shoal Creek Boulevard
Austin, TX 78757-6897
800/897-3202

Slosson Educational Publications
P.O. Box 280
East Aurora, NY 14052-0280
888/756-7766

Super Duper Publications
Department SD2000
P.O. Box 24997
Greenville, SC 29616-2497
800/277-8737

Thinking Publications
P.O. Box 163
424 Galloway Street
Eau Claire, WI 54702-0163
800/225-4769

10

Lessons Learned: Thirty Years of Applied Behavior Analysis in Treating Problem Behaviors

Richard M. Foxx

After almost 30 years of treating problem behaviors, many of which were severe, one gains a number of insights to share (e.g., Foxx, 1976a, 1976b, 1976c, 1977, 1980a, 1980b, 1982a, 1985a, 1990, 1991, 1992, 1993, 1996b, 1998a; Foxx & Azrin, 1972, 1973b; Foxx & Bechtel, 1983; Foxx, Bechtel, Bird, Livesay, & Bittle, 1986; Foxx, Bittle, & Faw, 1989; Foxx & Dufrense, 1984; Foxx & Livesay, 1984; Foxx & Martin, 1975; Foxx, McMorrow, Fenlon, & Bittle, 1986; Foxx & Shapiro, 1978; Foxx, Snyder, & Schroeder, 1979; Foxx, Zukotynski, & Williams, 1994; Martin & Foxx, 1973). Many of these observations relate to why behavioral programs are ineffective or fail in some settings. As a young behavior analyst, I believed that any well-designed procedure or program would be successful. Later I learned that a number of nonprogrammatic and programmatic factors can significantly hinder the process and maintenance of behavior change (Foxx, 1985a). Unfortunately, these factors have received little attention (Foxx, 1992).

This chapter is directed primarily at behavior analysts as an attempt to help them to be more successful in treating problem behaviors. For parents, knowledge is power and thus I hope that this chapter will provide an understanding of what a behavior analyst should consider when a program is developed to treat problem behavior.

Note. More extended discussions of some of the material in this chapter can be found in "Twenty Years of Applied Behavior Analysis in Treating the Most Severe Problem Behavior: Lessons Learned," by R. M. Foxx, 1996, *The Behavior Analyst*, *19*(2), pp. 225–235, and in "Twenty-Five Years of Applied Behavior Analysis: Lessons Learned," by R. M. Foxx, in press, *Diskriminanten*. Some of this material also was presented as an invited address at the Twenty-Fifth Annual Convention of the Norwegian Association for Behavior Analysis in Storefjell, Hoyfjellshotell, Norway (Foxx, 1998b).

Four general areas are covered. I begin by discussing why programs and individuals fail and suggesting solutions for achieving programmatic success. Next, to help the reader better understand problem behavior, I present some factors that can cause or influence it. I follow this with a discussion of some general program issues and considerations that relate to problem behaviors. I conclude the chapter with an overall plan for treating problem behavior and maintaining the successes that are achieved.

Why Programs and Individuals Fail and Suggested Solutions

The Reactive Treatment Model Is Used

The intervention model for most human services and special education systems is reactive rather than proactive. In the reactive model, nothing is planned or implemented until after a problem behavior has occurred. Hence, the programmatic thrust was to wait for individuals to do something wrong rather than teaching them to do something right.

Systems theory (Bertalanffy, 1968) explains why systems are inherently reactive and most concerned about their problematic children or students. Every system seeks to maintain a state of equilibrium and eliminate any noise within the system. Human services or educational systems seek to eliminate severe problem behaviors because they represent threats (i.e., noise) due to their potential to produce lawsuits, negative publicity, and disgruntled advocates and parents. A reactive system has little incentive to be proactive because positive outcomes do not create noise. A related problem is the client who is unresponsive to the system's attempts at positive behavior change. In this case, the system also is reactive because unresponsive individuals represent noise for the same reasons discussed for problem behavior. Accordingly, individuals regarded as untreatable or uneducable are typically transferred or shunted to the therapeutic or educational equivalent of Siberia.

Systems theory also states that (a) the older the system, the more resistant it is to change; (b) the more closed the system, the more resistant it is to change; and (c) closed systems die. These factors help explain parents' dissatisfaction with school systems and the emergence of home-based programming. Behavior change is best accomplished in young, proactive systems.

Proactive programming focuses on antecedents rather than consequences. It is a bit like playing chess. The more moves you plan ahead, the more likely you are to be successful in changing an individual's problem behavior. Good behavior change agents think like chess masters. They also always take what the child gives them. In other words, they change their behavior as the child changes his or hers. Its like a *pas de deux* in ballet. The change agent behaves in response to the child's behavior. In this behavioral therapeutic dance, the child always leads. Furthermore, as the child moves toward success, the dance steps keep changing.

The System Does Not See the Behavioral Approach as Relevant

The system may not understand how behavioral analysis will mesh with it or be used. In an article on the dissemination and adoption of innovative interventions, Backer, Liberman, and Kuehnel (1986) stated that the intervention must be viewed as relevant to the system's needs and must be readily translatable into tangible action appropriate to its environment. Another factor critical to adoption is the ease with which the system understands behavior analysis and its implementation. For adoption to occur, behavior analysis must be packaged in a format that enables the system to readily acquire the skills required for faithful application.

Not Every Setting Can Provide Effective Programming

The misconception exists that difficult problems and individuals can be treated and educated in every setting. Yet the environments in which clinical or educational interventions are conducted with difficult problems and persons rarely provide the necessary support to achieve success. Indeed, just as every hospital is not equipped and staffed to do high-risk heart surgery, some locations and behavior analysts are not necessarily suitable to treat problem behavior.

As a result, attempting to use a difficult, elegant, or cutting-edge procedure with a difficult behavior in a non-supportive environment is analogous to a heart surgeon attempting to operate on and maintain the health of a heart surgery patient in an unsterile environment. In such a case, any subsequent deleterious effects would be attributed to contaminating effects of the environment and not to the surgical procedure. Similarly, should one consider a behavioral program to have failed if the necessary environmental support was never provided? Individuals who display self-injurious and aggressive behavior represent the "heart surgery patients" of behavioral intervention and thus require a highly supportive environment.

If this support is not available, then the rationale for keeping the individual in a nonsupportive system must be questioned. Programming for very difficult behaviors and individuals must be limited to those settings where the necessary expertise and environmental support are available (Foxx, 1982a).

In Many Systems Reinforcement Is an Unnatural Act

High-quality reinforcement programs are crucial to successful intervention with problem behavior. Yet the most obvious missing ingredient in most systems is invariably positive reinforcement. Furthermore, few systems pay attention to the quality, variety, density, frequency, and subtlety of reinforcement.

Why do many people do a poor job of reinforcing? Clearly, it is not because the importance or need to reinforce has not been stressed, spoken, written, and modeled. I believe that reinforcement is an unnatural act for many people (Foxx, 1985a, 1993, 1996a). Most people entrusted to carry out reinforcement programs do not do so because they fail to see its relevance. Simply put, their lives are not very reinforcing and hence they do not view reinforcement as something particularly desirable or necessary.

Behavior analysts must continue to search for ways of teaching and motivating people to reinforce. To that end, the goal should change from trying to convince people to reinforce, to having them practice reinforcing until it becomes so automatic that they do not think about whether to reinforce but simply do it. Over time, the programmatic benefits of their use of reinforcement should become apparent. In effect, behavior analysts should be less concerned that people know *why* they are reinforcing than that they *are* reinforcing. The first question to ask oneself each time a student with autism is encountered thereby becomes "Is there a behavior I can go over and reinforce?" In this manner, change agents will think of themselves as bees and their students as a field of flowers (Foxx, 1996a).

No Behavioral Expertise Is Available

Successful treatment of a problem behavior requires behavioral expertise. When no one with the necessary expertise is available in a system, the typical result is a series of "treatment" failures followed by nontherapeutic "interventions" such as drugs and restraint. The solution is to hire someone with expertise or send the individual to a setting that has expertise.

There Is a Shortage of Behavioral Expertise

Behavior analysts have not always done a particularly good job of teaching intervener behavior and need to focus more on individual change agent behavior. Are special repertoires necessary for one to be a good behavior change agent (Foxx, 1985a)? Identifying such repertoires would help explain why some individuals have more programmatic successes than others.

Based on his work in teacher preparation, Sharpe (1994) described six stages in the development of expertise: novice, advanced beginner, competent, proficient, experienced proficiency, and virtuosity. Behavior analysts need to study what comprises expertise, what learning histories facilitate its acquisition, and how to train it.

Exceeding the Systems Skill Level: The Most Difficult Behavior Is Treated First

Even with access to behavioral expertise, many systems simply are not prepared to conduct and maintain a program for individuals with behavior problems. Their programs fail because they have no track record of success with less problematic behavior. As noted earlier, a reactive system is rarely concerned with intervening until an individual's behavior has escalated to a point where its disruptive effects on the system cannot be tolerated. Yet whenever there is a sense of urgency about a behavior problem, there is a high probability that something will go wrong programmatically. This is because there is a tendency to rush in and intervene without doing the necessary planning and functional analyses.

To avoid this pitfall the behavioral expert should select for treatment those students (a) whose behavior can be changed easily (e.g., with only minor environmental manipulations; Martin & Foxx, 1973) or (b) who have milder problem behavior (Foxx & Shapiro, 1978). Use of these strategies will ensure that the system has some success while also preparing it to treat more difficult behavior problems when its level of expertise is sufficient to do so. One key to being a successful consultant is the ability to recognize and select behaviors that are easy for the system to modify (Foxx, 1985a).

A good program designer is like a journalist or detective. All three ask the Wh– questions— who, what, when, where, why—and then how. What I suggested 15 years ago remains topical: "We need to teach staff to consider why clients misbehave, what circumstances or situations produce misbehavior and why programs fail" (Foxx, 1985a, p. 191).

The Behavioral Expert Does Not Conduct the Treatment or Is Used as a Circuit Rider

Failure can occur when the behavioral expert does not conduct the treatment. Many systems fail to use behavioral expertise properly. Their resident "experts" often function as circuit riders, spending most of their time traveling between sites attempting to put out fires rather than treating students or teaching staff. (Again, this demonstrates the reactive treatment model in operation.) Because these experts spend little time directly and actively participating in the behavior change process, their impact on the system is diluted and little actual change takes place. The circuit rider model guarantees that individuals with difficult behavior will receive very little direct intervention from the persons in the system most likely to be able to help them.

Many programs are evaluated in terms of what is written rather than what is being done because the people who do the evaluations, such as school principals, often have little, if any, programming background. The net effect is that individuals with expertise have been shaped to write programs rather than to conduct them. Imagine the mortality rate if thoracic surgeons spent most of their time developing written plans for surgery. What is needed is less saying and more doing.

The solution to these problems is to cease using the circuit rider model while freeing the expert from those duties and responsibilities (e.g., excessive paperwork and meeting attendance) that are incompatible with conducting treatment (Foxx, Bechtel, et al., 1986). In this way, the expert can spend the necessary time with the treated individual's program to train and shape staff to solve problems as they arise and give frequent corrective and positive feedback (Foxx, 1990). The expert would not move to the next case until the individual's program was stabilized and treatment staff had reached a desired level of programmatic competence. While it could conceivably require a fairly lengthy period to implement such an approach successfully in some large systems, the end product— successfully treated individuals and a high standard of uniform and sustained staff competence—would be well worth the effort.

The Recipe Approach Is Used

A program may not work for a problem behavior when it is created by a technologist rather than an analyst. A behavioral technologist is often someone who has learned a set of strategies, methods, and procedures and then applies them, often without much regard as to why. Conversely, a behavioral analyst sees each application of behavior analysis as a unique and individualized combination of events. The behavioral technologist is like a cook following a recipe, whereas the behavioral analyst is like a chef developing novel culinary concoctions through improvisation.

Journal Articles May Lack Critical Clinical or Educational Information

Sometimes important clinical or educational information may have been left out of an article used to support the intervention model (Foxx, 1996b). One should pay special attention to how long each day the program was conducted. Although some studies describe impressive interventions, a close reading reveals that the effects were achieved during brief daily periods. The question becomes, "What happens to these individuals during the vast majority of their waking hours?" Similarly, how severe were the individuals' problems? It would be helpful if journal authors were required to file, at some central repository, videotapes that contained a few vignettes of the intervention sessions. In this way one could view some of the subtleties in the treatment that are difficult or impossible to describe in an article. This could facilitate replication and would provide a clearer picture of what the treated individuals were like.

Occasionally I read an article that raises the question of whether the author(s) actually worked with the children. The descriptions in the paper simply go counter to my clinical experiences. The subjects do not seem real, procedures appear artificial and contrived, and the results are obtained too easily. Everything is a bit too pat. In effect, if it sounds too good to be true, it probably is.

Failure To Prepare the Treatment Environment Is Common

Programs fail if the environment has not been behaviorally prepared. Consider the following surgical analogy: No surgical operation is performed unless the environment is sterile, well-trained nurses are present, and an emergency generator is available in case the power should fail.

Behavior change agents need to prepare the environment before attempting to change behavior. For a problem behavior, such preparation includes ensuring the availability of behavioral expertise, having a high density and variety of reinforcement available, and programming the reinforcement of alternative, incompatible kinds of behavior. When this preparation is complete, the behavior change operation can begin (Foxx, 1980a, 1980b).

Making Programs Work Requires Administrative Clout

If a program is going to be successful, it must have the support of the person in charge, be it a principal, teacher, parent, or center director. Ideally, the behavior analyst also has supervisory or administrative powers and hence can simply mandate programmatic compliance (Foxx, Bechtel, et al., 1986). However, if the program designer is strictly a consultant or nonsupervisor, the program may not last because its success will become dependent on the designer's convincing people to carry out the program. This may be why successful consultants and program designers often have persuasive personalities.

I spend 10% of my time developing programs and 90% determining how to ensure that people will implement them (Foxx, 1976a). Many programs are unsuccessful because these percentages have been reversed. The issue often is not what program to use, but rather how to ensure that it will be delivered properly.

One way to increase accountability is to train and certify staff in all the interventions prior to program implementation. Such certification can be accomplished via videotaping practice sessions, role playing, and written and oral examinations. Grafting behavioral programming onto existing successful models also is useful. For example, in medical settings I arrange for behavioral programs to be conducted like the dispensing of medication. As with medication, individuals are assigned to dispense the behavioral program and attest (record) that they did, and there are negative consequences if they fail to carry out this assignment or do so incorrectly.

Some professionals in education and human services believe that, once they have been hired and certified, they have nothing new to learn. These individuals are often displeased and threatened when they must learn behavioral skills. This displeasure can lead to both active and passive resistance. This resistance is very unfortunate because many of them were ill prepared during their schooling for what they now are expected to do; that is, their current skills are no longer sufficient or useful.

Over the years my approach to this resistance has changed. Initially, I thought it could be overcome if people simply understood that using behavioral skills would make their jobs easier. This approach was not very successful. I now have a different strategy wherein I emphasize that behavioral skills are needed to meet one's job requirements. Simply put, in virtually every other type of work, employees expect to be required to develop, learn, and maintain whatever skills are necessary to perform their job. Companies train people to fit their needs. New employees expect this when they are hired. Later, if their job requirements change because of technological advancements, people easily accept and indeed hope for retraining. In education and human services, people need to understand that behavioral training is the result of scientific and technological advancements.

No One Conducts Programming for Long If It Is Not Working

No one conducts an ineffective program for very long. Most people's dedication and enthusiasm will wane quickly if no positive programmatic outcomes are apparent within a few days. A program is destined to fail if it is given only 2 to 3 months to work before a decision is made to continue or discontinue it. The behavioral expert's role is to help change agents see that they are having success during the early treatment days. This can even involve identifying why the program is working even though it may not appear to be. Some potential indications of early success with high-rate problem behaviors are that the duration of the behavior has become shorter over time, the time between behaviors has increased, or the time before the onset of the behavior has increased. Others strategies for maintaining change agent motivation are to show pretreatment videos and data, identify conspicuous collateral (related) improvements, and obtain input from the treated individual's significant others.

Problem Behavior Typically Worsens First

When change agents attempt to decrease a behavior, it typically worsens before decreasing. It is like the storm before the calm. A typical reaction in such cases is, "We've got to stop the program because it's making the child worse." The program is indeed making the child worse because he or she is displaying behavior that has been shaped and strengthened over time because it resulted in the discontinuation of programmatic efforts (Foxx & Dufrense, 1984). In effect, many students with problematic behaviors have been generously negatively reinforced for escalating.

Typically, individuals with fewer skills are likely to demonstrate behavioral escalation quickly, whereas individuals with high level skills tend to wait until the behavior analyst has become overconfident. One can never feel completely confident that a reductive program has worked until some behavioral escalation has occurred and then ceased. The key to programmatic success is the willingness to ride out the escalation.

The Problem Behavior Is Episodic

Episodic behaviors are difficult to treat because there are few opportunities to do so. There also is the potential for the treatment to be applied improperly. These problems can be overcome if the change agent views an episodic behavior as being akin to an emergency room or shock trauma unit situation. When someone stops breathing in an emergency room, treatment must be applied within less than 4 minutes. There is no time to go to the file cabinet to find the program on performing tracheotomies or applying oxygen. Accordingly, emergency room personnel know what to do because of repeated training and rehearsal. They recognize the antecedents that characterize respiratory distress.

To follow this model for episodic behavior, all treatment personnel must practice recognizing antecedents and applying the treatment during periods when there is no problematic behavior. Everyone should practice to the point where they react reflexively but appropriately when they encounter an episodic behavior or its antecedents.

Boredom and Routine Erode Maintenance Effects

Rigid adherence to successful treatment scenarios over an extended period of time can erode the maintenance of successful behavior change. The individual and staff become bored and fall into routines that make them less responsive when flexibility and variety are not programmed into daily routines (Foxx, Zukotynski, & Williams, 1994). Systematically and intermittently changing everyone's daily activities is one way of overcoming this problem.

Low-Functioning Clients Are Treated

A 10-year follow-up study (Foxx & Livesay, 1984) of eight persons treated by overcorrection procedures (Foxx & Bechtel, 1983) revealed that higher functioning individuals showed longer and better reduction of serious behavior than did lower functioning individuals. One reason was that the former individuals had more opportunities to obtain reinforcers and positive interactions with others because they had well-developed expressive language. In contrast, lower functioning individuals were dependent on others for such programming. To overcome this problem, more direct programming of competing reinforcers and activities is required in maintenance programs for lower functioning individuals (Foxx, 1982b).

Writing a Program Rather Than Interacting with a Client Has Occurred

Most programs fail because there is a tendency to simply write a program rather than interact directly with the individual (McMorrow & Foxx, 1986). A functional analysis is like an exploratory operation: One really does not know what needs to be done until he or she goes in and takes a look (Foxx & Dufrense, 1984).

An Earlier Successful Program Is Repeatedly Discovered

Often when reviewing someone's folder as part of designing a program, I am struck by a sense of déjà vu in that the current behavior problems have been successfully treated a number of times. Typically, the longer the period of time that passes between the treatment program and the return of problematic behavior, the less likely the original, successful program will be reinstated (Foxx & Livesay, 1984). Often the problem is that earlier successes are buried beneath reams of paper in the individual's files. One solution is to place a brightly colored sheet of paper in the front of the individual's chart that presents a description of previously successful programs and data supporting their effectiveness (Foxx, 1985a).

Understanding Problematic Behavior

Various factors can influence problem behavior. These factors include functioning level differences, physical problems, programmatic decay, equalizing attention from typical siblings or peers, and the nature of the tasks and situations that are presented to the person.

Functioning Level Differences

Generally, the individuals who present the most problematic behaviors are the most aware individuals in the setting. Because most systems operate from a reactive treatment model (Foxx, 1996b), these individuals have quickly learned that problem behavior offers the best means of predicting and affecting their environment, whether it be through attention (Martin & Foxx, 1973) or escape-related behavior (Foxx, 1990; Foxx, Bittle, & Faw, 1989; Foxx, Zukotynski, & Williams, 1994).

The Role of Physical Problems

I have often wondered what it must be like to be a nonverbal individual with limited language skills who has an excruciating headache, gas, or constipation, yet is unable to ask anyone for relief. Most people who suffer these minor but discomforting physical problems can seek relief from over-the-counter medications and ask others to reduce their performance demands. For example, a person might say to a coworker, "I don't feel very well today, so please don't expect too much of me."

Nonverbal individuals do not have these options. Their only recourse to escape a demanding situation when they feel poorly is to act out. This is where the perceptive sensitivity of the therapist comes into play. The sensitive therapist sees a droplet of mucus in the corner of a nonverbal child's nostril and thinks, "Perhaps Susie is acting cranky today because she is catching a cold. Let's reduce our learning expectations for her a bit today."

More serious problem behaviors such as self-abuse also can result from a variety of physical problems, including otitis media (ear infections), stomach ulcers, and abscessed teeth. It is critical that a thorough medical examination be given to anyone displaying self-abuse, especially if the onset of the behavior is quite recent.

Episodic or Cyclical Behavior: Physical Factors

The infrequent or episodic aggressive behavior of adolescents and some adults who are nonverbal or have limited expressive language skills can be very perplexing. One reasonable explanation for this aggression relates to physiological factors, given that the individuals have become sexually mature. For example, in young women the cause could be premenstrual syndrome (PMS). Given that a percentage of the "typical" female population suffers from PMS, it is quite reasonable to expect that some women with autism will also suffer from it. Such an assumption can be verified easily by determining if there is a very high correspondence between a woman's episodic acting out behavior and her menstrual cycle. If so, then the best way to begin treating her episodic behavior would be to keep accurate records of her cycle and simply reduce the demands on her prior to her menses.

Sexual tension may explain some of the episodic aggression that involves an attack on a favorite person such as a teacher. Both sexual arousal and aggression are controlled by the limbic region of the brain. The former requires some knowledge and experience if it is to be satisfactorily consummated, whereas the latter does not. Thus individuals with little or no awareness of what sexual arousal is or why they may be aroused may channel this arousal into aggression. Evidence for the thin line between aggressive and sexual behavior can be found in the prenuptial combat displayed by many animal species.

Episodic or Cyclical Problem Behavior: The Role of Programmatic Decay

The vast majority of episodic problem behavior may be primarily the result of programmatic decay. Consider the following scenario: A student displays a serious behavior and causes havoc within the school system (Foxx, 1996b). Everyone becomes very concerned about preventing future occurrences. Accordingly, the student is watched carefully, provided intensive programming, and given increased positive reinforcement in the form of attention, tasks, and activities. As time passes and no further behavior is displayed, everyone's concern and vigilance diminishes. The amount of attention given decreases, the consistency of programming wanes, and other students' crises occur to compete for and occupy everyone's attention and time. Eventually, the overall treatment effort decays to a point where the student, suffering from a low density of attention and other reinforcers, has to act out in order to restart the treatment process. Unfortunately, what has been created is a very lean intermittent schedule (Foxx, 1982b) that was attenuated unknowingly.

How Tasks Produce Problematic Behaviors

A good deal of an individual's problematic behavior is related to the nature of the tasks he or she is given because the person does not have the power to avoid or escape those tasks that are inappropriate. So, if the task is too easy, the person might act out to terminate it. The use of tasks that are too easy is not hard to explain. When professionals in the human services and special education fields find a task that a student will perform willingly, they tend to present it repeatedly. The student, becoming increasingly bored, has no choice but to act out because doing so will typically lead to the termination of the task or session. Thus, acting out is negatively reinforced by escape from the task. This problem is easily identified when someone says, "Bobby used to like to do _____, but he doesn't like to do it anymore." Change agents must constantly be alert to this programming pitfall. This problem can be avoided by establishing appropriate criterion levels of performance so that students are moved to the next step or program once they have demonstrated mastery of a task.

The same scenario can occur if the task is too difficult or if insufficient positive reinforcement is available for performing it. In the former case, a simpler task must be substituted or the task should be analyzed and broken down into more easily mastered steps (Foxx, 1982b). The solution to the latter case is to use sufficient positive reinforcement (Foxx, 1982b) as well as other training procedures (Foxx, 1984, 1985b).

Problematic Behaviors Serve To Equalize Attention

Imagine you are a nonverbal, echolalic (McMorrow, Foxx, Faw, & Bittle, 1986) or minimally verbal child sitting at the dinner table with your parents and two typical siblings. Your siblings are talking about what they did at school today. You cannot, or if you could, you might well be talking about doing the same things you did yesterday and last week. To whom are your parents going to attend? To their children who are more verbally facile. It is simple human nature.

The child with autism who is quiet and acts appropriately throughout the meal often receives little attention. However, this child can compete with siblings for attention by misbehaving. Throwing or spilling food, or perhaps making loud noises while drinking, can be very functional under the circumstances, because it will garner parental attention.

Problem behaviors occur not because individuals are malevolent, but because the behaviors work. When children with autism are being good citizens at the table is when it is most important to speak and interact with them.

Why Problematic Behaviors Do Not Occur in New and Exciting Places

Individuals with problematic behavior often are not exposed to many new or public situations because of the fear that they will act out. When brought into these situations, however, they often do not act out because, if they did, they would have to leave a stimulating environment and return to a less stimulating or challenging one. No one who is enjoying an interesting new setting wants to return to a dull one. Exposing individuals to new and exciting places can be worthwhile rather than risky, because there is a good chance they will not misbehave.

Programmatic Issues and Considerations

Having discussed why programs fail and what influences problematic behavior, I now turn to some programmatic issues that should be considered.

Behavior Contrast: A Source of Misunderstanding

Understanding problem behavior allows behavior change agents to anticipate what is going to happen in a treatment program and thereby maximize the chances of success. When change agents do not understand why something is happening, they become frustrated and the programs deteriorate. Consider the phenomenon of behavioral contrast (Foxx, 1985a, 1996b) as it relates to decreasing a problematic behavior. Simply stated, if a problematic behavior is successfully decreased in one situation, it will almost invariably become worse in untreated situations. Hence, if a teacher tells me that she has eliminated a child's problematic behavior at school, I am not surprised when she also tells me that the child's parents have told her, "I don't know what you're doing to my child but he acts worse at home." The parents are right; his behavior has no doubt become worse at home. In this case, it is the teacher's responsibility, prior to implementing the school program, to alert the parents to the possibility that behavior contrast could occur. Likewise, if parents seek to first treat a problematic behavior at home, they should alert the school about the home program because the potential for behavior contrast will exist. These situations can cause parents to become distrustful of their child's teacher, or vice versa.

Behavior contrast helps explain some of the distrust that can occur within an organization or across individuals responsible for someone's care and treatment, or why professionals sometimes dismiss the comments of parents or paraprofessionals. A knowledge of behavior contrast effects also can help managers and administrators identify those individuals and settings where programs are not being applied or are being applied less consistently. In effect, where programming is poor or nonexistent, escalations will be evident in the very problem behaviors that are showing decreasing trends in all well-programmed settings.

Behavior Knowledge

Someone responsible for changing behavior must have two types of knowledge. Working knowledge is what can be retrieved or used at any time. It is what you know about changing behavior without having any notes or books handy or what you would use in answering an attorney's questions in court. The other type of knowledge is knowing how and where to find information about behavior change by reading, asking questions, visiting the library, searching the Internet, or consulting experts.

Although both types are important, one's working knowledge essentially determines one's capabilities to change behavior and the limitations, both self-imposed and externally imposed, that should be placed on the change agent. Just as surgeons are expected to have extensive working knowledge regarding the operations they perform, so too must behavior change agents have extensive working knowledge. This is especially true if intrusive interventions are being considered. No change agent should ever conduct a program that he or she would not feel comfortable explaining scientifically, conceptually, and practically in a courtroom. Indeed, anyone who designs or conducts programs without the proper working knowledge is like a physician practicing without a license.

Individuals who cannot discuss the distinction between withholding and withdrawing a positive reinforcer should not be using extinction or time-out procedures. A trained behavior analyst knows that when using extinction a positive reinforcer is withheld, whereas in a time-out procedure a positive reinforcer is withdrawn contingent on the person's behavior (Foxx, 1982a). These definitional differences must be understood by change agents practicing a science of behavior. In a way, differentiating between extinction and time-out is a bit like differentiating between potassium chloride (KCl) and sodium chloride (NaCl). Extinction and time-out are similar in that both contain elements of extinction, yet they are separate operations. KCl and NaCl contain chloride, are white salts, and are necessary to sustain life, yet it is important to differentiate between them because too much of one, KCl, can be lethal. The same precision is important in differentiating behavioral procedures.

How Reducing Behavior Can Become Reinforcing

Early in my career, I was extremely bothered that my behavior analytic students usually scored highest on the reducing behaviors section of any course or workshop. This occurred even though I had spent most of my time talking about increasing behavior. Why did everyone seem to want to know more about how to decrease behavior?

The answer is provided by a functional analysis and what it reveals regarding the amount of effort that must be put into programming. Consider that when a successful program eliminates someone's maladaptive behavior, the problem is gone and there is often a return to the status quo. Conversely, when a successful positive reinforcement program increases someone's behavior, a new program must be developed to build upon the skill achievement that has been reached. This analysis suggests that future effort will be needed when building behavior because one is never done, whereas the elimination of a problem behavior requires no further effort. In effect, reducing behavior is reinforcing and increasing behavior is punishing. This analysis of therapist response effort helps explain why most questions directed to an expert concern reducing problem behaviors. To avoid these problems, one must constantly focus programming efforts on increasing behaviors (Foxx, 1982b) and always reinforce an alternative response when seeking to decrease a behavior (Foxx, 1982a).

The Importance of the Initial Breakthrough

One key to success in working with problem behaviors is to achieve some initial success with the main behavior of concern (Foxx, 1980a, 1991; Foxx & Dufrense, 1984). Once this initial breakthrough has been accomplished, subsequent reductions in other problem behaviors will become easier. However, the initial breakthrough can be very difficult if the individual has had a history of failed interventions.

Providing Respite Care for Parents

To appreciate the problems that the parents of a child with autism must deal with every day, therapists should care for a child home for the weekend. The therapists will learn that parents have to do all of the daily tasks that everyone must do *plus* be concerned about a child who may require a good deal of attention and assistance. Taking a turn providing a weekend of respite care will go a long way toward ending therapists' complaints that parents have difficulty being consistent.

Targeting Public Problematic Behaviors for Early Treatment

Many parents express concern, and rightfully so, about their children's problem behaviors that call attention to them in public. One of the nicest things that therapists can do for parents is to make those behaviors among some of the earliest that are targeted for change. Doing so will gain parental cooperation and support for later programmatic efforts. The children will benefit as well because reducing these behaviors will increase the likelihood that they will be taken out in public more often.

Interrupting Agitated Individuals Early

The typical reactions to individuals with a history of aggression or self-abuse when they become agitated is to hope that they will calm down and to simply leave them alone. This approach, however, often results in the opposite effect, namely an escalation of the behavior.

The better strategy is to attempt to distract or redirect the individual before he or she becomes too wound up. Such an approach makes sense both behaviorally and physiologically. Behaviorally, responses are weakest in the earliest parts of a behavior chain or before agitation is reinforced (Foxx, 1982b). Physiologically, it is difficult to calm someone down once he or she becomes highly agitated and has a lot of adrenalin coursing through his or her veins.

Selecting an Easy-To-Treat Behavior First

When there is a sense of urgency about a behavior problem, there is a good chance of something going wrong programmatically due to the tendency to rush in and treat without taking the time to do the necessary planning and functional analyses. In such cases, programs rarely work and staff are likely to burn out. A good rule to follow is to select first a behavior that is easy to treat, that is, that everyone can have success treating.

Undoubtedly, someone at a program meeting will question why more serious behaviors are not being treated first. The answer is that it makes no sense to treat a serious behavior until everyone's skill level is elevated by building the necessary expertise within the system.

Finding an Expert

Individuals who really know about changing behavior are willing to have others watch them do so. Be cautious of anyone who hands you a written program and says, "If you do this, it will work," but who will not conduct a demonstration if asked.

Just because someone has had extensive academic training does not necessarily mean that he or she can effectively change behavior (Foxx, 1996a). Although this is a common assumption, academia sometimes emphasizes skills and areas that are not very relevant to changing behavior. For example, in some settings, the typical psychologist has more of an evaluation and diagnostic function than a programmatic one. This is not surprising because diagnostics are what many psychologists are trained to do. Yet it is not terribly helpful for parents to be told that a child is afflicted with autism if they are not told how to treat it.

Sometimes individuals may be extremely well versed in behavioral principles, but have few or no skills in changing behavior. It does no good for parents to learn that their child's problems are related to conjugate reinforcement schedules if nothing is done to solve those problems.

An Overall Plan for Treating Problem Behavior and Maintaining Treatment Success

The successful treatment of problem behavior and maintaining treatment success require a consideration of the following strategies and factors (Foxx, Zukotynski, & Williams, 1994):

1. Use a hypothesis-driven treatment model (Foxx, 1996b) whereby interventions are designed after a formal functional analysis has identified the variables that control or cause the behavior. Because problem behavior is sometimes under the control of multiple motivational and setting events and hence cannot be definitely linked to specific consequences, conduct an in-depth analysis of antecedent and setting events (Romanczyk, 1996). This will help to determine whether the occurrence or nonoccurrence of the problem behavior is associated with environmental events that repeat themselves predictably with specific caregivers or activities or across times of the day or days of the week. For example, an analysis may indicate that an individual acts out during language training sessions at 10 a.m. every day, in all daily language training sessions, in the presence of particular therapists, or in the first training hour every morning following a 3-day weekend.

2. Ensure that the stimuli that can, at times, control appropriate behavior are present before, during, and after the problem behavior is treated. To help determine what procedures, skills, and activities to implement when persons are not misbehaving, survey all of their significant others for treatment ideas. Another tact is to enhance their preexisting skills so that they can be displayed more frequently and with more variety.

3. Employ a skill-building strategy wherein new behaviors are taught to serve the same function as the problem behavior. Emphasize behaviors that access the same reinforcers, especially communicative ones. Teach requesting behaviors that are functionally equivalent to the problem behavior but more effective in generating reinforcement. In effect, requesting behavior must be less effortful than problem behavior. For example, teach caregivers to respond consistently and rapidly to requests. Train caregivers to be knowledgeable about the individual's communication system.

4. Select staff to participate in treatment who are important to the treated person because they have been associated with positive reinforcement. In other words, select trainers who are familiar and liked by the treated person because a mutual affection exists.

5. Eliminate such situations as frustration, boredom, and protracted periods of inactivity that are known to cause problem behavior. This can be accomplished by varying tasks, activities, encouraging choice making, and increasing individuals' activity levels. In this way, problematic behaviors that produce attention or gain task or situation escape or avoidance will become unnecessary and thereby nonfunctional.

6. Follow the least restrictive treatment model wherein the least intrusive but effective procedure is selected based on a review of treatment literature (Foxx, 1982a). For example, before treating aggression, read the literature on the behavioral treatment of aggression. Pay special attention to treatments that were successful with aggressive individuals who are like the person you wish to treat and display their aggression in similar situations or environments. Also, consider the intensity, severity, frequency, and topography (form) of the aggression. Thus, if you wish to treat a 12-year-old's aggression toward his sister in the home, look for studies that describe the successful treatment of preteens' or children's aggression in home environments.

7. Do not allow problem behavior to produce escape from educational and vocational activities (Foxx, Bittle, & Faw, 1989). Require the individual to remain in the teaching situation and complete one or more requested tasks before ending the activity. This will prevent reinforcing escape-motivated problem behaviors and, instead, will provide escape for task completion.

8. Increase the complexity of social reinforcement and tasks as the individual's behavior becomes increasingly more appropriate (Foxx & Faw, 1992; Foxx, Faw, & Nisbeth, 1990; Foxx, Faw, & Weber, 1991; Foxx & McMorrow, 1983; Foxx, McMorrow, Bittle, & Ness, 1986). Over time, the density of naturally occurring positive reinforcement will correspondingly increase as the individual's behavior becomes more appropriate. The complexity and relevance of tasks should also be increased.

9. Actively encourage choice making (Foxx, Faw, Taylor, Davis, & Fulia, 1993) and problem solving (Foxx & Bittle, 1989; Foxx, Kyle, Faw, & Bittle, 1989a, 1989b). Choice making is a first step in teaching of self-control (Foxx, 1990) because granting someone choices is giving them control.

10. Actively encourage the participation of the individual's significant others (Foxx, Zukotynski, & Williams, 1994). Parents and family are wonderful sources of information because they know the individual's history of problematic behavior and reinforcement.

Maintaining Treatment Effects

It is equally important to plan for the maintenance and long-term assessment of treatment effects. Maintenance refers to treatment effects or improvements that remain stable even after the intervention is removed (Foxx, 1999). Rarely do the effects of a treatment maintain in the absence of programming. As a result, careful planning is required to ensure that clinical effects will endure. Some successful strategies for achieving maintenance effects include actively programming or planning for maintenance (Foxx, Bittle, & Faw, 1989; Stokes & Osnes, 1986); ensuring similarity between the treatment and maintenance programs (Foxx & Livesay, 1984); ensuring that there is change agent and system accountability (Foxx & Azrin, 1973a, 1973c); following a functional approach by strengthening alternatives to the undesirable behavior and using naturally occurring positive reinforcers (Konarski, Favell, & Favell, 1992); and considering social validity, that is, whether the program is beneficial to the individual and society (Wolf, 1978).

Whenever possible, treatment should approximate the individual's natural environment because it permits potential maintenance-inferring problems to be identified and corrected and maintenance-enhancing factors to be maximized (Konarski et al., 1992). Some behavioral methods that approximate the natural environment and that can be used to maintain therapeutic gains include intermittent reinforcement, reinforcement delay, shifting to natural consequences, fading of therapist control, teaching of self-control, developing of peer or sibling support, and fading in situations and conditions that previously provoked the behavior prior to treatment (Foxx, Zukotynski, & Williams, 1994; Konarski et al., 1992).

All of these methods can fail, however, if therapy decisions are based on factors other than clinical progress, decisions are not individualized to the client, or sound behavior methods are stretched to the point where they cannot work effectively (Konarski et al., 1992). For example, fading therapist control cannot be made on the basis of expediency (e.g., financial considerations rather than the client's progress). All maintenance-enhancing strategies are a combination of skill and artistry (Foxx, 1996a) because few empirical guidelines exist.

The need for long-term follow-up assessment is particularly critical in the treatment of problem behavior. Conclusions regarding the long-term effectiveness of any procedure designed to decrease behavior should be based in part on whether the procedure is needed to maintain the therapeutic effects, as well as on the size and duration of reduction (Foxx, 1990; Foxx & Faw, 1990; Foxx & Livesay, 1984). Ideally, the behavior should remain greatly reduced after the procedure is withdrawn (Foxx, Bittle, & Faw, 1989). Follow-up assessments should include repeated observations conducted over an extended period rather than a single behavioral observation (Foxx, Zukotynski, & Williams, 1994). The contingencies (conditions) in effect throughout the maintenance phase should be specified so that the factors that likely contributed to any durable effects can be identified (Foxx, Bittle, & Faw, 1989).

Finally, generalization and maintenance of treatment gains should be assessed independently because they are separable and measurable, and doing so will prevent confounding generalization records with maintenance records. Maintenance refers to continued positive outcomes after the intervention ceases, whereas generalization refers to positive treatment effects' being apparent even in settings, situations, and behaviors not involved in the treatment. Addressing generalization and maintenance also facilitates inclusion by allowing the determination of the existing functional and acceptable behaviors in the individual's social environment.

Although problem behavior represents a major obstacle to the successful treatment and education of individuals with autism, applied behavior analysis offers scientifically validated methods of overcoming it. Effective and long-lasting treatment is possible when the insights discussed in this chapter are combined with the science of behavior analysis.

References

Backer, T. E., Liberman, R. P., & Kuehnel, T. G. (1986). Dissemination and adoption of innovative psychosocial interventions. *Journal of Consulting and Clinical Psychology, 54,* 111–118.

Bertalanffy, L. von. (1968). *General system theory: Foundations, development, applications.* New York: Braziller.

Foxx, R. M. (1976a). Developing overcorrection procedures for problem behaviors: A strategy for individualizing treatment programs. In *Eighth Annual Proceedings of the National Society for Autistic Children* (pp. 102–133). Washington, DC: National Society for Autistic Children.

Foxx, R. M. (1976b). Increasing a mildly retarded woman's attendance and self-help skills classes by overcorrection and instruction. *Behavior Therapy, 7,* 394–396.

Foxx, R. M. (1976c). The use of overcorrection to eliminate the public disrobing (stripping) of retarded women. *Behaviour Research and Therapy, 14,* 53–61.

Foxx, R. M. (1977). The use of overcorrection avoidance to increase the eye contact of autistic and retarded children. *Journal of Applied Behavior Analysis, 10,* 489–499.

Foxx, R. M. (1980a). The behavioral treatment of a self-abusive man. In *Proceedings of the Kentucky Autism Conference* (pp. 47–63). Louisville: Kentucky Society for Autistic Children.

Foxx, R. M. (1980b). Working with the self-abusive individual. In *Proceedings of the National Society for Autistic Children* (pp. 47–60). Washington, DC: National Society for Austistic Children.

Foxx, R. M. (1982a). *Decreasing the behaviors of persons with severe retardation and autism.* Champaign, IL: Research Press.

Foxx, R. M. (1982b). *Increasing the behaviors of persons with severe retardation and autism.* Champaign, IL: Research Press.

Foxx, R. M. (1984). The use of a negative reinforcement procedure to increase the performance of autistic and mentally retarded children on discrimination training tasks. *Analysis and Intervention in Developmental Disabilities, 4,* 253–265.

Foxx, R. M. (1985a). The Jack Tizzard Memorial Lecture: Decreasing behaviours: Clinical, ethical, legal, and environmental issues. *Australia and New Zealand Journal of Developmental Disabilities, 10,* 189–199.

Foxx, R. M. (1985b). Social skills training: The current status of the field. *Australia and New Zealand Journal of Developmental Disabilities, 10,* 237–243.

Foxx, R. M. (1990). "Harry": A ten year follow-up of the successful treatment of a self-injurious man. *Research in Developmental Disabilities, 11,* 67–76.

Foxx, R. M. (1991). Decreasing severe behavior with punishment procedures: Discontinuing their use while maintaining long-term effects. In *Treatment of Destructive Behaviors in Persons with Developmental Disabilities* (pp. 48–51) (NIH Publication No. 91-240). Washington, DC: U.S. Department of Health & Human Services.

Foxx, R. M. (1992). Saying vs. doing: Some frequently discussed and underresearched issues. *Psychology in Mental Retardation and Developmental Disabilities, 18*(2), 1–4.

Foxx, R. M. (1993). An observational potpourri. *Psychology in Mental Retardation, 19,* 1–3.

Foxx, R. M. (1996a). Translating the covenant: The behavior analyst as ambassador and translator. *The Behavior Analyst, 19*(2), 147–161.

Foxx, R. M. (1996b). Twenty years of applied behavior analysis in treating the most severe problem behavior: Lessons learned. *The Behavior Analyst, 19*(2), 225–235.

Foxx, R. M. (1998a). A comprehensive treatment program for inpatient adolescents. *Behavioral Interventions, 13*(1), 67–77.

Foxx, R. M. (1998b). *Twenty-five years of applied behavior analysis: Lessons learned.* Paper presented at the 25th Annual Convention of the Norwegian Association for Behavior Analysis, Storefjell, Hoyfjellshotell, Norway.

Foxx, R. M. (1999). Long term maintenance of language and social skills. *Behavioral Interventions, 14*(3), 135–146.

Foxx, R. M. (in press). Twenty-five years of applied behavior analysis: Lessons learned. *Diskriminanten.*

Foxx, R. M., & Azrin, N. H. (1972). Restitution: A method of eliminating aggressive–disruptive behaviors of retarded and brain damaged patients. *Behaviour Research and Therapy, 10,* 15–27.

Foxx, R. M., & Azrin, N. H. (1973a). Dry pants: A rapid method of toilet training children. *Behaviour Research and Therapy, 11,* 435–442.

Foxx, R. M., & Azrin, N. H. (1973b). The elimination of autistic self-stimulatory behavior by overcorrection. *Journal of Applied Behavior Analysis, 6,* 1–14.

Foxx, R. M., & Azrin, N. H. (1973c). *Toilet training individuals with developmental disabilities: Day and nighttime independent toileting.* Champaign, IL: Research Press.

Foxx, R. M., & Bechtel, D. R. (1983). Overcorrection: A review and analysis. In S. Axelrod & J. Apsche (Eds.), *The effects of punishment on human behavior* (pp. 133–220). New York: Academic Press.

Foxx, R. M., Bechtel, D. R., Bird, C., Livesay, J. R., & Bittle, R. G. (1986). A comprehensive institutional treatment program for aggressive–disruptive high functioning mentally retarded persons. *Behavioral Residential Treatment, 1,* 39–56.

Foxx, R. M. & Bittle, R. G. (1989). *Thinking it through: Teaching a problem solving strategy for community living.* Champaign, IL: Research Press.

Foxx, R. M. Bittle, R. G., & Faw, G. D. (1989). A maintenance strategy for discontinuing aversive procedures: A 52-month follow-up of the treatment of aggression. *American Journal on Mental Retardation, 94,* 27–36.

Foxx, R. M., & Dufrense, D. (1984). "Harry": The use of physical restraint as a reinforcer, timeout from restraint in treating a self-injurious man. *Analysis and Intervention in Developmental Disabilities, 4,* 1–13.

Foxx, R. M., & Faw, G. D. (1990). Long-term follow-up of echolalia and question answering. *Journal of Applied Behavior Analysis, 23,* 387–396.

Foxx, R. M., & Faw, G. D. (1992). An eight year follow-up of three social skills training studies. *Mental Retardation, 30*(2), 63–66.

Foxx, R. M., Faw, G. D., & Nisbeth, I. (1990). Social skills training for inpatient emotionally disturbed children: An analysis of response generalization. *Child and Family Behavior Therapy, 12,* 11–37.

Foxx, R. M., Faw, G. D., Taylor, S., Davis, P. K., & Fulia, R. (1993). "Would I be able to . . ."? Teaching clients to assess the availability of their community living life style preferences. *American Journal on Mental Retardation, 92,* 235–248.

Foxx, R. M., Faw, G. D., & Weber, G. (1991). Producing generalization of inpatient adolescents' social skills with significant adults in a natural environment. *Behavior Therapy, 22,* 85–99.

Foxx, R. M., Kyle, M. S., Faw, G. D., & Bittle, R. G. (1989a). Problem-solving skills training: Social validation and generalization. *Behavior Residential Treatment, 4,* 269–288.

Foxx, R. M., Kyle, M. S., Faw, G. D., & Bittle, R. G. (1989b). Teaching a problem solving strategy to inpatient adolescents: Social validation, maintenance, and generalization. *Child and Family Behavior Therapy, 11,* 71–88.

Foxx, R. M., & Livesay, J. (1984). Maintenance of response suppression following overcorrection: A ten year retrospective examination of eight cases. *Analysis and Intervention in Developmental Disabilities, 4,* 65–79.

Foxx, R. M., & Martin, E. D. (1975). Treatment of scavenging behavior (coprophagy and pica) by overcorrection. *Behaviour Research and Therapy, 13,* 153–162.

Foxx, R. M., & McMorrow, M. J. (1983). *Stacking the deck: A social skills training curriculum for retarded individuals.* Champaign, IL: Research Press.

Foxx, R. M., McMorrow, M. J., Bittle, R. G., & Ness, J. (1986). An analysis of social skills generalization in two natural settings. *Journal of Applied Behavior Analysis, 19,* 299–305.

Foxx, R. M., McMorrow, M. J., Fenlon, S., & Bittle, R. G. (1986). The reductive effects of reinforcement procedures on the genital stimulation and stereotypy of a mentally retarded adolescent male. *Analysis and Intervention in Developmental Disabilities, 6,* 239–248.

Foxx, R. M., & Shapiro, S. T. (1978). The timeout ribbon: A nonexclusionary timeout procedure. *Journal of Applied Behavior Analysis, 11,* 125–136.

Foxx, R. M., Snyder, M. S., & Schroeder, F. (1979). A food satiation and oral hygiene punishment program to suppress chronic rumination by retarded persons. *Journal of Autism and Developmental Disorders, 9,* 399–412.

Foxx, R. M., Zukotynski, G., & Williams, D. E. (1994). Measurement and evaluation of treatment outcomes with extremely dangerous behavior. In T. Thompson & D. Gray (Eds.), *Treatment of destructive behavior in developmental disabilities* (Vol. 2, pp. 261–273). Thousand Oaks, CA: Sage.

Konarski, E. A., Jr., Favell, J. E., & Favell, J. E. (1992). *Manual for the assessment and treatment of behavior disorders of people with mental retardation.* Morganton, NC: Western Carolina Center Foundation.

Martin, P. L., & Foxx, R. M. (1973). Victim control of the aggression of an institutionalized retardate. *Journal of Behavior Therapy and Experimental Psychiatry, 4,* 161–165.

McMorrow, M. J., & Foxx, R. M. (1986). Some direct and generalized effects of replacing an autistic man's echolalia with correct responses to questions. *Journal of Applied Behavior Analysis, 19,* 289–297.

McMorrow, M. J., Foxx, R. M., Faw, G. D., & Bittle, R. G. (1986). *Looking for the words: Teaching functional language strategies.* Champaign, IL: Research Press.

Romanczyk, R. G. (1996). Behavior analysis and assessment: The cornerstone to effectiveness. In C. Maurice, G. Green, & S. C. Luce (Eds.), *Behavioral intervention for young children with autism: A manual for parents and professionals* (pp. 195–217). Austin, TX: PRO-ED.

Sharpe, T. (1994). Training recommendations for "expert" behavior analysts. *The ABA Newsletter, 17,* 13–15.

Stokes, T. F., & Osnes, P. G. (1986). Programming the generalization of children's social behavior. In P. S. Strain, M. J. Guralnick, & H. Walker (Eds.), *Children's social behavior: Development, assessment, and modification* (pp. 407–440). Orlando, FL: Academic Press.

Wolf, M. M. (1978). Social validity: The case for subjective measurement, or how applied behavior analysis is finding its heart. *Journal of Applied Behavior Analysis, 11,* 203–214.

11

♦ ♦ ♦ ♦ ♦ ♦ ♦ ♦ ♦ ♦ ♦ ♦ ♦ ♦ ♦ ♦ ♦ ♦

Never, Ever Give Up

Lora Perry

When a screening suggested that Jason and Joshua were autistic, we didn't believe it. The twins were only 18 months old, so it seemed early to conclude the boys were anything but late talkers, which we had anticipated because twin development normally lags behind that of singletons. Although the boys flew into terrible rages, everything we had read about raising twins warned that the toddler years could be tempestuous.

The only reason Jason and Josh were screened for a developmental disorder in the first place was because of a referral to Child Development Services (CDS) by our vigilant daycare provider, a provider who obviously, I thought, did not know the first thing about twin development. I wrote CDS a five-page letter detailing point by point why our children better fit the diagnostic criteria for *twinship* than for "autistic-like tendencies." Today, I realize my letter was more an exercise in denial than a work of child development scholarship.

But when the hospital-based developmental clinic's physicians and psychologists *also* diagnosed the twins with autism at 27 months, we could no longer deny the truth. Professionally, I was an educator at our state's flagship medical center. It's in my *nature* to respect appropriately credentialed medical and psychological professionals. I believed them. With great grief, I believed them.

The first few days after the diagnosis were my strongest. Better to know the diagnosis so we can fight it, I reasoned. Our family is one of never-say-die fighters. I am the wife, daughter, sister, and godchild of a long line of self-sufficient entrepreneurs. Some of these innovative risk takers are more successful than others, but the culture is clear: Our family fights for its own. Like the brave, bald little children flanked by even braver parents I saw marching in and out of pediatric oncology at the medical center, our family would stand up to autism.

In the back of my mind, however, something was happening. I was not the same person I used to be. A few days before, I was the ecstatic mother of healthy, beautiful twin boys with limitless futures. I tried on the identity of "mother of beautiful twin boys with autism," and found it to be very uncomfortable. I tried to shake it off, but it stubbornly stuck to me.

Naively, I expected the health care system to respond to autism the way it had responded to medical diagnoses all through my life: Diagnosis is followed by treatment. I called the hospital and inquired about next steps. There was an awkward silence; I left my name and number.

A day later Harold Longenecker called on a referral from the developmental clinic, which turned out to be one of the luckiest breaks we had throughout our journey with autism. Harold was a PhD candidate with a keen interest in treating children with autism. We made an appointment to see him in 10 days, Harold's earliest opening.

And then we waited.

At one level, life became a whirlwind after the day of diagnosis, which I could not keep myself from calling "D Day." I drew upon all of the resources my medical center employer had to offer. Embarrassed that somehow *I* may have caused the children to be autistic, however, I couched my inquiries in cryptic or misleading terms: language disorders, research for a patient, my master's thesis, a burgeoning interest in pediatrics.

Books and abstracts described autism as a disorder consigning my sons to a life of aloneness, void of imagination and meaningful communication. Autism would rob my sons of friends, school, a profession, marriage, parenthood. . . . On the plus side, maybe someday they could be toilet trained, and maybe they could live in a group home.

Treatment? We faced a dizzying array of choices, each accompanied by passionate proclamations of effectiveness, or of "appropriateness." Although choices gave us a comfortable feeling of empowerment, that feeling was offset by the equally uncomfortable realization that we did not know how to decide which treatment offered our boys the opportunity to reach their highest potential.

Standing up to autism, my husband and I agreed, was truly a fight for the quality of our sons' future and self-sufficiency. I went on emergency family medical leave for 3 months after confiding only in my immediate supervisor. My colleagues were stunned at my sudden departure, one for which no explanation was offered.

On my first day home as a full-time mother since maternity leave, I gazed at my children. They didn't seem very different from other kids to me, but what did I know? These were my only children. I had no others to compare them to.

I had stopped reading books about toddler development months before, when Jason and Joshua began missing developmental milestones. I realized I also had stopped keeping the baby books, and the photo albums and video camera about which I had been so meticulous the first 2 years of the boys' life had been untouched for months. Instead, I turned to other mothers of twins. Each mother assured me developmental delay in twins is the norm.

Maybe the doctors were wrong, I thought. Maybe this is just a bump in the road, and the kids will veer back onto that developmental curve. ("Whew," I fantasized about the future, "we had that little autism scare, but it turned out it was just a language delay. And those tantrums—well, we all know where they get that temper from!")

Day after day I tried to read to the boys, but they would not sit still. I tried to interest them in the hundreds of toys we had bought. It suddenly occurred to me we had a lot of toys for one household, even one with twins. Why did we have so many toys? Over their 2 years, Jason and Joshua had never responded to toys, but we kept buying and buying, hoping to find the one thing that would turn them around.

No imagination, no play skills—isn't that what the books said? As the boys napped, I sat in the middle of our playroom surrounded by useless toys, and it finally hit me: Our children *are* autistic. They do not play with toys. They will *never* play with toys. And I became overwhelmed with grief.

How could this happen to *me?* I sobbed and sobbed, moaning with a voice I did not recognize as my own. I pounded the floor with my fists, angrier than I ever recall being. How *dare* this happen to my charmed life! How could you *do* this to me, God? Is this payback for all I have done wrong? Did I deserve this for being too self-centered? Punish me, if you must, Lord, but stay away from my *children!*

I argued with God until, in a moment of exhaustion, I became alarmed at my recklessness. Tempting fate by yelling at God was probably not, I thought, a good idea. I paused, and looked around the room full of toys one more time, but nothing had changed. It was just too painful. For the next 3 hours, I numbly packed boxes full of toys and stored them in the attic. Although I have never cleaned out the closets of a loved one who has died, I imagine it must be like this. But there was a difference: The clothes and smells and personal items of a deceased loved one hold memories. The toys I packed away held no meaning, other than dashed hopes. Worse, the process was ghostlike: Phantom images of how my towheaded children could have played and learned with me, if they were typically developing, danced around each teddy bear, each puzzle, each musical instrument.

Then life came to a standstill, as I waited for the days to pass until it was time to meet with Harold. What do you do, as a mother, with two 2-year-olds who will not look at you, cannot talk to you, and refuse to be held by you? You change diapers, you feed, you bathe, you watch, and you wonder. I began each day by calculating how many hours there were until I could go back to sleep. I watched the clocks crawl through the minutes and hours, and contemplated a lifetime ahead of crawling clocks. When the clocks drove me crazy, I packed the kids into the car and just drove around; at least the boys were contained, and usually they'd fall asleep.

At times, the pain was unbearable. A part of me realized I was slipping into depression. The rest of me was just horribly depressed.

Finally we met with Harold, a tall, lean man with creases around his eyes from laughing. Harold's first question to Steve and me was, "So, how are you holding up?" I was touched; Harold's compassion—the first that had been expressed to us since the diagnosis—nearly caused me to lose my composure. Instead, I adopted my "We're Fighters" stance: "We're fine. We're grateful to have a diagnosis. We have some work to do. What do we do now?"

Harold explained that although there indeed seemed to be endless choices in autism treatment, only one approach has a solid foundation in peer-reviewed scientific literature documenting effectiveness: applied behavior analysis (ABA). At the time, I had no idea what a gift Harold's clear communication about that simple fact was to our family. Today, I know this knowledge so early after the twins' diagnosis played a key role in securing effective early intervention, and in securing effective treatment and education over the long term.

A study using the methods of ABA, Harold said, had produced recovery in almost half of the children in the study (Lovaas, 1987).

"They recovered half their normal functioning?" I asked.

"No," Harold said, "47% of the children in the study recovered from autism."

My stomach jumped. For the first time since the diagnosis, it seemed as though there was reason to hope. Steve and I looked at each other. As long as there was reason to hope, we would work hard. We would do whatever it took to help our children recover from autism. At the medical center where I worked, there were hundreds of photos of young children in the hall through pediatric oncology. We called it the Wall of Heroes. Jason and Joshua would be heroes, too.

Again, I imagined the treatment would follow procedures in health care I had come to expect. Harold would make a referral to a specialist, and the twins would undergo a course of treatment. Right?

Not exactly. There were no health care–based providers of applied behavior analysis in our state. And even if there were, referral to these providers could come *only* from CDS.

This was confusing to us. If our child had leukemia, the hospital would have consulted our primary care physician, who would then refer us directly to treatment specialists who would deliver the care. I had developed the impression that CDS was some sort of lead early intervention agency in the state. I was only half right; I later learned that CDS is the lead early intervention *educational* agency in our state. It reports through the state Department of Education. This may seem like a minor detail, but it is one of critical importance: *health care*–based early intervention and *educational* early intervention seek different outcomes. Our failure to understand that, the CDS system's failure to effectively explain that to us, and the fact that CDS was the "sole gatekeeper" of the services we sought combined to lead us down a litigious path.

I contacted CDS, and we arranged to have our first Early Childhood Team (ECT) meeting. Harold and his knowledge of the literature about recovery were lifelines for us, and I wanted Harold to attend the ECT with us. However, Harold would be out of town for several weeks with his doctoral adviser; this, combined with the tight schedules of CDS staff, meant the soonest we could hold the ECT meeting was 6 weeks away.

Again, I faced the dilemma of how to occupy my time with the children. I could not send the twins to day-care; we had been asked to leave two day-care centers because of the kids' tantrums and intense need for supervision. While other children played or participated in group activities, Jason and Joshua systematically threw every toy over the child safety gate into the next room. When staff tried to direct the boys toward something more functional, the twins raved. If by some miracle only one child raved, that in itself was sufficient to set the other one off. Day-care staff would report to me, "He hit his head against the wall again," "He bit his hand," "He bit another child," "He ate a book." The staff would look at me expectantly, like "Why do you teach them this stuff at home?" I kept asking myself, "What do you expect me to do?" Finally, administrators would say our children were too upsetting for both staff and other children to endure. Day-care was not an option.

We had no family locally with whom to share the burden. My friends consisted only of colleagues from the medical center, all of whom had typically developing children and had no clue what we faced; nor, I suspected, was I ready to share this story, this grief process through which we struggled. When I was working, there was so much to do and so little time. Now, autism rendered me inept. At Bookland there were dozens of manuals about parenting and children.

In other sections there were books about autism. But nowhere could I find books about parenting the autistic child. I was a first-time mother with no guidance at all. Now, there was much to do, and agonizingly too much time in which to do it, but I didn't know *how* to do it.

I began fervently praying for God to recover my children from autism. "Please Lord," I prayed, "please recover Jason and Joshua from autism." In a jolt, I recalled some of the prayers I offered while I was pregnant. One was, "Lord, we trust you. If you have to bring a special needs child into this world, I think we can handle it. You have given us so much to be grateful for. We can provide good care for a special child." It was sort of a sacrifice prayer, I think. Maybe if I offered to care for a special child, God would be appeased and ensure healthy children.

Today I prayed, "Please give the boys language, God, so that we may teach them in this world. Lord, you gave mankind the gift of language. You share your Word and your commandments using language. You have given Steve and me these beautiful children to parent, and yet you have denied us the most powerful tool with which to do this job. Please help us, Lord."

How ironic that God spreads his Word through the written and spoken language, yet we were denied those tools. I guiltily recalled my words of anger and rebellion to God only weeks before, and followed with a prayer of genuine apology, seeking forgiveness. It's not my job to understand God and His motives, I reminded myself.

The clocks continued to crawl.

Finally, we attended our ECT meeting. Steve, Harold, and I were led through a labyrinth of small offices at the CDS site, to a tiny room populated with kindergarten-sized chairs. I joked that the uncomfortable furniture was one way of ensuring meetings were conducted efficiently. There was a polite chuckle, and the CDS site director called this binding meeting to order.

Steve and I began to enthusiastically share the research we had done about autism, the hope for recovery using scientifically validated methods, the providers we had identified, and the ways in which this intervention might be delivered to our family. "Based upon the scientific literature," I said, "we are seeking a 30-hour-a-week home-based program using applied behavior analysis for the children."

The site director perched sternly in her kindergarten chair. "You should know," Ms. O'Brien[1] said, "parents have no choice in the methodology we choose to use with your children, nor in the providers we select."

This was sobering. We faced the biggest challenge of our lives, and it appeared we had few choices through CDS. "Perhaps we can meet our requirements without going through CDS," I ventured.

---

[1]The name Ms. O'Brien is a pseudonym.

"CDS is the sole gatekeeper for your sons' early intervention," the director announced.

Our empowerment to face this challenge was shrinking.

Harold tried to find some common ground. "What methodology and providers are you thinking of using?" he asked.

"We routinely put children with autism in our preschool for 15 hours a week. There, the children receive 1 hour a week of occupational therapy, and 1 hour a week of speech therapy. We do a lot of sensory integration therapy, because, as you know, these kids have serious sensory issues."

"To what degree do you use applied behavior analysis?" Harold asked.

The site director waved her hand. "I am a special education professional with over 25 years of experience," she said. "There are many ways to teach children with autism. No one thing works for all kids."

"Ms. O'Brien," Steve said, "we need you to understand something. We are very committed to our children, and we will do everything we can to recover them from autism. The scientific literature clearly suggests 30 to 40 hours a week of applied behavior analysis offers us our best hope."

Ms. O'Brien was silent for a moment. "Again," she said, "I've been in this field for more than 25 years. I have never seen a child recover from autism."

I wonder why, I thought.

"I know that must be difficult for you to hear," Ms. O'Brien continued, "but the fact is, we have limited resources to help children with special needs. At 40 hours per week per child, your family alone will use 80 therapy hours per week. That is simply unacceptable. As we do with all children with autism, we will start your boys with 15 hours a week. In addition," Ms. O'Brien said, "CDS is not mandated to help your children maximize their potential. We are only mandated to ensure they make *progress*."

Let me get this straight, I thought. At the moment, there is one scientifically validated method to help children with autism reach their full potential, and one gatekeeper in the state through which to access the treatment. But the gatekeeper is mandated, is *designed*, to make us fall short of the mark. How is that smart?

I could tell Steve was losing his temper, and I wasn't far behind him. Harold jumped in. "And will those 15 hours use methods of applied behavior analysis?"

"We'll try," Ms. O'Brien said brusquely. "I'm not sure where we can find a professional who can train staff and supervise an ABA program."

"Harold has offered to do that," I pointed out.

"We don't have a contract with Harold." The implication was that for some reason that was important.

Patiently, Harold asked, "Well, do you have a contract with someone who can train staff and supervise an ABA program?"

"No. That's why we don't use ABA."

This was a nightmare of circular logic. "Can you *write* a contract with Harold?" I ventured.

"We'll see," Ms. O'Brien said. "Is there anything else?"

I had plenty to say, but said nothing.

"I can only imagine how difficult this is for your family," Ms. O'Brien said. "But there is one more thing you need to think about. Your children are your children, and they have autism. Is it fair of you not to accept them for who they are? You need to love them even though they are autistic." Color flushed my face, and I became outraged. In my professional capacity, I stayed poised, civil, and sometimes even diplomatic in confrontations. But when it came to bargaining for my sons' futures, I became unsure and tongue-tied. What has this label done to my family? Jason is Jason, the child; Joshua is Joshua, the child. Every parent wants their children to become as independent and self-fulfilled as they can be. Helping children to overcome challenges is part of parenting a typically developing child. Why do some people think helping an autistic or any other special needs child to do the same equates to "I don't love or accept my children?"

I recalled lines from a speech Catherine Maurice (1998) once gave:

> We love our children, and we will love them forever, whether or not they are autistic. But most parents I know do not love autism, and we need to be free to say that. I am happy some people have made their peace with autism. But that does not mean the rest of us have to make our peace with anything, unless we choose to do so.

Maybe someday we would choose to make peace with autism. But right now we did not have to. Our children were very young, and their outcomes were far from predetermined. I adjusted my self-image: Now I was a mother of twins with autism whom some other people perceive cannot accept or love her children.

Disgusted, we signed a contract for 15 hours a week of something vaguely defined as "developmental therapy." We didn't agree with the outcome of the meeting, but at least it was *something*.

As we left the building, I could picture Ms. O'Brien folding her arms across her chest and smiling. I imagined her saying, "Guess we showed *them* who's boss."

I'd never felt so powerless in my life. In my mind, I gave Ms. O'Brien a nickname: "Evil O'B."

How could we compromise on our vulnerable children's care? Why was the Department of Education suddenly in such a position of power over the treatment our sons would receive based on a medical diagnosis? Parents faced with a serious medical diagnosis of 2-year-olds think in terms of treatment and early intervention, not education. We think in terms of maximizing the potential of a life that has barely started, not in terms of what progress the child may make in coloring or reading or math. We had something very powerful in our favor, however: We had received an early diagnosis, and the children were very young. Brain research has revealed that during the first few years of life, the human brain is receptive to an amazing quantity of input, something referred to as brain plasticity.

Kids begin kindergarten at roughly age 5. Steve and I figured we had about 3 years to work very intensively to remediate this brain disorder called autism.

"My commitment to you," Harold said, "is that we will do this with or without CDS. We'll find volunteers or hire people. I'll train therapists and supervise the program."

We were so blessed to have Harold in our lives. We tried to negotiate compensation for Harold, but he dismissed that. "I make a good living," he shrugged. "I'm happy to do what I can." Again, the depth of Harold's generosity and compassion was overwhelming.

Each night I haunted Internet sites about autism. I became increasingly aware of controversy. People are so *passionate* about this disorder, I realized. Is there as much controversy between gatekeepers and families, and between family members, when it comes to treating children with leukemia? I was not aware of it at the medical center. When a physician says your child's best chance to combat cancer is an aggressive course of radiation treatment and chemotherapy, the parents can take or leave that recommendation. However, most parents recognize that the physician is an oncology specialist, a specialty honed over years of academic and clinical education. We turn to physicians because we expect them to cure illness or dramatically improve patient outcomes using the most proven methods. The commitment to using the most proven methods of cure and care narrows the field of choice in treatment.

Based on the scope of peer-reviewed scientific literature, the same is true of autism treatment: Science-based treatment options are currently limited to applied behavior analysis. For some reason, though, we seem unable to reach consensus about effective autism treatment, or even about how to *decide* how to decide what is effective. This, I realized, impacts families, children, gatekeepers, and providers. We waste time, emotion, energy, human resources, and money. While we argue and drift from one "promising breakthrough" to another, that precious early intervention window of opportunity unwaveringly continues to close.

Reading the posts on some of the Internet autism lists was depressing and confusing: "Ten-year-old John is incredibly stimmie[2] tonight—flapping his arms and running in circles." "Quick—I have a major PET tomorrow and I need some advice. How can I fight the special educator?" "John had a major tantrum tonight and put his foot through the wall." "Has anyone tried Epsom salt baths?" "Help me, I'm desperate. Susan is 9 and still not toilet trained." I had

enough depression and fear of the future without adding this confusion to the mix. Within a month, I canceled subscriptions to all the lists.

"Evil O'B" recommended that we apply for Medicaid coverage for the boys under the Katie Beckett waiver, which does not consider family income in its eligibility determinations. Without really understanding why we were doing it, we followed her suggestion. Determination of eligibility followed in 45 days. As it turned out, this coverage later proved to be yet another lifeline in our journey.

CDS went through the motions of placing ads in the paper for "teachers." The few candidates who responded were woefully unqualified to work with young children. I wrote a letter to the CDS board president, Shirley Tawney, expressing my frustration with CDS's lack of preparedness to meet the needs of children with autism, as well as CDS's disregard for the scientific literature about effective intervention for children with autism. There was no response.

I couldn't do much about autism yet, but I could write letters and dial the phone.

I wrote a letter to the governor. Our state was failing children with autism. What would the governor do?

I called and introduced myself to Dan Joslyn, principal of the elementary school that would be responsible for Jason's and Joshua's education when they turned 5. Our small K–6 island school had a population of 81. "You have a stake in the outcome of the early intervention of these children," I said to Dan. It was a "heads up." "Please prepare for what may be coming your way in 3 years." When the boys became school-age, I desperately wanted to avoid the kind of life-draining conflict I had had with CDS.

Dan was immediately sympathetic and candid. "We've never had children with autism in the school before," Dan admitted.

"I figure I have 3 years to educate you then," I said charmingly.

Within a week, Dan came to our house to meet the children. Shortly thereafter, Jill Adams, the Special Education Director who would be responsible for the kids' education after age 5, followed. The president of the three-person school board, Don Cowing, caught up with us at the general store. "We really want to help," Don said. "I want you to know we have agreed we will work to help your children as if they were our own." It was the start of our community's ongoing commitment to our children and our family. For the next 3 years, Dan, Jill, or Don visited once a month.

But until the kids turned 5, CDS held all the cards. CDS made several false starts with unqualified candidates attempting to deliver services in our home. Considering ourselves on our own now, Steve and I wrote an open letter to our community's churches, seeking volunteers for Harold to

---

[2]"Stimmie" means engaging in self-stimulatory actions such as arm flapping, twirling, gazing, perseverative vocalizations, and other stereotypy.

train. We had briefly contemplated hiring staff ourselves, but simple math times two made it clear that was beyond our budget. We wrote to the churches about autism, effective treatment, and the need for 60 to 80 therapy hours between the two boys.

Some church leaders read our letter to their congregations. Others posted it on bulletin boards or ran it in church newsletters. Within a few weeks, we had 15 people who had volunteered to generously give of their time and hearts. In one case, three generations of a family who worshiped at St. Mary's Catholic Church volunteered: Eddie McQuire, his 17-year-old son Shawn, and Shawn's grandmother—Eddie's mother—Pat. As Harold opened our first training session, he asked each volunteer to share why they had come forward for this demanding but rewarding work. Each said they had been touched by our letter to the churches. One young businessman, a father of four, candidly confided his motivation was no less than a calling from God.

Steve and I were deeply, deeply moved by the humility and heroism of these people, these strangers who had committed to give our family so much. It was a faith builder, and a reason to renew our hope for the future.

When the last person left after training that night, Steve and I looked at each other, then began to cry softly. "People will help us," Steve whispered.

We could go on.

Slowly we began to learn more about this unwelcome stranger in our house called autism. We found that autism severely compromises the beautifully orchestrated typical parent–child relationship. Typically, a child has or expresses needs, and parents ache to fulfill these needs. The child provides reinforcement to the parents by becoming soothed or satiated, or by demonstrably expressing love and appreciation. The child learns to depend on the parents; in turn, the parents find it rewarding to care for the child.

With untreated autism, though, the warm fuzzies of parenting can be few. I'd have given anything for Jason just to *look* at me when he heard my voice. I had surrounded Josh with nothing but love since before he was born. Why did he stiffen so when I picked him up?

Without autism, what would you two be thinking and doing now, I wondered. If I could manage your tantrums better, we could do more: go to story time at the library or take swimming lessons. These growth experiences are denied you, my little ones, until we can get it together.

Our primary care pediatrician turned out to be another ally in our quest for 30 to 40 hours a week of ABA. Refreshingly candid about his lack of experience with autism, Dr. Enright nevertheless teamed up with an autism specialist, and together the pediatricians accepted responsibility for an outcome-based care plan for the twins. Now that the children were covered by Medicaid, we sought to discover whether their therapy could be covered by Medicaid without involving CDS.

This led us to two more helpful contacts. The first was an advocate. Jim Breslin was a fast-talking ex–New Yorker who did not mince words. He listened to our story. "It sounds like a clear case of health care discrimination based on the twins' disability. I think you should contact the media," he said.

"Oh, I couldn't possibly do that," I said. "I don't think I'm ready for that."

"Look," Jim said. "This isn't about you anymore. It's about those kids. There is no shame in having children with special needs. *I* have a kid with special needs. As a mother, you need to do *whatever it takes* to get those kids the care they need."

I didn't think I was *ashamed* of autism, but neither was I completely ready to adjust my public identity and self-perception from that of a professional at the medical center to that of "mother of the twins with autism." I began to understand that, aside from accepting autism into my life, I had to adjust my *entire* self-image. I had a new and unanticipated role. Jim's words echoed incessantly in my head. "You need to do whatever it takes."

My next phone call was to a woman named Vicky. Vicky's name was given to me as someone who used to work for Medicaid, and who now worked for the Department of Mental Health/Mental Retardation. "She might be able to help you to understand the system," someone said.

No matter how long I talked to Vicky, it appeared there was no way around CDS to access the method, frequency, and intensity of treatment for the twins' *medical* diagnosis, treatment that would be funded with *health care* dollars. *"Why are educators gatekeepers of health care?"* I finally wailed to Vicky, and burst into tears over the phone.

Vicky sat in stunned silence for a moment as I sobbed. "We do need to change the system," she finally said quietly. "I know that doesn't help you right now, and I'm so, so sorry about that." It was the first time anyone, anywhere in this ridiculously annoying, frustrating, and demeaning process had said "I'm sorry." Vicky seemed to be a woman of compassion and conscience, yet a woman who worked in state government! It was an unsteadying thought to me.

"We're working on change. Parents are primary stakeholders, and we need them to help us change."

I sighed. "Change" would take forever. "Change" was not my problem at the moment.

"I'm sorry to be so emotional," I said.

"You have every right to be," she responded.

A few days later Vicky called back and invited me to serve on the Medicaid Managed Care Steering Committee. The steering committee's mission was to review whether our state should manage Medicaid dollars in an outcome-based HMO style or in a fee-for-service type of managed care. At first, I wanted to decline. How could I possibly take on anything else? Didn't I have enough to do with two autistic kids and 80 hours a week of programming to fill?

But after Steve and I talked about it, we decided it would be strategic to more fully understand Medicaid, the major funding stream that would pay for our kids' long-term care. I agreed to participate.

Through the Medicaid Managed Care Steering Committee, I learned that our state's Department of Mental Health/Mental Retardation has a stated objective to pursue "long-term outcome objectives from a whole-life perspective." This means the state recognizes that an individual's life extends beyond the school years, and thus needs to prepare individuals to live their lives fully and with as much self-sufficiency as possible. This outcome-based perspective was completely different from the Department of Education's mandate to demonstrate a student's "progress" and "educational benefit" from services.

From what I heard at CDS and at Medicaid meetings, I realized that somewhere along the line, gatekeepers had lost focus on the distinction between medically necessary *treatment* for children with autism, and a free and appropriate *education* for children with autism. Medically necessary treatment is calculated to help patients recover from illnesses and disorders. If recovery is not possible, the medical community seeks to maximize a patient's potential. The medical community evaluates its excellence, and ethics, based on the patient's *outcome*.

In contrast, and according to definitions in our state's Medicaid Manual, education consists of "academic services in those traditional subjects as science, history, literature, foreign languages and mathematics." The education community evaluates its success in educating children with special needs based on the child's *progress*—not outcome. This progress is measured with varying degrees of accuracy, and is determined to be of educational benefit within a very broad range of interpretation.

I mused that, despite best efforts, not all children will recover from autism; nor, for that matter, will all children recover from leukemia. But families and practitioners still try to recover children from disorders and diseases. Studies suggest that if we do everything right, using ABA, autistic kids have about a 50/50 shot at recovery. But unlike children who have leukemia, children with autism will not die if we are not successful at recovery. Children with autism have the same life expectancy as their typically developing peers.

ABA has been documented as building skills in *every* domain: social, cognitive, communication, academic, play/motor, and self-care, among others. It also has been scientifically validated as highly effective in reducing problem behaviors, including self-injury, aggression, and perseveration.

Every minute we invest in trying to recover a child from autism is a verifiable investment in that child's future self-sufficiency and success, whether the child recovers or not. From a cost–benefit point of view, I found research that showed competently delivered, early, intensive behavioral intervention can produce levels of self-sufficiency in children with autism that are estimated to save taxpayers about $200,000 per child up to age 22, and 1 million dollars to age 55 (Jacobson, Mulick, & Green, 1998). Isn't that what outcome-based managed care is all about?

Yet we could not bypass CDS to gain access to the Medicaid funding stream for developmental therapy, under which ABA treatment for children under 5 falls in our state. We needed to approach the problem from a different angle.

For CDS to obtain reimbursement from Medicaid, the individualized service plan had to be signed by the pediatrician, signifying the doctor's agreement that the plan meets the child's medical needs. CDS submitted a document listing 15 hours a week of treatment. As far as we were concerned, this was similar to rationing rads of radiation therapy for cancer, or to cutting meds to control high blood pressure in half. It takes what it takes.

Citing research that concludes that 30 to 40 hours a week of treatment is necessary to produce the medically indicated outcome objectives for the children, Dr. Enright refused to sign the document. This outraged CDS, which pulled what few services they had managed to provide. I then called attorney Richard O'Meara, who specializes in special ed cases.

Steve and I also decided that managing treatment and education for our children was now a full-time job, and my family leave time was nearly up. I resigned from the medical center. While the decision had been no contest, it was still painful. I had finally found an employer and a profession I adored. While I'm sure my supervisors understood, I could not help wondering if I was perceived as disloyal or unappreciative for all of the opportunities I had been given by them over the years.

At almost the same time, I received a flyer in the mail from the Johnson Group.[3] Johnson was advertising home-based applied behavior analysis programs for children with autism. I had been aware of Johnson's center-based program, but Steve and I felt a home-based program was more in line with our values and needs. Even if we had chosen Johnson's center-based program, it was an hour away under ideal conditions. We did not feel comfortable having the twins transported that distance in a special ed van. For that matter, we did not feel comfortable transporting the young twins ourselves through snow and other weather. Even if we overcame that discomfort, what would we do in the city for 6 hours? But now a home-based option was within our reach.

Before we decided to seek services from Johnson, we got parent references. Some families raved about how lucky our state was to have this resource. Others warned that Johnson's reputation was one of "our way or the highway," and

---

[3]A pseudonym for the provider.

that collaboration with families and providers outside Johnson's employ was difficult.

After consultation with attorney Dick O'Meara, we decided to file for due process. We sought 30 hours per week per child of home-based applied behavior analysis delivered by a provider with appropriate academic and clinical qualifications to treat autism. Based on our research, the only provider in the state that met these criteria was the Johnson Group. Within days of Dick's filing, CDS settled the case by agreeing to our request. It would take time to hire and train staff, but soon Johnson would take our program over from the volunteers.

We finally got our core, consistent services into place in July, 8 months after the twins were diagnosed.

Our first indication of Johnson's resistance to "playing nicely with others" came when they refused to include Harold in any aspect of the twins' treatment, despite our request. Not only did we think Harold would be a strong, ongoing member of the team, but at the very least we thought he could offer some valuable transition perspective. Yet Johnson flatly refused any contact with Harold. Because Johnson was the only provider of ABA staff in the state, we had no other choice. We sadly explained the embarrassing situation to Harold, who was exceedingly gracious about it.

"Call me whenever you need me," he said.

This experience put us on high alert that a monopoly on anything is not healthy for anyone.

Then suddenly, 2 months later my mother died, at age 59. My mother had never really believed that the twins—her only grandchildren—were autistic. I can understand that; the boys were too cute in her view to be autistic. If Mom left this world without the weight of worrying about the boys and our family, I could live with that. My father, brother, sister, and I struggled to accept Mom's sudden death. Once again, I had to adjust my self-image. Yesterday, I had a mother. Today, I do not.

Johnson compassionately rallied around my family to provide logistical support. "We'll have staff there overtime," the director said, "so you can go bury your mother." I hadn't thought about it, but she was right: The twin's behaviors were unpredictable enough that I dared not take the boys to Mom's funeral.

While grieving over the next few months, I learned one more life lesson: Autism does not insulate us from the other realities of life. Despite the disproportionate difficulties autism placed on our parenting, loved ones still die, fade to Alzheimer's, struggle with cancer, have car accidents, or get fired.

But neither does autism deny us some joys in life. Intimacy with Steve deepened, as we rose to challenges. There was joy in the small steps of progress Jason and Josh made every day. Sunsets were still beautiful, and music could still soothe the soul.

With more consistent staff now, my role in advocacy and state policy development was expanding. Responding to increased controversy over effective education for children with autism, a group of special educators invited me onto a task force that would analyze interventions. Ironically, this invitation came from Shirley Tawney, who had been CDS board president when we filed suit against CDS. I was tempted to decline, because I was distrustful of the educators.

"Evil O'B will be on that task force too," I said to my Dad, who was visiting over the first Thanksgiving holiday since Mom died. "I can't stand the idea of being in the same room with her." Just mentally picturing this woman made me feel exploited and powerless over my own family's future.

"Did it ever occur to you people like Ms. O'Brien are not really evil?" Dad said thoughtfully.

Steve agreed. "Maybe they're just misinformed. To bring closure to this CDS suit, you have to stop being so bitter."

"Maybe you should do more educational outreach. Do some positive things. Help make change in the state. Work with these educators," my Dad suggested.

It was a novel concept, one that felt vaguely illicit. How many of my convictions would I have to swallow this time? Still, for now our children had some solid programming. These educators would convene their task force with or without me. Better to be part of the process, my family decided, than to be a victim of it. And as Steve said, maybe helping to make some positive changes for children with autism would help heal my grief over both the diagnosis of autism and the death of my mother.

At the first task force meeting, Shirley made a startling announcement: "I have volunteered to co-chair this task force because my great-nephew was diagnosed with autism last summer." I saw the pain in Shirley's eyes as she looked fleetingly at me. Another life lesson: Our children were not the first to be autistic, and they certainly won't be the last.

After the meeting, Shirley took me aside. "Would you be willing to talk to the mother?" she asked. "She's devastated."

"Of course," I said. What could I say to this mother, I wondered. I was becoming an "elder" in this carousel of diagnosis and coping already. Shirley hugged me, surprising me. My heart melted. Pain brings people together in strange ways.

One beautiful Saturday we put the boys in the Subaru for a drive. Before we'd gone 10 miles, the boys fussed. "Let's turn around," I said. "No sense taking chances." Steve pulled into Hawkes' Nursery and turned around.

Jason went ballistic. Josh went ballistic because Jason was ballistic. Even though the boys were confined to their three-point restraint car seats, they could reach each other. They pinched, scratched, and bit each other, and themselves. They kicked the backs of our front seats. I unclasped my seat belt, turned around on my knees, and tried to protect the boys from one another, taking the bulk of their blows myself. I began to bleed. "Do you want me to pull over?" Steve asked.

"Get—us—home," I hissed.

The event set us up for several hours of tantrum behavior that afternoon. Jason became so angry he put his foot through his bedroom door. When we finally went to bed that night, I cried myself to sleep.

The next evening Steve proudly led me to the Subaru. "I fixed it," he said. There, between the two car seats, was a plywood barrier. "Look," Steve said. "I even engineered it so as the kids get taller, we can add height."

I was grateful for a way to protect the children from each other in the car. But the idea of facing this as the kids "get taller" was sobering.

From time to time people would stop me in Shop'n Save's parking lot, pointing to the barricade. "Wow! Is that because your kids fight in the car?"

"Yeah."

"What a great idea. Where can I get one?"

I was invited onto more committees and work groups struggling to improve systems of care and education for children with special needs. These experiences were incredibly useful in understanding the mindset and culture of administrators who make important decisions about the care of our children. Some of the mindset and culture was, I learned, foisted upon our administrators through lawsuits and consent decrees. But on a good day, I could contribute an observation or logical argument that actually moved the needle closer to effective and family-friendly systems. State government became very good at "talking the talk." Could they "walk the walk"?

We were about to find out.

Despite having what many now considered to be a very comprehensive early intervention program in place for Jason and Joshua, some disturbing trends were emerging. Both boys remained nonverbal, despite intensive efforts with communications programs. The twins' inability to communicate frustrated them. In addition, the Johnson Group insisted on working with both boys in the same room. This added to the boys' levels of frustration and anguish. When one twin began to tantrum, the other would inevitably follow. No matter how many times I suggested that the twins should be separated—after all, a singleton would have less distraction in a home-based program—my request was denied on the logic that the therapists could support one another in the same room. Another disagreement we had with Johnson was that, although we wanted each 3-year-old twin to learn to wait quietly at the door before going outside, in Johnson's model both twins had to be quiet at the same time. This penalized the "good" twin when the "bad" twin was having trouble. Again, a singleton could learn to wait quietly without this added demand.

I was sufficiently frustrated that my increasing number of concerns were brushed aside that I retained a PhD behavior analyst from out of state to consult with the program every other month. Maybe I simply didn't have the qualifications

to have my input and requests respected, I thought. To ensure that the consultant had sufficient information with which to begin and provide ongoing consult, I copied all the programs and data, and sent videotape as well, each time before she arrived. The consultant made numerous helpful suggestions that would increase the strength of our program.

Consistent with Johnson's refusal to collaborate with outsiders, however, I eventually received a letter from Johnson's local director: "We are sorry the current arrangement is not working out. Please let us know if we can help you identify another provider." . . . A not so thinly veiled threat that if we wanted to use the expertise of others, Johnson would no longer work with our family. For a second time, we found ourselves in the powerless and embarrassing position of being forced to dismiss from our treatment team a professional for whom we have great respect. Intolerable? Of course it was intolerable. But in our rural state, there was simply no alternative.

I vowed to create alternatives. A monopoly was not in the best interests of children with autism.

Jason and Joshua began to add aggression, self-injury, and property destruction more routinely to their tantrum behaviors. I kept incident reports, along with photographs and videotapes of the increasingly frightening behaviors taking place in our home. We were appropriately instructed by Johnson to remain neutral through these horrendous events; we did not want to teach the boys that the way to get attention, or anything else, was by pinching, biting, or damaging our home. We became adept at not flinching when Josh pinched. There is one photograph of Steve wearing a short-sleeved shirt. His arms are covered with quarter- and dime-sized bruises ranging in color from yellow to blue to green. Another summer day I went to the autism task force meeting with a bruise the size of an orange on my upper arm. My colleagues were learning more and more about what autism can do to families.

Johnson conducted several assessments to try to pinpoint the function of these behaviors. The behaviors seemed to ebb and flow along with a variety of variables. In response to the incident reports, photographs, and videotapes, the Early Childhood Team twice volunteered another 5 hours per week per child, bringing each child's home-based program up to 40 hours a week. The boys' behaviors continued to escalate, however.

Johnson, which did not have an in-state PhD-level aberrant behavior specialist on staff, took data, videotapes, and lead staff to their main office two states away for guidance. By coincidence, on the same day, we had a meeting with Jill Adams, who would be the boys' public school special education director when they turned 5.

Because of the respect I was gaining for the educators on the autism task force and my regard for Jill, I discovered I would have to revise my view of special educators. Dad and Steve were right: Special educators are not evil. They needed to know that there was more to know about autism, and they needed a respectful guide to help them through.

The effects of powerlessness and perceived exploitation were beginning to heal. I dropped "Evil O'B" from my vocabulary.

I fanned the incident reports and photographs on the table in front of Jill and Robert, a professional from the Department of Mental Health/Mental Retardation. Jill and Robert watched the same videotape of the twins' aggression, tantrum, and self-injury behaviors that Johnson staff were using to make some decisions. They were alarmed at the intensity of these behaviors. Both were silent when the tape finished. "Lora," Jill whispered, "I have nothing for you. I have no idea how to respond to that level of behavior." Robert agreed. "We have to consider residential placement."

We knew there were no residential placements that offered ABA models of care and education in our state. The closest ones our team would consider were two states away.

A few hours later, the Johnson staff returned from their own consultation about the boys' behavior. They were ashen. "Our clinical supervisors think we need to consider residential care," the director said quietly.

Among the professionals, it was unanimous.

It was December 10, exactly 2 years to the day from when we had sat in Harold's office with renewed hope for our children's recovery from autism. The children were now 4.

However, the concept of residential treatment and education for Jason and Joshua was not unanimous among some of the funding streams. And the timing for this recommendation could not have been worse. One of my work groups was responding to legislation that demanded an interdepartmental, long-term outcome approach to the care of children with mental health, mental retardation, and autism diagnoses. Historically, our state spent most of the budget caring for these children with intensive needs at residential placements out of state. Not only did this fracture families, but what little data we could get suggested these placements were of questionable therapeutic value. From a pragmatic public policy point of view, these placements sent an astonishing number of jobs out of state as well.

Therefore, one of my work group's key objectives was to bring children back home to community-based resources that would keep families together and meet intensive needs. It was a concept I passionately believed in at a very personal level. How could I send my darling, beautiful, wonderful children away at the age of 4? Autistic or not, we love them! Contemplating Jason's and Joshua's empty beds each night would be heartbreaking. What if there was a fire at this "placement"? Who would soothe the boys when they were sick? What if a pedophile slipped into the ranks of staff undetected? How could we not be a part of the boys' daily progress? Who would charm the boys into those precious smiles, those hugs that came more and more easily now?

What would I do with myself all day if the boys left? Of course, I could go back to work, but we were called to *care* for these special children. I could just picture it: The children go to residential care, and I adjust my self-image from the mother of twins with autism to the mother of twins with autism who no longer even live in our home.

I struggled with the idea of residential placement. Of course, there are families and circumstances under which residential placement is the best course of action: single parent families, for example, or families in which siblings might be hurt by the violent behaviors of a child with autism. But we did not face these additional challenges. Residential placement simply did not seem right for our children.

Despite our discomfort, we numbly went through the motions of intake for the residential placements, simply to hold the slots.

I asked for a review before the Local Case Resolution Committee (LCRC), an outgrowth of some of the work done at the state level to improve systems of care and education for special needs kids. The LCRC was comprised of, among others, special educators; people from the Department of Mental Health/Mental Retardation, the Department of Human Services, and the Department of Corrections; and parents. The LCRC heard the toughest cases, and they had some pooled funding. This pooled funding allowed great flexibility with which to overcome systemic roadblocks.

I pleaded with the committee to help me find a way to keep the children in our home. The children needed intensive treatment and education, yes. But couldn't we innovate something that would provide it in the home and community?

Over 2 hours, the committee did not find solutions. But they offered support. If I could come up with a model that would work, they would help me make it happen. In the meantime, the LCRC authorized funding to increase services in the home to 12 hours a day, to keep the children safe and in a therapeutic environment. We retained the services of Jessica Irish, a certified nurse's assistant, who worked tirelessly with the boys, taking duty no one else wanted: a workday that began at 5 a.m.; emptying commodes; and making new therapy materials at the voracious rate at which we consumed them, with 40 to 60 objectives per child.

Johnson did not have staff for 12 hours a day, 7 days a week, so the increase was phased in over time, as staff was hired and trained. By June, the twins' self-injury and aggression had diminished substantially. In addition, a class action lawsuit settlement opened some Medicaid funding streams for intensive in-home supports for families like mine, boding well for the relative stability of our model.

Our team decided to defer residential placement. For now, at least, the boys could stay home.

By fall it was obvious that Jason was progressing in his treatment much faster than Joshua. Jason had taught himself to read using flash cards with a word on one side and a photograph on the other. With his behavior analytic speech therapist, Jason began using dialogue boards and the Picture Exchange Communication System (PECS; Frost & Bondy, 1994) to communicate. At first I was not supportive of these augmentative communication strategies. But Mark Hammond, the speech–language pathologist, made it clear: "Until this boy can talk, we'll invest in building his literacy." Who could be against literacy? When Jason began to talk, he was fully prepared with a good grasp of sentence structure and meaning. Mark was right.

Jason's first sentences were very simple:

MOM: Jason, who's cute?

JASON: Me.

MOM: Who's smart?

JASON: (Points to head) Me.

MOM: Where are you going to college?

JASON: M-I-T.

MOM: How are you going to pay for it?

JASON: J-O-B.

MOM: And what are you going to study?

JASON: Gheeshig (Engineering).

Josh, though, lagged behind. He had mysterious spells of what we called "sads"; inexplicably, Josh's mood would swing from happy to tearful. First his face would fall, then his eyes would water, and he would begin to cry. The staff speculated that these "sads" were associated with seizure activity, but our physicians could find no indication of this.

That one twin might recover and the other one might not posed a horrifying "Sophie's Choice" dilemma the first time the thought occurred to us: How could we rejoice in one twin's progress when the other was still so challenged? But how could we overlook the awesome miracle of one recovery, a beacon of hope that another may someday follow?

Eventually we realized we perceived Josh to be lagging because of the inevitable comparisons with Jason. Measured against only himself, Josh was making tremendous progress. There were still no guarantees of recovery, but each boy was making sure and steady progress.

From time to time a new disagreement between our family and the Johnson clinical staff arose. We sought to condition Josh to a convenient token reinforcement system, but Johnson claimed this was too "abstract" for Josh. We sought to use most-to-least prompting, or prescriptive prompting; but Johnson clung stubbornly to their institutional preference for least-to-most prompting, with correction trials that were very frustrating for Josh. Considering how much time we spent together and the position of control Johnson had over our children, these sorts of disagreements were probably to be expected.

The therapists were a dream. They were incredibly dedicated, talented, and persistent with the boys. They were well trained. But sometimes clinical decisions the staff were instructed to implement by their supervisors were illogical to us or uncomfortable for us, and we had great difficulty in getting those points across. For the most part, there was nothing dangerous, although when dealing with severe aggression and self-injury behaviors, there is always an element of danger to both staff and children. We squabbled with Johnson clinical staff over the efficiency of programming and about the level of detail we perceived to be missing from data that would help us make better decisions for the boys.

"We have a sense of urgency about addressing behaviors that interfere with growth in young children with autism," Dr. Mark Steege, our consulting school psychologist, said to me one day. "Those behaviors interfere with increased independence, communication, social interaction, academics, and leisure. When do people call big meetings?"

"When kids exhibit big problem behaviors?" I guessed.

"Exactly. We do not have the same sense of urgency about the rate at which positive behaviors are acquired. Why doesn't anyone call big meetings when the child is learning slowly?"

"It's my impression sometimes they've labeled the child a slow learner, or decided he can't learn the task at all."

"They blame the learner."

I found myself wishing more and more often that there was more than one provider of ABA services in the state. I found myself wishing we could replicate at least one of the outstanding programs in New Jersey, California, New York, or Massachusetts.

I realized that unless somebody in my state tried to do exactly that, we'd always be consumers without choice. In addition, the Johnson Group would never be able to serve every child with autism in our region well. There was one other provider starting an early intervention program using ABA for kids with autism, but the way things were going, it still wouldn't be enough.

The autism task force had completed its work. Our 2-year, evidence-based assessment of interventions for autism had concluded that applied behavior analysis is currently the only intervention validated as effective for individuals with autism by the scope of peer-reviewed science. When the report was released, demand for ABA services would likely skyrocket.

I called Shirley. "Let's develop some resources," I said. "We need more ABA choices for all these kids." Slowly, a dream took shape: the Center for Child Development (CCD). It would be a collaborative program partnering special education and the medical community. From what I could see, the medical community had abdicated responsibility for the treatment of children with autism to the special education system. No wonder our special education budgets were so inflated! CCD would educate the medical community about autism today, and invite them to resume their role in coordinating an outcome-based plan of care for the children. Special educators could use outcome-based medical resources to supplement progress-based programs, for better outcomes all around. It wasn't like we weren't already spending this money. We were. We were just not coordinating it or communicating with one another about it. This led to inefficient, counterproductive, incompatible, and inconsistent interventions. Maybe I saw the situation more clearly because we had two kids going through autism interventions at the same time. Why did we need to break the kids down into funding streams? Why did we have to have different sets of goals and objectives for each one? Why did we need a different case manager for every agency? This was crazy!

Then, tragedy struck. A family nearby had 6-year-old triplet boys with autism, as well as a typically developing 2-year-old girl. The children's father was a trucker. One afternoon while Dad was on the road, fire broke out in the home at 4 p.m. The triplets did not know what to do. Each child coped with this bewildering conflagration by retreating to his favorite place in the house: one body was found in the computer room, another in a bedroom. The third child was found on the first floor after the second floor caved in. All three boys perished. The mother was able to save the little girl, at considerable injury to herself.

Our communities were devastated, and we mourned with the parents. Well aware of our own vulnerabilities when it comes to safety, Steve and I mourned on a very personal level. I kept asking myself, "Why weren't these children in some sort of therapeutic after-school program?" I recalled an article about a 10-year-old boy with autism who climbed a high tension tower, but could not get down. His slightly older brother, who was afraid of heights, heroically climbed the tower to soothe the child until help could arrive. Why wasn't that child in some sort of therapeutic after-school program? On top of everything else, we need to keep our children *safe*.

We *needed* the Center for Child Development. Shirley and I began meeting weekly to build this dream. We brought others in when we needed them, then regrouped for different phases of the development. United in a common quest, Shirley and I found our friendship deepening.

Sometimes I'd see our original volunteers around town. They'd ask excitedly about the boys. I always had new pictures to share.

"The kids must have turned 5 by now," ex-volunteer John said one day.

I was pleased that he had tracked them so long and remembered such a minor detail after nearly 3 years.

"How could you possibly remember that?" I asked.

"Oh, I saw that the special ed budget at the school jumped way up this year. I figured that was you guys . . ." Suddenly hearing how that might sound to me, John turned red. "Not that that's bad, I just figured. . . ."

I laughed and gave him a hug. My community had embraced these children with their hearts, minds, time, and

pocketbooks, and we were eternally grateful. At town meeting time, the local paper thought this was unusual enough to comment about it:

> Voters were willing to pay more to meet the needs of schoolchildren. The town's $2.7 million budget was approved by a wide margin with little debate, even though it will raise the property tax rate from $13.20 for each $1,000 of taxable property value to $14.35. The difference will cost the owner of a $100,000 home $115 a year. Among the school expenses driving up the budget is an increase in special education costs for 19 students. . . ."

A year later, the Johnson Group called a meeting with our family to explore what they termed the "fragility" of our intensive, community-based intervention for Jason and Joshua. The fact was that the country's strong economy was making it difficult for Johnson to recruit and retain staff within their existing rate structure with the state. Slowly, our staffing hours began to ebb. Johnson tried fervently to staff these hours, but it became impossible for them. The boys' tantrum behavior and self-injury escalated proportionally.

"We strongly urge you to follow our recommendation of 2 years ago for residential placement," they told us.

At many points along this arduous path, it would have been easy to give up. Give up on what? The children's recovery from autism is one obvious answer. Even though the children are now 6 years old, we have not given up on the possibility of recovery.

First of all, I have reason to seriously disagree with people who say recovery from autism is not possible. What is recovery from autism? At its most basic level, it is when the individual once met but no longer meets the criteria for autism in the *Diagnostic and Statistical Manual of Mental Disorders* (American Psychiatric Association, 1994). As a parent, I will not dignify the contention that if the child recovers, he or she was obviously once misdiagnosed. The circular logic inherent in the idea that autism is by definition a lifelong disorder is an obstacle to improving outcomes. Emerging data show that definition may need to be changed.

Second, there is nothing wrong with pursuit of the ideal. People who say we should let autistic individuals be autistic have never faced my sons' self-injurious and perilously aggressive behaviors. No one can convince me it is humane or ethical to accept that these behaviors are simply part of my sons' natures.

Third, we know much more today about how individuals with autism can learn. I will not look to the past as an indication of what the future will bring. If we decide recovery is unattainable after the age of 6 and we stop trying, it will become a self-fulfilling prophesy. I might also point out that one of the children in the original Lovaas (1987) study required 6 years of treatment before he no longer met the diagnostic criteria for autism.

But perseverance is not only about recovery. It's about being the kind of family we want to be. It's about really understanding that all individuals with autism, regardless of age, can make significant, meaningful progress toward rich and independent lives using scientifically validated treatment methods. If recovery happens along the way, so much the better. I don't know if one or both of the boys will ever recover, and it doesn't mean as much to me as it once did. What is important to me is the peace in my heart that comes from knowing that we have done and will continue to do, as Jim Breslin said all those years ago, "whatever it takes" to help our children reach their full potential. We will never, ever give up.

Guided by the peace that also settled upon us after much prayer, Steve and I knew that the answer to Johnson's second call for residential placement was "No." We were blessed with the knowledge and the public resources that allow our children, who for now are very challenging, to remain in the home with us. We began working with another provider specializing in "virtual" residential treatment programs—essentially, a group home in the family home. The provider did not have ABA expertise, but we could buy that from consultants. Harold came back, and Mark Steege stayed on. What the new provider *did* have that was essential to keeping our family together was a residential model infrastructure. Johnson had heroically tried to cobble one together, and succeeded amazingly well for nearly 2 years. But they simply were not set up to do this under these emerging economic and clinical conditions.

It was time for a change. And we were ready to face the future as a family.

Dear Lora,

During my meditation time this morning, I found myself thanking God for autism, and especially for how my life has changed since knowing you and your family. Then I thought, "Wait a minute. This is not right. Thankful for **autism***?" But as I thought for a while longer, everything became very clear to me.*

I was about to experience a difficult transition to retirement in my life, but I had been unwilling to share my fears and feelings with anyone. Consequently, I was facing an unknown future that was without purpose; scary, and affecting me in more ways than I was aware.

You and I worked for almost 2 years as colleagues on the autism task force. As you know, my interest in autism began because my great-nephew was diagnosed as autistic.

Lora, I gained such profound respect and professional admiration for your commitment and hard work. When our autism task force completed its work, there was a void in my life. I was happy when you began work on the Center for Child Development. I challenged myself to learn as much as possible to help children with autism.

This commitment was precipitated by regret for my insensitivity to your family's needs and knowledge when I was president of Child Development Services. It was later affirmed when you explained why your family could not come to my home for lunch, because the boys did not yet have the skills necessary to succeed in that setting; instead, you invited me to your home for dinner. I realized that no one can understand what parents of children with autism face until you are in their home often. Thank you for inviting me and others into your home and hearts; this cannot always be easy for you and Steve.

When I finally read Catherine Maurice's (1994) book Let Me Hear Your Voice, it helped me feel the pain and understand more about parents of children with disabilities. I could say the rest is history, but that would not explain the depth of my story.

Because you shared your pain and honest feelings, I have been able to share mine with you; because your family has embraced me unconditionally as "Auntie Shirley," I have a new family to love; because of your commitment to making a difference in the lives of children with autism, I redoubled mine; because you shared your faith in God with me, I was moved to renew my faith and make a full commitment to God. At 64 years of age, all of these things have given me a new exuberance for life.

So perhaps I should not thank God for autism; but how would this all have taken place if Jason and Josh did not have autism?

Love, Shirley

Dear Shirley,
How can I possibly answer this? What are the right words?
Zkjskrjskhiyreh

Oops. It's hard to get any writing done right now. I'm at the laptop in our bedroom. The door to the attic is in here. Jason and Joshua discovered the virtual toy store in the attic a few weeks ago. I had forgotten all about it. Once I packed those toys away so long ago, I never thought about them. Now the kids act like they have won the lottery.
"Mama! Doggie!"
"Yes, Jason, it's a dog. Is the dog soft or hard?"
"Sssssft."
"Great, Jason! The dog is soft!"
How far we've come, Shirley, I thought. In 4 short years we have performed an evidence-based assessment of autism interventions; gained the cooperation and understanding of special educators about the importance of effective, intensive early autism intervention; invited the medical community to resume its role in outcome-based care management for children with autism; formed models to ensure that the dollars we invest to help children with autism achieve self-sufficiency are spent with accountability . . .

Don't let the word get out, however. Everyone fighting autism will want to move to this state. And that's not the right answer, is it? Imagine a world in which every family faced with a diagnosis of autism enters a service system that is family friendly, science based, and outcome driven, no matter where they live. There's nothing magic about this. It just takes work and commitment. If someone asked me, I'd say call your state Department of Education *right now,* and convene a task force to perform evidence-based assessments of autism treatments. Call your state Department of Mental Retardation and Developmental Disabilities *right now,* and form a group charged with developing service delivery systems that are responsive to families' needs. Call your Department of Human Services *right now,* and secure their commitment to the core value that a special child has the right to reach his or her highest developmental capacity.

And pray for guidance, strength, and resources. It works.

You're too busy to make change happen? We're all too busy. We need to make the time. We're in this for the long haul, for our children.

"Josh, did you find a toy?"

"Yeah."

Oh, it's a puzzle. "Puzzle."

Huge smile. "Puh."

"Awesome talking!"

What is it Margaret Mead said? "Never doubt that a small group of thoughtful citizens can change the world; indeed, it is the only thing that ever has."

References

American Psychiatric Association. (1994). *Diagnostic and statistical manual of mental disorders* (4th ed.). Washington, DC: Author.

Frost, L. A., & Bondy, A. S. (1994). *The picture exchange communication system.* Cherry Hill, NJ: Pyramid Educational Consultants.

Jacobson, J. W., Mulick, J. A., & Green, G. (1998). Cost–benefit estimates for early intensive behavioral intervention for young children with autism: General model and single state case. *Behavioral Interventions, 13,* 201–226.

Lovaas, O. I. (1987). Behavioral treatment and normal educational and intellectual functioning in young autistic children. *Journal of Consulting and Clinical Psychology, 55,* 3–9.

Maurice, C. (1994). *Let me hear your voice: A family's triumph over autism.* New York: Ballantine.

Maurice, C. (1998, March). *Effective intervention for autism: Clearing the path.* Speech presented at the Autism Intervention Movement Conference on Science in Autism Treatment, Pittsburgh.

Index

About the Authors

◆ ◆ ◆ ◆ ◆ ◆ ◆ ◆ ◆ ◆ ◆ ◆ ◆ ◆ ◆ ◆ ◆ ◆ ◆

William H. Ahearn, PhD, is a program director at the New England Center for Children and a clinical assistant professor in the Masters in Applied Behavior Analysis Program at Northeastern University. Ahearn completed undergraduate studies at the University of Miami and received his doctorate in experimental psychology at Temple University in 1992. He completed a postdoctoral fellowship in the Department of Behavioral Psychology at the Kennedy Krieger Institute and Johns Hopkins University School of Medicine, where he specialized in the functional analysis and treatment of severe self-injurious behavior and aggression in 1993. Ahearn then served as program manager for the Inpatient Pediatric Feeding Program at the Children's Seashore House in Philadelphia, then moved to the New England Center for Children in 1996. He has co-authored several studies on the treatment of pediatric feeding problems and several articles on other topics in applied behavior analysis and the experimental analysis of behavior. Ahearn currently sits on the board of editors for the *Journal of Applied Behavior Analysis* and *Behavioral Interventions*. He is also serving as the program chair for the Berkshire Association for Behavior Analysis and Therapy.

Pamela F. Dawson, BA, has a degree in economics from the University of Pittsburgh. Prior to the birth of her two children, she worked as an assistant vice president of operations for Mellon Bank. Since her daughter was diagnosed with autism in 1994, she has become an advocate for appropriate services for children with autism within the state of Pennsylvania. She has served on the boards of several nonprofit organizations that advocate for persons with disabilities, including the Autism Intervention Movement and the Arc of Westmoreland County.

Deborah Fein received her PhD in clinical psychology from Rutgers University and did postdoctoral training in neuropsychology at Boston University School of Medicine and the Boston V.A. Medical Center. She has had a long-standing interest in disorders on the autistic spectrum, publishing approximately 60 articles and book chapters in this area. Her research has been funded by the National Institute of Mental Health and the National Institute of Neurological Disorders and Stroke, and is currently being funded by the National Alliance of Autism Research and the March of Dimes. Major research projects at present concern the early detection of autism, cognitive impairments in autism, and neuropeptides in autism. She teaches in the clinical psychology program at the University of Connecticut and has a small private practice in Springfield, Massachussetts, where she lives with her husband and two daughters.

Edward C. Fenske, MAT, EdS, is the director of education programs at the Princeton Child Development Institute. PCDI is widely recognized for its contributions to the research literature of applied behavior analysis and autism intervention. This research has produced effective treatment models for persons with autism that are now being replicated nationally and internationally. Fenske's experience in delivering intervention to children with autism, support services to their families, and training and supervision to professional staff spans 25 years. His published works have addressed home programming, language development, and early intervention. He is a frequent presenter at local, state, and national conferences and has provided training and consultation services to parents and professionals in both public and private schools.

Richard M. Foxx, PhD, is a professor of psychology at Pennsylvania State University at Harrisburg and a clinical adjunct professor of pediatrics at the College of Medicine of Pennsylvania State University. Foxx has written five books, including *Toilet Training Persons with Developmental Disabilities, Increasing Behaviors of Persons with Severe Retardation and Autism, Decreasing Behaviors of Persons with Severe Retardation and Autism,* and *Looking for the Words: Teaching Functional Language Strategies.* All have been translated into other languages. He has written over 130 scientific publications, has made 13 training films, and has given over 1,000 talks on the use of behavioral principles to treat individuals with autism, mental retardation, mental illness, emotional disturbances, and typical development. Foxx is an internationally recognized expert in treating behavioral problems. He has lectured in 15 foreign countries and 47 states throughout the United States. He is editor-in-chief of the journal *Behavioral Interventions*. He was co-editor-in-chief of *Analysis and Intervention in Developmental Disabilities,* is on the editorial board of eight scientific journals, and is the consulting editor for the Research Press Special Education Series. Foxx is a Fellow in four divisions of the American Psychological Association, the American Psychological Society, and the American Association on Mental Retardation. He was president of the Society for the Advancement of Behavior Analysis; the Association for Behavior Analysis; and the Division of Mental Retardation and Developmental Disabilities of the American Psychological Association. He is a vice president of The Association for Science in Autism Treatment. In 1998 he received a Lifetime Achievement Award from the New York State Association for Behavior Analysis and was made an honorary member of the Norwegian Association for Behavior

Analysis. He has served as an expert witness in a number of court cases involving individuals with autism and developmental disabilities, including *Youngberg v. Romeo*, which was heard by the U.S. Supreme Court. He is a licensed psychologist and Board Certified Behavior Analyst. One of his books, *Toilet Training in Less Than a Day*, has sold over 2 million copies and has been translated into seven languages, and one of his training films, *Harry* (the treatment of a self-abusive man), has won numerous cinematic awards.

Gina Green received a PhD in psychology (analysis of behavior) from Utah State University following undergraduate and master's degree studies in psychology and educational psychology at Michigan State University. She taught in the Behavior Analysis and Therapy graduate program at Southern Illinois University for 3 years. Presently Green is director of research at the New England Center for Children in Southborough, Massachusetts; associate scientist at the E. K. Shriver Center for Mental Retardation in Waltham, Massachusetts; and clinical associate professor of psychiatry, University of Massachusetts Medical School. She has authored numerous articles, chapters, and abstracts on various topics in the education and treatment of individuals with developmental disabilities and brain injuries, and the experimental analysis of behavior. Green co-edited the book *Behavioral Intervention for Young Children with Autism*, published by PRO-ED. She has served on the editorial boards of several professional journals in developmental disabilities and behavior analysis, and currently serves on the Board of Trustees of the Cambridge Center for Behavioral Studies, the Board of Directors of the Association for Science in Autism Treatment, and the advisory boards of several autism programs and parent organizations. She is a Board Certified Behavior Analyst, and was president of the Association for Behavior Analysis for 1999–2000. *Psychology Today* named her the 2000 Mental Health Professional of the Year. Green lectures and consults widely on autism and related disorders, behavioral research, and effective interventions for people with disabilities.

Suzanne Jasper, MEd, has been working with children with autism for 11 years and currently serves as head teacher at the Alpine Learning Group in Paramus, New Jersey. In 1998 she was awarded the Teacher of the Year award from the Center for Outreach and Services for the Autism Community, New Jersey. She holds a master's degree in special education from William Paterson University. Jasper has presented at regional and national conferences and has co-authored several research articles related to autism treatment.

Patricia J. Krantz, PhD, is executive director of the Princeton Child Development Institute, a community-based, nonprofit program offering a broad spectrum of services to children, youths, and adults with autism. Krantz holds academic appointments at the University of Kansas, University of North Texas, and Queens College of the City University of New York. She is the author of many journal articles and book chapters; her current research focuses on stimulus control

procedures that increase spontaneous, generative language. She has made many international contributions to autism intervention, including lectures at The British Institute of Mental Handicap; the Congress of the European Association of Behavior Therapy; the Dean's Leading Edge Lecture at Deakin University, Victoria, Australia; and keynote addresses at the first conference on autism in the Soviet Union and at the Norwegian Association for Behavior Analysis.

Miriam Liss received her BA from Wesleyan University and her MA from the University of Connecticut. She is currently pursuing her PhD in clinical psychology from the University of Connecticut. For her dissertation, she developed a scale designed to measure sensory disturbances in children with autism. She was awarded the Collins scholarship from the Autism Society of America for this research. She has also investigated executive functioning and predictors of adaptive functioning in children with autism. She has taught abnormal psychology at both the University of Connecticut and the University of Hartford and psychology of women at the University of Connecticut. She is currently completing her clinical internship at the VA Consortium in Newington, Connecticut.

Gregory S. MacDuff, PhD, is the director of adult and community-living program at the Princeton Child Development Institute and adjunct professor at the University of Kansas. He has authored articles and book chapters on incidental teaching, photographic activity schedules, staff training strategies, prompt and prompt-fading procedures, and intervention models in residential settings. He has lectured nationally and internationally, and has provided consultation and training to a variety of public and private programs.

Catherine Maurice, who holds a PhD in French literature and literary criticism from New York University, is the author of *Let Me Hear Your Voice: A Family's Triumph Over Autism* (Knopf, 1993) and the principal editor of *Behavioral Intervention for Young Children with Autism: A Manual for Parents and Professionals* (PRO-ED, 1996, with Gina Green and Steven C. Luce, co-editors). In addition to her writing and editing activities, she serves on several boards, including the Association for Science in Autism Treatment, of which she is president, and the Behavior Analyst Certification Board. She is a founding member of the READ (Reading Excellence and Discovery) Board, an organization that works to bring direct instruction to inner-city children who are reading below grade level. Maurice lives in Connecticut with her husband and three children.

Lynn E. McClannahan, PhD, is executive director of the Princeton Child Development Institute. Nationally and internationally known, the Institute was one of the first community-based programs in the United States for people with autism. McClannahan's research on behavioral intervention, accountability systems, staff training and mentoring, and program evaluation has been recognized by the Senate of the State of New Jersey (commendation on research and service to persons with autism, 1988); by the National Teaching–Family Association (Outstanding Contributions Award, 1989); by the Norwegian Association for Behavior Analysis (featured interview in *Diskriminanten*, 1991); by Developmental Disabilities Services Managers (Annual Award for Outstanding Contributions in Management, 1992); and by Division 25 of the American Psychological Association (first Fred S. Keller Award for Distinguished Contributions to Behavioral Education, 1994). She and Patricia Krantz are co-authors of a recent book, *Activity Schedules for Children with Autism: Teaching Independent Behavior*.

Lora Perry earned her MS in business education from New Hampshire College. She and her husband Steve are the parents of twin boys who have autism. Jason and Joshua are treated and educated using supported inclusion principles of applied behavior analysis in home, school, and community settings. Perry is a board member of the Association for Science in Autism Treatment. She also continues to be involved in advocacy and resource development for science-based autism treatment, education, and research in her community and state, as well as nationwide.

Margery F. Rappaport, MA, CCC-SLP, is a speech–language pathologist in private practice in New York City. Having majored in theater at Boston University, she went on to receive a master's degree in speech–language pathology at Columbia University in New York. Rappaport has worked at the Morristown Memorial Hospital in Morristown, New Jersey, as well as New York City's Morrisania City Hospital, Montefiore Hospital and Medical Center's Center for Child Development, and the Head Start Program. Although Rappaport treats children with a variety of speech and language disorders, most of her practice involves working with children with autism and pervasive developmental disorders and their parents. She consults and lectures on communication in autistic spectrum disorders at schools, universities, and conferences in the New York metropolitan area and throughout the United States. Rappaport's work appears in Catherine Maurice's *Let Me Hear Your Voice* (Knopf, 1993). She also wrote a chapter on enhancing communication skills in the manual *Behavioral Intervention For Young Children with Autism*, edited by Maurice, Green, and Luce (PRO-ED, 1996). She has been on the Education Advisory Board of the Connecticut Center for Child Development since its inception.

Diana Robins received her BA in psychology and neuroscience from Oberlin College and her MA in clinical psychology from the University of Connecticut. She is currently a doctoral student in clinical psychology at the University of Connecticut. Her research is being funded by the U.S. Department of Education, the National Alliance for Autism Research, and the University of Connecticut Research Foundation. She is also the recipient of a predoctoral fellowship from the National Institute of Mental Health. Her current research involves the validation of the *Modified Checklist for Autism for Toddlers*, a screening instrument for the early detection of autism. She has been a lecturer at Trinity College and Sullivan County Community College.

Bridget A. Taylor holds a PhD in psychology from Rutgers University. She received her master's degree in early childhood special education from Teachers College of Columbia University in 1989. Taylor has specialized in the education and treatment of children with autism for the past 16 years. In 1988 she co-founded the Alpine Learning Group, a well-regarded education and treatment center for children with autism in Bergen County, New Jersey. She currently serves as director of educational programming. Taylor currently serves on the board of directors of the Association for Science in Autism Treatment. She has co-authored articles and book chapters related to autism and is a regular presenter at national and international conferences.

Lynn Waterhouse received her BA from the University of Chicago, and her MA and PhD in psychology and linguistics from the University of Pennsylvania. She has a long-standing interest in pervasive developmental disorders and has published extensively in this area since 1975. Her research has been funded by the National Institute of Mental Health, the Institute of Neurological Disorders and Strokes, and the March of Dimes. Current projects include studies of classification and longitudinal development of disorders on the autistic spectrum. She is currently a professor at The College of New Jersey, where she teaches courses on diverse subjects including philosophy, English, linguistics, and psychology.